Friedrich Schlegel and the Emergence of Romantic Philosophy

SUNY series, Intersections: Philosophy and Critical Theory
Rodolphe Gasché, editor

Friedrich Schlegel and the Emergence of Romantic Philosophy

Elizabeth Millán-Zaibert

State University of New York Press

Published by
State University of New York Press, Albany

© 2007 State University of New York

All rights reserved

Printed in the United States of America

No part of this book may be used or reproduced in any manner whatsoever without written permission. No part of this book may be stored in a retrieval system or transmitted in any form or by any means including electronic, electrostatic, magnetic tape, mechanical, photocopying, recording, or otherwise without the prior permission in writing of the publisher.

For information, address State University of New York Press,
194 Washington Avenue, Suite 305, Albany, NY 12210-2384

Production by Judith Block
Marketing by Michael Campochiaro

Library of Congress Cataloging-in-Publication Data

Millán-Zaibert, Elizabeth.
   Friedrich Schlegel and the emergence of romantic philosophy / Elizabeth Millán-Zaibert.
       p. cm. — (SUNY series in intersections—philosophy and critical theory)
   Includes bibliographical references and index.
   ISBN-13: 978-0-7914-7083-1 (hardcover : alk. paper)
   ISBN-13: 978-0-7914-7084-8 (pbk. : alk. paper)
   1. Schlegel, Friedrich von, 1772–1829. 2. Romanticism—Germany.
I. Title.

B3086.S54M55 2007
193—dc22   2006021934

10 9 8 7 6 5 4 3 2 1

For Leo and in memory of my grandmother (1916–2005)

Contents

Acknowledgments	ix
Introduction	1
Philosophy and Early German Romanticism	1
The Literary Dimensions of Early German Romanticism	5
Defining Romanticism	10
Schlegel's Antifoundationalism	18
Overview	20
1. Finding Room for the Romantics between Kant and Hegel	25
Idealism: From Misconceptions to Post-Kantian Variations	28
Searching for the Unity of Thought and Being:	
Idealist Jäger *versus Romantic* Spürhunde	32
Frank's Romantic Realists versus Beiser's Romantic Idealists	38
On Why Schlegel Is Not Hegel	44
Romantic Skepticism	48
2. Searching for the Grounds of Knowledge	53
Jacobi's Salto Mortale	54
Schlegel's Reaction to the Salto	57
Reinhold's Elementarphilosophie	62
Aenesidemus and the Shift from Principle to Fact	
of Consciousness	65
Fichte's Move from Fact to Act of Consciousness	68

3. Fichte's *Wissenschaftslehre*: A Tendency to Be Avoided?   71
The Foundations of Fichte's Wissenschaftslehre   72
The Clash between Schmid and Fichte   75
Fichte and Schlegel on Critical Philosophy   79
Fichte's Mystical Errors   86
The Spirit versus the Letter of Fichte's Philosophy   91

4. Niethammer's Influence on the Development of Schlegel's Skepticism   95
Niethammer's Skepticism   97
Niethammer's Appeal to Common Sense   101
Schlegel's Philosophical Debut   109
Schlegel's Critique of Niethammer's Appeal to Common Sense   111
Schlegel's Historical Taxonomy   114

5. Critique as Metaphilosophy: Kant as Half Critic   117
Revolution, Scientific Method, and Kant's Critical Project   120
Critiquing the Critical Philosopher   122
Away from Kant: Schlegel's Historical Turn   127

6. Philosophy *in Media Res*   133
The Wechselerweis *and the Search for Truth*   134
Philosophy "in the Middle": Between Fichte and Spinoza   137
Destroying the Illusion of the Finite: Schlegel's Critique of the Thing   141
Wilhelm Meister: Schlegel's Model of Coherence   150

7. The Aesthetic Consequences of Antifoundationalism   159
The Modern Spirit of Romanticism   160
Understanding, Misunderstanding, and Irony   165
Irony and the Necessity of Poetry   170

Notes   175
Bibliography   231
Index   249

Acknowledgments

My work on Schlegel began in 1993 when I was a graduate student at the State University of New York, Buffalo. The present book is a rather distant relative of my first attempts to come to terms with Schlegel's unconventional philosophy. I am grateful to many people who have helped me to develop work in a field that has only recently appeared on the radar screens of philosophers. Manfred Frank, with whom I first began my studies not only of Friedrich Schlegel's work, but also of the entire romantic constellation, shaped my philosophical development in important ways, and I hope that in the pages of this book, he can read the debt I have to him. I am also grateful to the German Academic Exchange Service, for the generous graduate fellowship they provided so that I could begin my initial explorations of early German romantic philosophy.

Rodolphe Gasché has supported my work from the beginning in many ways, and I am thankful for his support, not only in helping me to develop some of my views but also in helping me find venues to publish my work. I am also grateful to Jorge Gracia, who, while far removed philosophically from figures such as Kant and Schlegel, helped me develop my interests in German philosophy. Newton Garver read the entire manuscript in an earlier form and offered comments that much improved the current work. Barry Smith's work has always been a source of philosophical insights for me, and despite (perhaps because of) our philosophical differences, I always learn from him. Peter Hare's comments on an earlier version of the manuscript led me to rethink some of my claims regarding Schlegel's epistemology. Ronald Hauser led me to my first encounter with *Wilhelm Meister* and many other German literary treasures, and I will be ever grateful for the path he opened for me to the literary side of German Romanticism.

Acknowledgments

In 2001 I was fortunate to have the opportunity to participate in the NEH Summer Institute on Kant and early German Romanticism that was organized by Jane Kneller and Karl Ameriks. The discussions I had there helped me to clarify some of the points that I develop in the present volume. To Karl Ameriks I owe a special debt, for his encouragement of my work has been unflagging. At the NEH Institute I met Fred Beiser and Bob Richards, two thinkers whose work has been invaluable to the field of early German Romanticism and whose intellectual generosity is a true gift. Fred read my dissertation on Schlegel and sent me comments that led me to rethink several of my claims and to work harder to sharpen some of my points. The influence of his work is evident in the following pages, and I hope that my criticism of some aspects of his arguments does not overshadow the great admiration I have for his work. Bob Richards has been most supportive, and our discussions of Schlegel and other themes related to early German Romanticism have certainly helped me to sharpen my views. Thom Brooks read the entire manuscript, and his comments were of great value.

Versions of some of the chapters were presented at conferences or talks. Given the generous support of the Alexander von Humboldt Foundation, I was able to spend the 2004–05 academic year in Leipzig, Germany. I am grateful for the kind reception I received from the Department of Philosophy at the Universität Leipzig, and for the comments I received at a talk I gave there. The arguments I develop in chapter 1 were shaped considerably by those comments. My host in Leipzig was Pirmin Stekeler-Weithofer, and I thank him for his support. Chapter 3 developed out of a talk I gave for the North American Fichte Society, and I am grateful to Dan Breazeale, Tom Rockmore, and Arnold Farr for organizing that meeting and to the participants there for their comments. My views on Schlegel's reception of Kant came into focus as I prepared a talk for the North American Kant Association Session on Kant and Romanticism at the American Philosophical Association's Central Division Meeting in 2002. I thank Karl Ameriks for organizing that talk and Jane Kneller and Peter Foley for discussion that helped me to develop the material that became chapter 5 of the present book. Some of the ideas developed in chapter 7 were first developed for an article ("Romanticismo e postmoderno: variazioni incompresse sulla critica della modernità") that Nectarios Limantis and Luigi Pastore invited me to write for their collection *Prospettive sul Postmoderno* (Milano: Mimesis, 2006).

I would also like to offer thanks to Bärbel Frischmann, a fellow Schlegel scholar. Her work and friendship have shaped my work. I would also like to thank the students in the graduate seminars I have taught at the Universidad Simón Bolívar, in Caracas, Venezuela and at DePaul University in Chicago, for the many stimulating discussions which have helped me look in new directions and develop my ideas. Though distance separates us, I am deeply thankful for the friendship and support of my work from Rafael Tomás Caldera, Victor Krebs, Fabio Morales, and the late Luis Castro Leiva.

My gratitude also extends to the editorial staff at SUNY Press, in particular to the production editor, Judith Block, and to Marilyn Semerad, director of production, for their expertise in guiding the manuscript to its final form. I also wish to acknowledge David Prout, who prepared a thorough and detailed index, which contributes greatly to the usefulness of the book. I am also grateful for a grant from the University Research Council of DePaul University which helped cover the costs associated with the final preparation of the manuscript

My first philosophical investigations began by my grandmother's side, and they continue with the most supportive partner in all of my *Symphilosophie*, my husband and fellow philosopher, Leo, who has contributed to this book in more ways than I can properly acknowledge.

Introduction

Philosophy and Early German Romanticism

The value of early German Romanticism as a literary movement has been generally accepted.¹ The growing interest in the movement by philosophers is a more recent phenomenon; it is no overstatement to claim that there is currently a renaissance of interest in the philosophical dimensions of early German Romanticism.²

Stanley Cavell, Frederick Beiser, and Andrew Bowie were among the first brave souls in the Anglophone world to dare ascribe philosophical importance to early German Romanticism. Adjectives such as *brave* and *daring* are not out of place if one considers the checkered past of the reception of early German Romanticism: for it has been interpreted as *at best* a literary movement with excessive emphasis on the irrational forces of human life, in the words of no less an icon of German literature than Goethe, a sick movement to be avoided by anyone with a healthy spirit,³ and at worst, a movement sowing the seeds of something as diabolical as National Socialism.⁴ In what follows, I hope to show that Goethe's diagnosis of Romanticism was flagrantly wrong: by tracing the *Frühromantik* movement through Friedrich Schlegel's philosophical commitments, it will become clear that the adjective *romantic* describes a robust conception of philosophy from which we still have a great deal to learn.

Each of the three thinkers mentioned at the outset, Cavell, Beiser, and Bowie, has highlighted slightly different aspects of early German Romantic philosophy. In *This New Yet Unapproachable America: Lectures after Emerson and Wittgenstein*,⁵ Cavell writes of his discovery of early German Romanticism. Philippe Lacoue-Labarthe and Jean-Luc Nancy's *Literary Absolute*⁶ served to introduce Cavell to various writings from the

1

journal *Athenäum* (1798–1800), which the Schlegel brothers, Friedrich and August Wilhelm, coedited. Friedrich Schlegel's call for a new relation between philosophy and literature caught Cavell's attention, in part because of its challenge to the view most philosophers have of what an acceptable relation between philosophy and poetry should be: "I guess such remarks as 'poetry and philosophy should be made one' would not in themselves have been enough even in my day to have gotten one thrown out of most graduate programs in philosophy, but their presence, if used seriously, as a present ambition, would not have been permitted to contribute to a Ph.D. study either; and like vestigial organs, such ideas may become inflamed and life-threatening."[7] Cavell points to one central root of the pervasive exclusion of the early German Romantics from the philosophical canon: the privileged place they granted to philosophy's relation to poetry, a place that makes certain philosophers uncomfortable.

Cavell is most certainly *not* uncomfortable accepting an intimate relation between philosophy and poetry. Cavell's contribution to the study of early German Romanticism has not been through writing *on* the Romantics as much as by offering a model of what might properly be called "romantic" philosophy, especially, regarding the sort of skepticism to which it leads, a skepticism that generates questions such as: What is a philosophical result? What is philosophical activity? and his view of philosophy as "neither empirical generalization nor legislation, but rather reading, or criticism, or understanding from the inside."[8] Schlegel and Cavell share a philosophical concern for "understanding from the inside." (The meaning and importance of this phrase shall be discussed in chapter 6.)[9]

In the chapters that follow, I shall make a case for the *philosophical relevance* of the privileged place held by poetry and aesthetic experience in early Romantic philosophy. Two caveats are in order: I will be concerned in this book with a particular figure, Friedrich Schlegel, and with a particular period of German Romanticism, the early period. Early German Romanticism flourished in two cities, Berlin and Jena, between the years of 1794 and 1802. Yet Schlegel's romantic thought extended beyond these years, with 1808 (the year he converted to Catholicism) marking his break from many of the philosophical convictions that shaped his romantic phase. The romantic phase of Schlegel's thought continued during his periods in Paris and Köln, when he was separated from the thinkers who had come together in Jena to form the *Frühromantik* movement.

The leading figures of the early German Romantic movement were the Schlegel brothers, Caroline (née Bohmer) Schlegel Schelling, Dorothea (née Mendelssohn) Veit Schlegel, and Friedrich Daniel Ernst Schleiermacher, Friedrich von Hardenberg (Novalis), Wilhelm H. Ludwig and

Sophie Tieck, and Wilhelm H. Wackenroder. The philosophical dimensions of *early* German Romanticism were stronger than other romantic movements that followed it. Middle (or High) Romanticism (1808–1815) was shaped by the work of poets and artists such as Achim von Arnim, Clemens Brentano, and Caspar David Friedrich. Late Romanticism (1815–1830) was a more conservative movement and was led by figures such as Franz Baader, E. T. A. Hoffmann, Johann von Eichendorff, Friedrich Schelling, and the elder Friedrich Schlegel, whose work after 1808 underwent a major transformation. Early German Romanticism was breaking apart as a movement as early as 1802, for by that time, Wackenroder (d. 1798) and Novalis (d. 1801) were both dead, and Friedrich and Dorothea Schlegel had gone to Paris. After what has been dubbed "the Jena *Wunderjahr*" (1794–95), the early German Romantic movement never recuperated its momentum.[10]

Friedrich Schlegel is considered the leader of the romantic circle in the early period, and his work will be the focus of this book. In particular, I shall discuss the consequences of his skepticism regarding the feasibility of establishing a first principle for philosophy, which, I shall argue, is a central element of his romantic philosophy, a philosophy that is finally receiving due recognition on the Anglophone world.[11]

Frederick Beiser has written more on early German Romanticism than has Cavell and is, together with Ernst Behler, among the leading authorities on early German Romanticism in the United States. His historical and philosophical work on the period has enabled philosophers to have a context into which the early German Romantics can be placed. In addition to historical and hermeneutical work of the highest quality, Beiser has also provided bold and nuanced philosophical analyses of crucial ideas that shaped the period, providing, for example, a major analysis of the very meaning of German idealism, the relation between the *Aufklärung* and *Frühromantik*, and a philosophical account of the perennially elusive meaning of romantic *Poesie*.[12]

Andrew Bowie has also contributed to the growth of the field through his first-rate translations of Schelling and Schleiermacher[13] and through his original interpretation of several aspects of the *Frühromantik* movement. Bowie balances excellent historical detail with a broad, yet thorough knowledge of contemporary trends of philosophy.[14] In recent work, Bowie connects the work of the early German Romantics to trends in contemporary German and Anglo-American philosophy, showing us their relevance to problems still very much on the mind of contemporary philosophers both in Germany and in Anglophone countries.[15] In his article "John McDowell's *Mind and World*, and Early Romantic Epistemology," for a special volume of the *Revue Internationale de Philosophie*, in

Frühromantik, edited by Manfred Frank,[16] Bowie connects the epistemological insights of the Romantics with McDowell's work, thereby connecting the work of the early German Romantic philosophers (whom, I suppose, most would classify as continental philosophers) with the work of a leading contemporary analytic thinker.[17]

Long before Cavell, Beiser, and Bowie began to bring the contributions of the early German Romantics to the Anglophone world, Schlegel's work caught the attention of important German thinkers. Wilhelm Dilthey's work, for example, was informed considerably by Schlegel's view of philosophy as an essentially historical enterprise, even while he ultimately favored Schlegel's friend and one-time roommate in Berlin, Friedrich D. E. Schleiermacher.[18] Schlegel's philosophy was groundbreaking for the development of the field we know today as the human sciences (*Geisteswissenschaften*).[19] Walter Benjamin's dissertation on the concept of 'art criticism' in German Romanticism was primarily a study of Friedrich Schlegel, and Benjamin was one of the first philosophers to appreciate Schlegel's critique of modernity.[20]

In addition to the influence that Schlegel's work had on other thinkers, I wish to show that it is also important in its own right. For Schlegel's philosophy represents an important reaction to major German philosophers of the eighteenth century, in particular to the work of Kant and Fichte. With the "first generation of Kant readers," the group of thinkers of which Schlegel was a part, we find important challenges to defining philosophy in terms of mathematical and scientific models of necessity and certainty and a move toward incorporating history into philosophy and of bringing philosophy closer to poetry, in what was part of a more general move to establish a philosophical method for understanding the unity of all branches of knowledge. Contrary to standard philosophical wisdom, such a move marks not the beginning of the end of philosophy as a sober discipline that can bring us closer to truth but rather, as I shall argue, it is a constructive move that fortifies our search for truth.

The Romantics were challenging the very conception of what counted as philosophy, and this entailed the construction of an entirely new set of boundaries used to carve out what would count as the territory of philosophy and which disciplines would be its nearest neighbors. According to the map drawn by Schlegel, philosophy and poetry turn out to be at least as close as philosophy and science. (The implications of this intimate relation between philosophy and poetry will be discussed in chapter 7.)

Despite the recent revival of Anglophone interest in the philosophical relevance of early German Romanticism, the philosophical community has not quite rid itself of its lingering discomfort with any map of philosophy that places philosophy too close to poetry. One effective way to bring early German Romanticism into the philosophical fold is by reminding the philosophical public of encounters that the early German Romantics had with figures whose philosophical standing is unquestionable. Schlegel's skepticism regarding the possibility of a philosophy based on first principles led him to develop an alternative to both Kant's and Fichte's transcendental idealism and so to formulate an original definition of the goals and methods of philosophy. These contributions often go unrecognized and cannot be fully appreciated if we do not treat Schlegel's work as, first and foremost, a philosophical work.

Of course, my insistence regarding the the need to analyze the robustly philosophical dimensions of early German Romanticism more seriously in no way entails that there was not a vibrant literary dimension to the movement. The early German Romantics did produce much of literary value, and a large part of their enterprise was committed to questioning the role of art not only for philosophical enquiry but also for society as a whole. For this reason, it is perfectly legitimate, and indeed necessary, to understand the literary dimensions of this movement. Yet I hope to show that a deeper understanding of Schlegel's philosophical commitments sheds light on some of the themes that the early German romantic literary figures were addressing in their poems, plays, and stories, and, moreover, that neglect of the philosophical dimensions of Schlegel's thought endangers a proper reception of what early German Romanticism, in both its literary and philosophical dimensions, was ultimately all about.

The early German Romantics were seeking to redefine the categories of poetry and philosophy and hence they employed unconventional forms for the expression of their ideas. Most characteristic was the use of the fragment, a literary form that lends itself to creative interpretation. Yet this form does not preclude the possibility of conceptual analysis. It does make the task more difficult. I believe that this difficulty, coupled with Schlegel's frequent use of suggestive metaphor, where most philosophers would prefer a rigorous argument, has hindered philosophical investigations of his work, and in general, of the early German Romantics. Much work on the philosophical contributions of early German Romanticism is currently being done to correct the gaps in knowledge of the philosophical contributions of the early German Romantics, yet certain problems regarding the general image of early German Romanticism as an exclusively literary movement remain pernicious and pervasive.

The Literary Dimensions of Early German Romanticism

Ernst Behler was a leading authority on Schlegel and a case in point regarding the exaggerated literary interpretation of early German

Romanticism (and of Schlegel's work) to which I have alluded. Together with others, he compiled and edited the standard edition of Schlegel's works[21] and produced several influential works on Schlegel and Romanticism, and the criticisms of some aspects of his focus certainly are not meant to take anything away from the important contributions he has made to the field of Romanticism in general and to the work of Friedrich Schlegel in particular.[22] Behler's work tends to focus upon early German Romanticism as a literary movement and tends to view Schlegel as a man of letters rather than as a philosopher. To be sure, Behler gives a detailed account of the philosophers who influenced Schlegel and refers, here and there, to Schlegel as a philosopher. But this is insufficient; although in his work he does explore some of the philosophical dimensions of Schlegel's thought, especially, the latter's discussion of the relation between poetry and philosophy, Behler does not enter into a detailed analysis of Schlegel's philosophical positions and at times even suggests that Schlegel did not really have *that* much interest in philosophy anyway. In the introduction to *German Romantic Literary Theory*, Behler gives an account of three traditional views of early German Romanticism according to which early German Romanticism is understood to be: (1) an outgrowth of the classicism of Goethe and Schiller; (2) an extension of transcendental idealism; (3) or part of the encyclopedic tradition of the eighteenth century.[23] He shows why these views are incomplete or wrong, presenting his own characterization of the movement. He begins with a general claim that 1 and 2 "are common views of early German Romanticism in literary history. Both of them—the assumptions of a positive relationship on the part of the Romantics to the philosophy of transcendental idealism and the poetic world of Goethe and Schiller—emphasize important features in the new theory. Upon closer consideration, however, this firm location of early Romanticism in the intellectual landscape of the time dissolves, and a phenomenon much more complicated emerges which escapes final definition and location."[24] A few pages later, Behler becomes more specific, maintaining, "Yet, in the end, early Romanticism is just as little an extension of the idealism of Kant, Fichte, and Schelling as it is a mere offshoot of classicism and the classicist theory. Here again, the early Romantic mentality adopted an attitude that showed little interest in historical frameworks of philosophy, the content of philosophical knowledge, the results of philosophizing, or systems of thought. Instead, it departed from these reference points and arrived at its own medium of reflection, that is, at art, poetry and literature, independent of historical relationships."[25]

As shall become clear in chapter 2, while I agree with Behler that Romanticism was no mere extension of the idealism of Kant, Fichte, and Schelling, my reasons for supporting such a claim are entirely different from those of Behler. Behler's interest in distinguishing early German Romanticism from German Idealism is part of a move to distance the early German Romantics from philosophy, a move that effectively undermines any philosophical value the movement may have had. Behler not only makes claims about the literary theory that emerged from this movement but also reduces the movement to this literary dimension. This is wrong. Schlegel, for example, *was* interested in the historical frameworks of philosophy and even wrote a history of philosophy.[26] And Schlegel's lectures on transcendental philosophy are evidence of his interest in the possibility of philosophical knowledge, that is, on epistemology. While Behler acknowledges that the early Romantics showed some interest in philosophy, he does emphasize that they showed only "little interest," thereby dramatically obscuring the importance of philosophy for the early German Romantics. Behler's own claim is that early Romantic theory "[c]an be described as an interaction of the literary and the philosophical encyclopedia—not as their synthesis, to be sure, but as an attempt to think philosophy from the point of view of poetry and poetry from the point of view of philosophy."[27] Yet how can philosophy be thought from the point of view of poetry and poetry from the point of view of philosophy if there is merely *little interest* in the historical frameworks of philosophy, the content of philosophical knowledge, and the results of philosophizing? Surely there must be considerable interest (more than "a little interest") in these issues if such a new relation between philosophy and poetry is to be formulated. My story of Schlegel's romantic philosophy is an attempt to correct this misrepresentation of early German Romanticism as only minimally interested in philosophy.

Behler's characterization of Niethammer's *Philosophical Journal of a Society of German Scholars* is an example of another misunderstanding concerning the nature of early German Romanticism. He writes that it, "became the main organ for formulating the principles of transcendental idealism, and many of Fichte's and Schelling's early writings first appeared in it. Fichte later joined Niethammer as its editor." The *Philosophisches Journal*, at least while under Niethammer's guidance, was not devoted to formulating the principles of transcendental philosophy but rather to questioning the validity of such a philosophical project. The early German Romantic philosophical position was one of skepticism with respect to the feasibility of Fichte's philosophy. Behler's description of the journal, a journal that was the major vehicle for the expression of these criticisms, suggests that the early Romantics were *supporters* of Fichte's philosophy. But this is false, as I shall show in chapters 3 and 4.

Behler is aware that there is a relation between the early German Romantics and certain philosophical developments of their era, yet he is content to generalize about the philosophical developments in order to focus on the literary dimensions. Behler's literary focus, for all of the rich insight into the movement that it undoubtedly offers, has the perverse effect of neglecting the truly philosophical dimensions of the movement.

A more promising move is found in Frederick Beiser's attempt to come to terms with the philosophical dimensions of a key term that is usually considered to be the exclusive domain of Germanists so has not attracted the attention of most philosophers, namely, *romantische Poesie* (romantic poetry). Beiser admits that the question of what the young romantics mean by 'romantic poetry' "is no easy question," and he is not after "anything like a full explanation" of the term.[28] As he tells us, "I am going to set aside all questions about its etymology and suspend any discussion of its philosophical foundations. All I want to do now is to raise one very basic question about the meaning of this phrase. Namely, to what does it apply? Or, in short, what were the young romantics talking about when they spoke of romantic poetry?"[29] As Beiser correctly indicates, the concept of 'romantic poetry' was pivotal for the early German Romantics, providing an important "point of entry" into their set of concerns. Beiser's strategy is also quite sensible. He is after clarity regarding what the term *romantic poetry* refers to, and he hopes, with such clarification, to show that the traditional approach to *Frühromantik*, which has been guided by too narrow an understanding of what 'romantic poetry' applies to (namely, to a particular set of literary characteristics), has led to a serious neglect of the "fundamental metaphysical, epistemological, ethical, and political ideas that are the real foundation of early Romanticism."[30] I share Beiser's apprehension of the tendency to relegate analyses of key romantic terms to the literary realm, as if philosophers could not possibly have anything to say about them. Indeed, Beiser argues that the scope of references of 'romantic poetry' is much wider than the literary frame typically used to approach it: "First, [romantic poetry] refers to not only literature, but also all the arts and sciences; there is indeed no reason to limit its meaning to literary works, since it also applies to sculpture, music, and painting. Second, it designates not only the arts and sciences but also human beings, nature, and the state. The aim of the early romantic aesthetic was indeed to romanticize the world itself, so that human beings, society, and the state could become works of art as well."[31] For Beiser, 'romantic poetry' "designates not a form of literature or criticism but the romantics' general aesthetic ideal."[32] It is misleading to read 'romantic poetry' as a term that designates a specific literary form, whether prose or verse, and so on, and it is misleading, too, to read the term as merely a historical concept demarcating a particular period of literary creation. Beiser argues that 'romantic poetry' is a *normative* concept—

part of Schlegel's project to bring philosophy, poetry, science, indeed, all spheres of human inquiry, into contact with one another. It is the expression of the early German Romantics "striving for wholeness" and "longing for unity," a striving and longing that are part of a romantic project, backed by what Beiser calls a "holistic spirit," with the goal of recreating "the unity of all the arts and sciences" and of reestablishing the "unity of art and life."[33] Beiser is certainly correct to locate the most salient philosophical features of the early German Romantic movement in the quest for unity, a quest that is often overlooked because of Schlegel's unconventional method for approximating that unity. It must be emphasized, however, that Schlegel's "striving for wholeness" was not a haphazard striving, and in the following chapters, I will uncover the philosophical *method* that underlies Schlegel's romantic striving for unity, a striving that employed a variety of tools still shunned by most philosophers. Schlegel's romantic philosophical project is intimately connected to his conception of romantic *Poesie*, which, with Beiser, I read normatively, as an aesthetic *ideal*.

While interdisciplinary work is contemporarily all the rage, some two centuries after Schlegel campaigned for it, many philosophers still tend to read Schlegel's literary references as evidence of his *lack* of philosophical rigor. Yet this is often simply a prejudice. Schlegel's deep concern for particular novels (especially for Goethe's episodically structured *Wilhelm Meister*), for particular authors such as Shakespeare, Cervantes, and Goethe, and his interest in the multiperspectival richness of dialogues and fragments as literary forms were the result of his view of how humans approximate truth. Schlegel considered novels, poems, and other literary forms to be fertile sources for examining the structure of knowledge, in particular, to examine how humans justify beliefs. Therefore, it is a gross distortion to read Schlegel's interest in romantic poetry as in any way unphilosophical.

Slowly, research into the philosophical foundations of early German Romanticism is helping to correct the distorted view resulting from an excessive emphasis on the literary character of this movement. Dieter Henrich's work has contributed to this end. Henrich focuses primarily on the importance of Hölderlin's contributions to early German Romantic theory, but he also gives a reconstruction of the constellation of thinkers who comprised the group known as early German Romantics, showing their relations to the major philosophical currents of the time.[34] Moreover, Manfred Frank has provided a brilliantly detailed account of the philosophical foundations of this movement, and not only has he punctiliously shown the philosophical context from which the cluster of philosophical concerns with which they worked arose, but he has also made connections between the views of some of the early German Romantics and developments in contemporary analytic philosophy.[35] In the Anglophone world,

Frederick Beiser's work has, as mentioned above, helped to create a historical and philosophical context from which to read the early German Romantics as important in their own right, clearing the philosophical skies of the imposing shadow cast by Hegel's thought and helping to correct some of the distortions caused by the literary interpretations of the movement. Moreover, Andrew Bowie has helped bring the contemporary philosophical relevance of early German Romanticism into sharp focus, especially regarding its contributions to epistemology, reminding us of how much we still have to learn from the innovative thought of the early German Romantics. Recent scholarship on the movement has also helped to correct the lingering perception that "[t]he natural philosophical efforts of the Romantics did not exert any lasting influence on the further development of the natural sciences and medicine,"[36] showing that Schlegel's desire to join philosophy, poetry, and science was no pipe dream and that in fact, "Romantic thought gave shape to [nothing less than] Darwin's conceptions of nature and evolution."[37] To argue for Schlegel's particular contribution to the sciences is beyond the scope of the present book, but his contributions to *Naturphilosophie* and to the discussions of nature that took shape at the turn of the eighteenth century certainly deserve more attention than they have hitherto received.[38]

Beiser, Bowie, Frank, and Henrich have done much historical, philological, and philosophical work that has served to shed light on the philosophical contributions of the early German Romantics. They have begun to build a body of literature that treats the figures of this movement as serious philosophers.[39] Nevertheless, no work in English has been devoted exclusively to an analysis of Schlegel's philosophical position during the specifically romantic phase of his thought, and this is the main gap that the present book seeks to fill.[40] For although Schlegel is, perhaps, in some ways, a minor figure *when compared to* Kant, Fichte, Schelling, and Hegel, he is still a philosopher who merits serious attention, and an understanding of his unique philosophical position will give us deeper insight into the contributions of these more prominent figures and into the development of German philosophy in the immediate post-Kant period.

Defining Romanticism

As I have indicated, I am not attempting to offer a comprehensive treatment of Schlegel's philosophy but rather of a particular period of his thought, the romantic phase. There are various phases to Schlegel's thought, marked by important conceptual shifts.[41] We can make a broad classification according to the following phases: (1) the "Objektivitätswut"[42] or "classical" phase (1793–96); (2) the turning point or "romantic" phase (fall, 1796–1808); and (3) the conversion and late works or "conservative" phase (1808–29). *Vom Wert des Studiums der Griechen und Romer* (*aus dem Nachlass*, 1795–96) (*KA* 1, pp. 621–42) and *Von der Schönheit in der Dichtkunst* (aus dem Nachlass, 1795) (*KA* 16, pp. 5–31) are characteristic writings of Schlegel's "classical" phase. During this period, Schlegel's thought is marked by an interest in philological studies of the ancient Greeks. As the work of both Schlegel's early period and his late period depart in important ways from his "romantic" one, neither of these periods will be central to this book.[43]

In contrast to Kant who came to philosophy with a strong background in science, and to Fichte, Schelling, and Hegel who came to philosophy from a study of theology, Schlegel's background was strictly philological. The significance of this fact shall become clearer when we discuss his view of philosophy. We shall see that Schlegel's study of classical Greek and Roman literature and art evolved into a comparative study of ancient and modern history and aesthetics. It was within the context of his engagement with this comparative enterprise that his skepticism regarding the possibility of a philosophy based on first principles was first articulated.[44]

During the romantic phase, Schlegel was in Jena and Berlin. In the summer of 1796, he left Dresden in order to join his brother, August Wilhelm, in Jena. August Wilhelm had been invited there by Schiller to work on Schiller's journal *Horen*. Jena quickly became the center of early German Romanticism.[45] Between 1795 and 1797 Fichte was the most important philosopher in Jena, and Schlegel's contact with the rising philosophical star was tremendously important, yet, as shall become clear, Schlegel was hardly a blind follower of Fichte's idealist philosophy. During his romantic phase, Schlegel began to focus more upon modern literature and philosophy and to develop his own philosophical positions. In fact, the review he wrote of Niethammer's *Philosophisches Journal* (1797) was considered by Schlegel to be his own philosophical debut.[46] In this review, he makes explicit his skepticism regarding a philosophy based on first principles. This skepticism is a primary tendency of his "romantic" period.

Schlegel's reviews of Schiller's work were filled with irony and stinging criticisms.[47] Schlegel's polemic with Schiller made it difficult for him to remain an active and financially supported member of the Jena intellectual community, for Schiller controlled the most important journals in Jena. During his time in Jena, Schlegel had contributed to the Berlin-based journals *Lyceum der schönen Künste* and *Deutschland*, both edited by the Berlin *Aufklärer* C. F. Reichhardt.[48] In 1797, Schlegel left Jena for Berlin. This move provided him with new opportunities and exposed him to a broader circle of thinkers; accordingly, his philosophical activity increased.

In 1798, Schlegel and his brother founded *Das Athenäum*, a journal that became a major vehicle for the articulation of the ideas of the early Romantics. A. W. Schlegel, Friedrich Schlegel, Dorothea Veit, Caroline Schlegel, Novalis, Ludwig Tieck, Friedrich Schleiermacher, and others contributed to this journal.[49] The journal, which appeared between 1798 and 1800, was in part a reaction against what Schlegel viewed to be the conservative mood of journals such as those edited by Reichhardt. *Das Athenäum* was most unorthodox: the Schlegels wanted their journal to be open to innovative articles in both form *and* content. Friedrich Schlegel even went so far as to proclaim that all contributions that were polemical and "sublimely impudent" (displaying "*erhabene Frechheit*") would be included—that is, all contributions that were "too good" for other journals.[50]

Das Athenäum tested conventions; it was devoted to radical criticism. Although laudable as this polemical, somewhat negative aspect was, it was not the only aspect of the journal that deserves attention.[51] The key positive function of the journal was that it served to develop the theme that came to characterize this group, that is, the concept of 'the romantic.' Schlegel's journal was comprised of reviews and fragments.[52] The use and significance of the fragment in Schlegel's work has received much attention.[53] Schlegel's use of the fragment is largely the result of his ambivalent relation to creating a system for his ideas.[54] In *Athenäum* Fragment 53 he writes: "It is just as fatal for the spirit to have a system and not to have a system. Some way of combining the two must be reached."[55] According to Eichner, the medium of such a combination is precisely the literary form that the early Romantics favored, the fragment. This form, because it is not *necessarily* systematic, provides the space necessary for the free play of irony and facilitates the possibility that a single idea be approached from a plurality of perspectives.

These investigations into the significance of the literary form for understanding the philosophical content of a given philosophical work are important in their own right.[56] Nonetheless, I do not think that Schlegel's insistence of the tension of both having and not having a system and the ensuing attempt to reconcile these two states can be fully explained solely by reference to his use of the fragment. In chapters 3 and 5, I discuss the central role that the notion of tradition played in shaping Schlegel's very conception of philosophy and present his concern with history as an important element of his ambivalent attitude toward having and not having a system.

The use of the fragment and dialogue form was in keeping with the early Romantics' desire to call the traditional roles of poetry and philosophy into question. It is within the context of this challenge that the term *romantic* becomes significant in Schlegel's work. He did use this adjective in his early writings but then only as a term of literary criticism, to denote a certain class of writings or a certain period of the history of literature: romantic poetry was opposed to classical poetry, it was subjective and artificial (*künstlich*), whereas classical poetry was objective and natural. This early use of the term might explain, though not justify, the endemic mistake of considering early German Romanticism as merely a literary movement.

Schlegel's endorsement of the ancients changed around 1795, and it was around this time that his use of the adjective *romantisch* became central to his work, becoming an aesthetic ideal and indeed the catchword of a philosophical movement. 'Romantic' has been analyzed by many scholars, in part because before one can say anything meaningful about Romanticism, be it English, Russian, Spanish, or German, and be it romantic painting, literature, or philosophy that one wants to examine, there must be some clarity regarding the adjective that is drawing our attention to a given group in the first place.[57] A few authors have addressed the meaning of 'romantic' within the specific context of early German Romanticism. A. O. Lovejoy, for example, presents his view of the source and original meaning of 'romantic' in its use by the early German Romantics and of the sources and content of the aesthetic and philosophical ideas for which the word stood.[58] He contrasts his view to that of Haym (whose *Die romantische Schule*, 1870, is a classical attempt to define 'romantic' within the context of the German intellectual tradition). Haym claimed that 'romantic' poetry simply meant "*Romanpoesie*" or writings possessed of the qualities of Goethe's *Wilhelm Meister*. Haym equates 'romantic' with the German word for novel which is *Roman*. This, according to Lovejoy, is problematic for several reasons: (a) it does not explain then what the term could have meant as we find it in Schlegel's pre-*Meister* writings; (b) every modern novel may be romantic, but not everything romantic is a novel (Shakespeare's work is romantic, as are the medieval tales of romance, and some songs and poems); (c) to reduce the origin of 'romantic' to its relation with the novel is to limit its philosophical relevance. Lovejoy claims, "The genesis of Romanticism, then, is very seriously misconceived, when it is supposed (as by Haym and many others after him) that the conception of 'Romantic poetry' was formed by Schlegel only about 1796 or later, that he 'abstracted it' from *Wilhelm Meister*; that it implied a sort of apotheosis of the novel among the literary genres; and that Schlegel's first elucidation of it was in the *Athenäum* in 1798. The theory of Romanticism was, so to say, a by-product of the prevalent classicism of the early 1790s."[59]

According to Lovejoy, the most important text in Schlegel's conversion from classicism to romanticism was not Goethe's *Meister*, but Schiller's essay "Über naive und sentimentalische Dichtung" (published in *Horen* in 1795).[60] Schiller's essay, written in the aftermath of the Reign of Terror, 1793–94, is a vindication of the moderns, yet not far from Schiller's mind was the bitter taste of disappointment with certain aspects of how the project of modernity was being carried out. A way to avoid more errors is sketched in Schiller's essay "Über die ästhetische Erziehung des Menschen" (On the Aesthetic Education of Humans, 1795), which, as Dennis Mahoney has indicated, provided a kind of "cure for the ills of modern society."[61] While Haym is correct that *Wilhelm Meister* came to symbolize an almost perfect model of romantic art, Lovejoy's observation that Schlegel did not abstract his notion of the romantic from Goethe's novel is also true. Schlegel was already well on his way to developing his notion of the romantic by the time he wrote his essay, "Über Goethes Meister" (1798). As Lovejoy correctly indicates, the roots of Schlegel's development of 'romantic' are better placed in the influence of a figure with whom Schlegel had a much more tempestuous relation: Friedrich Schiller.

Although Schlegel and Schiller did not see eye to eye on many issues, Schlegel had great respect for Schiller's insights on the role of art for educating humanity, and his romantic project was, in many ways, an attempt to take Schiller's project a step further (and of course, to assimilate Schiller's thought on his own terms), that is, to use poetry to shape society into some sort of cohesive whole. Schlegel proved to be a much more progressive thinker than Schiller, and the two thinkers, though sharing much in the way of general goals for the progress of society, did not see eye to eye on the particularities of several key issues, especially regarding the role of women in society. The modern, progressive spirit of early German Romanticism, a spirit that created problems for Schlegel, especially among his more conservative colleagues, has not been fully appreciated, in part, because of the dreadful association between Romanticism and Nazism, but as I have already mentioned, such an association is based on misconceptions of early German Romanticism, and once the misconceptions are laid to rest, the progressive potential of the movement becomes clear. For Schlegel, political progress and the proper appreciation of poetry's value for society go hand in hand.

In 1797, Schlegel scorns his earlier *Objektivitätswut* and openly announces his romantic turn. Lyceum Fragment 7 offers an important hint of the new path his thought was to take: "My essay on the study of Greek poetry is a mannered hymn in prose to the objective quality in poetry."[62] It seems to me that the worst thing about it is the total lack of indispensable irony; and the best, the confident assumption that poetry is infinitely valuable—as though that were a settled thing."[63] This explicit endorsement of poetry and irony would shape Schlegel's philosophical method throughout his romantic period. As Schlegel's appreciation for the subjective elements of art, of the presence of the individual and the autonomy of artistic production developed, Schlegel no longer viewed the ideal of art as an accomplished state of perfection but as an eternal process of becoming. In the famous and oft-quoted *Athenäum* Fragment 116 we find Schlegel's announcement that "romantic poetry is a progressive, universal poetry."[64] Romantic poetry is an ideal, a poetry that is progressive because it is always in a state of becoming, never reaching completion.[65] As Beiser has argued, it is crucial that 'romantic poetry' not be limited to any literary realm, for it references an approach to reality and is as much a normative concept as it is a historical concept.

In his discussion of Schlegel and modernism, Behler links Schlegel's emphasis on infinite becoming (which as shall become clear in the following chapters, is the result of his conviction that one cannot begin philosophy from knowledge of first principles à la Fichte or from a blind leap of faith à la Jacobi), to the sense of modernity developed by the Romantics. Behler claims that the sense of modernity developed by Schlegel is "fully conscious of its separation from classical perfection and equally distant from any utopian goal of accomplishment."[66] As Behler correctly indicates, Schlegel's frequent references to "not yet," "as long as," and other gestures to the process of becoming do not designate a transitoriness that must be overcome, but rather the "actual state of our knowledge, its permanent form."[67] Behler claims that an entirely new concept of poetry and a "fundamentally new sense of modernity" had to emerge "when the classical model of literary creation was overcome and replaced by a notion of poetry involved in a process of infinite progression."[68] The application of infinite perfectability not only of poetry but of reality in all of its dimensions radicalized the notion of progress announced during the Enlightenment. The progressive critique of modernity articulated by Schlegel in his work will be addressed in chapter 7, when I discuss the aesthetic consequences of Schlegel's romantic philosophy.

Following Behler, we can understand the meaning of 'romantic' in two ways: chronologically and typologically.[69] Chronologically, 'romantic' "referred to a tradition of literature originating in the Middle Ages and pervading literary writing in modern Europe, but which was held in low esteem by neoclassicists and even excluded from the literary canon."[70] In his "Letter on the Novel" (1799), Schlegel himself puts this in the following way: "This is where I look for and find the Romantic—in the older moderns, in Shakespeare, Cervantes, in Italian poetry, in that age of knights, love, and fairy-tales where the thing and the word originated."[71] The "romantic" then belonged to an earlier period, and it did serve as a kind of historical concept to reference a tradition that

Schlegel and others (A. W. Schlegel, Schleiermacher, Novalis, etc.) hoped to revive as a means of understanding modern politics, aesthetics, and philosophy. The reason they looked to this period in order to address these issues becomes clear when we understand the typological meaning of the term. According to Behler: "The typological referred to certain exotic traits in literature, including compositional and structural ones, which were originally expressed in Romanesque literature, but which were now found everywhere."[72] Yet, while Behler's claim pins the romantic onto the literary realm, narrowing the application of the term, Schlegel himself was careful to stress that his use of 'romantic' should *not* be limited to any such narrow range of application: "According to my point of view and my use of the term, romantic is that which presents us with sentimental material in a fantastic form (that is, in a form determined by the fantasy)."[73] Schlegel's use of 'romantic' added an important new perspective to the debate of this period concerning the relation between the ancients and the moderns. Yet, as Beiser indicates, Schlegel did not exhaustively define the romantic in historical terms (though certainly, the romantic is, in part, a historical category). Instead of carrying out the debate between the ancients and the moderns purely in terms of chronological categories, Schlegel shifted the foundation of the discussion to a conceptual one, that is, to a discussion concerning the meaning of the classical and the romantic, yet not merely as adjectives to describe literature. Certainly, 'romantic' became a tool for classifying poetry, but more precisely, it became a way of comparing the past with the present in a way which superseded literary categories: it became a way of comparing the past with the present in a philosophical way. The "older moderns" to which Schlegel makes reference had not been overturned. They were not "thinkers of the past" who also belonged in the past, but rather dialogue partners for the present: they would serve as the orientation points that Schlegel and his contemporaries (A. W. Schlegel, Schleiermacher, Novalis, etc.) hoped to revive as a means of understanding modern politics, aesthetics, and philosophy. Furthermore, the "older moderns" would be complemented by the contemporary moderns, of whom Goethe was Schlegel's most widely referenced example: with Goethe's novel *Wilhelm Meister* enjoying the honor of being, together with Fichte's *Wissenschaftslehre*, and the French Revolution, one of the "greatest tendencies of the age."[74]

In the chapters that follow, I will argue that Schlegel's romantic project is intimately connected to the philosophical project of showing that the inherent incompleteness of romantic poetry has important consequences for the status of our knowledge claims (this is clear from Schlegel's reaction to many of the post-Kantian attempts to ground philosophy and secure an absolute foundation for our knowledge claims): according to

Schlegel we do not build knowledge deductively from absolute foundations but rather piece our claims together in a coherent scheme, so absolute certainty is not an appropriate epistemological goal. Greater and greater degrees of certainty are the most we can hope for. It is in this epistemological, antifoundationalist sense that Schlegel's philosophy is romantic.

The group of thinkers who contributed to *Das Athenäum* was introducing, via 'romantic,' a new, revolutionary description of an ideal not only of poetry but also of human knowledge in its boundlessness, an ideal that committed them to a certain philosophical method. However, this term was not, in their time, used to describe the thinkers themselves. According to Behler, *new school* or *Schlegelian school* was the most frequent designation.[75]

Schlegel remained in Berlin until 1799 when he returned to Jena, joining Schelling, Tieck, and Novalis. The year 1800 was not promising for the intellectual horizons of Jena: Fichte had been dismissed in 1799, a casualty of the Atheismusstreit, and in early 1800 Schelling left. With the departures of Fichte and Schelling, the university took a chance on a rather obscure figure, and after some discussion of his credentials, Friedrich Schlegel was offered a position as a lecturer at the university. Two lecture courses were announced: (1) "Über Transzendentale Philosophie," (2) "Über die Bestimmung des Gelehrten." (It is unknown whether the latter course was ever given and what precisely Schlegel intended to cover in these lectures: whether he came to praise or to critique Fichte's *Bestimmung*, which Fichte had presented in the summer semester of 1794.) Schlegel's course on transcendental philosophy attracted some seventy students, yet most did not stay until the end of the semester (23 March 1801).[76] Apparently, Schlegel's habit of speaking freely, without following any prepared comments, coupled with his lack of experience as a lecturer, made his lectures confusing, and many students were not motivated to continue attending the course. Schlegel preferred to place the blame for low attendance on the "intellectual laziness" of the students, rather than on his lecture style, and after the Jena Mißerfolg (failure) vowed never again to lecture publicly. The last lectures of his romantic period, the Köln lectures, *The Development of Philosophy in 12 Books* (1804–1806), were given to an intimate audience of three (Sulpiz and Melchior Boisserée and Johann Baptist Bertram), who in contrast to the "lazy" students of Jena, met patiently with Schlegel for two full years of instruction. During all of Schlegel's moves and activities in his romantic phase, and throughout his writings, one thing remained steady, Schlegel's skepticism regarding a philosophy based on first principles. That skepticism will be my focus as well as I present Schlegel's romantic philosophy.

Schlegel converted to Catholicism in 1808, but a shift away from his romantic phase can be observed as early as 1804, the year he left Paris.

Schlegel's conversion was one step in a series of many that signaled his growing conservatism.[77] He and Dorothea eventually settled in Vienna, and Schlegel became a counselor in Metternich's government. According to Beiser, when Schlegel attempted to account for his conversion to the Roman Catholic Church, he referred to the sense of belonging he felt within it. In 1817 he claimed that his intellectual career could be described as an attempt to attach himself to a whole greater than himself: "In my life and philosophical apprenticeship there has been a constant searching after eternal unity... and an attaching to something external, a historical reality or a given ideal... There was an attaching to the orient, to the German, to freedom in poetry, finally to the church, as everywhere else the search for freedom and unity was in vain. Was this attaching not a search for protection, for a final foundation?"[78] Already in a fragment from 1806, he had expressed his fondness for Catholicism: "To become Catholic is not to change one's religion, but to acknowledge true religion."[79] The pantheism of Schlegel's early period is now seen by him as the entrance to truth (*Eingang zur Wahrheit*) with Catholicism as the final goal. This shift was not unique to Schlegel, for many of the early German Romantics underwent similar conversions, transforming their early revolutionary goals into more conservative ones. While I will not investigate the causes of the conservative turn that Schlegel and many in his cohort underwent, it is an issue that does warrant attention.[80]

My focus in this book shall be on a particular period of German intellectual history, from 1794 to 1808, on the problem of grounding knowledge and Schlegel's solution to this problem. While the focus is limited, I believe that the investigation yields productive insights into aspects of the post-Kantian discussions that remain underexplored in the Anglophone world and that still have much to teach us about nothing less than the unity of knowledge.

Schlegel's Antifoundationalism

Schlegel was consumed with the problem of philosophy's starting point; his solution to this problem was informed by his general skepticism regarding the project of basing philosophy upon any absolute, single principle. This skepticism was the result of attempts, most notably of K. L. Reinhold and J. G. Fichte, to secure the "first principles" of Kant's critical philosophy. These "first principles," it was argued, formed the building blocks or ground of all philosophy. Hence, it was with these principles that philosophy must begin. Further, until these principles had been uncovered, philosophy would never be a science, that is, a unified whole but rather, merely a loose collection of parts. Schlegel's work challenged this view of philosophy. As we shall see, Schlegel did not support the view that before philosophy could begin, it was necessary to secure its first principles. Philosophy does not begin with a certain starting point from which all else is deduced. Schlegel argues that philosophy cannot proceed without a view of the larger context within which our knowledge claims take place. This in turn leads him to claim that philosophy cannot proceed without a history of philosophy and further that there are no single principles from which he can deduce truth with absolute certainty. Hence, he rejected anything like a Fichtean single, absolute first principle for all philosophy, and the line of deduction governing such a system, embracing instead a *Wechselerweis*, which, as shall become clear in due course, is Schlegel's term for holistic justification.

The *Wechselerweis* is part of Schlegel's vision of philosophical method, a method connected to a robust conception of organic unity and a plurality of starting points, rather than a method that departs from a single, absolute starting point. Deductive lines are replaced by a circle in Schlegel's view of philosophy and its method. In the chapters that follow I shall critically examine the sources and implications of Schlegel's romantic antifoundationalism. I have chosen to leave the term *Wechselerweis* untranslated. It consists of the German words *Wechsel* and *Erweis*, "change" and "proof," respectively. '*Wechsel*,' in the synthesis with *Beweis*, takes on the shade of a reciprocal, alternating, or mutual change in the process of confirming something, so perhaps the best English translation to capture what Schlegel is after with '*Wechselerweis*' would be something like "reciprocal," "mutual," or "alternating" confirmation.[81] The *Wechselerweis* is Schlegel's alternative to deductive, syllogistic proof structures.

Schlegel claims that "principles are always in plural, they construct themselves together; there is never just one as the fanatics of first principles think" (*KA* 18, 105, no. 910). Schlegel's references to a *Wechselerweis* are part of his conviction that no principle is comprehensible in itself but rather is in need of another principle, which is also in need of another principle for its clarification, and so on. What Schlegel is attempting to indicate with his references to the *Wechselerweis*, or the notion of justification as a process of mutual confirmation of beliefs, is that the search for truth is more like work on a crossword puzzle (to use Susan Haack's useful metaphor)[82] than it is like a deduction that leads us from a certain first principle to the truths that follow with certainty, and almost mechanically, from this principle. Armed with the *Wechselerweis* as the structure for evaluating evidence, our search for truth resembles our search for the word that best fits into a crossword diagram. We might think that the best five-letter word for a small body of water is *river* until we see that the word to be built has to have a *b*, so we go back and change the word to *brook*. Each solution we give to the crossword puzzle comes step by step and makes sense only as we find it coheres with the solution of other parts of the puzzle. Schlegel's references to construction are important, pointing to his coherence model of truth, to a process involving reciprocal confirmation of claims, which serves to lead us ever closer to truth, even while, as Schlegel does not tire of reminding us, our search for truth in life will (unlike the crossword puzzle) never be complete, which is why he emphasizes the infinite process of becoming that is an essential part of his romantic thought.

In what follows I shall present a systematic account of Schlegel's views concerning philosophy's starting point, although this was never systematically developed by him. For this reason, a critic could object to the procedure I follow. It is misleading, the critic could argue, to speak of Schlegel's thought in a systematic way at all because he claimed, against Fichte, Schelling, and Hegel, that philosophy is not a science, but a striving toward knowledge and thus can never attain systematic necessity. Both the content and the form of philosophy are, according to Schlegel inexhaustible (*unerschöpflich*).[83] This is consistent with his rejection of a philosophy based on first principles. If there is no absolute first principle upon which the science of knowledge rests, then philosophy cannot be endowed with systematic necessity.[84] Yet this does not entail that there is no structure to Schlegel's thought or that there is no system to be found within this structure. I think that there is, and although, as I have mentioned above, the form of Schlegel's thought does present the reader in search of arguments with certain problems, these problems are not insurmountable. This book is an attempt to come to terms with Schlegel's view of philosophy, and although his views and the way in which he presented them were unconventional, the conventional tools of philosophical analysis and systematicity are not misplaced in dealing with his work.

One clarification must be brought before the reader here. Throughout the book I shall be discussing various conceptions of philosophy, hence it is essential to be aware of the fact that for the philosophers of this period—immediately following the publication of Kant's *Critique of Pure Reason*—the foundations of knowledge *are* the foundations of philosophy as well, so a questioning of the foundations of knowledge was bound to result in a radically different view of philosophy itself.[85]

Overview

Understanding Schlegel's thought requires an appreciation of the philosophical commitments that shaped the early German Romantic movement. For this reason, chapter 1 will be devoted to distinguishing early German Romantic philosophy from a movement with which it is often confused (and under which it is all too often subsumed), classical German Idealism. As I have mentioned, Schlegel came to Jena in August 1796, and the time that he spent there is central to the development of his thought, not least of all because of his exposure to the controversies surrounding Reinhold and Fichte's attempts to revise Kant's philosophy. Schlegel worked out some of his most important positions in reacting to what he took to be the mistakes of figures such as Reinhold and Fichte. So, in chapters 1 and 2, the relevance of these thinkers to Schlegel's thought will be discussed. Another controversy that shaped Schlegel's thought was the so-called pantheism controversy or debate between Moses Mendelssohn and F. H. Jacobi regarding Lessing's alleged Spinozism. Jacobi equated Spinozism to atheism and condemned the German Enlightenment thinkers for taking a path that led to fatalism and atheism. His solution to the Enlightenment's dead end was a leap of faith that would jump-start our epistemological enterprises and free us of atheism and fatalism, the twin evils of Spinozism. Schlegel disagreed strongly with Jacobi's reading of Spinoza (and eventually embraced Spinoza's realism as a balm against the excesses of Fichte's idealism); moreover, he was just as opposed to Jacobi's appeal to faith as the starting point for philosophy as he was to Reinhold's attempts to move beyond the foundations of knowledge established by Kant in the *Critique of Pure Reason*. Schlegel's reactions to the controversies presented in chapters 1 and 2 will reveal the roots of Schlegel's skepticism regarding first principles and serve to show some of the ways in which early German Romanticism differs from the idealism of figures such as Fichte and Hegel.

Fichte's *Wissenschaftslehre* was heralded by Schlegel as one of the three greatest tendencies of the age.[86] In chapter 3 I shall examine the meaning of this claim, which amounted to far less than an uncritical embrace of all things Fichtean. As we shall see, though Schlegel's thought develops in reaction to Fichte's insights, there are nuances to his praise of Fichte. Schlegel was not the only one to react critically to Fichte's *Wissenschaftslhere*, and in chapter 3, I shall discuss some of the important critics that Fichte faced and in whose company Schlegel found himself. The first literary vehicle of this criticism was Friedrich Immanuel Niethammer's journal, *Philosophisches Journal*. The journal opened an important discussion of the feasibility of a philosophy based on absolute first principles. This, to repeat, became a central theme of the romantic philosophers. A careful examination of the journal's goals and contents reveals why and to what extent early German Romantic philosophy can be called a "skeptical" movement.

In chapter 4, I will discuss Niethammer's plans and objectives for the *Philosophisches Journal*. As its editor, Niethammer articulated the purpose of the journal in his announcement (*Ankündigung*) as well as in his preliminary report concerning the sorts of issues that the journal would discuss (*Vorbericht über Zweck und Einrichtung dieses Journals*), and both of these critical documents will be discussed. At the end of the chapter, I examine Schlegel's review of the first four issues of the journal (1795–96), for here we come to some important remarks by Schlegel regarding the nature of philosophy. The review was published in the *Allgemeine Literatur Zeitung* in 1797.[87] A study of the review reveals that although Schlegel shares with Niethammer the view that a philosophy based on a single, absolute first principle is untenable, he is as opposed to Niethammer's pragmatic appeal to common sense as he was to Jacobi's appeal to faith as the starting point of philosophy.

While Schlegel's critique of Niethammer gives us insight into his view of the relation between common sense and philosophy, Schlegel's critique of Kant, the great critical philosopher himself, gives us a clear view of Schlegel's notion of critique. In his writings on Kant, the central role that history and comparison play in Schlegel's conception of philosophy becomes clear. Schlegel's critique of Kant is the subject of chapter 5.

If philosophy cannot rest upon a single principle, how are we to ground our knowledge claims? According to Schlegel, all philosophy, and hence all knowledge, is always the result of a *Wechselerweis*, the central conceptual structure of his philosophy. This *Wechselerweis* and the view of knowledge from which it springs is the subject of chapter 6. Schlegel uses a cluster of metaphors to refer to the structure of knowledge and philosophy that emerges once we give up on the deductive model that relies on some absolute first principle. These metaphors all point to Schlegel's commitment to holism and a starting point for philosophy that need not be some clean, ahistorical starting point from above and from which all else can be deduced via a logical proof structure. Ultimately Schlegel will argue that our search for knowledge may begin anywhere as long as we see each starting point as part of a larger whole, as part of some sort of organic unity. One upshot of Schlegel's view of philosophy is that our knowledge claims will never attain a necessary, systematic unity. The form and content of philosophy are inexhaustible.[88]

Schlegel emphasizes change and endorses a "genetic" or "synthetic" method. This, I argue, is an essentially historical method in which change is primary. In order to clarify this, I present Schlegel's critique of paradigms of philosophy that rely upon the concept of the 'thing' as something ahistorical and static and discuss how this ties into his claims regarding the *Wechselerweis*. I then turn to Schlegel's review of Goethe's novel, *Wilhelm Meisters Lehrjahre*, which I present as not just a critical response to Goethe's *Bildungsroman* but also as a portrait of Schlegel's epistemological convictions and holism.

I conclude the book with an examination of the aesthetic consequences of Schlegel's thought (or what can be called, to follow Beiser's description, "the aesthetics of antifoundationalism").[89] Part of the reason for the dismissive view of early German Romanticism by philosophers has been its heavy dose of literary devices and the move to bring art and philosophy into closer conversation. Schlegel actually carried out his calls to unite poetry and philosophy (his experimental novel, *Lucinde*, is but one example of this), and he paid a steep price for this, shunned by both the poets and the philosophers, branded a mediocre poet and an unsystematic, dilettantish, sloppy philosopher. My assessment of him is more positive: I think that he was successful in leading us to rethink the structure of knowledge and in taking important steps to unify science, poetry, and philosophy. It is not my purpose in this book to show that Schlegel's philosophical project was infallible but rather to show that, right or wrong, Schlegel did have philosophical views. The worth of Schlegel's philosophy can only begin to be properly assessed after it is excavated from the forbidding surface of a tradition that buried it long ago.

Chapter One

Finding Room for the Romantics between Kant and Hegel

Philosophers have frequently modeled their work on the mathematical or natural sciences and distanced themselves from anything literary. The stereotype shaping this tradition is that philosophers, like scientists and mathematicians, are interested in truth and reality and poets in appearances, imitations of reality.[1] This stereotype has led many mainstream philosophers to identify themselves closely with the community of scientists and shun the company of poets. The upshot of this is a dry, technical style of philosophizing that pays little attention to literary devices that would detract the reader from the truth that is being shown by the argument of the philosopher. For, to resort to rhetorical flourish (rhetoric is, after all, merely *ars bene dicendi*, and philosophy is not an art but a science) is to leave the esteemed company of the philosophers and to enter the ill-reputed company of those who do not use language to uncover truth, but rather to persuade, like the sophists, or to deceive, like the poets.

One of the most reductionist views of philosophy put forth in the twentieth century was that of the logical positivists. An emblematic figure of the logical positivist movement was Rudolf Carnap. According to Carnap the domain of art belongs to the poets and the domain of theory to the philosopher. And for Carnap anyone who hopes to bring the two together, to be a kind of poet-philosopher, has confused art with theory and will only be able to generate nonsense. In order to produce theories, philosophers support their statements with arguments, claim assent to the content of these arguments, and polemize against philosophers of divergent persuasions by attempting to refute their assertions. Poets, on the other hand, "do not try to refute in their poem statements in a poem by another poet, for they know they are in the domain of art and not in the domain of theory."[2]

This view of the distinct task of the philosopher and the poet was met with a warm reception by philosophers who sought to give philosophy the reputable standing of a science. Though the star of logical positivism itself has dimmed almost to darkness, its spirit nonetheless continues to inform the way in which philosophy is done (especially in Anglo-American circles, where analytic philosophy holds sway) and the distance many philosophers like to keep from anything smacking of the literary. Seen through the lens of logical positivism, the post-Kantian period of German philosophy, with its talk of spooky concepts like *'das Absolute,'* *'das Sein schlechthin,'* *'der Geist,'* and other such things "measureless to man," looks like little more than an obscure pile of nonsense, nothing about which "real" philosophers have to trouble themselves.

Yet, there are some "real" philosophers who have attempted to defend the philosophical movements dedicated to analyzing such "non-sensical" terms. Richard Rorty is a well-known, even infamous, figure, who is well aware of the effects that reductionist views of philosophy have had upon the development of the field. He describes the legacy of positivism in his characteristically provocative way: "Logical positivists such as [Carnap] trained students to brush past romance and to spot nonsense. In the space of two generations, [. . .] dryness won out over [. . .] romance. Philosophy in the English-speaking world became 'analytic'—antimetaphysical, unromantic, highly professional, and a cultural backwater."[3] According to Rorty, the only way out of this stagnant water is to see that "Philosophy is best seen as a kind of writing. It is delimited, as is any literary genre, not by form or matter, but by tradition—a family romance involving, e.g., Father Parmenides, honest old Uncle Kant, bad brother Derrida."[4] Linguistic analysis, a method that Rorty had promoted early in his career, is not a method that goes along with a conception of philosophy as a kind of writing.[5] If philosophy is seen as a kind of writing, literary form no longer fades silently into the background, viewed with a resigned sigh: it takes on philosophical significance. Furthermore, once we begin to see philosophy as a "family romance," issues of "honest old Uncle Kant's" relation to "Father Parmenides" and "bad brother Derrida" may arise and with these, the act of comparing various stages of this family romance with other stages. In this way, the hermeneutical dimension of philosophy becomes more prominent. The task of understanding a philosopher's contribution will be more than simply a matter of getting the argument straight (although, of course, this will also be important). Rorty's conception of philosophy as a kind of writing goes hand in hand with certain aesthetic methods that involve issues of interpretation and historical contextualization. This, as we shall see, is much in keeping with Schlegel's view of philosophy as an essentially historical enterprise.

Philosophers who emphasize philosophy as a kind of writing are more open vis-à-vis the relation philosophy has to poetry and to disciplines other than mathematics and the natural sciences. Of course, philosophers should be cautious when entering these waters, for if philosophy becomes *merely* a kind of writing somehow reducing all reality to texts; that is, if philosophers give up the idea of an independent reality, then they are in danger of sinking into a kind of helpless relativism. Grim as it may be, philosophy as a cultural backwater would still be preferable to philosophy as a sea of relativism. Yet there is no reason to accept a false dichotomy: philosophy as *either* a set of verifiable propositions *or* merely as a kind of writing. There are many more models of philosophy available to us, models that need to be revisited.

The early German Romantics were one of the first groups of thinkers to seriously challenge the model of philosophy based on the natural or mathematical sciences, and, as a result, they faced then and continue to face now discrimination from "mainstream" philosophers. Insofar as they present their ideas systematically, it is much easier for philosophers who understand philosophy to be akin to science and to theory building to privilege the philosophy of Kant and Hegel; most philosophers remain suspicious of the use of fragments, dialogues, essays, and novels favored by philosophers such as the early German Romantics. Few philosophers are hospitable to a conception of philosophy that entails an intimate relation with the realm of art or a move toward making philosophy a cultural tool rather than a scientific tool.[6]

The unification of philosophy and poetry is threatening to philosophers because of the narrow way in which many of them conceive of *both* philosophy *and* poetry. On this narrow reading, philosophy is essentially an analytic exercise in clarity and critique, one that maintains an objective relation to an independent reality, whereas poetry tricks us with all sorts of semblances of reality, pulling us away from reality and into a never-never land of make-believe that obviously has nothing to teach us about how things are. More broad-minded views of both poetry and philosophy go a long way toward making us see that the two disciplines need not be "embattled adversaries."[7]

The early German Romantics endorsed just such a broad-minded view of both philosophy and poetry. Moreover, they did not appeal to poetry as a way of dragging us away from reality and confusing us with mere appearances. Indeed, their call for the completion of philosophy in and as poetry is the result of a deep-seated skepticism regarding the limits of philosophy and ultimately of human knowledge. And while Schlegel did not offer us a closed system, this does not entail that he was not serious about philosophy. Yet philosophers consistently disregard the work of the early German Romantics, precisely because of their innovative method and the fluid way in which they moved from philosophy to poetry, dismissing them in favor of the "grand system builders" of the period (esp. that almost holy trinity, Kant, Schelling, and Hegel). All too often, when the work of the early German Romantics is addressed, they are misread under the shadows of the more mainstream German philosophers of their period or even worse, demonized as the precursors of the Nazis.[8]

By clearly distinguishing the contributions of the early German Romantics from those of the more famous idealists of the period, I hope to go beyond the banal caricatures of the movement, which condemn the early German Romantics to a purely literary realm. In so doing I shall also carve a space for them that accurately depicts their philosophical contribution to the history of ideas and so to present them as something more than second-draft players on the great team of German Idealists (that famous line *from* Kant *to* Hegel, a teleological line according to which the problems introduced by Kant are solved by Hegel, in the culminating moment of the period). In short, then, one goal I have in presenting Friedrich Schlegel's romantic philosophy is to show that the period between Kant and Hegel contains a far greater diversity of philosophical controversies, ideas, and movements than can be seen if the only lens we use to focus on the "golden age" of German Idealism, roughly between 1781 (the year Kant published the first version of his *Critique of Pure Reason*) and 1807 (the year Hegel published his *Phenomenology of Spirit*), is that of the grand system builders.

Yet, before turning to Schlegel's contributions and the general philosophical thrust of early German Romanticism, we need to consider what is meant by German Idealism, a term that is all too elastic to serve us well if we are to attain a clearer understanding of the post-Kantian period. As idealism is a term that has been so often misrepresented, before beginning with a treatment of what the German Idealists were doing, it is worth clarifying some points regarding what the German idealists were not doing. For just as the Carnapian legacy has left philosophers with a suspicion of the nonsensical blending of philosophy and poetry, it has also left philosophers with a certain level of reserve against idealism, which is often read as a move away from reality.

Idealism: From Misconceptions to Post-Kantian Variations

All too often, idealism is associated with an antirealist position, in this sense, the *ideal* of idealism refers to that which is "not real." This sort of idealism is rooted in Berkeley's idealism and his famous *esse ist percipi* view of reality. According to this view, idealism is essentially a negative metaphysical doctrine. It was this sort of idealism that formed the basis of G. E. Moore's famous refutation. Yet, as Frederick Beiser has recently argued, the sort of idealism behind the German philosophical movements of the 1700s was rooted not in Berkeley, but in Plato. Indeed, Beiser's book *German Idealism: The Struggle against Subjectivism, 1781–1801* tells a story of German Idealism according to which this philosophical position is compelling *not* because it leads us to the subject, trapping us there in some sort of egocentric predicament that makes it impossible to determine whether our ideas of the world actually correspond to something objective in the external world, but rather because it leads to the development of a robust realism and naturalism.[9]

As the reception of German Idealism, especially in the analytic tradition, has suffered because of the general misperception that all forms of idealism amount to antirealism, we do well to keep in mind the following warning offered by Karl Ameriks:

> Anyone reading German Idealism should, at the very least, take note that the notion of idealism has carried with it both positive and not merely negative meanings and that the negative sense dominant in contemporary English is by no means to be assumed. The negative meaning of 'idealism' implies that most things that are commonly taken to be real are *not* in fact, that is, they do not exist at all, or at least not in the manner that has been assumed. The positive interpretation of 'idealism,' in contrast, involves seeing the term as *adding* rather than subtracting significance, as emphasizing that, whatever we say about the status of many things that are thought to exist at a common-sense level, we also recognize a set of features or entities that have a higher, a more 'ideal' nature.[10]

Beiser also stresses the importance of distinguishing between two quite different versions of idealism: "the two versions of idealism correspond to two senses of the term 'ideal,' the ideal can be the mental in contrast to the physical, the spiritual rather than the material, or it can be the archetypical in contrast to the ectypical, the normative rather than the substantive. Idealism in the former sense is the doctrine that all reality depends upon some self-conscious subject; idealism in the latter sense is the doctrine that everything is a manifestation of the ideal, an appearance of reason."[11] The dismissive reading of German Idealism would have the post-Kantian period represented as a slow eclipsing of the world by an overgrown subjectivity. Yet, according to Beiser's account, "the story of German Idealism becomes a story about the progressive *de-subjectivization* of the Kantian legacy, the growing recognition that the ideal realm consists not in personality and subjectivity, but in the normative, the archetypical, and the intelligible."[12] A major advantage of reassessing the philosophical commitments of the German Idealists in the terms suggested by Beiser is that the influence of Plato's thought on the movement comes into sharper relief. Plato was a pivotal figure not only for the German Idealists but also for the early German Romantics: Friedrich Schleiermacher translated his works, and, as I shall discuss in chapter 7, Schlegel referred to him with great admiration and modeled his own romantic irony on Socratic irony. Yet I ultimately remain unconvinced by Beiser's reading of the early German Romantics as absolute idealists of a Platonic or any other bent.

Despite some disagreements I have with Beiser's classification of the early German Romantics, I fully support his antisubjectivist reading of the German Idealists. To prevent general misunderstandings of the post-Kantian period, we do well to follow Beiser's advice and keep in mind that German Idealism is *not* a threat to a subject independent reality, *not* a breed of antirealism according to which all of reality depends on the subject, and so it is *not* a position that reduces all of reality to the mental or spiritual realm. Yet, it is certainly not sufficient, for the purposes of distinguishing German Idealism from early German Romanticism, that we know what German Idealism is *not*, we have to know something more about what it is.

In order to highlight the differences between German Idealism and early German Romanticism, what I am after here is not a definition of idealism in the basic sense of an ontological doctrine according to which things in the universe are dependent, in some way or another, on mental structures. In broad brushstrokes, what I shall do is present German Idealism as a response to the problem of knowledge introduced by Kant's critical philosophy. Obviously, I cannot offer an exhaustive account of the movement, which was incredibly diverse. And even my sketch in this chapter shall be limited to a focus on Fichte, Schelling, and Hegel's reception of Kant's philosophy, with special attention to how they attempted to solve the problem of Kant's troubling dualisms. In chapter 3 I shall return to the distinction between German Idealism and early German Romanticism, with a detailed focus on Fichte's idealism and Schlegel's critique of it.

Kant's transcendental idealism presented his contemporaries with a dualistic conception of human nature that was found to be highly problematic. What Kant sought to explain was how the mental and the physical, so utterly different in nature, were nonetheless related in such a way that it was possible for us to have knowledge of the external world, a world that was at once independent of us and yet accessible to us. In complicated ways, the term *transcendental idealism* brings together Kant's epistemological (the transcendental is that which lays out the conditions for the possibility of knowledge) and ontological (idealism is a position about the nature of the things in the world) commitments: commitments that are fully laid out only when we consider his system in its entirety as a combination of transcendental idealism and empirical realism. In working out his system, Kant was led to posit a duality between the *phenomenal* world, the world we can know, and the mind-independent or *noumenal* world, to which we can never have determinate access.

Much of the work of the post-Kantian German idealists was focused on overcoming the dualisms that they found troublesome in Kant's system, most notably, the one between intellect and sense, which is arguably *the* fundamental dualism in Kant's system (underlying the dualisms between, for example, concept and intuition, reality and appearance).[13] These dualisms were charged with landing us back in the very skeptical arena that Kant wanted to avoid with his critical philosophy. As Beiser has indicated, "[t]hough German idealism assumes such different, even incompatible forms, what all its forms have in common is the attempt to save criticism from skepticism."[14] It is my contention that a more careful look at the various attempts to save criticism from skepticism will help us to come to a better understanding of how to distinguish the unique contributions of the early German Romantics (Schlegel's contributions in particular) from those of the German Idealists who were their contemporaries.

Fichte, Schelling, and Hegel each addressed the problem of the sources and limits of human cognition. A decidedly idealist focus in the period can be found in the view that the role of reason is constitutive in shaping human experience yet that there must be some ground of reason, some unity underlying thought and reality that would enable us to move beyond Kant's troubling dualisms and so escape the threat of a skepticism that leaves us without clear access to the world as it is. Kant set limits to knowledge in order to avoid the mistakes of unreason (fallacies, amphibolies, antinomies, paralogisms, and other "monsters" born of the sleep of reason).[15] Furthermore, Kant saw his "critical method" as a way to provide an account of knowledge that would resist Cartesian and Humean doubts. Kant viewed his transcendental idealism as the only truly critical idealism, that is, the only position that would enable us to avoid the skepticism of whether or not our beliefs actually correspond to something in the world. Quickly, however, Kant's critics found problems with exactly how the sensible and intellectual realms, utterly different in nature, were supposed to interact. So began a host of well-known attempts to finish Kant's revolution, by tending to its true spirit (Fichte), providing the missing premises for his conclusions (Schelling), or finding a principle that truly grounded the critical philosophy (Reinhold).

Searching for the Unity of Thought and Being: Idealist *Jäger* versus Romantic *Spürhunde*

What most of the self-appointed Kantian revolutionaries shared was a certain search for the unity of thought and Being, something that would give us a way out of Kant's troubling dualisms and provide an answer to the age-old question of how mind and world connect. The unity of thought and Being is also known as the Absolute. Andrew Bowie characterizes the philosophical developments in the immediate post-Kantian period in terms of the German Idealists' goal "to articulate the relationship between mind and nature as a relationship between two ultimately identical aspects of a totality, the Absolute, thus overcoming the split between idealism and materialism."[16] One sensible way to approach the problem of clarifying the meaning of the German Idealist movement is to focus upon how the "big three" thinkers of the period, Fichte, Hegel, and Schelling, came to terms with the Absolute. Yet I want to avoid one standard reading justifiably criticized by Bowie and other scholars of the period, that is, the reading according to which "the move from Kant to Hegel via German Idealism and early Romanticism consists of the working through of a series of untenable attempts to deal with central Kantian problems, which are then largely resolved by Hegel."[17] Some of the problems posed by Kant's philosophy were addressed by the early German Romantics and in ways that, as Bowie points out, rejected "essential elements of German Idealism."[18] It is my view that an essential element of German Idealism that Schlegel rejects is that the ultimate origin of Being is transparent to reason. Schlegel and the early German Romantics accept a certain opacity of Being, which informs their skepticism and motivates their aesthetic turn, a turn too long underappreciated and dismissed as an irrational and unphilosophical move.

Each of the German idealists gives an account of the unconditioned or Absolute in order to overcome the split that Bowie refers to between idealism and materialism. Fichte's Absolute is pure being or the indifference point of the subjective and objective. Hegel's Absolute involves something like the establishment of the identity and nonidentity, the subjective and the objective, the ideal and the real in a correspondence that would explain the possibility of knowledge, all within the space of reasons generated by reason, and so, of course, transparent to reason.[19] Bowie goes on to characterize Hegel as arguing that "subjectivity and objectivity can therefore be thought of as grounding each other, without there being any need for a further ground. The Romantic question will be whether the position from which this can be asserted could actually be philosophically legitimated, rather than postulated as the goal of philosophy, which may not be attainable."[20] As Bowie suggests, the way in which the post-Kantians appropriate the Absolute will turn out to be pivotal for drawing a line between the German Idealists and the early German Romantics. Schelling is a protean figure, and for him, the absolute identity of subject and object is the work of art (a view that, as we shall see, links him closely to Schlegel, for whom the epistemological role of art was to be a central part of philosophy).

In order to deal with the Absolute, the German Idealists have to appeal to a nondiscursive mode of knowledge (nondiscursive in the sense of not being dependent upon the rules of thought provided by Kant's categories) in the form of intellectual intuition. This need arises from the somewhat paradoxical situation in which we find ourselves when we seek to *know* something about the unconditioned. As Schlegel put it: "To know already indicates a conditioned knowledge," so "[t]he unknowability of the Absolute is [a] triviality."[21] Schlegel's solution to the problem of the unknowability of the Absolute was to develop an alternative way to understand the structure of knowledge and reality, and it is in this development that Schlegel's romantic skepticism takes shape.

In contrast to the German Idealists, there is no attempt made by Schlegel to begin from or arrive at the original unity of thought and Being. The early German Romantics maintain a closer relation to what Günter Zöller has so aptly characterized as Kant's "oblique epistemological approach" and Andrew Bowie and Charles Larmore have described, using a somewhat different metaphor, in terms of an "opacity" in Kant (especially in reference to his talk of the imagination as "that art hidden in the depths of the human soul" and the enigmatic schematism as the way to circumvent the regress of rules for the application of rules).[22] As Bowie observes when discussing Kant's chapter on the schematism, a chapter that is uncharacteristically short and that has the function of explaining (in fewer than a dozen pages) nothing less than how we apply concepts of the understanding to objects of experience in order to form determinant judgments: "The functioning of judgment ... relies upon an aspect of spontaneity which cannot be conceptually articulated, because if it were to be brought under a concept it would lose its mediating status between intuition and concepts, receptivity and spontaneity."[23]

Since the functioning of judgment cannot be conceptually articulated, the way in which we come to apply pure concepts of the understanding to objects of experience in order to form determinant judgments remains an "art hidden in the depths of the human soul, whose real modes of activity nature is hardly likely ever to allow us to discover, and have open to our gaze" (*verborgene Kunst in den Tiefen der menschlichen Seele, deren wahre Handgriffe wir der Natur schwerlich jemals abraten, und sie unverdeckt vor Augen legen werden*" [A 141/B 180]). Claims such as these may have been what led Schlegel to characterize Kant as the *Spürhund* (or sniffer dog/sleuth) of philosophy and Fichte as the true *Jäger* (hunter) of philosophy; Schlegel himself is in this respect much closer to Kant than he is to Fichte, content to be aware that he is on the trail of the Absolute, without needing to grip it between his teeth.[24] An acknowledgment that there are aspects of our epistemological framework that remain elusive, that is, not open to our gaze, despite our most critical approach to philosophy, is something that Schlegel openly endorses, not, as has sometimes been claimed, as a detour away from the rationality celebrated by the Enlightenment thinking of Kant and his ilk, but rather as a humble acceptance of the limits of human cognition.[25] The German Idealists push for a crystal clear view of the Absolute as part of their effort to purify philosophy, understood as *Wissenschaft*, of any menacing shadows, anything that would not be open to our gaze, including, of course, the Absolute, or the unconditioned, and this sets them apart from their romantic colleagues. It is in this sense that Schlegel's seemingly lighthearted characterizing of Kant as the *Spürhund* and Fichte as the *Jäger* of philosophy takes us to a deeper philosophical point regarding what philosophers are able to achieve: the idealists go after and believe they have hunted down the Absolute, whereas the early German Romantics are convinced that we can be on the trail of the Absolute and get ever closer but never hope to capture it. This point has crucial ramifications for their view of knowledge and of truth.

To avoid possible misunderstanding of Zöller's position, generated by my references to his work, I should emphasize that Zöller, though concerned with presenting a counterimage to the Hegelian picture of German Idealism, is not interested per se in the early German Romantics and does not address Schlegel's work at all. Nonetheless, several of the points he makes regarding the radical critique of German idealism that he claims was carried out by Fichte, Schelling, and Schopenhauer can be used to help us gain clarity regarding the philosophical project of German idealism and the important contrast to this project we find in the work of the early German Romantics.

In his article "German realism: The Self-limitation of Idealist Thinking in Fichte, Schelling, and Schopenhauer," Zöller is concerned with filling out the story of post-Kantian developments in terms of the "realist self-supplementation" found in the work of three important members of the German idealist tradition.[26] Zöller's reexamination of German Idealism leads him to claim that "in placing reason in relation to a space on which it borders but that it cannot enter, Fichte, Schelling, and Schopenhauer, each in their own way, continue the Kantian project of articulating the grounds and bounds of reason. Like Kant they seek to strike a balance between the idealist recognition that the natural and social worlds reflect reason's demands and interests and the realist insight that the world is more than the work of reason."[27] The acknowledgment that "the world is more than the work of reason" means that those hunters of the unity of thought and being are never going to find such unity. They can only be on its trail (as the *Spürhund* is on the trail of the hunted animal). Zöller goes on to argue: "[T]o be sure, this reevaluation of reality does not amount to an outright cancellation of the idealist insistence on the constitutive role of reason. Rather, Kantian and post-Kantian idealism undergoes an emendation: the apparent self-sufficiency of reason is complemented, in fact completed, by being traced back to a dimension of ultimate origin or being that is beyond reason but without which there would be no reason."[28] The acknowledgment that Being cannot be fully uncovered via reason is no move to an irrational realm, but rather it "amounts to a radical critique of the system of absolute, purely rational idealism as developed by Hegel."[29] As Zöller indicates: "Throughout his development Schelling considers it philosophy's task to start with the absolute. This marks a departure from the oblique, epistemological rather than metaphysical approach introduced by Kant and still very much carried forward by Fichte. For Kant and Fichte, the absolute can come into view only from the perspective of the finite, human mind. Moreover, both Kant and Fichte insist on the essential limitations of the human mind in grasping the absolute, which can only be approximated by cognition and has to be rendered in images."[30]

The Fichte to whom Zöller refers is the later Fichte, who is much closer to Schlegel (more a *Spürhund* than a *Jäger*) than the early Fichte, who as we shall see in chapter 3, fell under sharp attack from Schlegel for his "crystal clear" reports of the foundations of knowledge. I am not here interested in entering a debate on how the later Fichte differs from the early Fichte. What I do want to highlight in bringing attention to Zöller's points is the emphasis that the critique of idealism put forward by Fichte (at least by the late Fichte), Schelling, and Schopenhauer, for all of their differences, shares a common point: the rejection of an absolute, purely rational idealism.

Each of the three thinkers discussed by Zöller, admittedly in strikingly different ways, admits some opacity with regard to just how much of the Absolute can be illuminated by reason alone. This point marks an important departure from full-blown idealism (that is an idealism according to which reason is entirely self-sufficient), even while each of the three critics maintains a certain commitment to idealism. The views of the period that granted reason full self-sufficiency in uncovering the ultimate origin of reason gave rise to a view that the Absolute, according to which it could be fully grasped by the human mind, that is, in a way that made the Absolute transparent to us. Schlegel rejected both the self-sufficiency of reason in connection with the problem of uncovering the ultimate origin of Being and the accompanying view that finite human beings could grasp the Absolute in its full light. The light of reason continues to shine for Schlegel and the early German Romantics, keeping us on the trail of our search for the Absolute, even while they argue that it alone cannot fully illuminate the ultimate origin of reason. Part of the philosopher's task is to help us find our way in the darkness, to give us a method for dealing with the opacity of the Absolute. Schlegel's rejection of the transparency of the Absolute is what gives rise to the most original aspects of his thought.

In contrast to Zöller, Charles Larmore and Andrew Bowie are both concerned with the early German Romantics in particular. Despite the different focus that they have, both Larmore and Bowie, like Zöller, refer to a departure from classical German idealism in terms of an acknowledgment that the Absolute "eludes" the grasp of reason. Larmore is interested in Hölderlin and Novalis' critique of Fichte, so he is interested in the early Fichte, the same Fichte that Schlegel critiques. In his article, "Hölderlin and Novalis," Larmore underscores the common philosophical convictions of Hölderlin and Novalis and how those convictions distinguish their philosophical contributions from those of Fichte.[31] His analysis clears space for a deeper understanding of the epistemically valuable aesthetic insights of the early German Romantics. As Larmore points out, Hölderlin and Novalis argued that our subjectivity "has its basis in a dimension of 'Being,' which eludes not only introspection but philosophical analysis as well . . . For both of them, philosophy runs up against limits that poetry alone can point beyond."[32] The opacity of Being is thus critical for understanding the difference between German Idealism (be it Fichte's, Hegel's, or Schelling's) and the philosophical project of the early German Romantics. Larmore's reading of Hölderlin and Novalis brings the unique contribution of the early German Romantics into focus, setting them apart from the German Idealists under whose shadows they are too often read.

Hölderlin and Novalis (and as we shall see, Schlegel too) agreed in opposing one of the leading assumptions of the idealism of the early Fichte and of Hegel, namely, "that reality is transparent to reason." As Larmore is careful to point out, Hölderlin and Novalis's move to deny subjectivity the status of a self-evident first principle does not entail that they dismiss subjectivity as an illusion, so the romantics are not heralding the "death of the subject."[33] What Hölderlin, Novalis (and, though Larmore does not mention him, Schlegel) do herald is an end to foundationalist approaches to knowledge and the beginning of a turn to poetry that is no embrace of the irrational but rather a turn toward aesthetic experience as a reliable and by no means irrational guide in our approximation toward the Absolute.[34] The early German Romantics do not make a typically German Idealist move to achieve a transparent look at the Absolute. And the most typical German Idealist, indeed the one against whom the contributions of the so-called secondary figures have too often been measured, is Hegel.

Andrew Bowie deftly captures the distinction between early German Romanticism and Hegelian idealism in the following way: "The core issue between the Romantic and Hegelian positions is, then, whether the Absolute really can, as Hegel thinks, be grasped by the power of reflection, and whether it therefore requires no presupposition external to reflection."[35] As Bowie goes on to claim, the early German Romantics do *not* think that the Absolute can in fact be grasped by the power of reflection alone, and this recognition gives rise to a view of knowledge markedly different from Hegel's: "The Romantic Absolute is not what philosophy can articulate by revealing the ultimate relativity of finite contradictions, because there can be no end knowable in advance to the contradictions generated in the structures we have described. The Absolute is, rather, what renders our knowledge relative and continually open to revision, at the same time as sustaining the goal of truth by assuring that revised judgement must be able to be predicated of the same world as the preceding now false judgement."[36] This point regarding the Absolute as that which renders our knowledge relative and continually open to revision is crucial to distinguishing *Frühromantik* from German Idealism. As we shall see, even the meticulously presented version of absolute idealism that Beiser presents overlooks this, which is part of the reason that he insists that the early German Romantics are absolute idealists.

Terry Pinkard's "Hegel's *Phenomenology* and *Logic*: An Overview," also makes reference, albeit it not entirely explicitly, to a kind of "oblique epistemological approach," in Hölderlin's work, as he traces several of Hegel's insights back to this tragic figure who for far too long has been neglected by philosophers.[37] According to Pinkard, Hegel's *Phenomenology of Spirit* is a reaction to Hölderlin's original insight that all mediated knowledge (all judgments we make) presupposes an original unity of thought of Being (something that cannot be judgmentally articulated): "The original, primordial unity of thought and being was reconceptualized by Hegel as an *intersubjective* unity constituted by patterns of mutual *recognition*, from which other conclusions could indeed be derived. However, Hegel also believed he had to motivate such a change in direction in idealist thought by showing that this conception itself had historically come to be *required* of us, that it was not simply one philosophical option among others."[38] While Pinkard does not himself derive from his argument ways of distinguishing between *Frühromantik* and German Idealism, the elements are there to draw such differences (so our task is much easier than Schelling's—we do not have to look for the missing premises of a given conclusion, just to draw the conclusion from clearly presented premises): the early German Romantics accept the opacity of Being, whereas idealists such as Hegel develop an absolute idealism that allegedly provides a transparent glimpse of Being.

Hegel, good German idealist that he was, could not accept the epistemological opacity that is a hallmark of romantic thought. He instead, according to Pinkard, developed a notion of judgment as taking place within the whole of the "space of reasons," or the "absolute I," which is what articulates the original unity of thought and being that Hölderlin (and the early German Romantics) insisted could not be articulated via judgment.

Frank's Romantic Realists versus Beiser's Romantic Idealists

Like Bowie, Larmore, Pinkard, and Zöller, Manfred Frank traces classical German Idealism to its articulation by Hegel that consciousness is a self-sufficient phenomenon, one that is able to make the presuppositions of its existence comprehensible by its own means. Frank contrasts this kind of idealism and the accompanying view of the self-sufficiency of consciousness to the conviction that characterizes the early German Romantics, namely, that self-being owes its existence to a transcendent foundation that cannot be made fully transparent by consciousness, claiming, in no uncertain terms, that it is a mistake to read *Frühromantik* as a mere appendage to German Idealism.[39]

Frank offers the following (admittedly *ad hoc*) definition of early German Romanticism:

> The thought of Hölderlin and that of Hardenberg (Novalis) and Schlegel *cannot be* assimilated to the mainstream of so-called German idealism, although these philosophers developed their thought in close cooperation with the principle figures of German idealism, Fichte and Schelling (Hegel, a late-comer to free speculation, played at that time only a passive role). The thought of Hölderlin, Novalis, and Schlegel implies a tenet of basic real-

ism, which I will provisionally express by the formula, that that which has being—or, we might say, the essence of our reality—cannot be traced back to determinations of our consciousness. If *ontological* realism can be expressed by the thesis that reality exists independently of our consciousness (even if we suppose thought to play a role in structuring reality) and if *epistemological* realism consists in the thesis that we do not possess adequate knowledge of reality, then early German Romanticism can be called a version of ontological and epistemological realism.[40]

Frank emphasizes the strong connection between the romantic position that the true foundation of self-being is a puzzle that cannot be handled by reflection alone to the early German Romantics' privileging of art and aesthetic experience. Frank's reference to the puzzle posed by the problem of Being, the "oblique epistemological approach" alluded to by Zöller, and the "opacity" of Being to which Bowie and Larmore refer, each points to a characteristic feature of romantic philosophy, an acknowledgment that our epistemological limitations make it impossible for us to get a transparent, crystal clear look at the Absolute: aesthetic experience allows us to approximate the Absolute. This epistemological humility contrasts rather sharply with the confidence exhibited by the German idealists of the period, (the early) Fichte and Hegel, both of whom are led in their philosophical endeavors by the belief that Being is, ultimately, transparent to reason.

The epistemological humility that is a hallmark of romantic thought and to which Frank appeals in distinguishing early German Romanticism from German Idealism should not be confused with a move away from reason, a confusion that seems to affect Beiser. Beiser characterizes Frank's strategy for distinguishing between early German Romanticism and German Idealism as one that brings us back to the misleading view that the early German Romantics were anti-*Aufklärung* thinkers, reviving the "distinction between the aestheticism of *Frühromantik* and the rationalism of the *Aufklärung*," by maintaining "that the romantics' first principle is suprarational and presentable only in art."[41] This in turn leads Beiser to make the rather puzzling move of classifying Manfred Frank, a philosopher who is more interested in the affinities between early German Romanticism and analytic philosophy (that is, in analyzing the connections between say, Novalis or Schlegel in relation to Donald Davidson, Hillary Putnam, or Thomas Nagel) than he is in tracing the connections between early German Romanticism and the work of Jacques Derrida or Paul de Man, as a postmodern interpreter of early German Romanticism.[42]

Yet Frank does not claim that the Romantics' "first principle is suprarational and presentable only in art." Frank, in fact, argues that the early German Romantics abandon the project of a philosophy based on first principles altogether; their Absolute is not a first principle of any sort but rather a *regulative idea.* Moreover, their turn to aesthetics is no "suprarational" move. Frank explicitly distances early German Romanticism from postmodernism, by emphasizing the role that the notion of the Absolute plays in the development of early German Romanticism: "*Without* the tendency towards the Absolute philosophy could not act 'polemically' towards the finite. Therefore he who wishes to mark the beginning of the truly radical modern (or even post-modern) with the dissolution of the notion of the Absolute is in error. Were it not for the orientation of a non-relative One, then the different interpretations which surface in history could never contradict one another and so also not annihilate one another."[43] Frank underscores the pivotal role that the notion of the Absolute plays in the romantic conception of knowledge: the Absolute is that which renders our knowledge continually open to revision. In his discussion of Novalis' conception of the Absolute, Frank emphasizes that according to Novalis' view, the Absolute can only be known negatively, which is why Novalis calls "searching for the first principle" a futile activity, "the squaring of the circle," and "from the impossibility of ultimately justifying the truth of our conviction [Novalis] draws the conclusion that truth is to be replaced with probability." Probable is what "is maximally well connected," that is, what has been made as "coherent as possible without there being an ultimate justification to support the harmony of our fallible assumptions of an evident Archimedean point of departure."[44] But this emphasis on coherence as a criterion for truth claims hardly amounts to an irrational move.

If we follow Frank's portrait of the early German Romantics, we come to a view of them as realists who nonetheless bid farewell to certainty as an epistemological goal and who embraced something like a coherence view of truth, built around a conviction that absolute justification is an impossibility, an attempt to square the circle, yet who are thinkers who strive for ever more knowledge and who drew important aesthetic consequences from the lack of any absolute grounding for our knowledge claims, not as part of any move away from reason and the progress of knowledge, but rather to serve both.

Fred Beiser, in part perhaps because of his belief that Frank's portrait of early German Romanticism lands us in an irrational realm, paints a strikingly different picture of the early German Romantics: they are not realists but absolute idealists. Beiser carefully unpacks what he means by the term *absolute idealsim*: "True to its name, absolute idealism was first and foremost a doctrine about the absolute, or to use some synonyms, the unconditioned, the infinite, or the 'in itself.' Like the term 'absolute idealism,' however, 'absolute' is rarely explicitly defined or explained [by the early German Romantics]."[45] After telling us that absolute idealism is a mixture of monism (not a plurality of substances, but a single substance exists), vitalism (the single, universal substance is an organism, which is in a constant process of growth and development), and rationalism (this process of development has a purpose or conforms to some form, archetype, or idea), Beiser tells us: "In absolute idealism a distinction is finally made between two senses of the ideal that had constantly been confused before Kant and by Kant: the distinction between the noumenal and archetypical on the one hand, and the mental and spiritual on the other."[46] Beiser claims that Frank's classification of the early German Romantics as realists is based on too narrow an understanding of idealism:

> Frank makes a sharp distinction between the philosophy of early romanticism and absolute idealism. Frank uses the terms 'absolute idealism' to designate the doctrine that 'the basic facts of our reality are mental (even ideal) entities' (*Unendliche Annäherung*, op. cit., p. 27). In this sense it is certainly correct to claim that the early romantics were not absolute idealists. However, it is important to see that the romantics themselves did not use the term in this sense, and that they did sometimes espouse a doctrine they called 'idealism.' Furthermore, it is misleading to place the romantics outside the idealist tradition entirely, as Frank would like, because they still adhere to some of its central principles.[47]

But it is incorrect to claim, as Beiser does, that Frank places the Romantics "entirely" out of the idealist tradition. In fact, Frank emphasizes, for example, some of the basic convictions that Schlegel shared with his idealist contemporaries, Hegel and Schelling, in particular, the insight that "the concept of finitude is dialectically bound to that of infinity and cannot be isolated from it."[48] Frank does observe, however, where Schlegel departs from Hegel and Schelling (and from an important strand of German Idealism), namely, in his conviction that we cannot represent the Absolute positively in knowledge.

Besier points us to Schlegel as the first romantic to use 'absolute idealism,' yet Schlegel's references to absolute idealism do not lend great evidence to Beiser's case that the best way to categorize the early German Romantics is as absolute idealists, for Schlegel never claims that absolute idealism alone would be enough to give us a clear understanding of the mind or the world. He in fact emphasizes that idealism must always be complemented by a strong breed of realism. And the fact that Schlegel emphasizes this seems to contradict Beiser's claim that absolute idealism, of the sort that characterizes the romantics, amounts to a kind of realism, for if Schlegel agreed with this, why would he insist that absolute idealism had to be complemented by realism? Consider the following fragments which Beiser offers as evidence of Schlegel's commitment to absolute idealism: "Absolute idealism without realism is spiritualism,"[49] or "The half-critic is more an idealist—Kant, Fichte—or more realist—Jacobi, Mohr, for to be an absolute [idealist or realist] in opposition and separate from the other is impossible. Only the absolute idealist is an absolute realist and vice versa."[50]

The most important element in Beiser's defense of early German Romanticism as a kind of absolute idealism is the Platonic heritage he ascribes to their breed of idealism: "This Platonic heritage means that— in one form or another—the absolute is identified with the logos or telos, the archetype, idea or form that governs all things. The absolute is not transcendent being, which is somehow presupposed by reflection and consciousness and so can never be its object."[51] Yet, as I will discuss in chapter 6, Schlegel is not receptive in general to a fixed, unchanging realm of being (except as we shall see, to provide rules of thought (logic) and laws to explain the motion of the cosmos (mathematics)), so Beiser may be treading on thin ice if he wants his classification of the early German Romantics as absolute idealists to rest on a Platonic heritage understood in terms of a philosophy guided by teleological principles.

Finally, Beiser claims that his appeal to the Platonic legacy of *Frühromantik* allows several important features of the movement to come to light, while avoiding the irrationalist readings of the movement, which have hindered a proper reception of its philosophical dimensions. He again takes Frank's reading to task for too easily slipping onto a path of irrationality:

> One of the most important [respects in which awareness of the Platonic legacy of *Frühromantik* leads us to revise our understanding of the movement] is recognizing that romantic aesthetic experience is not a kind of suprarationalism, a form of inscrutable awareness of the "mystery of being," which somehow presents the unpresentable only by virtue of the inexhaustible interpretability of a work of art. This assessment of romantic aesthetics, which finds its most powerful spokesman in Manfred Frank, suffers from several fatal difficulties. It is blind to the Platonic concept of reason in *Frühromantik*; it neglects the close connection between romantic aesthetics and *Naturphilosophie*, where the ro-

mantics did attempt to provide holistic explanations of nature; and, more important of all, it injects an unnecessary element of obscurantism into *Frühromantik*, which makes it vulnerable to all the old charges of antirationalism.[52]

While I take issue with aspects of Beiser's reading of the early German Romantics, I have deep admiration and respect for his work and for what he has accomplished with it. He has brought the early German Romantics into the canonical historical fold and has revealed crucial features of their work. Finally, philosophers are in a position to realize that questions such as, Can philosophy provide an exhaustive answer to the question of the nature of the self/mind (subjectivity) and its relation to the world? Must we give up the hope of exhaustive, certain answers to our questions and accept that limitations, deficiency, and a lack of absolute synthesis is part of the human condition, so philosophy will always have the epistemological opacity articulated by Kant, an opacity that art helps us to address? were addressed by the early German Romantics. A serious study of their unique contributions brings us to greater clarity regarding fundamental issues concerning the nature of human knowledge and the relation between mind and world. Nonetheless, in his attempt to save the early German Romantics from the allegedly obscurantist readings, I do believe that Beiser falls into a trap of a different sort, the dangers of which he is only too well aware:

> Someone might object that my Platonic interpretation of *Frühromantik*, with all its emphasis on holistic explanation, is proto-Hegelian. But I am tempted to turn this objection against itself: it is more a romantic reading of Hegel than a Hegelian reading of the romantics, for it shows just another respect in which Hegel was indebted to the romantic tradition. Specifically, it shows how Hegel's absolute idealism grew out of the romantic tradition; it was indeed only the most obscure and cumbrous expression of the absolute idealism that had already been worked out by Novalis, Schlegel, Hölderlin and Schelling... Still I admit that there is some point to this objection. Any proto-Hegelian reading of *Frühromantik* is problematic if it sees the romantics as system builders like Hegel... I think that my Platonic interpretation of *Frühromantik* avoids this pitfall. It still permits, indeed insists upon, a fundamental difference between *Frühromantik* and Hegel: namely, Hegel affirms, while the romantics deny, that it is possible to create a complete system of philosophy. In other words, Hegel affirms and the romantics deny that there is a single

conceptual elaboration and demonstration adequate to the intuitive insights of reason. In the romantic view, which again only follows the Platonic tradition, the discursive performance of reason will always fall short of, and never do full justice to, its intuitive insights. The romantics deny, in other words, that there is such a thing as the system of absolute knowledge; they read such a system as only a regulative goal, which we can approach but never attain through infinite striving.[53]

In stressing the romantic emphasis on the notion of system as a regulative goal, "which we can approach but never attain through infinite striving," Beiser's characterization of the early German Romantics begins to sound quite similar to Frank's reading, the one that Beiser rejects as irrational and inaccurate. Ultimately, I do not think that Beiser's reading of the early German Romantics as absolute idealists escapes the proto-Hegelian reading, which may unwittingly lend support to Frank's move to distance the early German Romantics from the German Idealists, well aware that without this distancing the Hegelian snare threatens.

The Hegelian snare is dangerous in terms of the reception of the early German Romantics, for when the early German Romantics are compared to Hegel, they are too often read as rashly scribbling down what the plodding Hegel systematically carried to the finish line, winning the philosophical race.

On Why Schlegel Is Not Hegel[54]

One important reason why the early German Romantics have gone unnoticed by most philosophers is that their work is read as part of the tradition of classical German Idealism, and in the company of grand system builders such as Fichte, Schelling, and Hegel, their work, which was not designed to result in grand theories at all, is often dismissed as incomplete and unimportant, as nothing more than a collection of dilettantish efforts either to do some strange version of poetic philosophy or to deal with philosophical problems that were much more "professionally" addressed by their contemporaries, Fichte, Schelling, and Hegel.

Encouraging this misreading of the early German Romantics as, at best, second-rate philosophers we find teleological historical narratives of the type initiated by Richard Kroner in his influential study of German Idealism (1921), *Von Kant bis Hegel*. Kroner presents the period from Kant to Hegel in terms of a teleological process culminating in the "universal synthesis of all prior views and standpoints that is Hegel's system."[55] Fortunately, in the years since the publication of Kroner's work, we have moved away from this Hegelian way of reading the period, and, as a result, the contributions of other thinkers of the period have come into sharper focus. Fichte, for example, has finally received the attention he deserves.[56]

Nonteleological readings of the period such as Beiser's *German Idealism: The Struggle against Subjectivism, 1781–1801* clear much-needed space on the map of philosophy for the early German Romantics.[57] Beiser privileges the early German Romantics in his tale of German Idealism, claiming that his study is "a reaction against the Hegelian legacy" and that Hegel was a "tortoise among hares,"[58] the hares being his predecessors in Jena, who never created grand systems, and who were treated with contempt in Hegel's rewriting of the history of philosophy. Beiser rejects the teleological reading of history that followed in Hegel's wake. One consequence of this rejection is that Beiser does not read German Idealism as a progression toward Hegel or a decline from Kant but rather as a much more nuanced movement and looks carefully at the contributions of individual thinkers on their own terms.

Nonetheless, vestiges of the Hegelian approach to history taint Beiser's reception of certain aspects of the Romantics. He claims that the Romantics' use of the fragment was part of a disorganized way to present their idea; the fragments lacked systematicity and completeness, which would be provided by the likes of Schelling and Hegel: "What was merely fragmentary, inchoate, and suggestive in Hölderlin, Novalis, and Schlegel became systematic, organized, and explicit in Schelling"[59] and "[w]hat Hölderlin, Schlegel, and Novalis... had left in fragments—what they regarded as a mystical insight transcending conceptual articulation—Schelling would now try to rationalize and systematize."[60] Although Beiser seeks to clear space on the map of ideas for thinkers squeezed out by Hegel, he claims, nonetheless, that "in unsurpassed fashion [Hegel] summarized and integrated into one system all the themes his less scholastic and organized contemporaries had left in fragments or notebooks."[61] With claims of such tenor, Beiser, for all of his insistence on the need to look at the post-Kantian period in a nonteleological way, seems to fall back into reading the period precisely in the Hegelian way he so strongly (and justifiably) criticizes. Beiser, in effect, reduces some of the Romantics' achievements, including their rejection of closed systems for the presentation of their ideas, to mere imperfect forms that awaited completion by system builders such as Schelling and Hegel.

The early German Romantics did have systematic ambitions, yet their conception of system had a rather special architecture, few were (and few continue to be) capable of appreciating. As I mentioned at the outset, philosophers continue to underestimate the role of literary form in philosophy, which hinders an appreciation of the philosophical contributions of the early German Romantics. The work of the early German Romantics was not work that awaited completion, even culmination, in Hegel or Schelling. The themes of incompleteness and incomprehension we find in their work are reflected in the literary forms they used to present it: the use of the fragment, for example, was *not* a result of a lack of resolution, a blameworthy incompleteness, in the sense of something that was meant to be finished and never was. Early German Romantic philosophy is incomplete not because the Romantics *failed* to finish their work but rather because they were convinced that a complete system could not be built.

As we have seen, many of the fragments published in *Das Athenäum*, the journal edited by Friedrich and August Wilhelm Schlegel between 1798 and 1800, reflect a skeptical attitude concerning the "proper startingpoints" of any scientific investigation and the possibility of certain results and of complete systems for the presentation of those results. We shall return to the aesthetic implications of Schlegel's antifoundationalism in chapter 7.

Yet, even before I give a detailed analysis of the romantic move to put philosophy and poetry into closer company, it is worth emphasizing at once that a major point of difference between the early German Romantics and the German Idealists is found precisely in that underappreciated element I have mentioned: literary form. The German Idealists favored conventional systematic approaches to their problems: the *Wissenschaftslehre*, the *System des transzendentalen Idealismus*, the *Phänomenologie des Geistes*, each, while by no means in strictly conventional ways, has systematic ambitions based on a view of philosophy as a discipline that should aspire to be like a science [*Wissenschaft*]: the literary form that Fichte, Schelling, and Hegel use is not open or playful (even while it is innovative). It guides the reader via strict argumentation to the conclusions that will authoritatively establish the theses defended. Rüdiger Bubner stresses that the Romantics, more concerned than their idealist contemporaries with commentary, criticism, and interpretation, also developed a different model of system. For the early German Romantics, "[t]he relevant model... is not a godlike creation of a system *ex nihilo*, as it was for the early idealists, but rather an actively sympathetic response of the part of the critic and the philologist to the significant creative works of the past."[62] As we shall see, Schlegel does indeed explicitly reject attempts to ground philosophy "ex nihilo" in ahistorical first principles, stressing the intimate relation philosophy has to history and tradition and searching all too often in vain for an active and sympathetic response to his own work, which was slow in coming.

Schlegel's view of philosophy is strikingly different from the view of philosophy shared by his Idealist contemporaries. It is a view shaped by his skepticism regarding our ability to grasp the Absolute through reflection alone and the ramifications of this insight, namely, that philosophy needs aesthetic tools to gain clarity regarding the ground of Being and that the search for the Absolute will never come to an end, so philosophy, as indicated in *Athenäum* Fragment 116 is a kind of infinite process of becoming, an infinite "*Sehnsucht nach dem Unendlichen*" (longing for the infinite) that will never be satisfied. The literary form that Schlegel favored to reflect that open-ended nature of philosophy was the fragment. Schlegel's use of the fragment is not to be read as an abandonment of an idea he was too lazy to systematize or not clever enough to fully develop, something in need of completion by a more systematic thinker, but rather his way of having and not having a system. For according to Schlegel: "It is equally fatal for the spirit to have a system and to have none. It will simply have to decide to combine the two."[63] I will return to this fragment several more times in my discussion of Schlegel's work, because an understanding of this rather cryptic fragment contains important clues for unpacking Schlegel's conception of philosophy itself. One point that Schlegel develops in this fragment is that every philosopher must have a system, for to make claims and construct arguments, we must assume some system, for we need limits, but this must be done with the recognition that any particular system is a part of a plurality of other systems. This is one important sense in which one must be within a system and without it. And instead of a closed system presumptuous enough to offer a last word on the nature of knowledge, what the philosopher has is a tendency, a path she follows to greater and greater degrees of probability, but never to certain truth. Philosophy does not require certainty, and those who dogmatically insist it does lead us only to error. Philosophy cannot be a science; it is more like an art. And as Andrew Bowie has observed, "[a]rt reminds us that the conceptually inarticulable can still be intelligible and may even be conceptually intelligible,"[64] so the move to put philosophy and art in closer relation, a move reflected in the use of the fragment, is not a move to an unintelligible, nonsensical realm.

The romantic skepticism that Manfred Frank stresses in his interpretation of the early German Romantics, that is, the skepticism regarding our knowledge of the Absolute, brings into view central aspects of the romantic philosophical project. The skepticism did not make the Romantics less philosophical, even while it made them more interested in the aesthetic dimensions of experience. It did lead them to experiment with innovative forms for philosophy, to experiment with form because they did believe that literary form was related to the very conception of philosophy and so related to a search for truth, which could best be reached via experimentation rather than by the decree of first principles.

Schlegel's concerns with the notion of system in philosophy arise as a consequence of his attempts to come to terms with the nature of human knowledge, which, once he had abandoned foundations and deductive method, was revealed to be anything but certain. According to Schlegel, the only truly critical philosophers were those who were willing to critique philosophy itself. So, while the German Idealists of the period tried to save criticism from skepticism, for the romantic Schlegel, the more important task was to take skepticism up a level to create a fully critical philosophy. One might then read the literary form of the fragment as a reflection of this skepticism rather than an as a heap of disorganized ideas awaiting systematic organization from a more "accomplished" system builder.

Romantic Skepticism

Schlegel was most emphatically *not* interested, as many of his German idealist contemporaries were, in finishing the revolution Kant had allegedly begun but had allegedly not finished. Indeed, as we shall see in chapters 3 and 5, Schlegel called into question the very level of "criticism" present in Kant and Fichte. The truly critical philosopher needed a heavier dose of skepticism than the German idealists had (and a heavier dose of historical attention than Kant, the great critical philosopher himself, had demonstrated).

According to Schlegel and his fellow romantics, no theory of the self will reveal us to ourselves as we are "in ourselves" or as we are absolutely. This view marks a significant departure from Fichte's idealism, and in many respects it marks a decisive break between early German Romanticism and German idealism overall. The elusive opacity of Being means that the notion of truth is going to look different than the conception of truth born of a system that presumes to have a transparent view of Being. Schlegel's "higher skepticism," or what Bowie has called Schlegel's "romantic skepticism" (contrasting this to Hegel's *Aufhebung* of skepticism), is addressed by Schlegel not only in his fragments but also in his lectures on *Transzendentalphilosophie* (delivered in Jena in 1800–01). In these lectures he claims that "All truth is relative, all knowledge is symbolic, and philosophy is infinite."[65] Yet the Romantics did not endorse the helpless relativism to which I made reference at the beginning of this chapter, a relativism that severs ties with objective reality. Schlegel was aware that his claim regarding the relativity of truth presented problems: "The claim that all truth is relative could easily lead to a general skepticism. For example, if all truth is relative, then the very claim that asserts that all truth is relative would also be relative. If everything is correctly understood, then one can concede this point. Nothing is thereby gained;

one can concede not only this claim, but also the claim that the entire system of philosophy is relative."⁶⁶ A philosophy that acknowledges the Absolute or some mind-independent reality, even if there is no crystal-clear access to it, even if we need the help of aesthetic tools, such as symbolism, metaphors, and a hermeneutical framework to come to an (ever-incomplete) understanding of it, is not the vulgar kind of relativism some postmoderns would like to locate in early German Romanticism and that Beiser would like to locate in Frank's reading of the early German Romantics. From the fact that the Absolute is not transparent to consciousness, it does not follow that there is no Absolute, which is, after all, a nonrelative orientation point if ever there were one.⁶⁷ Yet philosophy despite the presence of a nonrelative orientation point, philosophy, given the limitations of human knowledge, can never hope to come to an end, to reach a complete understanding of infinite reality. Schlegel notes "Absolute truth cannot be given, and this is the certificate for the freedom of thought and of spirit. If absolute truth were found, therewith the occupation of spirit would be complete, and it would cease to be, for it exists only in its activity."⁶⁸ Philosophy is a search for truth; yet it is no threat to the integrity of philosophy to point out that absolute truth will never be found, and that if it were, philosophy would come to an end. Schlegel's references to the relativity of truth point to a conception of truth claims as uncertain but not indeterminate. His view of truth is not antirealist, though; it is more like a coherence theory of truth than like a correspondence theory of truth. Schlegel's acceptance of uncertainty does not amount to an abandonment of a shared, objective reality against which we may measure our claims.⁶⁹

This point is essential to keep in mind if we are to be fair in our reading of other claims that Schlegel makes with respect to the nature of philosophy. For example, in *Athenäum* Fragment 84, he claims that "philosophy, like epic poetry, begins in the middle" (*die Philosophie, [fängt] immer in der Mitte an, wie das epische Gedicht*).⁷⁰ As claims of this tenor join others like "poetry and philosophy should be made one," it is tempting to read Schlegel as calling for a turn to the merely subjective and away from the objectivity of the world. Yet nothing could be further from the truth: Schlegel's emphasis on beginning in the middle and the relation between philosophy and poetry are part of his concern with the nature of philosophy and the result of his conviction that we cannot grasp the Absolute through reflection alone.

Since we cannot have knowledge of the Absolute, certainly we cannot use any absolute first principle as the foundation for our philosophy. Schlegel's talk of the relativism of truth is part of his view of philosophy as an infinite activity. In the first book of the lectures on the history of philosophy, entitled *Die Entwicklung der Philosophie in Zwölf Büchern* (Köln, 1804-05), Schlegel addresses the problem of where we begin when we philosophize: "To desire to provisionally prove what the beginning point of philosophy is, concerns separating out the first principle of philosophy (if there is such a principle), as is actually attempted in some scientific introductions. One can admit that in a tentative treatment the point from which one must begin to philosophize will be searched for and proved."[71] Of course, if there is no such principle, it will only be searched for and never found. In several fragments and in an essay, "Über die Unverständlichkeit," Schlegel stresses the value of incomprehension.[72] Because our knowledge claims are never rooted in an absolutely certain foundation, we cannot be so arrogant as to think that we will ever have the last word on the meaning of any given event or text or idea. The remainder is that which is incomprehensible. Schlegel's emphasis on incomprehensibility is part of his concern with what it means to understand a text, that is, with the hermeneutical dimensions of philosophy. His contemporaries were not well equipped to appreciate this aspect of his thought, however, which is why it became a fashionable mockery to claim that "what one does not understand, must have been written by a Schlegel" (*was man nicht versteht, hat ein Schlegel geschrieben*). Schlegel played with language in order to question nothing less than what Bowie has called "its world-disclosing function," yet philosophers have been very slow to see the critical potential in Schlegel's ironic approach to deep philosophical problems.

Schlegel's antifoundationalism and accompanying skepticism regarding the absolute certainty of our knowledge claims allow for plenty of play room in our epistemological attitudes. Irony finds a home here. Schlegel's good friend and fellow romantic Novalis described the communication of a thought as a fluctuation between "absolute comprehension and absolute incomprehension" (*Blütenstaub* 2), and Schlegel echoes this idea in many of his fragments, especially in *Lyceum* Fragment 108, where he claims that Socratic irony "contains and arouses a feeling of indissoluble antagonism between the absolute and the relative, between the impossibility and the necessity of complete communication." The best case for a Platonic legacy to be found in the early German Romantics can be made from "the ironic smile of Socrates" that Beiser claims is found "beneath the surface of Schlegel's skepticism about first principles and complete systems"[73] rather than in Plato's theory of ideal forms. I shall address that aspect of the Platonic legacy in chapter 7, where I will analyze the philosophical significance of Schlegel's emphasis on incomprehension and irony. Yet here I do want to note that irony, and the problem of understanding and misunderstanding is part of Schlegel's questioning of the very nature of philosophy itself and proved to have important ramifications for the question of philosophy's relation to hermeneutics and aesthetics.

As we shall see in the following chapters, Schlegel's embrace of incomprehensibility and uncertainty contrasts sharply with the views of the German Idealists, who were his contemporaries, especially Fichte's. Yet, all too often, if early German Romanticism even appears on the radar screens of the philosophers, it is often mischaracterized as a breed of German Idealism. According to this historical narrative, eighteenth-century German philosophy begins with Kant and reaches its culmination in Hegel: German philosophy develops *from* Kant's transcendental idealism, through Fichte's subjective idealism, *to* Hegel's majestic absolute idealism. But this "from . . . to" narrative, provides an order to the various philosophers of the period at too high a cost: if the idealism of the period reaches its culmination in Hegel, all of the thinkers between Kant and Hegel can only be read as parts of a greater path toward what only Hegel would properly accomplish. Under such a reading, the fragments, essays, and dialogues of the early Romantics, along with their talk of approximation and becoming, are erroneously read as unfinished projects that would be completed by the grand system builder Hegel.

The contributions of the early German Romantic philosophers can be fully appreciated only if we come to an understanding of them not as a breed of the more famous absolute German Idealists of the period, but on their own terms, through an understanding of their skepticism, a central root of early German Romanticism.[74] Schlegel's skepticism regarding our ability to have a clear look at the ground of Being led him to reject any attempt to ground philosophy upon a first principle and to embrace the notion of philosophy as finding its completion in and as poetry.

Romantic philosophy takes us out of the unromantic, cultural backwaters into which reductionist movements such as the logical positivists pull us as they dismiss art as having any relevance to philosophy. Indeed, Schlegel even goes so far as to claim: "In a critique of philosophy, philosophy must be treated as art."[75] Furthermore, he says, "There is reality that one cannot handle better than handling it as poetry. Animosity, so-called misfortune, mishandlings. There is much such poetry in the world. All middle things between humans and things are poetry..."[76] Reality that is handled *as poetry* does not become any less real, yet in handling it as poetry, we are reminded of the opacity born of our epistemological limitations, and critical philosophy is ultimately about the limits that must be set to our knowledge claims so that we can avoid nonsense and all of the other monsters born of the sleep of reason.

One consequence of treating philosophy *as* art is the use of literary devices that leave aesthetic play room for the reader. Schlegel's call to view philosophy as an art is part of his characteristic *Frechheit*, yet he wanted to do more than provoke. Schlegel's call to bring poetry and philosophy into closer company and his use of unconventional literary forms were part of a serious project dedicated to a very old-fashioned conception of philosophy as the search for truth. Schlegel's use of the essay and the fragment mirrored certain views of truth that he was developing.[77] While the stern system builders of the German Idealist movement were much more bound to the notion of philosophy as a science, protecting the dignity of philosophy from capricious aesthetic elements, the early German Romantic movement opened philosophy's borders with poetry, and not because of any disregard for reality or for truth, but rather as a result of a serious reflection upon the nature of both.

An understanding of the family romance that is philosophy can be better understood if we begin to pay more attention to the critique endorsed by the early German Romantics, which can only come into view once we begin to pay attention to their contributions, according to their own merits, instead of reading them under the shadows of the grand systems of the German Idealists. Philosophers do not really need to be afraid of poetry. It does not threaten truth or reality, but may, in fact, offer us keener insight into the nature of both.

Of course, while I have argued that we would do well to learn to read Schlegel's work on its own terms, this in no way entails that we do well to read his work in isolation from the major controversies that shaped his generation. And it is to just such controversies that we shall now turn.

Chapter Two

Searching for the Grounds of Knowledge

Schlegel's thought took shape in response to a "community of themes"[1] that emerged from the major events that set the agenda for much of the philosophical discussion in the last two decades of the eighteenth century of German thought, a period shaped by one fundamental problem: the grounds of knowledge.[2] The formative events of the period were: (1) the controversy between Mendelssohn and Jacobi (1780–85) concerning Lessing's alleged Spinozism and the subsequent publication of Jacobi's *Über die Lehre Spinozas in Briefen an Herrn Moses Mendelssohn* (*On the Philosophy of Spinoza in Letters to Moses Mendelssohn*) (first edition, 1785, revised and expanded, 1787); (2) the publication of Kant's *Critique of Pure Reason* (A version, 1781; B version, 1787), and (3) Reinhold's attempt to establish a foundation for the *Critique*, which was developed in his *Elementarphilosophie*, in his *Versuch einer neuen Theorie des menschlichen Vorstellungsvermögens* (*Essay towards a New Theory of the Faculty of Representation*) (1789, 1795), and in his *Über das Fundament des philosophischen Wissens* (*The Foundation of Philosophical Knowledge*) (1794).

Schlegel's reactions to Jacobi and Reinhold's work give us important insight into the emergence of his skepticism. In his skeptical response to the attempts of Jacobi and Reinhold to establish a first principle for philosophy, Schlegel joined the company of an important skeptic who provoked Fichte to develop a more resistant strain of foundational philosophy than the one offered by Reinhold. After presenting Schlegel's confrontation with Jacobi and Reinhold, I shall turn to the pivotal role played by the mysterious skeptic Aenesidemus, pen name of Gottlob Ernst Schulze.

Jacobi's *Salto Mortale*

A formative event of eighteenth-century German thought, which can accurately be characterized as "the true acid test for someone's loyalty to reason in late eighteenth-century Germany"[3] was the debate between Friedrich Heinrich Jacobi and Moses Mendelssohn concerning Gotthold Ephraim Lessing's philosophical loyalties.[4] The issue debated by Mendelssohn and Jacobi was whether Lessing, a well-known member of the Berlin Enlightenment, was really a Spinozist. A "Spinozist" would grant reason absolute authority, even if that meant denying authority to the claims of faith. Because Spinoza was famous for his pantheism, the debate became known as the pantheism controversy. Inasmuch as this name suggests that pantheism was the central theme of the controversy, it is not an accurate description of the event, for what was really at stake in the debate was the issue of whether faith or reason should have the upper hand in human knowledge. This is why one's response to this controversy became a kind of litmus test of one's philosophical loyalties.

The story surrounding the controversy is not lacking in drama, a drama that in the twenty-first century seems almost unbelievable. As the story is told, Jacobi claimed that on his deathbed, Lessing had confessed his allegiance to Spinoza's philosophy and hence to the fatalistic trappings of Spinoza's rationalist system. Jacobi used this alleged confession to further his critique of the Enlightenment's faith in reason. Mendelssohn was an important member of the Berlin Enlightenment and as such, a staunch defender of the claims of reason. In 1781 he was working on a tribute to his friend and fellow philosopher Lessing, and it was at this time that Jacobi informed him of Lessing's confession.[5] Mendelssohn quickly realized that Jacobi planned to use Lessing as a symbol for the model of reason propounded by the Berlin Enlightenment and then, by equating it with Spinozism, to demonstrate the fatal consequences it had for religion and morality.

Jacobi developed his claims regarding Lessing's alleged Spinozism in a series of letters published in 1785 and entitled *Über die Lehre Spinozas in Briefen an Herrn Moses Mendelssohn*.[6] An expanded edition of the letters was published in 1787 and came to be known as the *Spinoza Büchlein*. The core of Jacobi's argument against Spinoza's system is to be found in the Supplement 7 to his *Spinoza Büchlein*. It is in this section of the work that he announces, "All demonstration ends in fatalism" (*Alle Demonstration gebe in Fatalismus aus*). Jacobi's view of demonstration as ending in fatalism rests upon his view of knowledge. Jacobi understood knowledge in causal terms: to know x is to know the cause of x. The search for the cause of x leads us to y, which leads to search for y's cause and so on, until we find the first cause, or the uncaused cause. But we cannot know this uncaused cause, for to know it would be to know its cause, and we would no longer be dealing with an uncaused cause. Something that is uncaused is by definition unknowable.

Jacobi goes on to argue that it is absurd to claim that the foundation of knowledge is a principle that can be known to us, for if we had knowledge of this first principle, we would know its cause, and if the first principle has a cause, it cannot be a first principle. Jacobi showed that there was an infinite regress involved in any attempt to *know* the first principle of knowledge. Clearly, an "enlightened" thinker would shirk the futility of infinite regresses and certainly not call upon them to establish a foundation for knowledge. Yet, by linking Spinoza's uncompromsingly rationalist system to Lessing, a prominent member of the Berlin Enlightenment, Jacobi hoped to show that "enlightened" thinkers were indeed on a path that would lead to the sort of infinite regress that he sketched in his *Spinoza Büchlein*.

Jacobi, of course, had an alternative to the atheistic and fatalistic consequences of the rationalist model of reason. He suggested that we give up the attempt to establish a first principle for philosophy on the basis of reason and instead accept the certainty with which we begin any chain of reasoning as an act of faith, not of well-grounded reason. For Jacobi, our edifice of knowledge must rest upon a foundation of self-justified beliefs, and these must be taken on faith, for to take them on the basis of anything else would be problematic along the lines sketched above. With this move, Jacobi challenged one of the central tenets of the Enlightenment—the primacy of reason. This is well expressed in these words from Jacobi to Mendelssohn:

> My dear Mendelssohn, we are all born in faith and must remain within this faith, just as we are all born in society and must remain within society. *Totum parte prius esse necesse est.* How can we strive for certainty when certainty is not known to us in advance; and how can it be known to us, other than through something that we already recognize with certainty? This leads to the concept of an unmediated certainty, which stands in no need of explanation (*Gründe*), but actually excludes all such explanation, and solely and alone with the represented things is the corresponding representation itself. Conviction based on argument is second-hand conviction. Reasons are only properties of the similarity with things of which we are certain. The conviction which brings these about arises from a comparison and can never be totally certain or complete. If faith is an act of holding something to be true without

relying upon argument, then the very security we place in arguments of reason must be rooted in faith and so arguments of reason must take their strength from faith.[7]

Of course, for Mendelssohn, reason was the uncontested foundation of knowledge. Yet in this passage, Jacobi inverts the relation between reason and faith, rooting reason in faith. According to Jacobi, what one can grasp with the intellect is not nearly as vivid or certain as what one "grasps" through faith. This is because the claims of faith are accepted on the basis of feeling, which is immediate, and stands in no need of mediation via demonstration. Jacobi's emphasis on faith was a challenge to the Enlightenment's emphasis on the role of reason in the structure of knowledge and its progress.

While charging the Enlightenment thinkers with the absurd move of positing an absolute foundation of knowledge that could be explained through reason, that is, in pointing to the *irrationality* of their very rational enterprise, would it be far-fetched to accuse Jacobi of committing an even more condemnable form of irrationality—of altogether abandoning reason and substituting it with faith?

Some of Jacobi's contemporaries thought that the one who could properly be charged with offenses against reason was Jacobi himself. Now these are charges not to be taken lightly, for they are the first step toward dismissal from serious attention. Hence, it should come as no great surprise that Jacobi has his share of defenders against such charges. Arguably the best contemporary defender that Jacobi has is George di Giovanni. Di Giovanni, who has translated several of Jacobi's works into English and is a leading authority on him, has tried to show why it is not accurate to classify Jacobi as an irrationalist. He has objected to portraits of Jacobi that paint him as an anti-Enlightenment, irrationalist thinker. According to di Giovanni's reading of Jacobi, Jacobi actually rehabilitated reason, by "acknowledging it as the source [. . .] of what he had called the certitude of faith—not the reason of the philosophers [. . .] but an inward-looking reason that had immediate access to the divine in us."[8] Di Giovanni even goes so far as to compare the "inner light" that Jacobi invokes, to Descartes' notion of reason with "the innate idea of God as its standard of perfection."[9] Obviously, such a comparison functions to link Jacobi with rationalism instead of with the various breeds of irrationalism that have been associated with him. Di Giovanni insists that Jacobi's move to reinterpret reason as inner light in no way signals a break with rationalism or implicates Jacobi in any anti-Enlightenment or irrationalist moves. Di Giovanni emphatically states that "Jacobi never intended to foster irrationalism."[10] Di Giovanni's reading of Jacobi cannot be ignored or easily dismissed. Yet it does contrast quite strongly with another interpretation of Jacobi's project put forward by one of his contemporaries.

According to this other reading, Jacobi's conclusion that our knowledge begins not with a first principle that can be demonstrated but rather an absolute first principle that we must accept by an act of faith, reveals his foundationalism and his irrationalism. In claiming that feelings and sensations did more justice to the complexity of reality than philosophical reflection would ever be capable of doing, Jacobi parts company with Spinoza's rationalism and embarks upon a path leading to a blind leap of faith or *salto mortale*.[11] According to this interpretation of Jacobi's work, Jacobi's spirited defense of the claims of feeling and faith involves him in a serious abuse of the rights of reason.

One of the strongest, most fertile sources of this reading was Friedrich Schlegel. Schlegel was among the first to challenge what he dubbed Jacobi's "odd concoction" of foundationalism and irrationality. And even if this is a misreading of Jacobi, that is, even if di Giovanni is correct that Jacobi was not moving away from reason, much can be gained from a careful consideration of Schlegel's criticisms of Jacobi. Even if we do not gain a greater understanding of Jacobi's philosophical project, once we begin to understand Schlegel's response to Jacobi, we are well on the way toward a proper understanding of what his romantic philosophy was about.

Schlegel's Reaction to the *Salto*

Friedrich Schlegel's critique of Jacobi's appeal to faith clearly illustrates the distance between what he classified as Jacobi's irrational leap of faith and the more reasonable and rational challenge that the early German Romantics posed to the problems with the rationalist foundationalism of the period. To view the romantic reaction to this foundationalism against the background of the pantheism controversy is a sensible and convincing way of doing justice to the early German Romantic movement. The early German Romantics sought to show the inadequacies of the mainstream views of the Enlightenment project. But they also sought, and this much more vociferously, to show the inadequacies of what they dubbed the "irrationalist attacks" on the Enlightenment. Thus, romantic doubts concerning enlightened reason were not a rejection of reason but a refinement of it.

Although Schlegel agreed with Jacobi regarding the unknowability of the Absolute, claiming that "[t]o know already indicates a conditioned knowledge" and that "[t]he unknowability of the Absolute is an identical triviality," he did not accept the consequences that Jacobi drew from this observation.[12] Schlegel did not substitute knowledge of the Absolute as the starting point of philosophy with an appeal to faith that would secure the Absolute as the first principle of philosophy. Schlegel's move was more radical and yet rational. Schlegel's solution to the problem of the unknowability of the Absolute was to develop an alternative way to understand knowledge and reality, and it is in this development that Schlegel's antifoundationalism takes shape.

The Absolute, which as we saw in chapter 1, was a term of art during the post-Kantian period, is, pace Schlegel, by definition unknowable, for to know x is to know the cause of x, its condition. (Causes are subtypes of conditions.) Nonetheless, Schlegel's acknowledgment of the unknowability of the absolute first principle does not force him into Jacobi's camp, as many have hastily assumed.[13] In sharp contrast to Jacobi and reacting against what he perceived to be Jacobi's *irrationalism*, Schlegel avoided the infinite regress caused by the search for an absolute foundation of knowledge while he championed the cause of objective truth against subjectivity. He attempted to do this by parting company with any foundational philosophy whatsoever. Schlegel avoids the infinite regress that Jacobi halted in his appeal to faith by looking to another way to understand the structure of our knowledge. Schlegel moves away from the line that leads to the regress and embraces the circularity of our attempts to establish a foundation for our claims to knowledge. Schlegel does not replace reason with faith. He transforms the very conceptual structure used to understand the basis of knowledge. This comes to light in his confrontation with Jacobi's *salto mortale*.

Schlegel's confrontation with Jacobi's *salto mortale* is found in various fragments in which Schlegel directly addresses specific problems of Jacobi's philosophical position and in his review of Jacobi's novel *Woldemar*.[14] In this fragment from the *Athenäum*, Schlegel ridicules Jacobi's futile attempt to advance knowledge, which is objective, by turning inward to faith, which is subjective:

> The renowned *salto mortale* of the philosophers is often only a false alarm. In their thoughts they take a frightfully long approach run and then congratulate themselves on having braved the danger; but if one only looks a little more closely, they're still sitting on the same old spot. It's like Don Quixote's flight on the wooden horse. Jacobi too seems to me someone who, though he can never stop moving, always stays where he is: caught in a squeeze between two kinds of philosophy, the systematic and the absolute, between Spinoza and Leibniz, where his delicate spirit has gotten to be rather pinched and sore.[15]

According to Schlegel, Jacobi appeals to a measureless increase (*Steigerung*) of subjectivity, which he directs outwardly and which is posited infinitely as God but is really only a leap into one's own subjectivity and hence a false alarm. Faith cannot be the foundation of knowledge, for it does not lead us outward to reality but inward to our own subjectivity. Hence, it does nothing to explain how our beliefs come together to form knowledge claims.

In Schlegel's critique of Jacobi's *salto*, we find an echo of a criticism that had been raised by Mendelssohn, who was a pillar of the Berlin Enlightenment. Mendelssohn had charged Jacobi with offenses against reason in *Morgenstunden*. In lecture eight, he claims that there can be no duty to believe. The "spirit of inquiry" had to be kept alive and alert at all times for "blind faith" leads to superstition and fanaticism.[16] According to Mendelssohn, the gains of the Enlightenment, which were based on reason, and the simple truths of universal religion, which were anchored in common sense and not in the extravagance of mystical faith, should be protected from irrationalist attacks such as Jacobi's. Needless to say, Mendelssohn's commitment to rationality has never been questioned, though of course Schlegel's commitment to rationality is endemically overlooked.

Schlegel found much to object to in Jacobi's thought. His critique of Jacobi was more than just an observation on the sort of suicide into subjectivity toward which Jacobi's *salto* leads us. Schlegel also finds problems with the sort of dualism that underlies Jacobi's entire understanding of the tensions between reason and faith. Schlegel does not accept the false dichotomy that Jacobi sets up between knowledge and belief, nor Jacobi's way of reconciling it. First, Schlegel questions this dualism by asking: "Isn't belief and knowledge a completely false antithesis?"[17] Jacobi wants to overcome the primacy of reason over faith, but he never questions the traditional dualism that separates the two. Schlegel does question this dualism, and it leads him to a most original solution regarding philosophy's starting point.

Schlegel's review of *Woldemar* (1796) reveals Schlegel's commitment to objectivity. He writes: "Truth cannot be extorted (obtained) and he who numbs his reason only in order to believe what his heart desires, ends, as is only fair, with a mistrust of the beloved truth itself."[18] In this review, Schlegel defines philosophy as a search for truth, guided by a "pure interest in knowledge and truth," which stands in direct opposition to Jacobi's characterization of philosophy in terms of an experience of revelation. Moreover, Schlegel demands of a philosopher argument-logical rigor. *What* the philosopher claims is just as important as *how* she maintains it. A thinker who allows his own subjectivity to guide the search for truth, placing what he wants to find before what is there to be found, is not a philosopher, but a sophist.[19] For this reason, Schlegel says "*Woldemar* is really an invitation to an acquaintance with God, and this theological work of art ends, as all moral *Debauches* end, with a *salto mortale* into the abyss of divine mercy."[20] According to Schlegel, Jacobi is not a philosopher, for philosophers are guided by truth. We must presuppose that truth exists (*Wahrheit soll sein*) and let our investigations be guided by what we find, not by what we want to find. Jacobi does not do this, and so is a sophist, a thinker guided by what he wants to find. Schlegel objects to Jacobi's position on the grounds that it presupposes individual truths and therefore distorts reality and corrupts truth.[21] Schlegel writes: "The elastic point from which Jacobi's philosophy departed was not an objective imperative, but rather an individual option."[22]

According to Schlegel, philosophy is the striving for truth and knowledge, which must be an objective search; it must not be subjectivized by an appeal to faith. Strangely, here Schlegel's criticism echoes a claim made by one of Jacobi's supporters. Di Giovanni has claimed that in Jacobi's work, by means of faith, reality is revealed as irreducibly individual, in direct opposition to the universalizing function of conceptualization.[23] Di Giovanni sees promise in this move, for it clears a space for a historical dimension to philosophy. Schlegel was also aware of the move to the individual in Jacobi's work but saw this as a move away from reason and philosophy, not as an enhancement of either. Schlegel, however, did highlight the historical dimension of philosophy, not by using faith to reveal an "irreducibly individual" reality, but by refining the traditional philosophical approach to reality.

Schlegel's critique of Jacobi's *salto mortale* clearly shows that he was not willing to embrace revelation as a criterion for accepting a given claim. In his review of *Woldemar*, Schlegel rejects Jacobi's subjectivization and individualization of truth and then poses a question that opens the path to the development of his own position. He writes: "[Jacobi's] positive theory of faith can by no means be counted as philosophical . . . (That which Jacobi holds: 'that every proof presupposes something proved'; holds only for those thinkers who depart from one, single proof. What if, however, an externally unconditioned yet at the same time conditioned and conditioning *Wechselerweis* were the foundation of philosophy?)"[24] This important question, which Schlegel poses within the humble confines of a parenthetical remark, opens a clearing for his own position. It is a position that rejects the possibility of establishing a single, absolute foundation as the basis for our knowledge but that does not, in any way, amount to a form of subjectivism or sophism. Schlegel's antifoundationalism is philosophical—that is, it is part of his commitment to an objective search for truth. While Schlegel shares with Jacobi a concern about the problem of the pretense to knowledge of the Absolute, he is nevertheless opposed to Jacobi's solution to this problem. Schlegel saw Jacobi's solution as one that involved a break with reason while maintaining a strong commitment to foundations. Schlegel, in contrast, opts to break with foundations and stay with reason.

Schlegel's critique of Jacobi's *salto mortale* clearly shows that Schlegel's romantic thought was not, as the commonly held misperception regarding the nature of early German Romanticism would have us think, a reaction against Enlightenment thought *tout court*. Mendelssohn, the famous "rational" thinker, and Schlegel, the allegedly dreamy romantic, agreed that Jacobi's appeal to faith was an offense against the primordial philosophical task of defending rationality. The early German Romantics were not willing to forsake the objectivity of reason for the subjectivity of faith. They wanted to diversify the "light of reason" but not extinguish it. Hence, they were not working against the current of thought established by the Enlightenment thinkers. Their commitment to objectivity manifested itself quite differently but should not blind one to the fact that there is an underlying common goal.

Schlegel's romantic critique of Jacobi's *salto mortale* reveals that he viewed reason as the ultimate touchstone of knowledge. It further reveals the uniqueness of this much-maligned movement, for while the early German Romantics do not abandon reason as the ultimate touchstone of knowledge, they do abandon the idea that philosophy begins with any first principle whatsoever.[25] Romanticism was antifoundationalist through and through; and it was so in an attempt to capture the inherent incompleteness of philosophy and knowledge. This inherent incompleteness puts philosophy, Schlegel believed, in contact with aesthetic experience and poetry.

A first step toward an accurate understanding of Schlegel's contributions to post-Kantian philosophy is to recognize the difference between solutions to the problem posed by the Absolute, which end in something like Jacobi's *salto*, and Schlegel's much more sober antifoundationalsim. This is not only of historical relevance. For, under this light, the Romantics could be seen as holding the view that coherentism was the epistemological posture that best captured how, given our epistemological limitations, we come ever closer to grasping that which is without limits, the Absolute. I shall return to this in chapters 6 and 7, where I shall show that a defense of coherentism, even if it is coupled with a certain privileging of aesthetic experience, is not to be dismissed as unphilosophical.

Now we shall turn to Schlegel's reaction to another key controversy of the period, the one surrounding Reinhold's *Elementarphilosophie*.

Reinhold's *Elementarphilosophie*

Reinhold made his name known by the publication of his *Letters concerning the Kantian Philosophy* (*Briefe über die kantische Philosophie*, Vol. 1 1786–1787; Vol. 2 1792).[26] This publication did more to popularize Kant's critical philosophy than Kant's own attempts had (cf. Kant's *Prolegomena* 1784).[27] Reinhold, however, did not long remain merely a commentator on Kant's philosophy; his interpretation of Kant's philosophy led him to discover what he considered to be a serious flaw present in Kant's work.

According to Reinhold, the results of the *Critique of Pure Reason* rest upon the concept of 'representation' (*Vorstellung*), something that Kant never fully explicates. If the purpose of the first *Critique* is to analyze the conditions and possibility of human knowledge, and if this analysis rests upon *Vorstellung* without ever trying to develop a theory of representation, then Kant can be accused of question begging (or premise stealing). Reinhold attempted to fill in this gap and provide Kant's philosophy with a firm foundation. The result was Reinhold's first original contribution to philosophy, *An Attempt at a New Theory of the Human Faculty of Representation* (*Versuch einer neuen Theorie des menschlichen Vorstellungsvermögens*, 1787). His more important doctrines, the principle of consciousness (*Satz des Bewußtseins*) and his philosophy of elements (*Elementarphilosophie*) are not, however, contained in this first work. Two works that followed were more influential in charting the course of post-Kantian philosophy: *Beyträge zur Berichtigung der bisherigen Mißverständnisse der Philosophen* (1790), in which he revised most of the doctrines in the *Versuch* and *Über das Fundament des philosophischen Wissens* (1791) which Beiser describes as "Reinhold's manifesto for the *Elementarphilosophie*."[28] These works generated a heated discussion regarding the feasibility of a philosophy based on first principles. Below, I shall present an outline of the claims Reinhold defends in these works and then look at the critiques by Schulze (Aenesidemus) and Fichte and at Reinhold's attempt to answer his critics in the second volume of the *Beyträge* (1794), for these were discussions that shaped Schlegel's romantic thought.[29]

Whereas Jacobi, in his search to establish a starting point for philosophy, begins with the "*Es ist!*" that is, with a kind of commonsense realism, Reinhold begins with Kant's principle of consciousness, which he saw as a kind of apogee of philosophical development:

> Philosophical reason seemed finally to have come to a standstill when, in the person of a man in whom are combined the systematic spirit of Leibniz and the skeptical one of Hume, Locke's sound faculty of judgment and Newton's creative genius, it made

> advances such as were never made by any single thinker before. Kant discovered a new foundation of philosophical knowledge that includes the truth found scattered, in one sided-forms, in the previous expositions of that knowledge, yet excludes their falsity. Like all his predecessors he too assumed immutability, which is the hallmark of truth, to be the essential characteristic of the foundation of philosophy as well; unlike Locke, however, who tried to obtain it from the simples borrowed immediately from experience, and unlike Leibniz, who tried to obtain it from innate representations, he derived it rather from the possibility of experience which is found determined in the mind prior to all experience.[30]

Reinhold celebrates Kant's work on the basis of the foundation for the possibility of experience established therein.[31] Yet, despite Reinhold's obvious admiration for Kant's achievements, he departs from Kant's transcendental method; he is not content to establish the conditions of the possibility of knowledge; he claims, "This science of the faculty of cognition would have to be preceded by another that establishes its foundation." This, claims Reinhold, would be the "science of the entire faculty of representation as such."[32]

> For this science, which I name general Philosophy of the Elements (*Elementarphilosophie*) because it serves as the common foundation to both theoretical and practical philosophy, the *Critique of Reason* has indeed provided the materials, but never the idea, let alone the actual foundation. And if it is ever to be realized, philosophical reason must press forward yet another step in its analysis past the point attained in the *Critique of Reason*. This is the final step that philosophical reason can take, proceeding analytically, on its way to higher principles, through it, and it alone, is the ultimate and proper foundation of PHILOSOPHY discovered.[33]

Reinhold wants to establish the *logical* relation (as opposed to Kant's goal of establishing the *transcendental* conditions) between actual knowledge and its cause and arrive not at a *principle* of consciousness, but a *fact* of consciousness. To accomplish this goal, he develops the concept of representation, thereby making reference to a thing-in-itself obsolete. On Reinhold's model, the establishment of objective truth no longer requires any object that is not already a representation. "Every possible demonstration of objective truth would call for a comparison between a representation and an object different from it; but at the same time this comparison could only take place through representations, and indeed it would have to be between the one representation that consists in the impression itself, and the other through which the impression is represented; consequently, the comparison would never be set up between a representation and an object that is not already a representation."[34] Reinhold believes that he has found the most fundamental concept of 'knowledge' and 'truth,' the very concept that must be secured if philosophy is to be a science. According to Reinhold, the first principle of philosophy must be one that secures and defines representation and that can be represented. Reinhold's *Elementarphilosophie* was an attempt to place epistemology on a metaphysical foundation. The premises of Kant's *Critique* became the conclusions to be deduced in the *Elementarphilosophie*.

As Beiser indicates, Reinhold's project was guided by the following convictions: (1) philosophy must be systematic; (2) it must begin with one self-evident principle; (3) only phenomenology can fulfill the ideal of a "first philosophy." If philosophy is to be systematic, it must be deduced from one principle, which must be a self-evident principle, for if it were in need of a demonstration, it could not be absolute. But if only phenomenology can fulfill the ideal of a "first philosophy," then this principle must be a fact. This fact of consciousness is the first principle of Reinhold's philosophy. It is expressed in his *Satz des Bewußtseins*: "A representation is what is distinct in consciousness from object and subject and related to both" (Eine Vorstellung ist was im Bewußtsein vom Objekt und Subjekt unterschieden und auf beide bezogen wird). Reinhold's examination of the methods and presuppositions of Kant's critical philosophy led him to this fact of consciousness, which he posited as the starting point of all philosophy.

Schlegel was among the first to voice discontent with this claim: "Reinhold, the first of the Kantian sophists, was the first organizer of Kantianism and the one who perpetuated misunderstandings of it."[35] According to Schlegel, the *Letters* are what make Reinhold a sophist, a mere popularizer of Kant's philosophy, rather than a thinker who does something to improve or move beyond Kant's critical philosophy. The *Fundament* is responsible for generating misunderstandings of the critical philosophy. For, as Schlegel remarks in another fragment: "Kant does not begin with the fact that 'Experience is,' as Niethammer, Reinhold and Erhard have misunderstood him; but rather from the undemonstrated yet demonstrable principle that experience MUST BE as Beck, Schelling and Fichte have properly understood. This principle must be fully demonstrated."[36] On Schlegel's reading, Kant's transcendental conditions for the possibility of knowledge become, in Reinhold's *Elementarphilosophie*, the causes of knowledge. Hence, the structure of Kant's transcendental argument and its transcendental method are undermined and replaced by Reinhold's phenomenology.

Schlegel was not, however, the first to find fault with Reinhold's claims and arguments, and his fragmentary remarks were not nearly as devastating as the attack that was published anonymously in 1792: *Aenesidemus or Concerning the foundations of the Philosophy of Elements issued by Prof. Reinhold in Jena together with a defense of Skepticism against the Pretensions of the* Critique of Reason (*Aenesidemus, oder Über die Fundamente der von dem Herrn Professor Reinhold in Jena gelieferten Elementarphilosophie*).[37] This attack upon Reinhold's philosophy was an attack on Kant's critical philosophy and was responsible for a revival of Humean skepticism in the post-Kantian generation of philosophers.

Aenesidemus and the Shift from Principle to Fact of Consciousness

The author of the attack was soon discovered to be Gottlob Ernst Schulze (1761–1833), a professor of philosophy at the University of Helmstadt.[38] *Aenesidemus* is written as a collection of letters in which Hermias, an enthusiastic admirer of critical philosophy, declares to Aenesidemus his complete conviction (founded especially upon Reinhold's *Elementarphilosophie*) of the truth and universal validity of this philosophy. Aenesidemus responds to these enthusiastic claims with a skeptical examination of both Reinhold's and Kant's philosophy.

Aenesidemus claims "The Philosophy of the Elements, by deriving actual representation from a faculty which it takes to be something objectively actual, and by defining it as the cause of the representations, contradicts its own principles as well as the results of the *Critique of Reason*."[39] The problem expressed here is similar to the problem that Schlegel finds in Reinhold's attempt to ground Kant's critical philosophy, but Schlegel's criticism is not as broad. He does not claim that Reinhold contradicts himself, only that he contradicts the principles of the *Critique* because he shifts the discussion of knowledge from the conditions of its possibility to its actual causes. Why does Aenesidemus claim that Reinhold contradicts his own principle? Reinhold claims that the form of representations must be produced, which presupposes an active subject. Consciousness is presented by Reinhold as an intentional relation to objects. Of course, this leaves us with the problem of self-knowledge. If there is no unthing-like consciousness, if the very structure of consciousness consists in "something that is conscious and is called the subject, and something of which one is conscious and is called the object and something through which one is conscious of [something else] and is called representing,"⁴⁰ then we cannot have any knowledge of the subject as subject but only of the subject as object, thereby making self-consciousness impossible. If the first principle of philosophy is a fact of consciousness that cannot explain self-consciousness, then we are in need of another principle to explain self-consciousness, which is clearly at odds with Reinhold's claim that he has discovered the first principle of philosophy.[41] Moreover, according to Aenesidemus, Reinhold's fact of consciousness cannot explain the most basic act of consciousness we have, intuition. "The definition of the faculty of representation laid down in the Philosophy of Elements could only make comprehensible those representations that 'are referred to an object and subject and are distinguished from both,' if indeed it explained anything at all; for it is drawn only from this type of representation. It would not, however, establish the possibility of anything in us which, even without being referred to an object or subject and being distinguished from both, is nonetheless a representation and rightly deserves to be called so."[42] Again, a first principle that is capable of explaining *some* rather than *all* acts of consciousness is no first principle at all. Ultimately, Schulze, through his mouthpiece Aenesidemus, claims that Hume's skeptical attacks on the possibility of uncovering the origin of representations have left us without any materials with which to build a system of philosophy and therefore without a means of saying anything about the origin of human knowledge.[43]

These were charges to which Reinhold was compelled to respond. This response is found in the *Beyträge zur Berichtigung der bisherigen Misverständnisse der Philosophie, Vol. II* (1794).[44] In the section entitled "Über den Unterschied zwischen dem gesunden Verstanden und der philosophierenden Vernunft in Rucksicht auf der Fundamente des durch beyde moglichen Wissens," we find Reinhold's responses to Schulze's criticisms. In the foreword, Reinhold announces that his purpose is to seek out the sources of the misunderstandings generated by his philosophy, adding that he will seek these first in his own work and then in the mistakes of the accepted foundations of previous philosophical systems (*angenommenen Fundamente bisher bearbeiteter philosophische Wissenschaften*).[45] He also informs his readers that he had completed this part of the work before the appearance of Aenesidemus' review in the *Allgemeine Literatur Zeitung*. Nonetheless, Reinhold claims that Aenesidemus's objections have been answered: "Aenesidemus will find that his desire not to remain within the confines of my previous foundation for the *Elementarphilosophie* is also my desire."[46]

If Reinhold does not wish to remain within the confines of the foundation developed in the *Philosophy of Elements*, then where does he want to go? Eventually Reinhold, like Jacobi and Schlegel, came to realize that any attempt to establish a first *principle* for philosophy would be futile, yet he was led to quite a different conclusion than either Jacobi with his *salto* or Schlegel with his thoroughgoing skepticism. It was futile, Reinhold concluded, to attempt to establish a first *principle*, but his *Satz des Bewusstseins* was not a first principle but a fundamental *fact* of human knowledge. So, Reinhold does not give in to the skeptic's view that any attempt to establish a secure starting point for philosophy is futile; the starting point of philosophy cannot be a principle but a fact. Reinhold's strategy does not address the skeptical doubts regarding the possibility of finding philosophy's starting point, but it does address the problem of beginning with a principle. In shifting the discussion of the grounds of knowledge from principles to facts, Reinhold, the great popularizer of Kant, undermines the very methodology of Kant's critical philosophy.[47]

Reinhold continues to hold that representation is the most fundamental concept, the one that must be explained if we are to establish a first principle for philosophy, yet in light of the criticisms of his work, he does acknowledge that the structure of his argument must be revised. In this restructuring, the relation between common understanding and philosophizing reason takes on a new meaning. Reinhold defines understanding and reason in terms of outer and inner experience, respectively. He defines understanding thus: "Understanding in the strict sense of this word, is the faculty of our power of thought which deals directly with sensible representations; and produces from these new representations which are called concepts in the strict sense and are the combination of sensible representations."[48] The outer conditions of representation are the real, existing subject and the actual object of which the subject has the representation, that is, the cause of the representation. Understanding is common both to philosophers and nonphilosophers.[49] Understanding begins in the physical-historical world, common to all thinking subjects.[50] In contrast, reason provides the inner conditions of representations, the formal, a priori conditions. "Reason in the strict sense is the faculty of our power of thought which above all deals with supersensible representations and produces new representations which are called ideas."[51] Understanding is common because it functions within the realm of the given, that which is common to all. Reason functions within the realm of causes for what is given, and Reinhold describes the function of reason as the search for causes. He calls this "philosophizing reason." Both understanding and reason are indispensable to human experience; Reinhold even speaks of a culture created by both.[52] He uses this to suggest a kind of process at work, the process of uncovering the first cause of all knowledge. Until this is discovered, common understanding and philosophizing reason will be "out of joint with each other."[53] "As long as philosophizing reason has not yet, through its gradual progress, discovered the given, absolute first causes, it holds relative first causes to be absolute, merely assumed causes to be the given causes; this is a misunderstanding which is announced through the disharmony of reason with itself and in the quarrels between its representatives and the different ways in which these assumed first causes are put forth."[54] In order to overcome this problem, common understanding and philosophizing reason must work together. Reinhold makes the strong claim "In the search for a first cause, philosophizing reason must depart from the convictions of common understanding through which first causes can be deduced only insofar as this common understanding is healthy."[55] Where do we look for the foundation of philosophy? We look in both outer experience, that is, in human happenings, and in inner experience, namely, our conceptual structure. The direction of inquiry is not unidirectional; we move between the given facts of the empirical-historical world and the formal, a priori ahistorical world of ideas, of reason. So, in his analysis of the structure of human knowledge, Reinhold is no longer dealing with pure reason but with reason and its relation to history, psychology, and even physiology. He is no longer interested only in the conditions for the possibility of knowledge but also in the archaeology of knowledge itself, its actual causes.

Fichte's Move from Fact to Act of Consciousness

In his response to his critics, Reinhold focuses upon the justification of his fact of consciousness and how this differs from a principle of consciousness and then goes on to develop a new way of viewing the relation between common understanding and philosophizing reason. But another critique of Reinhold's work would show this line of defense to be the wrong one. In a review of Aenesidemus' criticisms (*Allgemeine Literatur Zeitung* 11, 12 February 1794), Fichte defends Reinhold against all the claims made against him by Aenesidemus, and this defense marked an important turning point in post-Kantian philosophy.[56] "It appears to emerge from what has been said so far that all the objects of Aenesidemus are groundless in so far as they are to be taken as directed against the truth of the principle of consciousness as such, but that they are relevant to it as first principle of all philosophy as mere fact; thus the objections make a new justification necessary."[57] According to Fichte, the problem is not the search for a first principle for all philosophy but with Reinhold's presupposition that the most fundamental concept is that of representation and the ensuing attempt to locate the principle in a *fact* of consciousness. Fichte criticizes Aenesidemus for failing to aim his skepticism against Reinhold's claim that representation is the most fundamental concept of philosophy. For Fichte, the most fundamental concept is not representation.

> It remains dubious in the eyes of this reviewer whether philosophy itself would benefit from their [Reinhold and Aenesidemus'] unanimity as regards the second point [that the first principle of philosophy must be that principle that defines and secures the concept of representation]; it might turn out, some time in the future, that what can be justifiably said against the principle of consciousness as the *first* principle of philosophy as a whole will lead to the suspicion that there must be for the whole of philosophy (and not just for theoretical philosophy) yet a *higher* concept than that of representation.[58]

Throughout the review, Fichte uses his criticisms of both Aenesidemus and Reinhold to clear openings for his own thought. On the issue of whether Reinhold's *Satz* is analytic (Reinhold, of course, claims it is) or synthetic (as Aenesidemus claims it is), Fichte finds himself in the middle and is led to a question that his philosophy will answer.

> Suppose that no consciousness can be thought without these three parts [subject, object, representation]; then these parts would certainly be contained in the concept of consciousness, and in regard of its logical validity the proposition specifying them would certainly be, as a reflective proposition, analytical. But obviously the performance of representing, the act of consciousness is itself a synthesis all the same, for it differentiates and refers; indeed, it is the highest synthesis, and the ground of all other possible ones. And with this consideration there arises, then, the very real question, how is it ever possible to trace back all the performances of the mind to the one [act of] putting together? How is *synthesis* to be thought without the presupposition of *thesis* and *antithesis*?[59]

This concern with the acts involved in consciousness became the basis of Fichte's conceptual framework. In addressing another point of contention between Aenesidemus and Reinhold, that of whether Reinhold's *Satz* is an abstract proposition expressing what *some* manifestations of consciousness have in common or what *all* of them share, Fichte finds another opportunity to introduce his own solution to the problem of securing a first principle for philosophy. If the principle is abstracted from empirical self-observation, then the principle is based on an abstraction, and this hints that the proposition must be based on something more than a mere actual fact. "This reviewer at any rate has convinced himself that the proposition is a theorem based upon another principle, but that it can be rigorously demonstrated a priori from that principle, and independently of all experience."[60] Fichte is in agreement here with Aenesidemus's critique of

Reinhold's claim that his proposition of consciousness is based on no abstraction at all, for insofar as Reinhold claims that we come to it from empirical self-observation, it must be based on an abstraction. Nevertheless, Fichte does not accept Aenesidemus's ensuing skepticism regarding the fate of all first principles.[61] For as Fichte suggests above, if the principle can be demonstrated a priori and independent of all experience, then the problem of its being an abstraction is removed. (Fichte does indeed believe that he can remove this problem and establish philosophy as a science.) According to Fichte, both Reinhold and Aenesidemus err in believing that philosophy's starting point can be found in a fact of consciousness. "To be sure, we must have a real principle, and not merely a formal one; but—if I may venture a claim which can be neither explained nor proven here—such a principle does not have to express a fact just as content (*eine Tatsache*, actual fact); it can also express a fact as performance (*eine Tathandlung*, actual deed)."[62] Reinhold's attempt to establish an absolute starting point for philosophy was met with skepticism by both Schulze and Fichte. Yet the skepticism involved was different. For Aenesidemus, the fact that Reinhold had failed in his attempt to secure a first principle for philosophy amounted to evidence of the impossibility of any such attempt. For Fichte, Reinhold's failure meant only that a first principle for philosophy could not be a fact of consciousness (for a first principle would have to be demonstrated a priori and independently of all experience), and furthermore that a concept more fundamental than representation must be found.

Reinhold's failure incited Fichte to respond with his own attempt to establish an absolute starting point for philosophy that he believed answered the skeptics. Just as Schlegel found Jacobi's value in having provoked Fichte, he sees Reinhold's value in having provided grist for Fichte's mill. He characterizes Reinhold's contribution to philosophy as a propadeutic to Fichte's philosophy: "As a propadeutic to the *Wissenschaftslehre*, Reinholdianism is very good, and should be allowed to campaign for its cause."[63] The ideas of both Jacobi and Reinhold were a propaedeutic to Fichte's philosophy, and the scrutiny with which each of these thinkers questioned philosophy's starting point led to a reorientation of post-Kantian philosophy. Familiarity with Kant's critical work would continue to be essential, but after the discussions inaugurated by Jacobi and Reinhold regarding philosophy's starting point, and Fichte's attempts to complete these discussions, the debate would cease to be held on Kantian terms. A profound restructuring of the course of the debate had been initiated.[64] We will examine this in the next chapter as we look at the structure of Fichte's idealism.

Chapter Three
===

Fichte's *Wissenschaftslehre*
A Tendency to Be Avoided?

As noted at the end of the previous chapter, after Schulze's attack revealed the shortcomings of Reinhold's attempt to secure an absolute first principle for philosophy, Fichte was led to develop his own solution to the problem of philosophy's starting point.[1] With Reinhold, Fichte held that in order to be a science of knowledge, philosophy must be based upon an absolute first principle. With Schulze, he believed that Reinhold had not provided this basis. But for Fichte, this was not because the search for a first principle was misguided but rather because Reinhold's approach was wrong. The *Wissenschaftslehre* is Fichte's attempt to solve the problem of philosophy's starting point and thereby to establish the foundation for Fichte's own version of Kant's transcendental idealism. The problem that Reinhold had failed to solve became the task Fichte set forth for himself. In Fichte's attempts to secure an absolute first principle for philosophy, the skeptics found a new target for their doubts regarding the feasibility of a philosophy based on an absolute first principle.

According to Fichte, the task of philosophy is to provide us with the ground of all experience. This ground is absolute, that is, not part of experience. The ground of experience cannot be encountered within experience. Fichte is very clearly an idealist, and his view of philosophy and of philosophy's starting point is determined by his idealism, that is, by his belief that the ground of experience is something that is not encountered within experience. And it is his breed of idealism that set the stage for Niethammer's appeal to common sense and Schlegel's romantic counterreaction. In this chapter we will look at the structure that underlies Fichte's idealism, so we will be in a position to evaluate Niethammer's and Schlegel's responses to it. Because we are dealing with a specific reception of Fichte's philosophy and its influence on the development of Niethammer's turn toward common sense and Schlegel's turn toward history, we shall limit our study of Fichte to his early philosophical writings, in particular the *Grundlage der gesammten Wissenschaftslehre* (1794) and to two of his contributions to the *Philosophisches Journal*: "A comparison of Prof. Schmid's system with the *Wissenschaftslehre*" ("*Vergleichung des vom Hrn. Prof. Schmid aufgestellten Systems mit der Wissenschaftslehre*") (1796) and "Attempt at a New Presentation of the *Wissenschaftslehre*" ("*Versuch einer neuen Darstellung der Wissenschaftslehre*") (1797).[2] In 1796 Fichte became the coeditor of this journal, and when he began to publish his lectures on the *Wissenschaftslehre nova methodo*, he did so in a series of installments for this journal. This was not because the journal was sympathetic to Fichte's philosophy. Fichte's coeditorship was a clever maneuver on the part of F. I. Niethammer who did not want to alienate one of the most influential (and temperamental) thinkers of the period. Many of the contributions to the journal were attacks on Fichte's philosophy to which Fichte was compelled to respond.[3] By making Fichte coeditor, Niethammer could safely publish articles that expressed strong arguments against Fichte's breed of idealism and then invite Fichte to respond.

The Foundations of Fichte's *Wissenschaftslehre*

In his review of Aenesidemus, Fichte had hinted that there was a real principle for all philosophy, one that did not express only a fact as content (*eine Tatsache*) but also a fact as action (*eine Tathandlung*). In his review he neither explained nor proved this, yet almost all that he wrote afterward was an attempt to do just this or to defend this claim from its detractors.

Fichte's philosophy is based upon one principle consisting of three logical propositions. As Dieter Henrich points out in his small but powerful book, *Fichtes ursprüngliche Einsicht* (*Fichte's Original Insight*), Fichte's unique discovery was that he saw that self-consciousness, which had long since been assumed to be the ground of all knowledge, can only be thought under certain circumstances.[4] These are expressed in three logical propositions and together constitute the principle of all knowledge. The three logical propositions are identity, contradiction, and synthesis. According to Fichte, the principle of identity is presupposed in every act of consciousness. But A=A is a logical fact (*Tatsache*), not yet any act of consciousness (*Tathandlung*). There must be, Fichte argues, something that posits this fact. This is the self-positing I.

This self-positing I then goes on to posit a Non-I, for in the act of self-positing, there is an active I that perceives itself as an object of consciousness and hence as a Non-I. Here we come to the second principle, that the I cannot be at one and the same time the non-I: this follows from the logical principle of non-contradiction (A and non-A is always false, that is, false in virtue of its very form). Yet, in the act of self-consciousness, we are aware of ourselves as an I and hence identical with that I (I=I) and as an I having as its object an I that cannot be identical to the positing I (I = Non-I). These two moments come together. The I posits itself, and it posits a Non-I, resulting in knowledge of the I as self-positing and the I as the Non-I or as the object of the self-positing I. This synthesis is effected by knowledge, a knowledge grounded on the transcendental unity of the I and the Non-I.

The fundamental principle of the *Wissenschaftslehre* is contained in the sentence, The I posits itself purely and simply (Das Ich setzt sich schlechthin). For in this formulation we find the primacy of the I not merely as thinking subject, but as active subject. For Fichte, reality consists in pure activity, an activity of the I. Fichte's idealism begins with a self-positing I, hence with an act (*Tathandlung*) of consciousness rather than with a fact (*Tatsache*) of consciousness: "If philosophy begins with a fact, then it places itself in the midst of a world of being and finitude, and it will be difficult for it to discover any path leading from this world to an infinite and supersensible one. If, however, philosophy begins with an Act, then it finds itself at the precise point where these two worlds are connected with each other and from which they can both be surveyed in a single glance."[5]

Fichte calls this most fundamental self-positing, which is presupposed by all facts of consciousness but is not itself a fact, an "act" (*Tathandlung*). The I posits itself, and upon doing so posits the Non-I as well. This Non-I serves to limit the I, which gives the I its reality. For, according to Fichte, a pure I, one that would exist unconditionally (that is, without limits), would be indefinite and unreal.

Fichte saw his contribution as an extension of Kant's philosophy, in particular of Kant's transcendental deduction, for it is there that the establishment of objective validity through the subjective conditions of representability is carried out. Fichte was also addressing the problem of Kant's positing of a thing-in-itself as the necessary source for all experience. Fichte believed that this thing-in-itself was unnecessary. Roger Scruton observes: "For Fichte, Kant's great achievement was to have shown that the mind has knowledge only through its own activity; in an important sense, the objects of knowledge are a *product* of that activity."[6] Those philosophers who did not see this and who insisted that the thing-in-itself was a necessary condition for the possibility of objective knowledge were dogmatists. According to Fichte, there are only two possible consistent explanations of experience: dogmatism (materialism) and critical philosophy (idealism). For

Fichte, dogmatism is that philosophical position that believes itself to be in possession of cognitions of things-in-themselves, and so is a type of metaphysical realism. This has the dangerous consequence of ending in a kind of determinism or fatalism (like Jacobi, Fichte mentions Spinoza as an example of this type of philosopher). This philosophical position focuses upon the thing rather than the I, on substance rather than on the active subject. The I is posited as part of being.[7] Critical philosophy, however, asserts freedom as its starting point, hence the I takes priority over any concept of the thing, the subject is understood as activity rather than as substance, and being is understood in terms of the activity of the I. In Fichte's idealism (which, of course, is a form of critical rather than dogmatic philosophy), the Non-I is not a Kantian thing-in-itself beyond the reach of knowledge but something that is opposed to the I by force of this I and hence very much within reach of the I.[8]

There is a problem here that I will now point to but that will be fully addressed within the context of Schlegel's criticisms of Fichte's idealism. The problem has to do with what is posited in Fichte's act of consciousness (*Tathandlung*). As Verweyen points out: "The option to be moral cannot be derived from an act that contains less than morality. But precisely this seems to be the problem in Fichte's early *WL*."[9] He continues: "The most fundamental ground of all consciousness is an act which precedes both theoretical and practical reason . . . But the evidence of the act of the ego that absolutely posits itself, Fichte's first principle, does not logically presuppose a moral option. Will not the step from the mere *Tathandlung* to an act of "ought"—which somewhere has to occur in the transcendental system—be an unwarranted leap to quite another level of discussion?"[10] The problem that Verweyen points out is something Schlegel had already addressed in a fragment from 1797: "The I posits itself not because it posits itself, but rather because it ought to posit itself; there is a big difference between the two."[11] Schlegel was aware of the problem that Verweyen points out, namely, that unless Fichte includes the moral imperative (should) in his original self-positing of the I, he cannot account for freedom. Schlegel's awareness of this problem was an important step in the development of his own philosophical position. Ultimately it led him to the more radical claim: "The *I posits itself* and the *I should posit itself* are not deduced from a higher proposition, one is as high as the other; they are two principles, not one. *Wechselgrundsatz*."[12] I shall discuss the implications of this claim in chapter 6. Here I shall simply point out that once again, Schlegel's criticisms of the search for a first principle lead him to suggest a move away from *Grundsätze* and the linear, deductive scheme that they are used to govern and toward a *Wechselgrundsatz*, which is a uniquely romantic alternative to all such first principles for philosophy.

The Clash between Schmid and Fichte

Schlegel was hardly Fichte's only critic. The *Philosophisches Journal* published several articles that addressed the problems other philosophers found with Fichte's work. Here I shall present one such critique, which was relevant to the development of Schlegel's views, and Fichte's response to it.[13] Schlegel was familiar with the exchange between Schmid and Fichte, and more important, some of the skepticism expressed by Schmid was shared by Schlegel, so our investigation of this exchange will further clarify the nature of Schlegel's skepticism.

Schmid's contribution to the journal was not a direct attack on Fichte (although Fichte was to perceive it as such) but rather a series of questions that reveal a deep skepticism regarding the possibility of establishing a first principle for philosophy. The title of his article, "Pieces from a Text on Philosophy and Its Principles" ("Bruchstücke aus einer Schrift über die Philosophie und ihre Prinzipien"), alerts us to the fact that this will not be a systematic treatment of the problem of philosophy's starting point, but rather an exploratory set of questions regarding the relation between philosophy and its principles. Schmid begins with a series of questions. A first principle is searched for: if we do not yet know where to find it, is it unknown? What is the status of philosophy if we cannot locate a first principle for it? Is philosophy determined by the first principle, or is the first principle determined by philosophy? If the first principle determines philosophy, then when we look for the principle of philosophy, we also look for philosophy. One of the primary issues embedded in the issue of the starting point for philosophy is the very definition of philosophy itself. Fichte, Niethammer, and Schlegel each takes a different position regarding the starting point of philosophy, and hence each thinker comes up with significantly different definitions of philosophy itself.

After opening these questions related to the definition of philosophy, Schmid makes some definitive claims regarding the foundation from which we begin to philosophize. His philosophical primitives are representation, will, and object. He writes: "[T]hat we represent something, that we have a will, that there are objects: all of this can be known immediately and does not lend itself to philosophical proof."[14] Philosophers must not attempt to go beyond these primitives (i.e., the facts that we have the faculties of representing and of willing and that there are objects). For Schmid, the proposition, I am, or, The I exists (*Ich bin* or *Das Ich ist*), is the foundation from which all philosophizing begins.[15] All principles of philosophy presuppose a thinking subject who represents and wills and an empirical world of objects. Pure philosophy, if pure philosophy is to be defined as having no dependence upon the physical world, is an "empty and foundationless Philosophy" (*leere und grundlose Philosophie*), a "lazy creature of the mind" (*müssiges Hirngespinst*).[16] Schmid finds the attempts to establish a single, absolute first principle for philosophy to be an exercise in futility. He describes this in the following way:

> The new and bold attempt to bring together the beginning and endpoint of all philosophizing by attributing an idealistic absolute to the concept of a knowing subject, an absolute which would be found in all acts of self-consciousness, and from this fictional infinity (*erdichteten Unendlichkeit*) draws each time precisely as much as one believes to be necessary in order to deduce all that is found in self-consciousness. In this way, philosophy becomes an infinite work of fantasy (*unendliche Dichtung*) and the philosopher elevates himself to the rank of a self-creator of a world, of the substance of all things which originate in him and for him.[17]

Obviously, Fichte's philosophy is a prime example of one such "new and bold attempt" to create a foundation for philosophy, one that falls into the category that Schmid classifies as an "infinite fiction" with the philosopher as the creator of the world and a philosophy that is not really any philosophy at all. For Schmid, it is not a mistake for the philosopher to begin with facts. The mistake is to begin with a self-positing act of consciousness and leave the empirical world behind. Schmid accepts an a priori fact of consciousness as a legitimate principle of philosophy: "That there is understanding and a will and that through these two faculties a manifold of activity and actions are possible: this is a fact—something given, but given a priori—an object of reason—absolutely *a priori*."[18] Yet understanding and will cannot be understood in purely a priori terms, but rather also as faculties of nature in union with nature and from this perspective—given *a posteriori*.[19]

Hence, according to Schmid, the goal of philosophy is to isolate the most primitive conditions necessary for cognition. In this, he is in good company with most of the post-Kantian philosophers of this period. Yet he parts company with Fichte—indeed, he sets himself up for a sharp attack from Fichte—insofar as he claims that the objects of philosophy are a priori and a posteriori facts. This means that the method of philosophy cannot proceed in isolation from empirical experience. The world is a combination of consciousness and physical objects—facts given by reason and those given by nature. Schmid's claims here are in stark opposition to Fichte's, and in fact he classifies Fichte's breed of idealism (although he never mentions Fichte by name in his article) as a type of empty fiction, a self-indulging philosophy that could only describe a particular subjective world, never the objective world.

Fichte was quick to respond to Schmid. He did this in an article for the *Philosophisches Journal*, "Comparison of the System Presented by Prof. Schmid with the *Wissenschaftslehre*."[20] The title sounds innocent enough, but it hides what has been described as an act of annihilation, a vituperative attack by Fichte against Schmid's very tentative questions regarding the need for first principles in philosophy.[21] After presenting the major points of Schmid's article, and reminding us that not everyone (esp. not Schmid) has the talent necessary to do philosophy, Fichte goes on to give a new presentation of his *Wissenschaftslehre*: "In my opinion, the question which philosophy must answer is the following: how are our representations joined to its objects, to what extent can one say that these objects are independent and correspond to something outside of us?"[22] According to Fichte, the goal of philosophy is to give an account of the status of our representations, and hence the objects of philosophy are *Tathandlungen* (acts of the mind) rather than facts. His method is purely rational, leading him to a subjective idealism. He claims to have settled all of these claims in the *Wissenschaftslehre*. Yet Schmid's flagrant misunderstandings have made him realize that he must reacquaint readers with his system.[23] He informs us that his principle task in the *Wissenschaftslehre* was to determine whether our representations correspond to something outside of us. He writes:

> What are the reasons for our claim that our representations correspond to something external to us? To address this question is the task of all philosophy and the *Wissenschaftslehre* takes this task on and answers this question in the following way: The representation and the object which should correspond to it are one—indeed the same—only looked upon from two different perspectives. That it [the representation] must be looked upon from these two different perspectives lies in the knowing and representing nature of reason, this is necessary and is to be seen as necessary. The *Wissenschaftslehre* provides insight regarding how and why the rational being distinguishes both, even though they are one, and then later must judge that both are completely equal, accounting for the quality of freedom which the representation as such has and necessity which the object as such has.[24]

This identity is uncovered in the self-positing I. Fichte claims that the method of the *Wissenschaftslehre* is simply the method of abstracting from all contingent parts of the I and thereby uncovering it as a pure activity. He describes it thus (and in not-so-subtle parenthetical remarks reminds his readers of Schmid's deficiencies as a thinker—most of Fichte's critics turned out to be unfit for philosophy, at least from Fichte's perspective):

> The method of the *Wissenschaftslehre* is the following: It demands all to note what they generally and absolutely necessarily do when they say to themselves—"I" (everything depends on this, but precisely this arrival to the absolute with complete abstraction from all individuality is what few humans can achieve). The *Wissenschaftslehre* postulates: everyone who really takes on the demanded task will find that he posits himself, or what might be clearer to some, that he is both subject and object. In this absolute identity of subject and object consists I-ness.[25]

The I is that which cannot be a subject without at the same time being an object, and vice versa. This identity is the starting point of Fichte's philosophy. He writes: "Through this identity of ideality and reality, critical idealism has its beginning. This is not an idealism in which the I is only a subject nor a dogmatism according to which the subject is treated only as an object."[26] Fichte presents his idealism as critical rather than absolute (in which case the I would be only a subject) or dogmatic (in which the I would be only an object). Fichte's claim is that he has discovered an identity that gives unity to knowledge (hence the title of his work, *Science of Knowledge*) and to philosophy. This is why he claims "The *Wissenschaftslehre*, with its first principle, displays not only all of philosophy, but also the conditions for all philosophizing. It dismisses not only everything, but everyone, who does not belong within its boundaries."[27] According to Fichte, all of philosophy begins with and is determined by reflection upon the I: "What does one think when one thinks this principle? If the philosopher continues with this question, he finds that the exhaustive answer to this is the entire domain of philosophy."[28]

Schmid had claimed that any attempt to go beyond the primitives—will, understanding, and the givenness of objects—was bound to lead to confusion, to empty, unjustified claims. To this Fichte replies that the goal of the *Wissenschaftslehre* is not to justify a system of things (*Dinge*) but to describe a series of acts (*Handlungen*).[29] Fichte does not deny that he must address the problem of the status that representations have, but this, he claims, is something quite different from giving an account of things as facts.[30] Indeed, Fichte claims (against Schmid) that it is not a fact of consciousness that there are things such as humans, animals, and trees. Rather, it is a fact of consciousness that this particular human, this particular animal, this particular tree, which moves before my eyes, exists. According to Fichte, every general concept presupposes not a thing but rather an abstraction that the mind performs because it is free.³¹ The "I" is not a fact, for a fact is, on Fichte's account, something found, and the I is never found (it is the finder, the very condition necessary in order for anything to be found at all). Hence the I must be pure activity, a *Tathandlung* rather than a *Tatsache*.³² According to Fichte the objects of consciousness are the result of our freedom to abstract (*Freiheit der Abstraction*) and the formative powers of our imagination (*Bildung durch die Einbildungskraft*).³³ The process of abstracting from a particular tree that I see to the concept of 'tree' in general is the product of the imagination in its freedom (*Product meiner Einbildungskraft in ihrer Freiheit*).³⁴ Fichte goes on to argue that the same process that guides our formation of concepts of things guides our formation of our concept of ourselves that is of our faculties of understanding and will.³⁵

According to Fichte, the task of the *Wissenschaftslehre* is to place together what has been separated through abstraction.³⁶ This is because if we proceed via abstraction, we may miss certain links in the chain; this cannot happen when we bring different elements together.³⁷ He characterizes Reinhold's philosophy as one that begins with facts and then looks for underlying principles and describes his own philosophy as the inverse of this.³⁸

Fichte and Schlegel on Critical Philosophy

In his *Attempt at a New Presentation of the* Wissenschaftslehre (1797–98), Fichte develops his claim that the identity of the I as subject and as object is the fundamental foundation of all knowledge.³⁹ He even claims that "a systematic derivation of consciousness as a whole (or, what amounts to the same thing, a philosophical system) would have to begin with the pure I."⁴⁰ In order to explain consciousness, Fichte believed, we need to posit a consciousness in which subject and object are not parted, but rather united. Only such a unity stops an otherwise infinite regress. For if we think an object only as the product of a representing subject, the representing subject can be thought of as the object of another representing subject, ad infinitum. Yet, if we can isolate a moment in which subject and object are one, we will have reached an absolute starting point, an unmediated consciousness of our self. And true to Schlegel's characterization of Fichte as the *Jäger* of philosophy, Fichte hunts down the unity underlying all of our cognitive activity in the unmediated consciousness of our self as insurmountable (*unhintergehbar*) and as an activity (not a fact).⁴¹ This move freed him, or so he thought, from the criticisms that had been leveled against Reinhold by Schulze. Fichte defines philosophy in terms of this identity. He writes:

> All possible consciousness, as objective and belonging to a subject, presupposes an unmediated consciousness in which what is subjective and what is objective are simply [*schlechthin*] one and the same. Otherwise, consciousness is simply [*schlechthin*] incomprehensible. One will look in vain for a connection between subject and object if one does not grasp their unity. Hence, all philosophy which does not depart from the point at which they are united is necessarily shallow and incomplete and cannot explain what it should explain and so is not philosophy at all.[42]

Fichte cannot conceive of philosophy that is not grounded upon a principle that guarantees a certain starting point, which in turn guarantees a completeness that would not otherwise be available and that is required for something to *be* philosophy. As we shall see, Fichte's rejection of openness and incomprehensibility is not shared by Schlegel, who embraces both, that is, who believes that philosophy must contain incomprehensible aspects and is inherently incomplete.

Schlegel was well aware of Fichte's deeply dismissive attitude toward those who did not follow his method, describing Fichte as one who "idealized his enemies to model representatives of pure non-philosophy" so that whoever was not engaged in philosophy in the sense in which Fichte defined it was not engaged in philosophy at all. Anyone who was not an idealist according to Fichte's terms was not a philosopher. Moreover, for Fichte not just any form of idealism will count as philosophy. The task of philosophy is to indicate the basis of experience (here Fichte shows his deep connections to Kant's transcendental idealism), but this does not entail any commitment to experience (here, in an attempt to avoid Kant's troubling dualisms, Fichte breaks rather violently from Kant's empirical realism). Fichte claims that the identity of the I as both subject and object cannot be part of experience, yet it is the ground of all experience. For this reason "experience is not something with which idealism is, as it were, acquainted in advance and which it keeps in view as the goal at which it has to arrive. In the course of its derivations, idealism knows nothing of experience and takes no heed of it whatsoever. It commences from its own starting point, and it proceeds in accordance with its own rule, without the slightest concern for what may ultimately result."[43] Fichte saw his philosophical contributions as an extension of Kant's philosophy, in particular of Kant's transcendental deduction. That is, he believed that his work helped solve the problem of establishing objective validity through the subjective conditions of representability. Fichte claims to be answering the same questions as Kant's philosophy, even more completely (and successfully) than Kant had.

Schlegel, in a review of the first volumes of the *Philsophisches Journal*, faults Fichte for not having given a "complete proof" (*einen vollständigen Beweis*) of this claim.[44] And Fichte attempts to complete his proof in section 6 of the second introduction to the *Wissenschaftslehre*. Fichte not only believed that his system was "none other than the Kantian system," but also that it completed Kant's revolution.[45]

To complete the revolution begun by Kant, the problem of Kant's positing of a thing-in-itself as the necessary source for all experience needed to be addressed. Fichte believed that this thing-in-itself was unnecessary. As I discussed earlier, those philosophers who did not see this and who insisted that the thing-in-itself was a necessary condition for the possibility of objective knowledge were dogmatists. Recall that for Fichte, there are only two possible consistent explanations of experience: dogmatism (materialism/realism) and critical philosophy (idealism). Dogmatists believe that they are in possession of cognitions of things-in-themselves, so they endorse a type of metaphysical realism. This realism is defined in terms of determinism so from Fichte's perspective, amounts to a flagrant affront to the concept of the 'freedom of the self-positing I,' which he champions in his own philosophy. Like Jacobi before him, Fichte sees in Spinoza's philosophy a model of the sort of determinism/fatalism that he finds threatening to the well-being of philosophy. For Fichte, Spinoza was a thinker focused upon things rather than the I, on substance rather than the active subject. In Spinoza's system, the I is posited merely as a mode of being, subject to the laws of nature, with no access to the supersensible realm, and thereby robbed of its freedom.

Critical philosophy, on the other hand, turns dogmatism on its head. It asserts freedom as its starting point, hence the I takes priority over any concept of the thing, the subject is understood in terms of its activity rather than as a mere mode of being, and being is understood in terms of the activity of the I. As I have emphasized, in Fichte's idealism (which he insists is a form of critical rather than dogmatic philosophy), the Non-I is not a Kantian thing-in-itself beyond the reach of knowledge but something that is opposed to the I by force of this I and hence very much within the reach of the I.

Despite Fichte's insistence that his version of idealism was the only truly critical version of idealism, and that those who did not do philosophy according to the method indicated in the *Wissenschaftslehre* were dogmatists, Schlegel insisted that Fichte was indeed the dogmatist. He tells us, "In the *Wissenschaftslehre* the method must be critical: but Fichte is not critical."[46] Why isn't Fichte critical? Because "absolute idealism without realism is mystical," and the mystic is certainly no critic![47]

Mysticism is no more than a proxy for philosophy that Schlegel describes as the abyss in which reality gets lost.[48]

Critical philosophy must fuse idealism and realism, Fichte with Spinoza, odd bedfellows if ever there were such; yet contra Fichte, we must remember that an odd match is not necessarily an inconsistent match. The blending of Fichte and Spinoza, however discordant it might seem, is for Schlegel a necessary strategy in order to understand nature as an organic whole. This understanding is mediated by consciousness (the only realm, pace Schlegel, that Fichte can tell us anything about) and the infinite realm of being (the domain of Spinoza's philosophy). Consciousness and the infinite are the two poles of reality, and the philosopher must find a way to incorporate both poles into his method, otherwise he remains dogmatic, cut off from one aspect of reality or the other. Beiser, then, has good reasons for appealing to holism in order to explain the romantic push to join Fichte and Spinoza: "[The early German Romantics] held that idealism and realism are one-sided perspectives, which are both true and false: they are true about one aspect of the whole but they are false about the whole itself. If nature is an organic whole, it is not possible to say with idealism that it is completely *inside* consciousness nor with realism that is entirely *outside* consciousness. Rather, it is both and neither."[49] Hence, on Schlegel's reading, Fichte's philosophy is one-sided, and ultimately cannot accomplish what it needs to accomplish. Fichte goes both too far and not far enough in his *Wissenschaftslehre*. He goes too far in pushing to establish the foundation for all of philosophy. He is searching for an absolute ground of knowledge, yet such a search is both unnecessary and futile; it is unnecessary because, as we shall see, philosophy begins "in the middle," and it is futile because "[t]o know already indicates a conditioned knowledge," so "[t]he unknowability of the Absolute is an identical triviality."[50] Yet, insofar as Fichte remains inside consciousness, he does not go far enough in his attempt to explain reality. As Schlegel himself puts this, "[Fichte] wants to demonstrate far too much and then far too little."[51]

Fichte's confusion about how much and how little he should demonstrate can be traced to a misconception regarding the nature of philosophy. Fichte just does not see that philosophy need not, indeed cannot be grounded in an absolute, first principle. Schlegel endorsed antifoundationalism in an attempt to capture the inherent incompleteness both of our knowledge and of philosophy itself. In the first book of the lectures on the history of philosophy, entitled *The Historical Characteristics of Philosophy according to Its Successive Development*, Schlegel addresses the problem of where we begin when we philosophize: "To desire to provisionally prove what the beginning point of philosophy is, concerns separating out the first principle of philosophy (if there is such a principle), as is actually attempted in some scientific introductions. One can admit that in a tentative treatment the point from which one must begin to philosophize will be searched for and proved."[52] Of course, if there is no such principle, it will only be searched for and never found. In several fragments and in an essay, "On Incomprehensibility," Schlegel stresses the value of incomprehension. Because our knowledge claims are never rooted in absolutely certain foundations, we should not be so arrogant as to think that we will ever have the last word on the meaning of any given event or text or idea. The remainder is that which is incomprehensible.

Because Fichte believes that philosophy begins from an absolute foundation, pure and certain comprehensibility is not only possible but demanded. Recall that he defines philosophy in terms of the "absolute comprehensibility" of consciousness. Because Schlegel rejects the possibility of an absolute foundation for philosophy, he embraces incompleteness and incomprehensibility and charges that those who want to explain everything become like popes in their own small domains, exhibiting the dogmatism born of *imposing* truth rather than *seeking* it. Even the literary form that Schlegel favored for the expression of his ideas reflects his commitment to nondogmatic approaches to philosophy; the fragments defy a notion of a complete system, making the incompleteness of philosophy transparent at the level of literary form.

Schlegel's particular breed of antifoundationalism also has consequences for the role of history in philosophy. Schlegel's position is that we never begin with the certain knowledge that there is any first principle; instead we must begin with what we have—a history of what has been thought by other philosophers before. According to Schlegel, an introduction to philosophy can only be a critique of all earlier philosophy. His first lecture of *The Historical Characteristics of Philosophy* concerns the problem of introducing philosophy, which is ultimately the problem of the beginning of philosophy. According to Schlegel, any attempt to begin with a pure point of certainty is impossible: "To entirely abstract from all previous systems and throw all of this away as Descartes attempted to do is absolutely impossible. Such an entirely new creation from one's own mind, a complete forgetting of all which has been thought before, was also attempted by Fichte and he too failed in this."[53] Prominent representatives of the modern European philosophical tradition such as Descartes and Fichte sought the foundation for philosophy in a lonely cogito or *Ich*, but Schlegel rejects this move and any attempt to isolate a single, fixed principle (whether that principle is understood as an activity or as a fact) underlying all of our knowledge claims. To "throw away" everything that has been developed by other philosophers or to "completely forget" all that has been thought before is to presume that philosophy can be done without attending to the history of philosophy. It is, according to Schlegel, impossible to do philosophy critically without doing the history of philosophy. This point, again, is intimately connected to his antifoundationalism. He writes: "Our philosophy does not begin like the others with a first principle—where the first proposition is like the center or first ring of a comet—with the rest a long tail of mist—we depart from a small but living seed—our center lies in the middle."[54]

A philosophy such as that of Fichte, which is based on first principles, provides a perspective from the outside, that is, from a point that establishes all that follows from it. Such a position is foundational, with the first principle or foundation standing outside of the matter that it serves to explain. The first principle is fixed, static, and presumably explains all the changing, living matter in the world, matter that, in Fichte's words, it need "take no heed of whatsoever."[55]

Schlegel's view of philosophy represents a radical departure from Fichte's foundationalist, ahistorical view of philosophy. Schlegel's reference to a "small but living seed" is an important metaphor. His particular breed of antifoundationalism commits him to something like life as the framework for understanding reality. Schlegel himself describes his philosophical method as genetic or synthetic as opposed to deductive or syllogistic.[56] The opposition of his genetic method to the deductive one underscores the historical dimension of Schlegel's approach: the very term *genetic* is connected to a coming into being, to an evolutionary development, and to understanding the development or genesis of an idea. To understand how a given thing comes into being, we do well to look at its various phases of development or its history.

Since we have no access to an obvious starting point for philosophy, we must begin with what we do have, a rather messy heap of what has been thought before. In *Athenäum* Fragment 84, Schlegel claims that "philosophy, like epic poetry, always begins *in media res*."[57] When we do philosophy, we are not starting from a position outside the ebb and flow of philosophical ideas, but in the midst of this dynamic process itself, *in media res*. Schlegel's move to "the inside" or "the middle" is a move toward taking the history of philosophy seriously and toward reconceptualizing the very notion of critical philosophy in historical terms.

Schlegel describes the various philosophical systems that comprise the history of philosophy as links in a coherent chain, with an understanding of any given philosophical system requiring some understanding of the chain to which it is connected.[58] And for Schlegel, though wholes are important to him, a philosophical system has little to do with a "systematic derivation of consciousness as a whole," in part because as we saw above, such a system, positioned "within consciousness" would remain one sided. Moreover, Fichte's conception of system overlooks elements that are crucial to Schlegel's view: "System is an integrated, connected whole of the matter of knowledge [*wissenschaftliche Stoff*] in a continuous mutual confirmation and organic coherence—a whole of a plurality that is in itself perfected and unified."[59] In Schlegel's conception of a philosophical system, change and interaction are stressed, and organic coherence is the goal, a goal that no systematic derivation or single system will achieve for us. The philosopher must work from a single system, that is, from one link in the chain of all systems, but always with a view toward the unity of which each system is but a part. This fluency between one's own system and the greater whole of which it is a part is stressed by Schlegel in the following fragment: "Every philosopher has his own line or tendency which is his departing point and his cycle. He who has a system is as lost as he who has none. One must therefore reconcile both."[60]

What is the philosopher to do with such a dilemma? Schlegel seems to damn the philosopher for having a system yet doom her if she is without one. Beiser understands the dilemma presented by Schlegel in the following way: "On the one hand, it is dangerous to have a system, because it sets arbitrary limits to enquiry and imposes an artificial order on the facts. On the other hand, it is necessary to have a system, because unity and coherence are essential to all knowledge and it is only in the context of a system that a proposition is justifiable."[61] Beiser's emphasis on the relations among system, unity, and coherence is quite useful in helping us to understand the horns of Schlegel's dilemma, a dilemma that never even surfaces for a thinker like Fichte, whose system, standing in isolation from all else, is endowed with the certainty that a first principle and accompanying foundationalist method can grant.[62] In contrast, Schlegel's antifoundationalism leads him to see philosophy as consisting of a plurality of systems, each of which can offer a piece of the whole of the system of knowledge, but never the complete system. No individual line or tendency constitutes a system in the sense of the "integrated, connected whole of the matter of knowledge" to which Schlegel makes reference. Since Fichte, like Kant, believed that there was one system that could capture all truths, there was no pressing need to look to other systems, for at best they could offer partial truths and at worst, merely a collections of falsehoods. And there was an important sense in which for both Kant and Fichte the notion of system stood outside of the matter that was explained by the system, as a bedrock of sorts that holds unconditionally and provides the "secure path of the science" to the searchers of truth. Schlegel's view of the situation is quite different. He does not think that a philosophical system exists outside of the truths that are captured by it.

Schlegel rejects a foundationalist approach to the problem of knowledge and emphasizes the importance of coherence: we never have the last word on how to justify a claim, but we must try to bring our claims into some coherent scheme or whole. What goes for our own body of knowledge holds too for the body of knowledge that philosophers construct. And construct they do, but not via systematic derivations anchored in a firm foundation. Schlegel reads Fichte's emphasis on systematic derivations as an embrace of deduction, claiming that his demonstrations work by way of deduction, and deduction is never as strong as construction.[63]

So, on Schlegel's reading, Fichte's critical idealism is not all that critical after all; it is dogmatic. The truly critical philosopher will blend idealism with realism in order to avoid the limitations of one-sided approaches to reality. Moreover, philosophers who wish to avoid dogmatism will simply have to come to terms with the fact that there is no anchor to moor our beliefs and endow them with certainty. Now let us turn to the details of the position that Schlegel offered in the wake of his break from first principles, details that become clear in his critique of Fichte's philosophy.

Fichte's Mystical Errors

Schlegel displayed a high degree of characteristic *Frechheit* in his claims regarding the limitations of Fichte's philosophy, but this should not overshadow the great respect he had for both the work and the person. *Athenäum* Fragment 216 nicely captures Schlegel's admiration for Fichte: "The French Revolution, Fichte's philosophy, and Goethe's *Meister* are the greatest tendencies of the age," he announces. Given that Schlegel considered the French Revolution and Goethe's novel to be paramount historical events, to include Fichte's philosophy in this trinity is a noteworthy tribute. Indeed, Schlegel believed that Fichte's work had done for philosophy what the French Revolution and Goethe's *Meister* had done for political structures and literary form, respectively: Fichte's *Wissenschaftslehre* had revolutionized the field of philosophy, setting it on a path that celebrated human freedom, a path which every subsequent philosopher would have to traverse.

Yet Schlegel had far from unconditional approbation for Fichte: already a cursory look at the key term *tendency* in Fragment 216 cited above leads us to the root of a tension that would inevitably arise between the philosophical approaches of these two thinkers. Despite Fichte's insistence to the contrary, his philosophy was "merely" a tendency, a "temporary venture" (as Schlegel puts this), but not anything like "the secure path of a science." A tendency does not stand in isolation from that which came before it or from that which will inevitably come after it. It is something that is shaped by the past and will shape the future. A tendency is much like a tradition. It is formative, but not in any absolute sense, and its boundaries toward the past and the future are open. In the wake of a departure from first principles, tendencies are an important part of what we have to guide us in our search for truth.

Tendencies are far too provisional for Fichte's taste. A tendency could never support the architecture of the *Wissenschaftslehre*. Yet it was precisely tendencies, with their share of uncertainty, that were the very fabric of Schlegel's critical philosophy. This is, I believe, a fruitful point of comparison between Fichte and Schlegel's critical philosophy: Fichte's critical philosophy was a kind of pure foundationalist idealism (Fichte, after all, stressed that any attempt to fuse idealism with realism was doomed to be an "inconsistent enterprise"),[64] whereas Schlegel's critical philosophy was not a pure form of idealism at all; it was, rather, a unique antifoundationalist hybrid of idealism (à la Fichte) with realism (à la Spinoza) that was coherentist (and coherent) through and through.

Schlegel's critique of Fichte was not carried out as an attempt to finish something started but not completed by Fichte (as Fichte was allegedly carrying out the revolution Kant had begun but had not finished). Schlegel was interested in a reform of the very conception of philosophy that was shaping the post-Kantian period. He sought to move philosophy away from its moorings in science and the concomitant deductive method that had taken hold, and to bring it into the company of art and history. Schlegel thus endorsed a progressive and never-ending method for philosophy, based on the view that our knowledge claims would never be endowed with the certainty granted by absolute foundations but rather would only have increasing degrees of probability. They would, as it were, tend toward truth. An infinite search or longing for the infinite (the totality of all truths) replaces any model (not just Fichte's) that departs from an absolute first principle.

Although this never-ending story of our longing for the infinite might superficially appear as a fairy-tale-like approach to philosophical problems, it was, in fact, a much more sober alternative than the one Fichte offered. *Sober* is intended here in more than one of its connotations; for Schlegel likened Fichte's attempts to explain the foundations of our knowledge to those of a drunk who never tires of the futile activity of mounting and then promptly falling from the horse that is supposed to take him to his destination and is always left just where he began without having moved any closer to where he wants to go.[65]

According to Schlegel's view of philosophy, the philosopher can point to tendencies, to probable states of affairs, to beliefs that cohere with one another, but she cannot uncover the absolute foundation of all knowledge. But, according to Schlegel, Fichte held that in order to be a "science of knowledge," philosophy must be based upon an absolute first principle, and the *Wissenschaftslehre* is his attempt to secure this principle and thereby solve the problem of philosophy's starting point. In that work, Fichte does not tire of reminding the reader that "philosophy has to display the basis or foundation of all experience." This contrasts rather sharply with a theme that will be examined carefully in chapter 6, namely, Schlegel's insistence that philosophy always begins *in media res*.

As we have seen, Schlegel was aware of the importance of Fichte's *Wissenschaftslehre*, and he dedicated several sets of fragments to this work.[66] These fragments present some hermeneutical problems for the reader, for they may seem to be announcements of problems rather than systematic arguments presented to show the flaws of Fichte's approach to philosophy. Yet it would be a mistake to dismiss them on the grounds of their "unsystematic form" without first attending to the philosophical commitments from which they stem.

Schlegel faults Fichte for his attempt to deduce all of reality from the self-positing act of consciousness. This, says Schlegel, is based upon a flawed view of the nature of philosophy: "If one postulates a system of knowledge (*Wissenschaft*) and searches for the conditions of its possibility, one falls into mysticism and the most consequential solution—the only possible one—from this point of view, is *the positing of an absolute I*—through which the form and content of an absolute theory of knowledge are given at once."[67] Contrary to Fichte's own claim that the only truly critical philosophy had to be his version of idealism, Schlegel finds in Fichte's approach to philosophy heavy traces of dogmatism and mysticism and very little critical philosophy at all. He in fact, again with characteristic *Frechheit*, likens Fichte to the pope, who arbitrarily posits what he will and can easily explain everything; he, after all, has "infallible power to open heaven and hell."[68] If Fichte were the pope, Schlegel would have been burned at the stake as a heretic, for he is quite explicit regarding the errors of Fichte's approach to philosophy: "Philosophy in its proper sense has neither a first principle, nor an object, nor a definite task. The *Wissenschaftslehre* has a definite object (I and Non-I and their relationships), a definite principle (*Wechselgrund*) and therefore a definite task."[69] Fichte's deductions work, as any deductive system must work, only if one accepts his absolute starting point, the axiom from which all else follows. Yet, according to Schlegel, no one is convinced by this, and instead of argument, Fichte resorts to what Schlegel calls "papal-like" declarations of the truth of his claims.[70] Fichte claims that the task of philosophy is to indicate the basis of experience yet that this does not entail any commitment to experience. Further, he claims that those who disagree with him do not understand him, probably because they are not engaged in philosophy at all.

A critic might say that the only one who seems dogmatic in this story is Schlegel himself, who thinks that he can drop some punchy, provocative lines and thereby destroy his opponent's position. Part of the reason the early German Romantics have been neglected by philosophers is because their arguments are not presented in ready-made systems, like those of Kant or Fichte. Schlegel has arguments for his claims against Fichte, but they must be woven together carefully, pieced together into a coherent scheme, for any system Schlegel developed is in keeping with his aforementioned claim: "He who has a system is as lost as he who has none. One must therefore reconcile both." Schlegel's attempts at just such a reconciliation create more work for the reader but do not take any rigor away from his position. In addition to the fragments, we have several collections of lectures that Schlegel delivered that help to shed light on the details of some of his arguments against Fichte, in particular, his claim that Fichte was a mystic.

Following Schlegel's historical taxonomy, mysticism is dogmatic.[71] The dogmatism emerges because mysticism begins with an arbitrary positing of some Absolute. Even worse, insofar as mysticism begins with a single, absolute principle of all knowledge, it begins with a contradiction. This is the case because of the intrinsic unknowability of the Absolute. Any attempt to limit the Absolute is bound to end in contradiction, for then the philosopher is claiming both that there exists an Absolute and that there exists knowledge of the Absolute, hence the Absolute is not Absolute after all.[72]

Fichte's mystical errors can be avoided. He must take account of history and science so that his view of knowledge is not isolated from human reality. Idealism is empty if it is not connected to the concrete realities of the world. Schlegel defines philosophy as the "essence of all sciences": it cannot be solely concerned with the structure of consciousness with no regard for experience; mystical idealism leaves us with philosophy as a "sophistical art." Such a view of philosophy disregards history and other empirical data and is sharply at odds with Schlegel's view of the nature of philosophy.[73]

Schlegel critiques Fichte's disinterest in any science that has an object and his corresponding antipathy to history, arguing that history is an essential part of philosophy and the search for knowledge. In fact, as we shall see in chapter 5, Schlegel accused Kant, the great critical philosopher himself, of being only a "half-critic" because of his neglect of the history of philosophy and his inability to critique philosophy itself. Schlegel's conception of philosophy committed him to metaphilosophy, to coming to terms with the nature of philosophy itself. A Critical Age that criticizes everything except itself is not a fully critical age; one could say that it is "half-critical." Schlegel is after a critique of critique, a philosophy of philosophy, attempting, through his conception of historical critique, to achieve a metaphilosophy, a way of looking critically at philosophy itself, as a discipline that has developed through history.

The very first fragment of the *Athenäum* gives expression to Schlegel's concern with making philosophy the subject of philosophy: "Nothing is more rarely the subject of philosophy than philosophy itself."[74] To appreciate this claim, we must keep in mind that Schlegel was interested in making the *entire* tradition of philosophy the subject matter of philosophy, for he was well aware that other philosophers, even those who thought philosophy could begin with a first principle (e.g., Descartes and Fichte), had reflected on the nature of philosophy itself in developing their methods. But this was not enough: one had to approach philosophy historically in order to get a view of the whole and to *really* make philosophy the subject of philosophy. With characteristic irony (of just the sort that led so many of his contemporaries to misunderstand him), Schlegel describes his push to criticize philosophy as just retaliation: "Since nowadays philosophy criticizes everything that comes in front of its nose, a criticism of philosophy would be nothing more than justifiable retaliation."[75] Schlegel's charges against the limits of Fichte's "critical philosophy" are rooted in his desire to develop a critical philosophy of philosophy itself.

Schlegel's emphasis on history as essential to critique is part of his general view of philosophy as framed by life, as beginning *in media res*, in the midst of change. Accordingly, the object of philosophical critique is also something changing and growing, and the philosopher must be equipped to handle this teeming mass of material.

Fichte does not blend his philosophy with the philosophy of philosophy, which is part of the error-riddled path that leads him to his ahistorical method.[76] A critical (as opposed to a dogmatic or "half-critical") philosopher must be engaged in a history of philosophy in order to go beyond his own particular system. According to Schlegel, Fichte does not do this. Behler nicely expresses a central aspect of Schlegel's critique of Fichte: "Schlegel raised the question of Fichte's own historicity or the historicity of what was going on in his system and felt that what was proclaimed here as absolute Ego or absolute thought was nothing more than J.G. Fichte in Jena, including all his personal idiosyncrasies and prejudices."[77] Indeed, as Schlegel himself wrote, "The *Wissenschaftslehre* is a Fichtean presentation of the Fichtean spirit in Fichtean letters," with both the spirit and the letter leading to foundationalism.[78] So Fichte's philosophy is a tendency of the age, that is, Fichte's influence is undeniable, and his emphasis on the importance of human freedom in coming to an understanding is to be lauded. Yet, given Schlegel's reservations against a philosophy based on first principles, that is, given Schlegel's antifoundationalism, what are we to make of Fichte's foundationalist project? Fichte's emphasis on freedom is a tendency we should follow; whereas his misguided, mystical quest for absolute foundations is tendency best avoided, for it is, in the end, just one more version of the foundationalist philosophy that Schlegel rebukes.

The Spirit versus the Letter of Fichte's Philosophy

There have been, as is to be expected, dissenting voices on this matter of Fichte's alleged foundationalism, and I think it only fair to end this chapter with a more sympathetic reading of Fichte than the one offered by Schlegel. In an article from 1994, Tom Rockmore argued that while the letter of Fichte's early thought commits him to a foundationalist tendency, the spirit of his early thought is antifoundationalist:

> [I]n Fichte's early thought, . . . we can discern foundationalist and antifoundationalist tendencies. Fichte is better known for his foundationalism, which apparently corresponds to the letter of his view. Yet there is also a nascent antifoundationalist aspect corresponding to the spirit of his thought, which has not often been studied . . . I am convinced that we can best be true to the spirit of Fichte's transcendental philosophy not in defending his own form of foundationalism but in abandoning it for the exciting new conception of antifoundationalism that he advances in his idea of ungrounded system.[79]

Rockmore raises several points that are relevant to the story of Schlegel's critique of Fichte that I am telling here. Rockmore emphasizes the important role that notions such as circularity, system, and antifoundationalsim played in the development of post-Kantian philosophy. Yet, while Rockmore discusses post-Kantian thinkers such as Hamann, Herder, Jacobi, Maimon, and Schulze in connection with general reactions to Kant's critical philosophy and the foundationalist conception of system that Fichte elaborated in the wake of the critical philosophy under the influence of Reinhold, he makes no reference at all to Schlegel's views on these matters. Moreover, Schlegel developed rather sophisticated criticisms of both Kant and Fichte's philosophy.

Rockmore is certainly correct in pointing to an important area of investigation in post-Kantian philosophy, an area that has for too long been neglected: namely, the epistemological systems that developed in this period, as thinkers attempted to reconstruct or even revolutionize the critical philosophy, which was, in essence always an attempt to uncover the structure of our knowledge. As Rockmore indicates, although *antifoundationalism* has only recently become a fashionable term, philosophers have been offering it as an alternative to foundationalism for centuries, and there were quite original versions of it presented in the period between Kant and Hegel. Like Schlegel, Rockmore finds a prototype of foundationalism in Descartes:

> At least since Descartes, the whole weight of the modern discussion is directed in an obvious way to the demonstration of claims to know in order to resist skepticism in any form. The conception of foundationalism introduced by Descartes is intended as a strategy to provide indefeasible claims for knowledge, that is, claims resistant to even the strongest forms of criticism. Descartes specifically states that the *cogito* is intended as the Archimedean point, and hence as a place to stand, as a foundation on which to construct the scaffolding of knowledge.[80]

Like Schlegel, Rockmore links foundationalism to a "view of knowledge as a permanent, ahistorical framework or matrix of reality."[81] Also in company with Schlegel, Rockmore finds a strong foundationalist thrust in Fichte's theory, particularly in "the idea that from a self-evident principle we can identify the first principle of human knowledge and hence we can ground knowledge."[82] Yet, in his move to characterize Fichte as an antifoundationalist, Rockmore and Schlegel part ways.

According to Rockmore, Fichte claims that "every science requires a foundation that cannot be proven within it but that must be certain. Since knowledge depends on a foundation that is not susceptible of proof, Fichte asserts that it is simply certain because it is certain."[83] Following Schlegel's characterization of Fichte, this would be the papal-like Fichte speaking, declaring that something is certain because it is certain and because he says so. Yet, pace Rockmore: "[t]his claim is an admission that knowledge takes the form of an ungrounded system."[84] Philosophy has both a hypothetical character and a circular nature, both pointing to the same conclusion, namely, "although philosophy requires certainty, it can never reach this goal. Philosophy cannot yield certainty, although knowledge requires it. In other words, what we can know is that the search for knowledge is an endless task because the theoretical requirement of a foundation, in other words of a linear, noncircular form of reasoning, cannot be met in practice."[85]

On Rockmore's reading, Fichte's foundationalist "letters" come as a result of his view of philosophy as *complete system* in need of a foundation; the antifoundationalist spirit is born of Fichte's acknowledgment that certainty is not possible and that our search for knowledge is never ending or infinite.

The affinities between Schlegel's antifoundationalism and the antifoundationalist "spirit" that Rockmore imputes to Fichte are striking. This is a sympathetic reading of Fichte, and in comparison, Schlegel's criticisms may seem unduly harsh and indeed not in tune with the spirit of Fichte's philosophy. I find myself in the peculiar position of agreeing with the praise Rockmore lavishes upon antifoundationalism as much more in tune with the human condition, and for his general annoyance with thinkers who would like to ignore the larger picture that the history of philosophy affords us. Nonetheless, I resist his move to uncover the roots of this turn away from grounded system and foundationalism in the spirit of Fichte's philosophy.

At the end of his essay, Rockmore tells us that: "Fichte stands at the crossroads of modernity: He participates in the Cartesian enterprise that holds that only if we can ground knowledge that there is any to be had; and he further participates in the anti-Cartesian movement following from the realization that whatever knowledge there is can only arise within a process that has no foundation, and hence no certainty."[86]

Schlegel would endorse the first half of the claim, namely, that Fichte's philosophical approach puts him precisely in the company of Descartes, with both guilty of attempting to create philosophy anew, from the solitary mind, completely "forgetting" all that had been thought before and doing philosophy as if it could be done in complete isolation from the world of unfolding events. The anti-Cartesian movement that Rockmore describes is precisely the movement of which Schlegel was a part, but Schlegel did not see this as part of Fichte's idealist project.

Schlegel was deeply concerned with the problem of form in philosophy, which is reflected in many of his comments on the vexing problem of the role of system in philosophy. And while the conception of system need not have a relation to the issue of grounds or foundations of knowledge, in Schlegel's case it did. Schlegel's concerns with the notion of system in philosophy arise as a consequence of his attempts to come to terms with the nature of human knowledge, which, once he had abandoned foundations and deductive method, was revealed to be anything but certain. According to Schlegel, the only truly critical philosophers were those who were willing to critique philosophy itself and who were, moreover, committed in spirit and letter to the antifoundationalism that he believed provided the best general view for understanding human knowledge, a knowledge that would never end in anything like final words or absolute truths, and certainly never began with them either.

Ultimately, I think that Schlegel is justified in calling Fichte's level of "criticism" into question. Fichte may indeed be an antifoundationalist in spirit, dedicated to the infinite search for knowledge, which can only get under way from acknowledging our inability to achieve certainty, but in letter, I think it is fair to call him to task for dogmatically clinging to the view that even if philosophy cannot yield certainty, knowledge requires it. The truly critical philosopher, on this reading, is not the German idealist, but the romantic skeptic. Now let us turn to another skeptic who, while no romantic, did influence Schlegel's thought.

Chapter Four
================

Niethammer's Influence on the Development of Schlegel's Skepticism

Jacobi, Reinhold, and Fichte was each concerned with the problem of philosophy's starting point. They were trying to overcome the paradox involved in giving a rational account of the Absolute or unconditioned. Jacobi believed that the paradox could only be overcome through a leap of faith, hence the claim that our knowledge is grounded upon a feeling rather than a principle. Schlegel rejected this appeal to faith as contrary to the search for truth essential to philosophy. Yet Schlegel did not support attempts, such as Reinhold's or Fichte's, to secure an absolute first principle for philosophy. For Schlegel, philosophy begins neither with a leap of faith nor with the awareness of a first principle (whether that principle be described as Reinhold's *fact* of consciousness, or Fichte's *act* of consciousness). According to Schlegel, philosophy does not begin with any *one thing* at all, but always with an interaction between *at least two principles*. Schlegel defends a *Wechselerweis* as the structure from which philosophy departs. Schlegel's *Wechselerweis* structure is best understood as an alternative to the proposed solutions to the problem of philosophy's starting point that we have hitherto discussed. It is an alternative to those views that appeal to first principles and lead to a view of philosophy as a deductive or systematically derivative enterprise. According to Schlegel's view, change is primary, and the way to understand it is through a synthetic/genetic method as opposed to a deductive one.

As we saw in chapter 2, Schlegel was not alone in his skepticism regarding attempts to base philosophy on an absolute principle: Schulze's skepticism raised questions to which both Reinhold and Fichte were compelled to respond. Schulze was not a lone voice crying in the wilderness, in fact, a fairly strong movement against foundationalist philosophy took shape in the period: there was even a journal devoted almost exclusively to questioning the feasibility of a philosophy based on first principles. This was Friedrich Immanuel Niethammer's *Philosophisches Journal einer Gesellschaft teutscher Gelehrten*. Schlegel's view of philosophy shares much with the type of skepticism that is formulated in the statement of purpose of this journal. As editor of the journal, Friedrich Immanuel Niethammer (1766–1848) articulated the purpose of the journal in his announcement ("Ankündigung") as well as his preliminary report concerning the sorts of issues that the journal would discuss ("Vorbericht").[1] In these texts a certain (albeit quite subtle) skepticism regarding the feasibility of a philosophy based on an absolute first principle is to be found. The journal was to have a significant influence on the development of Schlegel's views of philosophy.

In December 1794, Friedrich Immanual Niethammer took over Carl Christian Erhard Schmid's *Philosophisches Journal für Moralität, Religion und Menschenwohl*, which under his guidance became *Philosophisches Journal einer Gesellschaft teutscher Gelehrten*.[2] Under Niethammer's direction, not only the title but also the purpose of the journal changed. We will look at Niethammer's announcement and report. We will then turn to his first article for the journal, "On the Claims of Common Sense for Philosophy" ("Von den Ansprüchen des gemeinen Verstandes an der Philosophie").[3] These writings will serve to illustrate the line of thought that was to be developed in the various issues of the journal and can be read as an introduction to the journal itself.[4] From these three texts we find that Niethammer intended to establish a journal that would be guided by two themes: (1) skepticism regarding the project of basing philosophy upon first principles and (2) the problem of reconciling philosophy with common sense, that is, reconciling discursive reason with intuitive reason or, what Niethammer terms "philosophizing reason" (*philosophierende Vernunft*) with common understanding (*gemeiner Verstand*).[5] These two issues are closely related for they lead to a metaphilosophical questioning of the tasks of philosophy: Can philosophy be valuable at all if its foundation has not been absolutely determined, that is, if it does not begin with an absolute first principle? If philosophy does not begin with an absolute first principle, can it begin with common understanding and thereby attempt to approach the ideal of a complete science? In grappling with these issues, Niethammer was on his way to developing a view of philosophy that was not based on an abstract, absolute first principle, but rather on the claims of common sense.[6] This chapter will focus on how Niethammer develops these views and consider the influence of Niethammer's skepticism on Schlegel's thought, an influence that is well documented in a review Schlegel prepared of the first four issues of the journal as well as in fragments from notebooks he kept during this period.[7]

Niethammer's Skepticism

Before turning to a discussion of Niethammer's public position as articulated in his contributions to the journal, it is worth looking at some of his correspondence with other thinkers from the period immediately preceding the appearance of his public writings regarding the futility of establishing a first principle for philosophy. As Dieter Henrich indicates, Niethammer's essay, "Von den Ansprüchen des gemeinen Verstandes an die Philosophie" must be read in conjunction with the "Ankündigung" and the "Vorbericht" and must include an examination of his private exchange with Herbert and J. B. Erhard. The private exchange is particularly important because, in these letters, Niethammer could afford to be much more candid regarding his skepticism concerning the project of a philosophy based on first principles than he could be in his public writings.

In his letters to Herbert and Erhard, for example, Niethammer openly rejects the project of establishing an absolute first principle.[8] In this correspondence, these are the two prevalent themes: (1) a turn toward a new authority for philosophy, that is, a turn away from Kant's emphasis on pure reason; and (2) a turn toward an appeal to common, healthy understanding (*gesunder Menschenverstand*), a turn that implied an explicit rejection of a philosophy based on first principles.

On 4 May 1794, Franz P. von Herbert responded to Niethammer with the following advice:

> Where is Kant's first principle in the *Critique of Reason*, if you do not have enough of it, there is no help for you! Indeed, my dear Niethammer, I implore you, I beg you, use your exceptional talent to clearly present Kant's theory. In order to do this you need, in Reinhold's, Fichte's, and your own way to make this clear and have it serve your needs; then you will be the advocate of good things, only protect healthy human understanding (*gesunden Menschenverstand*) from a single absolute principle, for, if there were one at all, it would be superfluous. [...] From now on I pronounce myself to be the irreconcilable enemy of all so-called first principles of philosophy and those who need one to be fools, who, when they are attacked by a paroxysm, deduce and syllogize from their first principle. In my opinion, the maxim and first principle of each human and philosopher should be 'I would like to be a moral being' and this should offer us the matter, both apriori and aposteriori (when it is necessary) which the human

faculty of representation needs, that is, if these thoughts can be cleansed of all contradictions, so has he done all that must be done.⁹

For Herbert, Kant's first principle in the *Critique of Pure Reason* is the fact that "Experience is the foundation of all experience and knowledge cannot go beyond experience." This sort of first principle does not, according to Herbert, threaten healthy, human understanding, presumably because it does not displace it by some speculative starting point that we can never experience directly. Erhard was supportive of Herbert's mandates. Excerpts from two letters express his agreement with Herbert's general position, one supportive of Kant's critical philosophy and completely skeptical of attempts to move beyond it. Erhard argues that Kant had defined the general territory of human knowledge and hence provided us with a reasonable point of orientation, while Reinhold and Fichte, in their moves to uncover some absolute first principle for philosophy, misguided us, taking us to a realm beyond experience. In a letter from Erhard dated 4 May 1794, we find the following words to Niethammer:

> If we are concerned with knowledge, it is impossible to move beyond Kant; yet we can move beyond Kant if we are concerned with an overview of knowledge. These higher principles are neither principles of being nor of knowing but merely of representing [...] and there I stand and must continue climbing if I want to view an infinite horizon but if I am concerned with encountering actual objects, I must descend. If I care to remain in my high region, then I have space for all logical possibilities but I must not be annoyed when those standing below me shout up at me that these are not actual/real.¹⁰

Any "higher principles," that is, any principles that move beyond what we can in fact know, cannot be principles of being or knowledge as such. They can only be principles of representing. These "higher principles" give us an overview of knowledge, but Erhard does not find the essence of philosophy in this overview. Philosophy must first be concerned with knowledge itself, with the actual or real, and from there ascend to these higher principles. In the way he has presented things here, it is clear that Erhard finds any attempt to locate a first principle for philosophy to be inherently flawed. One cannot begin with an overview and then come down to the objects of experience: philosophers must begin with experience and then ascend to higher principles. A "higher principle" cannot serve as the foundation for philosophy.

In another letter from 19 May 1794, Erhard writes: "From one perspective, Herbert is completely right regarding the problem of first principles. Philosophy which departs from one principle and attempts to deduce everything therefrom remains always a sophistical work of art, only philosophy which rises to, and does not deduce from, a highest principle and presents all else in perfect harmony, is the true one."[11] A philosophy that departs from one principle begins where no human is or can be and hence is sophistical. A philosophy that rises to a highest principle begins with human experience and is then guided by an ideal of unity to begin to unify the claims regarding this experience. Here we find the first hints of the project to transform philosophy from a program of deduction from a highest principle to one of infinite approximation toward an ideal that can never be attained, a regulative idea.[12]

This transformation of philosophy as a program that proceeds by deduction from a highest principle into one of infinite approximation toward an ideal that can never be attained had already been initiated by Schulze's critique of Reinhold's attempt to develop a philosophy based on an absolute first principle. As Manfred Frank points out, Reinhold was forced by Schulze's critique to acknowledge that foundational subjectivity (*gründende Subjektivität*) must be a representation of an unattainable idea— merely regulative. For, according to Reinhold's principle of consciousness (*Satz des Bewusstseins*), all consciousness involves an act of representing an object, so self-consciousness must be an act of representing an object as well. But this presents problems, for the object represented is the self that is no mere object: the self should not be objectified.

The only way out of this objectification of the subject is to give subjectivity a regulative rather than a constitutive function. Reinhold's concept of 'subjectivity,' which he still wants to maintain as his first principle, then ceases to be a firmly established foundation and becomes an ideal which we can never establish but which guides our conceptualization of the world. The skeptical attacks on Reinhold's philosophy had forced Reinhold to recognize the futility of his early approach. And while Fichte, for example, was not convinced by Reinhold's admission that the terms of his original project were flawed, the correspondence between Herbert, Erhard and Niethammer indicates that they were indeed convinced that Reinhold's initial project was fatally flawed and more generally, that *any* attempt to establish a first principle for philosophy was futile.

In his letters to Erhard and Herbert, Niethammer quite openly announces his support for a move away from a philosophy based on first principles. In a letter dated 2 June 1794 Niethammer comments upon how devastating Schulze's *Aenesidemus* has been to Reinhold's philosophy, comparing Schulze's criticisms to a "fatal downpour which has washed away Reinhold's general foundation."[13] In the letter, Niethammer continues to discuss the issue of locating a first principle for philosophy in terms of the futile attempts to locate the bedrock of all knowledge, comparing such efforts to the cosmologists' attempts to locate the resting point of the earth on the back of the elephant, and the elephant on the back of a turtle, whose resting place is not given, for, the quest to locate the absolute can always be pushed up another level. In his letter, Niethammer asserts that the question of first causes can be sensibly posed and answered within the realm of the natural sciences. If we want to pose the question of whether there is a foundation for philosophy, we must look for the answer in Kant's *Critique of Pure Reason* and not beyond it. For the *Critique* has done us the great service of demonstrating that "we and the world are only insofar as we represent, think and sense; and where we do not represent, think or sense, we and the world (at least for us) cannot be."[14]

According to Niethammer, Kant has provided a solution to the problem of empty speculation by clearly delineating the scope of human knowledge and more importantly of human action. For Erhard, Herbert, Niethammer, and the thinkers who supported the project of Niethammer's *Philosophisches Journal*, philosophy can never proceed merely speculatively; it must go hand in hand with human action and praxis. Ultimately, Niethammer concludes that a highest and single principle for all knowledge is not necessary. Underscoring his agreement with Herbert, he claims that "the first principle of every human and philosopher should be: 'I wish to be a moral being.' "[15] He writes: "With this conviction that a highest and single principle of all knowledge is dispensable, I can look on at all philosophizing judgments and its representatives in peace. I, as a human being, am not at all affected by the success or failure of establishing the beginning of all knowledge."[16] Although Niethammer, in his concern with philosophy as a practical activity (hence his claim that the problem of the beginning does not mean anything to him as a human being), sees no usefulness in the establishment of an abstract principle upon which to base philosophy, he does not deny that the search for such a principle has produced some beneficial results for philosophy.[17] These attempts have not been completely useless, Niethammer contends, because they have led to some advancement in the unification of philosophy, but they have only been useful insofar as they have been recognized as *attempts to search* for a first principle. The *search* for a first principle is necessary in order to endow philosophy with some sort of outer unity, the ideal of having one basis upon which to rest the edifice of our knowledge.[18]

Problems arise when philosophers mistakenly believe that they have secured such a principle or that such a principle must be secured *before* any progress in knowledge can be made. Such philosophical beliefs are illusory, because where we cannot represent, think, and sense, the world is nothing for us. Those philosophers who believe that philosophy must rest upon certain first principles commit us to a sphere beyond our cognitive capacities; to leaps of faith or dogmatism. Such a view paralyzes any progressive movement in philosophy, for according to such a view, before philosophy can move forward, we must secure its first principle, and attempts to secure this first principle become more important than searching for truth. For Niethammer and his circle, the search for a first principle is important, but its deduction or proof is an exercise in futility. They do think that such principles exist yet that such principles will never be a constitutive part of our knowledge but will serve, rather, as guideposts, as regulative ideals.

From the exchanges among Niethammer, Herbert, and Erhard, we begin to see the sorts of issues that were to guide the discussions that took place in Niethammer's journal. Niethammer was dedicated to developing a philosophy that was based in human experience, not in empty speculation. He develops this more fully in his announcement and report of the journal and in his article on the relation between philosophy and common sense.

Niethammer's Appeal to Common Sense

In the "Ankündigung" and the "Vorbericht," Niethammer states that the goal of philosophy is to create a unified system for all knowledge. In this he is in close company with Fichte. Fichte, too, had claimed that the goal of philosophy was to create a unified system for all knowledge. In fact, as I discussed in chapter 3, his *Wissenschaftslehre* or *Science of Knowledge* was an explicit attempt to do just this. Yet Niethammer parts company with Fichte regarding the way in which this unified system is to be attained. According to Niethammer, philosophy should strive to develop its relation to common experience rather than losing itself in empty speculation. This view determines his method and is clearly at odds with Fichte's view that philosophy can be a science only after its first principle has been proved.

According to Niethammer, in order to achieve the goal of creating a unified system of knowledge, two tasks are central: the *search* for (rather than the establishment of) a foundation of all knowledge (outer unity) and the consolidation of each individual branch of knowledge (inner unity). The first task establishes philosophy as a science, the second as the science of all sciences. In both texts, Niethammer observes that skeptical attacks and the quarrels among the defenders of Kant's critical philosophy serve to show that philosophy has not yet attained this goal of unity. Niethammer also indicates that in these attempts to make philosophy into some sort of unified science there has been a prevailing tendency toward speculation and a neglect of empirical data (*Empirie*).[19] This is misguided because, according to Niethammer, to work toward the perfection of philosophy as a science means to make philosophy useful, and speculative philosophy does not do this.[20]

Philosophy must be a system that can reliably guide human inquiry. If philosophy remains a mere aggregate of one-sided opinions, unproved principles, and unreliable/shifting (*schwänkende*) concepts, it cannot do this. Hence, Niethammer emphasizes the goal of making philosophy into a unified body of knowledge, that is, into a system, a science of knowledge.[21] The central point made by Niethammer in the *Ankündigung* is that the major problem facing philosophy is the attempt to move beyond Kant (here he reiterates the points made in his exchanges with Herbert and Erhard); in this context he makes mention of two trends inspired by Kant's critical philosophy: (1) *Transcendentismus*, or the attempt to transcend Kant's philosophy (here Fichte is the implicit perpetrator), and (2) *Hyperkriticismus*, or the mere parroting of Kant's critical philosophy (this is probably a reference to Schmid, who was best known for having written a dictionary of Kant's philosophy and Reinhold who was best known as the popularizer of Kant's critical philosophy).[22] The result of such attempts to either move beyond Kant or to make Kant's philosophy the subject matter of philosophy is that philosophy moves further and further away from its actual subject matter, the realm of human experience.

Niethammer claims that the goal of philosophy is to establish the unity and universality of our knowledge so that philosophy can serve to guide us in our thinking. But inner and outer unity are not enough. The results of such unity must be applied to the individual sciences.[23] Each science postulates principles and concepts, which it is philosophy's task to deduce.[24] To make philosophy popular or to popularize philosophy is to make it useful (*not* to make it readily accessible to all). And we cannot wait until we have found a first principle in order to begin to apply philosophy to the problems that it is meant to solve. For "the perfection of philosophy as a science is an idea which we can only approximate with gradual steps."[25] We must work for the perfection of philosophy as a science and at each point in which we come closer to this goal, apply our broadened overview and increased certainty/definition (*Bestimmtheit*) to the individual bodies of knowledge.[26]

In the *Vorbericht*, which is the lengthiest and most detailed of the texts, Niethammer spells out how philosophy is to be brought closer to human experience so as not to become lost in empty speculation. He repeats that, instead of moving on to make useful applications to other fields of knowledge, philosophy is continually paralyzed by the problem of its foundation, the problem of philosophy's starting point. This in turn has led some thinkers to question whether there is such a foundation at all.[27] We have seen that in his private correspondence he openly admits that he is one of these thinkers. In this public text he merely states that some thinkers have questioned whether there is any foundation for philosophy at all, being careful not to identify himself with this group. Throughout the article, Niethammer states his position tentatively. The search for a first principle of philosophy *may not* be the best way to establish philosophy as the science of all sciences. *Perhaps*, suggests Niethammer, the idea of a science of all sciences is a goal that can never be reached (*ein nie erreichbares Ziel*) and must be a never-ending search. His private correspondence reveals a stronger position, a rejection of any attempt to secure a first principle for philosophy.

The fact that we cannot establish a first principle for our knowledge need not keep us from making progress in the perfection of philosophy as a science of knowledge because, insofar as we think and sense, we have a place to begin, namely, in experience. The relation between the claims we make based upon experience and those claims substantiated by the theoretical perspective and conceptual apparatus afforded us by philosophy is the subject of Niethammer's article, "Von den Ansprüchen der gemeinen Verstand an der Philosophie."

Niethammer's "Ankündigung" and "Vorbericht" present a view of philosophy as the science of all sciences, one that must strive toward a systematic unity of knowledge. The two-fold task of philosophy is the systematization of our knowledge and the application of any progress made to this end to the existing individual bodies of knowledge or sciences. Niethammer reminds us that as long as philosophers remain enmeshed in the project of attempting to establish a first principle for philosophy, the fulfillment of both of these tasks will be thwarted. Without a principle that is apodictically certain, we can never achieve a system of knowledge whose claims are absolutely certain. Niethammer's article on the relation between common sense and philosophy is one in which he publicly expresses his rejection of any attempt to secure a first principle for philosophy. Niethammer concludes that "in the entire breadth of our complete knowledge there is no principle to be found which has the required apodictic, unconditioned certainty which would serve as the foundation for a system of our knowledge which would then be complete in each of its parts, and whose principle likewise would be completely indubitable and absolutely certain."[28] If we do not have this principle, if we can never establish it, can we speak of knowledge or truth at all? According to Niethammer, such principle is not necessary before we can speak of knowledge and truth. Like Jacobi, he recognizes the futility of establishing anything about that which is unconditioned. Absolute certainty would only be possible if we could determine the unconditioned, that which conditions all of our knowledge claims. Like Jacobi, Niethammer claims that this is impossible. Unlike Jacobi, however, he does not suggest any leap of faith and a positive affirmation of truth based on a faith dissociated from reason. Niethammer turns instead to an appeal to common sense. After we understand the nature of his appeal we will be in a position to understand why he can claim that, even if we can never establish a first principle for philosophy, we can speak of truth and create a unified body of knowledge and thus make progress in philosophy.

Knowledge begins with the claims of common sense, that is, according to Niethammer, with claims regarding the bedrock of our experience, our being in a spatial-temporal world, which are those claims that, if doubted, lead to self-defeat. Yet our investigation of knowledge leads us beyond experience to determine whether any of our claims regarding this experience are in fact endowed with universality and necessity. According to Niethammer, we begin with experience and move from there to a questioning of how this experience is possible, and only in this latter line of questioning do we come upon necessary and universal validity. Hence, only after we have subjected the claims of common sense to a philosophical analysis can we be certain that they are universally valid and necessary.

Building from some of Reinhold's later insights, Niethammer views philosophizing reason and common understanding as working together. For Niethammer, common sense and philosophy need each other. Because the claims of common sense are self-evident and are in no need of proof or demonstration,[29] it seems that common sense can do without philosophy, for philosophy serves to ground the general validity of our knowledge and action, and the claims of common sense are in no need of such a grounding.[30] From this perspective it would seem that in the relation between common sense and philosophy, common sense should have the last word, so if a philosophical claim contradicted a claim of common sense, then the philosophical claim should be rejected. Yet according to Niethammer, the claims of common sense carry with them no necessity, and hence we are presented with a problem: how are we to know that a given claim of common sense will always hold?[31] There is certainly a significant difference between the feeling we have that our common sense claims are universal and necessary and the actual universality and necessity of this feeling itself. How then, asks Niethammer, are we to ascertain that our feeling that the claims of common sense are universal and necessary is in fact so?[32] Common sense cannot answer this question. Common sense claims are merely descriptive; in order to speak of universal validity and necessity, analysis of these claims must be carried out. This is the task of philosophy. Whereas in the "Vorbericht,"

Niethammer spoke of a two-fold task of philosophy, in the "Von den Ansprüchen" article Niethammer claims that the proof of the universality and necessity of the claims of common sense is the authentic and single task of philosophy (*eigentlich und einzig Aufgabe*).

The claims of common sense are the claims we make regarding our experience in the world. According to Niethammer, common sense cannot claim to present any positive criterion of truth for it is in need of confirmation from philosophy, which provides the positive criterion for truth, which endows our claims with universality. As negative criterion, common sense has the last word and must as such be respected by philosophy. According to Niethammer, the claims of common sense are present to consciousness immediately, and they are accompanied by a feeling of absolute universality and necessity, which is present in the human spirit and cannot be usurped by any philosophy and may not be contradicted by it either.[33]

In examining how it is possible to establish the universality and necessity of the claims of common sense, Niethammer (following the advice given him by Herbert) turns to Kant's *Critique of Pure Reason* and his transcendental method. Yet he does not uncritically follow Kant's line of argument. Niethammer argues that philosophy must begin with experience and that we must establish the transcendental conditions of this experience (i.e., the conditions of its possibility) but never be led to conclude that experience is somehow a product of some a priori conceptual framework and that experience is secondary, while some a priori first principle is primary. Niethammer argues that we begin with experience, not with a mere manifold of sense impressions that are in need of the categories of understanding in order to count as experience. Hence, although he turns to Kant, he also voices a strong criticism of Kant's transcendental method. He writes: "Is the proper conclusion drawn from the fact (of experience)? Are the conditions which explain and clarify the fact and which the *Critique* presupposes to be necessarily in the subject, really the necessary and only conditions of this fact? Is experience only possible in this way? Everything depends upon proving that the law of a certain condition a priori holds universally for a given a posteriori conditioned."[34] According to Frank, Niethammer here anticipates a contemporary critique that is often leveled against transcendental arguments. Transcendental arguments look for apodictic conditions for the possibility of a given something, yet these conditions are deduced from that which is conditioned and hence originate always in something that is nonapodictically certain, that is, from theory-relative propositions.[35]

The issue here is the truth of our claims and the validity of our arguments. We begin always in the world, with experience, but we do not end there. Experience is not per se dependent upon any transcendental deduction; we are in need of an investigation of the a priori conditions that make experience possible only insofar as we want to establish the universality and necessity of this fact.[36] Hence, these transcendental conditions do not form the foundation of philosophy, but experience forms the basis of philosophy. Niethammer writes: "Philosophy cannot begin a priori, and then from an a priori, unmediated certain principle, something which is in itself unconditioned, move synthetically forward in the chain of conditions and thereby endow everything connected to this chain of conditions with the same unconditioned certainty. Rather, it must first go synthetically forward, from something conditioned in the chain of conditions in order to find the necessary conditions from which it can then first move forward to form a system which has universal validity."[37] Like Jacobi and Schlegel, Niethammer is concerned with the paradox of explaining the unconditioned. His solution is to turn toward the fact of experience as his starting point and to move away from a model of philosophy whereby it is understood as a series of deductions from some absolute starting point outside of experience, the point that endows our knowledge claims with absolute certainty. Such a starting point creates a gulf between the theoretical framework of the philosopher and the world of experience that we share. In the *Ankündigung* Niethammer voiced his complaint concerning the widespread neglect of *Empirie* in philosophy; in his article on the claims of common sense, he develops a position that places *Empirie* at the beginning, the most fundamental place, of philosophy.[38]

Niethammer's appeal to common sense leads him to posit experience as the starting point of philosophy. Niethammer criticizes those defendants of the critical philosophy who have attempted to move from the fact that there is experience to a higher place (*höhern Standort*). He claims that the fact that there is experience gives us the only foundation we need (*der einzige Standort*) from which to begin philosophizing. Attempts to begin philosophizing that start beyond experience, open philosophy to all sorts of skeptical attacks.

With this as his starting point, Niethammer thinks he has overcome the paradoxes of philosophical methods that attempt, in some way or another, to condition the Absolute and has presented a view of philosophy that saves it from the destructive attacks of the skeptics.[39] Moreover, he has grounded philosophy in historical, material reality, thereby helping to correct the problem of the widespread neglect of empirical experience in philosophy. That there is experience is a claim of common sense, and it is true even if we cannot establish with certainty how it is true. (Establishing how such a claim is true is an issue of how the proposition should be analyzed.) Niethammer does not believe that we must agree upon one method of analysis before we can make claims that are true nor that the primitive claims of common sense are dependent upon any one philosophical system.

What does it mean to transform philosophy from a project of establishing an absolute first principle and then deducing all else from this into a project that abandons the model of deduction from an absolute starting point and instead endorses a view according to which the first principle is merely regulative? It means among other things that our knowledge claims can never be claimed to be universally valid and that a claim can be true even if it has not been established to be universal and necessary. "We will submit the claims of common sense to philosophy and must admit that only when philosophy can provide a universally valid and complete proof of these, can a complete conviction of the universal validity of our knowledge take place."[40] This of course never takes place. In order to have absolute certainty, we would have to locate the absolute first principle of all knowledge. "Everything here depends upon the extent to which philosophy can determine its own certainty and this depends only upon the principles upon which it rests. A judgment is proved (demonstrated) when I deduce its universal validity which had been assumed directly, and perform this deduction indirectly via a deduction from the universal validity of another judgment."[41] If we could find the first judgment, the first principle from which all other judgments could be deduced, then we could create a system of absolutely certain knowledge. Then nothing at all, not even a claim of common sense, could be accepted as true that contradicted the system of propositions that we could deduce therefrom. But Niethammer questions this possibility: "The question arises as to whether there is such a completely unconditioned first principle which we could lay down as the first principle of our complete system of knowledge."[42] If there is no such first principle, what sort of power do our claims to knowledge carry? According to Niethammer, the most widespread mistake of philosophers has been to assume that, because the certainty of the claims of common sense is unmediated, it is not a strong enough foundation for our knowledge. They then look to a first principle for this foundation, believing that without absolute certainty, we have nothing (no truth) at all. But Niethammer believes that the claims of common sense do form the foundation for all else. We do not end with them, for we attempt to transform them into philosophical claims, that is, into claims that we can show to be universal and necessary. They are more like the "middle" to which Schlegel makes reference than like indubitable first principles, the lonely *Ich* or cogito that Schlegel believes have led us only to isolated systems of philosophy that only give us half the story of reality.

In fact, at the end of his article Niethammer states: "At a later time we will discuss whether this lack of apodictic certainty could be fulfilled by positing a principle from which the entire system of our knowledge could be deduced and through its success, i.e., by showing that the system deduced therefrom was a whole of which the principle was the midpoint through which all radii of the circle passed, could prove itself to be first principle. This is the issue of whether the mere form of philosophy as a science can establish the sought after apodictic certainty of our knowledge."[43] Niethammer's speculation here will be taken up by Schlegel as he develops his *Wechselerweis*, which is a presentation of philosophy as a system that is understood in terms of wholes and parts. Of course, for Schlegel, our knowledge will never be apodictically certain, but that does not mean it cannot serve to bring us closer to truth.

For Niethammer, our knowledge begins, as he so explicitly expressed in his letter to Herbert, in the world, with experience and claims regarding this experience. In Niethammer's article concerning the relation between common sense and philosophy, common sense is understood as a kind of foreknowledge (*Vorkenntnis*). He claims that the certainty of the claims of common sense are present "before all, and without any, scientific theories and thus completely independent of these."[44] The certainty of the claims of common sense is "unmediated" (*unmittelbar*) and precedes all scientific investigations. Here we are reminded of Jacobi's *salto mortale*. This too was a kind of appeal to unmediated certainty as the basis of our knowledge. However, Jacobi's realism is not based upon common sense but upon his leap of faith. Whereas Jacobi posits the unmediated certainty of being, Niethammer maintains that there is an unmediated certainty of some primitive knowledge claims that we make.

As we saw in chapter 2, Schlegel found fault with Jacobi's leap of faith insofar as it was a leap that led to an individualization of reality, something that then exonerated, instead of discovering or demonstrating, truth, and also insofar as it was a leap that set up a false dichotomy between faith and knowledge. In chapter 3 we observed Fichte's attempts to go beyond the limits established by Kant, albeit in the name of freedom rather than faith. Niethammer and his cohort were skeptical of all such attempts to define philosophy in terms of a first principle, be it a principle of faith or freedom. For this group of thinkers, philosophy does not begin with a secure principle that can be proved to be the necessary condition of all knowledge. Such a principle is operative in our quest for knowledge, but not as a foundation. The principle is regulative not constitutive, and philosophy can never achieve the unity of a science. Philosophers must, however, strive for such unity in order to come to an ever-fuller understanding of the world. This view of philosophy as an infinite task shaped Schlegel's thought. Schlegel was against an approach like Fichte's, which sought to establish definitively the absolute starting point of philosophy. He was much closer, in this respect, to Niethammer. However, Schlegel voiced many concerns with Niethammer's emphasis on common sense.

Schlegel's Philosophical Debut

Niethammer's appeal to common sense and the implications that this move held for the issue of philosophy's starting point and Niethammer's view of the task of philosophy are important to an understanding of Schlegel's romantic philosophy. Schlegel's response to Niethammer's view of philosophy was articulated in a review of the first four issues of Niethammer's *Philosophisches Journal*. This review was published in the *Allgemeine Literatur Zeitung*, 1797. Schlegel considered this piece to be his philosophical debut. In a letter to Novalis he writes:

> I am satisfied with the review of Niethammer's Journal, not because it has been praised, but rather because with it I have completely realized my intention. That is indeed what I wanted: that Niethammer should understand me but not Fichte. Every person should understand the review, but each in a different way. Entirely clear and infinitely deep. More on this in person. Because it was my debut on the philosophical stage and because I was limited by countless external chains—you will allow this light formation to be seen (for as a review and according to the goals of a review, I consider this to be better than any other of my writings) as an important advancement of my mind. Everything which I wrote before (you know which catastrophes I refer to) I now see as children's play.[45]

Schlegel had published important pieces before this review.[46] Hence, it is significant that he marks this particular piece of writing as his "debut on the philosophical stage." It is not idle curiosity that leads us to ask why Schlegel should have held this review of Niethammer's journal to be his philosophical debut. Is there a position developed here that identifies him as a philosopher with a unique project? If we consider the review together with the fragments that he wrote during this period, we do find such a position. Schlegel's philosophical project puts him in closer company with Niethammer and further from Fichte, which may be why he claims that Niethammer should understand him, but not Fichte.

The review of Niethammer's journal opens with praise for it. Schlegel describes the journal as containing a wealth of important essays, which everyone interested in the developments of philosophy should not only read, but study.[47] Schlegel includes a detailed account of seven articles,[48] yet of greatest importance for coming to an understanding of Schlegel's ultimate rejection of Niethammer's appeal to common sense are his remarks on Niethammer's article, "Von den Anspruchen des gemeinen Verstandes an die Philosophie." The review reveals that although Schlegel is in company with Niethammer in rejecting a philosophy based on an absolute first principle, he is opposed to Niethammer's appeal to common sense as a criterion of truth in philosophy. At issue in this opposition to common sense as a criterion of truth for our knowledge claims is the problem of how we are to evaluate philosophy at all.

We begin our discussion where Schlegel ends his, with his reflections upon the difficulty of judging philosophy at all, that is, the problem of writing a review of a philosophical text. In a fragment from 1786 Schlegel writes: "Every philosophical review must also be a philosophy of the review, that is, review 1/0."[49] The reason why a philosophical review involves an infinite task is because, according to Schlegel, judgments of philosophy cannot be scientific judgments, for philosophy is not a science. If philosophy is not a science, then before we can judge any given work of philosophy, we must begin with a questioning of how are we to proceed, what our method should be, that is, our starting point and our ending points. He writes: "How can there be scientific judgments where there is not yet a science? Indeed, all other sciences must oscillate as long as we lack a positive philosophy, one in which there is at least something relatively firm and generally valid. Nothing is yet established (*ausgemacht*) in philosophy; this is something the present state shows us. All foundation and ground is still lacking . . . Where then, should a philosophical review begin and end?"[50] This is a strong statement of the present state of philosophy as Schlegel viewed it. In spite of the efforts put forth by Jacobi, with his fearless *salto*, Reinhold, with his tenacious variations on a foundation for philosophy, and Fichte in the relentless presentations of the *Wissenschaftslehre*, philosophy was still far from being a complete science. According to Schlegel, no firm foundation has yet been established that would allow us to defend one system as the only feasible system and thereby generate the criteria for judging all other attempts to solve philosophical problems. This being the case, it would seem that all judgments of philosophy would be system relative. And, as there are as many philosophies as there are philosophers, there would also be a multitude of possible judgments to be made regarding any given philosophical system. Ultimately, as we began to see in his critique of Fichte and which shall come into even sharper view in his confrontation with Kant's "critical" philosophy, Schlegel argues that what is missing from philosophy is a metaview of the field itself, a perspective that would enable the critic of philosophy, the writer of a review, to respect a given individual contribution to the field without losing sight of the whole to which it belongs. It is within the context of such a view that we must approach Schlegel's criticisms of Niethammer's appeal to common sense.

Schlegel's Critique of Niethammer's Appeal to Common Sense

A look at Schlegel's "review" of Niethammer's *Vorbericht* and "Von den Ansprüchen" reveals him to be in agreement with Niethammer in rejecting a speculative philosophy based on absolute first principles, yet highly suspicious of Niethammer's appeal to common sense. Schlegel endorses Niethammer's attempts to bring philosophy closer to the world of human happenings, but he finds many problems with the details of how Niethammer proposes to make the move, especially problematic for Schlegel is Niethammer's appeal to common sense. What Schlegel proposes as a better solution to the problem of philosophy's beginning point is a historical turn.[51]

After stating that Niethammer gives more space to common sense than is customary, Schlegel notes, "This tendency (of clearing more space for the claims of common sense than is customary) must be felt most strongly by a philosopher who loves justice, for in this process of judging of the claims of common sense, defendant and judge are the same, and this because the claims of common sense and the claims of philosophy are presented as quarreling parties. That this is the case is precisely what this reviewer doubts."[52] Schlegel goes on to justify his remark by presenting two views of common sense (*gemeiner Verstand*), one according to which common sense is simply the healthy sense (*gesunder Verstand*) of reasonable men with a general education, but without any speculation. According to this view, philosophy and common sense would have no positive influence on one another; indeed, they have a duty not to interfere with one another. The soundness of the conclusions reached on the basis of common sense should not lead us to conclude that a speculative investigation or conceptual exploration is meaningless or unnecessary any more than that a philosophical investigation of the conceptual framework surrounding common understanding would lead us to view common understanding as somehow deficient. Schlegel also provides a view of common sense according to which common sense is the essence of all unmediated claims that are not only believed to be universally true but are indeed universally true. According to Schlegel, these two views are at odds with one another:

No one is in a worse position to judge; indeed, no one is less interested in what common understanding (in the latter sense) [as the essence of all unmediated claims that are not only believed to be universally valid, but are indeed universally valid] wants and says, as common understanding (in the first sense) itself. To not only deduce the claims of common sense but to sort them from the innumerable claims and to present them fully is not an easy task; but only the philosopher can do this, and only through philosophy. This is indeed a circle. Hence, common understanding says something different in every philosophy and usually it tends to agree with this philosophy.[53]

As already noted, Niethammer maintains that philosophy begins with the claims of common sense, for these claims are primitive. Yet these claims carry with them only the feeling that they are true; their universality and necessity can only be demonstrated after an analysis carried out by the philosopher. This view, according to Schlegel, presents a problem. The philosopher's task is to begin with the claims of common sense and then through his system, determine whether these claims are indeed true. Yet, as soon as the claims become the object of the philosopher's analysis, they are subject to the whims of his system, and the primitive nature of the claims is endangered, for the claims are then already a product of the system that is judging them. According to Schlegel, the way to correct this would be to determine the truth of the claims of common sense in a historical way, that is, by comparing the claims with various systems and so independently of the speculative efforts of any one philosophical system. For then philosophers could not so easily dismiss certain claims of common sense by arguing that their systems proved that these claims were not universally true.

In a fragment from 1796, Schlegel claims that the principle of the empiricists is that what is universally accepted is universally true, but the claims of unphilosophical understanding can only be investigated through the positive principles of philosophy, and hence those who appeal to common sense are caught in a vicious circle, for that to which they are appealing is not really common sense at all, but insofar as it is to be some universal common sense, it must already be some product of speculation.[54] Schlegel argues that, if we could compare the claims of nonspeculative understanding (i.e., common sense) with the claims of several philosophical systems, then it would become clear to philosophers that if there were a discrepancy between the claims produced by their systems and those of common sense, the error would lie with their philosophy and not with common sense.[55]

Another dimension of Schlegel's critique of Niethammer's appeal to common sense is to be found in the problem he sees with applicability as a criterion for philosophy. Schlegel views the support of this criterion as part of an attempt to make philosophy into a purely descriptive, pragmatic discipline. In a fragment from 1796, he writes: "Applicability is so little a criterion of true philosophy as communicability. He who makes it a criterion presupposes that the philosophical solution to a certain task should serve to fulfill a certain goal, and contradicts himself."[56] These criticisms of the appeal to common sense and to applicability as a criterion in philosophy are consistent with Schlegel's view of philosophy as something that cannot be reduced to one principle, object, or activity.

Both Niethammer and Schlegel resisted the idea of a philosophy based on a single, absolute first principle. Their skepticism led them to develop quite different alternatives to the problems they found with any attempt to secure such a first principle. In turning away from a philosophy based on absolute first principles, Niethammer turned toward common sense: philosophical claims are acceptable if they do not contradict the claims of common sense. Niethammer's appeal to the claims of common sense is an attempt to prevent philosophers from empty flights of speculation, for it is in these flights that philosophers (e.g., Reinhold, Fichte) often make claims that contradict common sense. According to Niethammer, even if we cannot secure an absolute first principle for philosophy, we can still have a ground upon which to build a system of knowledge. This ground is our experience and the claims drawn from this experience. Yet Niethammer overlooks the problem that Schlegel points out, namely, that what counts as a claim of common sense, and then of course whether this claim is useful and coheres with other claims, depends upon a given philosophical system so is not primitive. A fragment that Schlegel wrote in 1796 expresses this well: "A philosophical quarrel can only be settled before a philosophical bench of justice, a philosophical judgment can only be made by a philosophical judge; those who appeal to healthy, human understanding provide a public confession of their non-philosophy or they deny the possibility of philosophy at all. Indeed, not every quarrel with a philosopher regarding his philosophy is philosophical."[57] Schlegel is aware that philosophy must respect the claims of common sense, but that these claims cannot form the bedrock of philosophy. Schlegel's turn away from a philosophy based on a single, absolute first principle is not a turn toward the claims of common sense, but rather a historical turn. He sees in a historical approach to philosophy the possibility of looking in from the outside at the various attempts to systematize knowledge and to search for truth. Such a historical perspective might be a balm against those quarrels between philosophers that are more about territory than about anything philosophical. One could object here that, even if we grant Schlegel the objectivity of his historical, neutral taxonomy—one that would indeed unify the various contributions of philosophers—he has not thereby solved the problem of a system-relative critique but only moved it to another level.[58] In order to explore this objection and provide a response to it, we shall now look closely at what Schlegel actually attained in his attempt to provide a system of classification and comparison of different philosophical systems.

Schlegel's Historical Taxonomy

Schlegel's assessment of various philosophical systems is shaped by his view of philosophy in general. He views philosophy as an infinite task that cannot be defined with respect to one task. "Philosophy should be an end in itself and so it cannot define itself through the task of defending the claims of common sense from skeptical attacks or through finding the scientific unity of all knowledge without thereby losing its high worth."[59] The value of philosophy is the search for knowledge it undertakes. This is the essence of philosophy, and any view of philosophy that attempts to narrow or reduce this search is not true philosophy at all. This view led him to classify most contributions to philosophy as dogmatic "non-philosophy": "The essence of philosophy is the search for the totality of knowledge. This entails the negation of all arbitrary positing (this is opposed to knowledge) and all contradictions (these oppose unity and totality). Hence, skepticism, empiricism and mysticism are only types of philosophizing non-philosophy."[60]

In chapter 3 I presented a quick glimpse of Schlegel's historical taxonomy, in order to show why he categorized Fichte's philosophy as a breed of mysticism. Let us now look more closely at Schlegel's critique of skepticism, empiricism, and mysticism. Early in his work, in fragments, and later, in a more systematic way, Schlegel was committed to creating a history of philosophy.[61] He was interested in creating some sort of philosophical taxonomy so that each philosophical system could be understood according to its own merits or faults. The fragments in which Schlegel discusses his taxonomy can be best understood as skeptical satires of the breeds of what he took to be the two major branches of philosophy: critical philosophy and dogmatic philosophy.[62] He claims that mysticism, skepticism, and empiricism are dogmatic.[63] This is because they begin with an arbitrary positing of some absolute.[64] This is all part of the same sickness, that of partializing and narrowing the view of knowledge and truth. According to Schlegel, insofar as each of these positions begins or ends with a single, absolute principle of all knowledge, each of these philosophies begins or ends in contradiction. As we have seen, the contradiction is the result of the intrinsic unknowability of the Absolute: any attempt to limit the Absolute is bound to end in contradiction, for then the philosopher is claiming both that there exists an absolute and that there exists knowledge of the Absolute, and hence the Absolute is not absolute. In another fragment from the same period Schlegel continues with his condemnation of the three major groups of philosophers: "The most consequential skeptics, mystics, empiricists, are those who really and indeed stop philosophizing... Mysticism produces itself. Its ESSENCE and also its BEGINNING is the arbitrary positing of an absolute. The essence and beginning of consequential eclecticism is the arbitrary annihilation of the absolute unlimited, the arbitrary positing of an absolute limit."[65] These three species of philosophy have created only a history of error.[66] The skeptic ultimately defeats himself, for ultimately he must hold something in order to refute others on the charge that nothing holds and hence the consequential skeptic, the one who follows his position through to its logical end, contradicts himself. The mystic posits an absolute first principle and then easily deduces all else from this principle. This approach also defeats itself, though not in the same way as the skeptical position does. Mysticism is self-defeating because it is sophistical and cannot ultimately tell us anything about the world.[67] Schlegel presents mysticism as a kind of idealism that disregards history and science.[68] The eclectic empiricists are bound to the historical and natural world and are realists. They begin with the claims of common sense, which are unlimited, and then proceed to limit these claims. This is because they view philosophy in a limited way, as a practical activity, whose only worth can lie in its applicability.[69] These errors can be overcome. The mystics must take account of history and science so that their view of knowledge is not isolated from human reality. The mystics are idealists, but their idealism becomes empty if it is not connected to the concrete realities of the world. The empiricists are realists, yet their realism cannot lead them to reduce philosophy to a purely empirical science, for then they reduce philosophy to a finite task and cease to be philosophers.[70] Empiricism is too much of an "evident science," mysticism is too much a "sophistical art," and philosophy, according to Schlegel, is far more than either of these; any philosophical system that can be reduced to one principle will lead to error.

The content and form of philosophy are inexhaustible. Therefore, according to Schlegel, philosophy is not a science, nor should that be its aspiration. Philosophy is the essence of all sciences: "Philosophy in itself is no science—insofar as all branches of knowledge form a system and should be handled philosophically, one could call the essence of all of these philosophy."[71] Hence, philosophy is far more than a deductive science.[72] If it were a deductive science, once we had isolated its first principle, we would have determined the form of philosophy. Treating philosophy as if it were a deductive science is the greatest error of most philosophers. Moreover, such a view of philosophy makes it difficult if not impossible to assess the contributions of other philosophers, for such a view of philosophy ties the philosopher to one system as the right system. There is no way to compare the contributions of various philosophical systems—only a way to classify all other systems as the wrong ones, without being in a position to appreciate their possible merit. Now, as we have seen, Schlegel, even within his peculiar historical taxonomy, is in a position to judge various breeds of philosophy as based on error, yet he does not dismiss them. He suggests ways in which these errors could be overcome. Hence, it is not that he believes that mysticism, empiricism, or skepticism is inherently flawed, only that there have been mistakes committed by their adherents. Each philosopher is entitled to her own system, yet she must also be in a position to understand and perhaps appreciate the contributions of other systems. A leitmotif of Schlegel's holistic view of philosophy sounds once again: "Every philosopher has his own line or tendency which is his departing point and his cycle. He who has a system is as lost as he who has none. One must therefore reconcile both."[73] Every philosopher must have a system, for to make claims and construct arguments, we must depart from a system, but this must be done with the recognition that this particular system is part of a plurality of other systems, which belong to the history of philosophy. It is in this sense that Schlegel believes his historical taxonomy frees him from the confines of any one system and puts him in a position to critique the various contributions of other philosophers. In the formation of this historical taxonomy he does depart from a determined definition of philosophy, namely, that philosophy is infinite and begins with infinitely many principles, never with only one absolute principle. Yet, insofar as this view is coupled with an admission that one must always have and not have a system—that is, have a point of reference, but also an awareness that enables one to compare this point of reference with other points of reference—his historical taxonomy is not system relative in any pernicious way. It is never merely a means of classifying philosophical systems (though insofar as it does, it is indeed relative to a specific view regarding the nature of philosophy) but also provides a means of comparing various systems. Schlegel's commitment to doing philosophy historically led him to take issue with the level of criticism of the great critical philosopher himself, Immanuel Kant, and it is to that critique that I now turn.

Chapter Five

Critique as Metaphilosophy
Kant as Half Critic

In order to understand and assess the value of Kant's critical project, we have many sources to which we can turn. Surely, there is no scarcity of published material on this topic. Starting with the first wave of the reception of Kant's thought, two influential philosophers we have already discussed stand out: Reinhold, who believed that he had discovered the first principle (the infamous *Satz des Bewußtseins*) upon which Kant's philosophy ultimately rested, and Fichte, who rather arrogantly announced that he understood Kant and his critical project better than Kant himself. As we have seen, these two members of the first generation of Kant readers accepted that Kant's critical philosophy was a major breakthrough for philosophy, and each saw his own philosophical contributions as improvements (even if sometimes highly revisionist ones) upon Kant's philosophical project.

Famously, Kant described his own critical project as a revolution of sorts, analogous to the Copernican revolution. Kant believed that he had shown how a priori concepts apply to experience but are not derived from it. The revolutionary kinship with Copernicus consisted in the discovery of the truth regarding center and orbit, not, of course, in Kant's case, of the sun and the earth, but of mind and world: Kant's revolutionary discovery (or so he thought) was that objects of knowledge conform to the categories of our mind, rather than our mind being shaped by objects of experience.

Reinhold and Fichte believed that Kant's philosophical program was indeed revolutionary and that their own fine-tuning would complete the revolution that Kant had begun but had not finished. That is, Reinhold and Fichte believed that their efforts would result in a definitive answer to the intractable question they believed Kant's philosophy did not answer:

how do a priori concepts apply to experience if they are not derived from it? Critical philosophy was all about setting out limits to knowledge claims so that nonsensical metaphysical claims could be averted and the legitimacy of our knowledge claims would be settled once and for all. If no definitive answer could be given regarding how a priori concepts applied to experience, Kant's critical philosophy would never be complete.

Many examples show that often the "revolutionary" thinkers who claim to be finishing what was started by someone else end up hijacking the revolution and distorting its goals. It is my contention that such was the fate of the two Kantian revolutionaries I have just mentioned, who ultimately end up distorting, rather than completing, Kant's critical project. Reinhold and Fichte thought that Kant's revolution was incomplete because it lacked a foundation that would provide the definitive answer to the problem of how a priori concepts applied to experience. They accepted Kant's general view of philosophy as modeled on the natural sciences and as an activity that need not have any intimate connection with history,[1] yet they misread his philosophical project as one that called for some sort of absolute foundation. It was this last point that led to some of their excesses. They made the mistake of confusing criticism with the construction of a deductive system. Bubner clearly articulates the kind of misunderstanding that plagued many a post-Kantian understanding of "criticism":

> The proof of the legitimacy of understanding, which is the task of a transcendental deduction, does not follow from a higher principle which permits insight beyond our understanding of [empirical] reality. Since the legitimization of empirical knowledge does not rest upon a dogmatic principle, we must conclude that the expectation of a strict and logically compelling deduction is groundless... People used to read the deduction as a strict and ultimate logical justification. Anyway, such an undertaking would be contrary to the critical restrictions of transcendental philosophy as a whole. Criticism is by definition something different from the construction of deductive systems. Historically speaking, this misunderstanding was already present in Kant's lifetime. Since Reinhold or since Fichte at least, an urgent need has been felt to complete or improve the basis of deduction, if the full claim of an absolutely convincing deductive legitimization of all our knowledge is actually to be supported.[2]

Based on the sort of misunderstanding sketched by Bubner, certain post-Kantian revolutionaries reasoned that if the first principle of Kant's critical philosophy could be found, then Kant's revolution would be complete, for that first principle would explain how concepts that are not derived from experience can be applied to experience. Even if their approaches were misguided, both thinkers offered original contributions to the development of classical German Idealism in the wake of Kant's critical philosophy. Moreover, there has been plenty of attention paid to Fichte's idealism and his relation to Kant. Reinhold remains somewhat of a marginal figure in philosophical circles. Yet even he has received more attention from philosophers than Schlegel, who was just as influenced and excited by the publication of Kant's *Critique of Pure Reason* in 1781 (and its subsequent revised version of 1787) as those mentioned earlier and who, I have been arguing, offered original philosophical reactions to the major controversies of his period. As we have seen, Schlegel held Fichte's *Wissenschaftlehre*, Goethe's *Meister*, and the French Revolution to be the tendencies of his age. If Kant was such an important figure for Schlegel, as I claim he was, why is he missing from the famous trinity Schlegel announced in *Athenäum* Fragment 216? An investigation of this question leads us to a further refinement of Schlegel's view of philosophy and of critique.

As we have already seen, like Reinhold and Fichte, Schlegel belonged to the first generation of Kant readers. Yet, in contrast to these two and to many of his other contemporaries, Schlegel was not interested in showing that he had understood Kant better than Kant himself, or in searching for the missing premises of Kant's arguments. In short, Schlegel did not see himself as one who could carry out the revolution that Kant had begun but had not finished. Schlegel was quite influenced by Kant's critical project, yet he found problems with the general view of philosophy that Kant endorsed. In short, he believed that Kant's critical philosophy was fine as far as it went, but it just did not go far enough. With Schlegel, we find an important call toward the completion of critique *in* philosophy via a critique *of* philosophy itself. In other words, we find an important voice critical of the great critical philosopher himself. Hence, like Reinhold and Fichte, Schlegel was interested in a revolution but not so much in Kant's allegedly unfinished one as in his own.

Schlegel endorses a move to connect philosophy with its past: he does not see the past as something that confines us, and certainly his commitment to doing philosophy historically did not keep him from endorsing the most important revolution of the eighteenth century, the French Revolution. Schlegel's claim that "the French Revolution was an excellent allegory for transcendental idealism"[3] already gives us a hint of where Kant and Schlegel might part ways: Kant was much more interested in scientific revolutions than in the political ones, and Kant's political and historical myopia is something that troubled Schlegel and formed the basis for his critique of Kant. For example, Schlegel's critique of

Kant's concept of 'republicanism' and his rejection of democracy is highlighted in his "Versuch über den Begriff des Republikanismus" (1796), which was part of his attempt to uncover some of the shortcomings of Kant's view of the Enlightenment.[4]

Schlegel wanted to get to a higher level of criticism than the one Kant had reached, but not, as Reinhold and Fichte had tried to, by establishing a principle higher than the one given in Kant's transcendental deduction, that is, by establishing an *absolute* or unconditioned principle, which by definition would be beyond the conditions of knowledge set out by Kant in the *Critique of Pure Reason*. Schlegel understood that Kant's view of critique did not lead to the construction of deductive systems of philosophy. What Schlegel sought was a historical critique of philosophy—what we can call a "historical turn." His work brought attention to the limitations of the notion of critique offered by Kant in his First Critique and to the benefits of a framework that would allow the philosopher to look critically at philosophy itself (such a framework, as we shall see involved incorporating history into the very activity of doing philosophy).[5]

In this chapter, I shall present Schlegel's charge that Kant was a "half-critic" and analyze the role that Schlegel's antifoundationalism played in shaping his critique of Kant.[6] Before I begin, some brief, preliminary remarks concerning the relation between revolution and scientific method in Kant's critical project are in order to set the stage for an appreciation of Schlegel's critique of Kant's general approach to critique.

Revolution, Scientific Method, and Kant's Critical Project

Taking my lead from one of Schlegel's insights, namely, that "A good preface must be at once the square root and the square of its book"[7] (which is one more provocative attempt by Schlegel to bring attention to underappreciated aspects of a philosopher's system) let us begin with Kant's preface to the *Critique of Pure Reason* for our clues regarding the nature of his critical project. In a note to the preface of the first edition of the *Critique* he announces: "Our age is, in especial degree, the age of criticism, and to criticism everything must submit. Religion through its sanctity and law-giving through its majesty, may seek to exempt themselves from it. But they then awaken just suspicion, and cannot claim the sincere respect which reason accords only to that which has been able to sustain the test of free and open examination (Axi, note)."[8] Philosophy is the tool to carry out the critique, so there is an important way in which critique can be equated with philosophy: Kant's transcendental version of it, of course. Kant goes on to specify the meaning of his use of the term *critique*, continuing to press his view that critique serves as a kind of tribunal: "I do not mean by this [critique of pure reason] a critique of books and systems, but of the faculty of reason in general, in respect of all knowledge after which it may strive *independently of all experience*. It will therefore decide as to the possibility or impossibility of metaphysics in general, and determine its sources, its extent, and its limits—all in accordance with principles" (A xii). Critique, for Kant, is a kind of method for determining the limits and boundaries of pure reason. Pure reason is, by definition, not conditioned by anything empirical. Hence its critique can have nothing to do with something as dependent upon the empirical as history. Kant looked to the natural sciences for his models of how the philosopher should proceed. As Kant explicitly states in the preface to the second edition of the *Critique*, he is interested in placing metaphysics upon the "secure path of a science" (B vii). It is only after the limits and boundaries of pure reason have been established that metaphysics will discover the path of science, and only then will the activity of the metaphysician be transformed from that of "random groping" (*ein bloßes Herumtappen*) (B vii) to one of enlightened investigation, for with the help of these limits, metaphysicians will be led by principles that are known with certainty in advance, that is, by principles whose truth can be demonstrated a priori and that do not depend upon the empirical realm. In the dramatic setting of the preface to the second edition of the *Critique*, the shift from the groping to the enlightened stage of thought is brought about by a revolution. Why, asks Kant, has the "sure road to science" not been found for metaphysics? Where is the revolution that will herald the shift from blind groping to certain progression toward knowledge? He answers: "The examples of mathematics and natural science, which by a single and sudden revolution have become what they now are, seem to me sufficiently remarkable to suggest our considering what may have been the essential features in the changed point of view by which they have so greatly benefited" (B xvi). The methods of the mathematicians and the natural scientists offer clarity and progress. It is only by following their lead that philosophy will be liberated from its dark age and become a progressive discipline. Such a liberation is possible only through a revolution, and Kant describes the purpose of his First Critique in terms of a revolutionary shift in thinking: "This attempt to alter the procedure which has hitherto prevailed in metaphysics, by completely revolutionizing it in accordance with the example set by the geometers and physicists, forms indeed the main purpose of this critique of pure speculative reason" (B xxii). Revolution, scientific method, and critique go hand in hand. When in the preface to the first edition of the *Critique* Kant speaks of the "secure foundation" (A xi, note) upon which the sciences rest, he does not have in mind the absolute first principle that Reinhold and Fichte thought had been heralded by Kant but never really delivered. The foundation Kant refers to is an a priori deductive method that has close kinship to the methods of mathematicians and natural scientists, methods that promised to bring progress to philosophy.[9]

While Kant embraces an ahistorical, deductive method for critical philosophy, he does *not* claim that criticism is equivalent to the construction of deductive systems, which would entail that there would have to be some absolute first principle to support the critical philosophy. Reinhold and Fichte misread Kant's critical project as a deductive project in which the first principle from which all else was to be deduced was missing and which each of them, using different strategies (Fichte of a decidedly idealist bent) would supply. In sharp contrast to his contemporaries, Schlegel did not misread Kant in this way, in part because of his antifoundationalism. A closer look at *what* about Schlegel's antifoundationalism led him to: (1) avoid Reinhold and Fichte's mistake of confusing criticism with the construction of deductive systems and (2) to reject Kant's ahistorical model of philosophy is now in order.

Critiquing the Critical Philosopher

Recall that in *Athenäum* Fragment 84, Schlegel claims that "philosophy, like epic poetry, always begins *in media res*."[10] As such a claim joins others like "poetry and philosophy should be made one," it is tempting to read Schlegel's as calling for the destruction of all venerable methods that had made philosophy a discipline in the first place, which may be why in the not so distant past philosophers shunned such claims as insalubrious to the field. But as I have insisted, Schlegel's call is not a *destructive* one, but a *productive* one calling for the creation of a new map of inquiry whereby the kinship between poetry and philosophy is made visible: he is after a unified theory of knowledge.

Schlegel's emphasis on beginning the search for knowledge in the middle and the relation between philosophy and poetry are part of his concern with the nature of philosophy, and it is here that he departs from Kant. Nonetheless, Schlegel's departure from Kant does not entail a complete abandonment of Kant's Enlightenment philosophy, and certainly it does not entail a rejection of reason, as too many scholars (even some who are sympathetic to early German Romantic philosophy) have argued.[11]

Schlegel, for example, is in agreement with Kant concerning the limits of our knowledge. As we have seen, Schlegel claims that knowledge of the Absolute is impossible, because it is something that is by definition unconditioned, and we have knowledge only via the conditions that we ourselves impose on objects.[12] Hence, for both Schlegel and Kant, there is something inherently absurd in chasing after knowledge of that which is by definition unconditioned. Despite this point of agreement, Kant certainly would not have had any sympathy for claims such as, "philosophy, like epic poetry, always begins *in media res*." Kant used philosophy, and philosophy understood as the queen of all *sciences*, to frame and ultimately to understand reality. Schlegel's claim that philosophy beings *in media res*, that is, in the midst of change, flux, and processes suggests that something other than philosophy alone frames reality. Claims calling for the union of philosophy and poetry and comparisons between the methods of philosophy and those of poetry lead some to dismiss the Romantics as anti-Enlightenment thinkers, more interested in feelings and art than in reason and rigor, yet to embrace poetry as a way of knowing is by no means irrational.

While the early German Romantics do not abandon reason as the ultimate touchstone of knowledge, they do abandon the idea that philosophy begins with any first principle whatsoever (the upshot of their antifoundationalism) and the view that philosophy, understood as a solitary system standing outside of change, outside of history, can frame reality. Once we understand this move away from philosophy understood as the production (in the form of system) of an isolated thinker created ex nihilo, as the ultimate frame for all of reality, we can begin to understand the concerns that underlie Schlegel's interest in beginning philosophy in the midst of a philosophical tradition that has much to teach all thinkers who seek truth. Schlegel's historical approach to doing philosophy is rooted in a conviction that philosophy, insofar as it is a search for truth, can never come to an end. "[P]hilosophy is more a searching, a striving for a system of knowledge [*Wissenschaft*], than a system of knowledge itself."[13] While Schlegel is critical of Kant's distant relation to the history of philosophy, and his lack of metaphilosophical perspective, he does not reject Kant's critical project wholesale, and he certainly does not abandon reason as a touchstone for truth.

Schlegel's endorsement of antifoundationalism gave way to a view of philosophy as inherently incomplete. As we have seen, in the first book of the lectures on the history of philosophy, entitled *The Historical Characteristics of Philosophy according to Its Successive Development*, Schlegel addressed the problem of where we begin when we philosophize, questioning the very possibility of beginning with a first principle on the basis of doubts regarding its existence. From his doubts regarding the existence of a first principle for philosophy, Schlegel develops a view of philosophy as an infinite activity, for if there is no such principle, it will only be searched for and never found. Schlegel's position is that we never begin with the certain knowledge that there is such a principle; instead we must begin with what we have—a history of what has been thought by other philosophers before. Recall that Schlegel's first lecture concerns the problem of introducing philosophy, which is ultimately the problem of the beginning of philosophy (this connection between introductions and starting points helps to explain what is behind his remark concerning prefaces as the squre root of books).

According to Schlegel, an introduction to philosophy can only be a critique of all earlier philosophy. Abstracting entirely from previous systems, beginning ex nihilo, is no way to begin to do philosophy, for history and tradition are necessary guides for the philosopher. Schlegel is critical of any philosophy that begins with a disconnected I, which is part of why he ultimately rejects Fichte's philosophy. To "throw away" everything that has been developed by other philosophers or to "completely forget" all that has been thought before is to presume that philosophy can be done without attending to the history of philosophy. It is, according to Schlegel, impossible to do philosophy without doing the history of philosophy. This point, again, is intimately connected to his anti-foundationalism and his view of the importance of the evolution or development of ideas. What does Schlegel offer in place of a first principle, in place of something like Fichte's *Ich*? As we have seen, he offers a "small, but living seed."[14]

Schlegel's antifoundationalism leads him to reject any attempt to reduce philosophy to a deductive science according to which the successful philosopher would be the one to uncover the first principle upon which the entire deduction rested. So Schlegel parts company with Reinhold and Fichte's push to complete Kant's philosophy through establishing an absolute first principle. Schlegel describes the various philosophical systems that comprise the history of philosophy as links in a coherent chain of connections, with an understanding of any given philosophical system requiring some understanding of the whole chain to which it is connected.[15] The philosopher must work from a single system, that is, from one link in the chain of all systems, but to critique other systems, to critique philosophy itself, the philosopher must be able to see beyond his own system. Recall Bubner's description of the historical method that Schlegel initiates in terms of "an actively sympathetic response on the part of the critic and the philologist to the significant creative works of the past," a view that gives rise to a model of doing philosophy that contrasts sharply to the models of the German idealists, who saw philosophical systems as "godlike creations," which were, of course, ahistorical.[16]

Kant, of course, does have references to earlier thinkers in his work, but that hardly amounts to a serious consideration of history, for those references serve only as examples of errors that must be overcome. Kant emphasizes that if his views are the correct views, the erroneous views of his predecessors have been overcome and ultimately, certain aspects of philosophy's past have also been overcome, for he has provided the definitive answers to questions regarding the pure categories of the understanding of intuition, how the mind works to form knowledge, and other such issues central to the structure of knowledge. Of course, Schlegel was not mad, so he would agree completely with Kant that the erroneous views of past philosophers (and of present and future philosophers, for that matter) could be ignored, and that in the evolution of ideas, there is a sense in which the past is overcome. Where he strongly disagrees with Kant is on the point of the absolute certainty Kant can have that he has made study of his predecessors unnecessary, for such an unconditioned rejection of past philosophers is only born of unconditioned or absolute speculation. Schlegel favors what he refers to as "conditioned speculation," which is born of historical philosophy.[17]

For Kant, just as contemporary students of medicine have no need (other than historical interest) to study Hippocrates, philosophers would have no need to study the views of Plato or Berkeley, for Kant would have solved the problem of the structure of knowledge and solved it definitively, giving us the secure path that would enable us to find truth. The very last lines of Kant's *Critique of Pure Reason* assure the reader that the thirst for knowledge (*Wißbegierde*), which had until then gone unsatisfied, might now be able to be completely satisfied (a state of *völligen Befriedigung* having been reached).[18] As Schlegel stresses the importance of the *Wißbegierde* as a kind of motor in our search for knowledge, any complete satisfaction of it would run counter to the very purpose of philosophy as a kind of thirsting for knowledge, for if the longing were gone, why would we search anymore?

Certainly Kant does not directly encourage any interest in history or historical development of ideas as relevant to his critical project.[19] Schlegel, without naming the culprit in this instance, takes Kant to task for neglecting the history of philosophy in his quest for a pure philosophy:

> There have been philosophers, who have taken what is clearly a very important claim, namely that the philosopher must be a *Selbstdenker*, and exaggerate the claim so much, that they go on to claim that the philosopher need not bother himself at all with the opinions and ideas of others let alone allow himself to be influenced by these, so that his philosophy can be created in a completely *pure* way, with his own way of thinking developing toward the highest perfection in complete independence from foreign teachings, with absolute independence/sovereignty.[20]

In contrast to Kant's conception of philosophy as a field of inquiry that has no need of the past (except to provide examples of what should be avoided in the future) and that the correct system (his own) would make all others dispensable, Schlegel's call for a critical look at philosophy itself is part of his conviction that no single philosophical system can ever offer the final word on truth, so an examination of other systems is of great value. The historical critique of philosophy is what Schlegel offers to free us from the confines of any one system and to increase our chances of coming closer to truth. Indeed in the *Lectures on Transcendental Philosophy*, which he delivered in Jena (1800–1801) in his short-lived career as university lecturer, Schlegel sharply distinguishes philosophy from other sciences in virtue of its dependence on past ideas: "*Philosophy is an experiment*, and therefore each person who wants to philosophize, must always start again from the beginning. (In philosophy it is not the same as in the other sciences; that one may take what has already been accomplished in the other sciences, and build on it. Philosophy is a totality that exists for itself [*ein für sich bestehendes Ganze*], and each person who wants to philosophize must simply start at the beginning [*schlechthin vorne anfangen*]."[21]

The totality to which Schlegel makes reference is a tradition of philosophy, a history of ideas that we need in order to progress in our search for truth. And his appeal to simply start at the beginning must be read in combination with his other claims that his philosophy "begins *in media res*" and "with a living seed," so we are not here going back to Descartes' lonely cogito or Fichte's authoritative, world-forgetting *Ich*, as starting points that would serve as first principles from which the apparatus of all else that we could possibly know could be deduced. Starting simply from the beginning is no call to foundationalism.

Despite Schlegel's push to incorporate history into philosophy, he does not thereby *reduce* philosophy to history. According to Schlegel, because philosophy concerns the investigation, explanation, and judgment of ideas, opinions, and thoughts, philosophy is best understood via a historical critique of these ideas, opinions, and thoughts.[22] Schlegel emphasizes that this investigation is not a "matter of history, but rather of critique" (*nicht Sache der Geschichte, sondern der Kritik*). By now it should be clear that this matter of critique is certainly not identical to Kant's notion of critique, infused as it is with hermeneutical tools that Kant did not see as central to the task of the philosopher, and certainly not part of the identity of the queen of all sciences.

What does Schlegel's romantic conception of critique amount to? A closer look at Schlegel's charges against Kant will reveal the essence of the critique born of Schlegel's antifoundationalism and historical turn.

Away from Kant: Schlegel's Historical Turn

Schlegel shared with Kant the view that theirs was the age of criticism. Yet he did not believe that Kant's "critique" went far enough. For a critical age that criticizes everything except itself is not a fully critical age. One could say that it is "half critical." Schlegel is after a critique of critique, a philosophy of philosophy, attempting, through his conception of historical critique, to achieve a metaphilosophy, a way of looking critically at philosophy itself, as a discipline that has developed through history. As I have already noted, it is significant that the very first fragment of the *Athenäum* gives expression to Schlegel's concern with making philosophy the subject of philosophy: "Nothing is more rarely the subject of philosophy than philosophy itself."[23] With characteristic irony (of just the sort that led so many of his contemporaries to misunderstand him), Schlegel describes his push to criticize philosophy as just retaliation: "Since nowadays philosophy criticizes everything that comes in front of its nose, a criticism of philosophy would be nothing more than justifiable retaliation."[24]

Schlegel's charges against the limits of Kant's "critical philosophy" are rooted in his desire to develop a critical philosophy of philosophy itself. Just as the critical age criticizes all but itself, Kant does not criticize his "critical philosophy," so Schlegel calls Kant a "half critic," later explaining: "[A] critique of philosophizing reason cannot succeed without a history of philosophy. [This] is proved to us by Kant himself. His work as a critique of philosophizing reason is not at all historical enough even though it is filled with historical relations and he attempts to construct various systems."[25] A successful critique of philosophizing reason is a critique that places a given philosophical system into a context that allows for a full understanding (or at least an approximation to this full understanding) of its place in the history of ideas. And while certain philosophical points from different philosophical systems can be meaningfully compared in an ahistorical manner, to develop a critique of philosophy itself, one must trace the development and genesis of ideas (recall Schlegel's description of his method as genetic as opposed to deductive) and compare the development of various philosophical systems with others. A successful critique of philosophy requires a history of philosophy. When history is incorporated into the very method of philosophy itself, we can assess a given contribution of a philosopher, not only by *classifying* her arguments as valid or invalid, sound or unsound, but by *comparing* the merits of the contribution to other contributions made by other philosophers from different periods.[26] Schlegel equates the philosopher who is merely able to classify arguments as a "natural science observer" (*naturforschender Beobachter*) of philosophy, someone who may indeed, for the purposes of good classification, make some historical suggestions, take the preliminary steps toward the development of a history of philosophy, but who, because of being trapped within one system, is unable to do philosophy historically.[27]

Schlegel's emphasis on history as essential to critique is part of his general view of philosophy as framed by life, as beginning *in media res*. Accordingly, the object of philosophical critique is also something changing and growing, and the philosopher must be equipped to handle this teeming mass of material. The history need not be expansive, after all, Schlegel praises Fichte for making Kant's philosophy the subject of his own philosophy, hailing him as "Kant raised to the second power" so that "the theory of knowledge [is] much more critical than it seems to be" because "the new version of the theory of knowledge is always simultaneously philosophy and philosophy of philosophy."[28] Fichte was hardly a model of a philosopher who took the history of philosophy seriously, but he was a philosopher who saw that philosophy evolved and changed and saw that philosophers had to look critically at philosophy itself. The various versions of the *Wissenschaftslehre* form a kind of history all their own, which is enough to fulfill Schlegel's call for philosophy to be historical, at least in a minimal sense of developing (even in a rudimentary way) some philosophy of philosophy.

Historical critique is the result of acknowledging that philosophy is *not* like a natural science. It is more like a historical or human science. If philosophy is not like a natural science, argues Schlegel, then the judgments we make cannot be scientific judgments. They are more like what Schlegel calls "philosophical judgments of art" (*philosophische Kunsturteile*).[29] Read against this background, we find more philosophical punch to Schlegel's calls to unite philosophy and poetry. Philosophy and poetry should come closer together in part because of the hermeneutical framework that they share.[30] Yet, just as applying a historical method to philosophy does not reduce philosophy to history, the use of *philosophische Kunsturteile* does not reduce philosophical criticism to aesthetic judgment, but rather it gives rise to a richer notion of critique in philosophy. Walter Benjamin, with the perspicuity that characterizes his philosophical vision, observed that it was first with the early German Romantics that the expression "art critic" (*Kunstkritiker*) replaced "art judge" (*Kunstrichter*). His work on this subject develops the nuances of the early German Romantics' contributions to the development of the notion of critique, but mainly in the area of art.[31] However, it was not only within the realm of art that criticism came to be of central importance for the early German Romantics.

As stated already, in the preface to the first edition of the *Critique of Pure Reason*, Kant characterizes his age (circa 1781) as the "age of criticism," understanding criticism as a kind of tribunal that would subject all within its jurisdiction to a "free and open examination." Schlegel supported Kant's call to subject everything and everyone to "free and open examination," yet he did not believe that Kant's "critique" (that is to say, what counted for Kant as "free and open examination") went far enough.

When Schlegel calls Kant a "half critic" (*halber Kritiker*), that is, a partial or incomplete critic, he is pointing to the limitations of Kant's critical project. For although Kant's notion of philosophy does not limit the task of philosopher to that of a judge evaluating the logical validity of certain arguments and the truth of certain claims, neither does his transcendental method have the historical perspective that Schlegel argues is necessary in order for the philosopher to be in a position to evaluate other systems, to provide a free and open examination of philosophy.[32] Without a historical perspective, claims Schlegel, when we come to judge other systems, we can only judge them according to our own system. Hence, all assessments of other systems are ultimately self-referential. So Kant is unable to critique his critique: he can claim the legitimacy of scientific knowledge only within his own system. Schlegel believes that the philosopher must also be a philologist and a historian in order to be a good critic.[33] Kant, he claims, failed to incorporate history and philology into his critique:

> The critic has much in common with the polemicist; only he is not concerned with destruction but rather merely with sorting out (*sichten*), with cleansing prior philosophies of their waste (*Schlacken*). Kant's aim is not polemical, he says that the critic must attempt to place himself in the most varied and universal way of each system, grant each system its due rights, yet this does not often occur in Kant's work. The idea, nonetheless, that a critique must precede philosophy itself is entirely Kant's discovery and is certainly useful: he approximated his ideal here and there, this would have happened much more often had he been more of a philologist and had paid more attention to the philological, critical history of philosophy.[34]

Sympathy and praise for the path opened by Kant's critical philosophy mix with clear criticism of the failure on Kant's part to develop critique fully enough, to connect philosophy to history, to develop a historical critique, in short, to develop a hermeneutical framework for philosophy. Schlegel takes Kant to task for not granting each system its due rights, that is, not fully engaging with the systems that preceded his historically. Kant's historical myopia is what leads Schlegel to claim that "Kant is in principle highly uncritical"[35] and that "philosophy must be critical but in a much higher sense than in Kant."[36] The higher sense to which Schlegel refers is a historical sense, not the "higher" sense alluded to by Reinhold and Fichte in their quixotic chase after the Absolute. Schlegel's objections reveal that he understood that for Kant criticism did not amount to the establishment of a first principle for philosophy.[37] This understanding eluded prominent philosophers of the post-Kantian period (our "revolutionaries," Reinhold and Fichte, in particular).

Some of the confusion on the part of Reinhold and Fichte can be traced to a basic misunderstanding of Kant's critical project, a misunderstanding that did not hinder Schlegel's reading of Kant. We have already seen that a misunderstanding of the transcendental deduction as something meant to be "strict[ly] and logically compelling" led Reinhold and Fichte to posit absolute starting points for philosophy, to convert philosophy into an absolute, deductive system. In effect, these thinkers hijacked Kant's revolution, that is to say, his critical project, transforming it from a project designed to lay down limits and boundaries to the claims of knowledge to one of a search for an absolute first principle, from which *all* of our knowledge claims could be "strictly and logically" deduced.

In sharp contrast to his contemporaries, Schlegel, the sober Romantic, understood that Kant's view of critique did not lead to the construction of deductive systems of philosophy. As I indicated at the beginning of this chapter, Schlegel, unlike the figures who receive most of the attention of philosophers interested in post-Kantian philosophy, understood that it was futile to try to get at a principle higher than the one given in Kant's transcendental deduction, that is, to an absolute or unconditioned principle.[38] The sense in which Schlegel wants to get to a higher level of criticism is not the misguided sense in which Reinhold and Fichte strove to do this.

In the age of criticism, an appeal to objective criteria in order to evaluate a given philosophical system is not enough to achieve a complete critical approach to that system. According to Schlegel, in order to fully appraise the work of any philosopher, we need more than the objective rules of logic. We need a richer context in which to place the philosophical system; in short, we need a history of philosophy, a historical critique of philosophy. Moreover, critique should not stop at a single system; philosophy itself needs to be critiqued. The history of philosophy puts all philosophers in the position of appreciating the goals and tendencies of *all* philosophical systems.

Unlike Reinhold and Fichte, Schlegel had no need to transform Kant's critical philosophy into a deductive philosophy and to complete Kant's revolution by establishing an absolute, first principle. Schlegel was, in fact, not at all interested in establishing foundations for philosophy. He did not misread Kant's critical project in this way. His charge that Kant was a half critic stemmed from a view he had of the task of the philosopher and the nature of philosophy itself. Schlegel viewed philosophy as something inherently incomplete, something that was ever developing and as a discipline that would best be modeled on something less ahistorical than the natural sciences. Moreover, Schlegel was committed to making philosophy itself the subject of philosophy, arguing that a serious engagement with the history of philosophy was necessary in order to fully critique philosophy itself. The remedy to the problems left by Kant's half critique is a historical critique of philosophy itself, a philosophy of philosophy. Schlegel's metaphilosophical concerns were ultimately part of his deep concern for the nature of philosophy itself, and it is to his view of philosophy that I now turn.

Chapter Six

Philosophy *in Media Res*

As discussed in chapter 2, Schlegel's defense of coherentism, because it is coupled with a certain privileging of aesthetic experience, is often dismissed as unphilosophical. This may be why philosophers who wish to highlight the philosophical relevance of Schlegel's work tend to emphasize the kinship between his views and the views of philosophers whose philosophical credentials are impeccable. For example, Manfred Frank and Andrew Bowie have made the innovative move of joining the inquiries of the early German Romantics with those of some contemporary analytic philosophers. This is a complicated move, for the levels of inquiries are quite different, yet both Bowie and Frank have shown that productive overlaps exist, especially in the area of epistemology and views regarding how we justify our beliefs about the world and how truths are collected under the single name of science (*Wissenschaft*). Their work shows that interest in the early German Romantics not only has historical value, as an interesting chapter in post-Kantian philosophy, but that the early German Romantics grappled with problems still very much on the minds of contemporary philosophers and that their work merits a careful reassessment in part because it rewards us with new insights on issues still of concern to us.

Fred Beiser has placed the contributions of the early German Romantics into the tradition of classical German Idealism, arguing that the Romantics' contributions have as important a role as those of Hegel himself, a philosopher whose contributions are taken to constitute the culminating moment of the post-Kantian period. The way that Beiser weaves the early German Romantics into the story of German Idealism is by defining them as absolute idealists in the Platonic sense. Robert Richards has recently told the story of the important contributions of the early German Romantics in terms of their impact on the development of the life sciences, tracing some of Darwin's insights back to romantic *Naturphilosophie*.

I think that each of these approaches is quite valuable in shedding light on the philosophical contributions of the early German Romantics and of showing just how relevant their thought remains. Yet, to fully appreciate Schlegel's philosophical contributions, I believe it is also valuable to look more carefully at Schlegel's own forays into the practices that he preached, that is, to look at how he applied his own philosophical views to his critical practice. In order to offer just such a look at Schlegel's critical practices, after presenting Schlegel's *Wechselerweis* and ensuing view of philosophy, I will present his reading of Goethe's *Meister* and argue that he was drawn to that novel because of the model of coherence he found within it, how it showcases the epistemological commitments he endorsed.

The *Wechselerweis* and the Search for Truth

Throughout this book I have made reference to Schlegel's *Wechselerweis*, and it is just now that I am in a position to fully explicate it. From the preceding chapters, it should be clear that the *Wechselerweis* is Schlegel's proposed alternative both to absolute first principles, which transform philosophy into a deductive enterprise, and to appeals to common sense, which reduce philosophy to a purely pragmatic enterprise. Schlegel did not view philosophy as a deductive science nor as a practical science but rather, as we saw, especially in his confrontation with Kant's philosophy, as a historical, comparative science that would remain open-ended.

References to the *Wechselerweis* are found scattered throughout Schlegel's writings, in his fragments, essays, and lectures. Perhaps the most compact presentation of this idea is to be found in the second appendix to fragments that appeared under the title *Philosophical Apprenticeship*,[1] twenty-four fragments concerning the nature of philosophy in general and Schlegel's view of its starting point in particular. In these fragments, not only is Schlegel's skepticism regarding the feasibility of a philosophy based on first principles explicitly expressed, but so is his insistence that the only way to proceed in philosophy is via a *Wechselerweis*. Consider the following claims:

> Infinite are the steps forward which yet remain to be taken. Not only is the content inexhaustible, but also the form, every concept, every proof, is infinitely perfectible. Even mathematics is not excluded from this, cannot be excluded from this. The perfectibility of mathematics is of extreme importance for philosophy.[2]
>
> *Bildung* is the only thing that protects against *Schwärmerei*. There are no principles, which could be universal, purposeful companions and leaders towards truth.[3]

> Not only a *Wechselerweis* but a *Wechselbegriff*, must ground philosophy. One may ask with each concept as with each proof, for another concept and another proof. Hence, philosophy must, like an epic poem, begin in the middle and it is impossible to present it piece by piece, so that the first piece would be completely grounded and explained. It is a whole and the way to understand it is not through a straight line but rather through a circle. The whole of this science of all sciences must be deduced from two ideas, principles, concepts, intuitions, without further ado.[4]
>
> [...]The refutation of all other [positions] and complete inner coherence [vollendete innere Zusammenhang] are the authentic criteria of a system...[5]
>
> In my system the first principle is truly a *Wechselerweis*.[6]

Each of these claims expresses an idea that shaped Schlegel's very conception of philosophy, namely, that the content of philosophy, as well as its form, is inexhaustible. No principles can lead us to truth not because there is no truth to be found; rather because the use of a first principle, especially à la Reinhold or Fichte, can only lead us to error, premised as each approach is on the belief that some indubitable first principle will enable us to spin a web of certainty. Schlegel's view of philosophy, that is, his view of the structure of knowledge, is one according to which what we need is not a first principle but a *Wechselerweis*, that is, an interaction between at least two ideas, principles, concepts, intuitions, underscoring the ways in which our beliefs find mutual support and are constructed into knowledge claims that lead us ever closer to Truth (understood as the totality of individual truths).

The above fragments also express that the *Wechselerweis* is intended as a method to understand reality as a whole, which is constantly changing. Most important, the above fragments make it clear that philosophy does not begin with anything certain, that is, with some proposition that can be proved. Uncertainty is intrinsic to philosophy, which is indicated in Schlegel's reference to the infinite perfectibility of the form and content of philosophy. Truth is indeed a goal of inquiry, and a heavy dose of optimism shades Schlegel's view of our ability to progress, that is, to grasp individuals truths and come ever closer to Truth, yet his optimism does not overtake him, as he consistently reminds us that a grasp of the whole (that is, the totality of individual truths) will forever elude us. Furthermore, as there are no first principles that can be reliable leaders in our search for truth, we must depend upon human judgment (something that Kant called a "special talent" that could not be taught but only practiced),[7] so the emphasis on the formation of the human (*Bildung*) takes on a central role for Schlegel, for only a well-formed human being is capable of exercising the "special talent" of judgment, and that talent is the only secure guide in our search for truth.[8]

Part of what Schlegel is attempting to capture in the expression *Wechselerweis* is something that he often repeats, that is, that there is no first principle. So, for example, in Fichte's philosophy, The I posits itself and The I should posit itself are each fundamental for what follows. Each is as important as the other; they mutually support one another in order to help us understand the idea of human freedom. Fichte's claim to have isolated the absolute, single first principle for philosophy, a claim that amounts to having had discovered the point of certainty upon which all other knowledge claims rest, is, for Schlegel, an illusion. As I discussed in chapter 3, Schlegel's response to Fichte's claim is to counter that The I posits itself depends upon another proposition and is thus not self-sufficient, but rather that it depends upon another proposition, The I should posit itself. These two propositions affect each other reciprocally/mutually and change each other and what follows. They mutually confirm one another. Thus, change is essential to the nature of reality, and any proof structure in philosophy must be equipped to capture this change.

As we have seen in the preceding chapters, Schlegel's study of his contemporaries is primarily a critique of their inability to grasp philosophy's true starting point. Schlegel's criticisms of Reinhold are basically criticisms of Reinhold's attempts to secure a first principle for philosophy. Schlegel's critique of Jacobi is a critique of what he took to be Jacobi's obstinate insistence that though knowledge of the Absolute was impossible, philosophy needed to depart from it anyway, even if via a *salto mortale*, which endangered objectivity and truth. Fichte, whom Schlegel mockingly compares to a drunk in his misguided efforts to secure a first principle for philosophy, is presented as a philosopher who ends up endorsing a rather misguided, mystical version of idealism, which Schlegel finds wanting due to its flagrant negligence of anything other than the stuff of consciousness.

Yet it is important to keep in mind that Fichte was a philosopher under whose spell Schlegel once fell and for whom he maintained a great degree of respect; yet Schlegel never let deference stand in the way of critical portraits even of the most revered figures of his time. Even Kant, the great critical philosopher himself, does not, on Schlegel's reading, deliver what he promises: he fails to critique critique. One might think that Niethammer, with his strong skepticism regarding the possibility of establishing first principles for philosophy, would be free and clear of Schlegel's stinging criticisms, yet Schlegel disagrees strongly with what he takes to be Niethammer's almost flippant acceptance of the claims of common sense as the starting point for philosophy. Schlegel presents the period of post-Kantian philosophy as scandal of scandals, a history of errors! How does Schlegel's *Wechselerweis* help set us on the right path?

The *Wechselerweis*, as a structure to understand how principles work together to lead us to truth, is related to Schlegel's holism and his endorsement of a coherence view of truth. For Schlegel, nothing is known in isolation but always as part of the whole of the parts that comprise it. All elements of our system of knowledge interact with one another. This denial of deducibility is Schlegel's metaphysical or methodological holism and is the central structure of Schlegel's antifoundationalist philosophy. The *Wechselerweis* is an open structure, one that allows philosophy to begin "in the middle," to pay due attention to both poles of reality, consciousness, and the infinite and thus free us from one-sided approaches to reality.

Philosophy "in the Middle": Between Fichte and Spinoza

Let us take a look at some of Schlegel's more systematic presentations of one cornerstone of his philosophy: the claim that philosophy must begin "in the middle." In his *Lectures on Transcendental Philosophy*, Schlegel provided the first attempt at a systematic presentation of his thought. Given Schlegel's acutely ambivalent attitude toward systems in general, these lectures represent an important moment in his own philosophical development and finally provided something that Novalis had pleaded for from his friend, namely, "to finally give a whole, where no part need be supplemented."[9] In the opening paragraphs of the lectures, we find a distinction that is of central importance in piecing together an understanding of Schlegel's holism: "Knowledge of the origin or primitive gives us *principles*. And knowledge of the totality gives us *ideas*. A principle is therefore knowledge of the origin. *An idea is knowledge of the whole.*"[10] Manfred Frank has pointed out that with this distinction, Schlegel distinguishes between that with which philosophy begins (principles) and that with which it can be sufficiently grounded (an idea).[11] Principles provide the origins of our knowledge, and ideas give us conceptual access to the whole, which is infinite and not graspable by any one concept. As Schlegel consistently claims (whether in fragments, reviews, essays, or lectures) philosophy is not a finite activity but rather an infinite one. It is the search for the principle of all ideas and the idea of all principles. For this reason, Frank suggests that one possible way of understanding the *Wechselerweis* is as an exchange between a principle of consciousness and an idea of the infinite. In order to fully appreciate why this exchange between a principle of consciousness and the idea of the infinite is an important clue in understanding the *Wechselerweis*, we have to have a clear notion of Schlegel's view of consciousness and his skepticism regarding any static conception of the world around us. According to Schlegel, the infinite exists only as posited, so there must be a positer. Hence in addition to the infinite there is a consciousness of the infinite. This is why Schlegel goes on to claim: "And so we now have the elements which philosophy offers us; namely, consciousness and the infinite. These are the two poles around which all philosophy revolves."[12] These two poles form the structure of reality. Indeed, Schlegel claims: "These two elements form a closed sphere in whose middle reality lies."[13] We have already seen this meeting before, in Schlegel's critique of Fichte, where he argued that Fichte's idealism needed to be complemented by Spinoza's realism. The two poles around which all philosophy revolves revolve, thus, around two philosophers: Fichte (the pole of consciousness) and Spinoza (the pole of the infinite). As Schlegel tells us, "Fichtean philosophy has to do with consciousness. In contrast, Spinoza's philosophy has to with the *infinite*."[14]

Fred Beiser discusses what he calls this "strange wedding plan," that is, the attempt to bring together Fichte's idealism with Spinoza's realism, in an attempt to see whether in this marriage of opposites, some underlying affinity can be found. On why the early German Romantics even attempt to bring Fichte and Spinoza together, Beiser says:

> What attracted the romantics to Fichte was his radical concept of human freedom, according to which the self posits itself, making itself what it is. It was this concept of the self-positing self that rationalized the French Revolution, giving to the self the right to remake laws and institutions according to the demands of reason. As supporters of the Revolution in France, the young romantics could only embrace the concept behind it. What the romantics admired in Spinoza was his synthesis of religion and science. Spinoza's pantheism seemed to resolve all the traditional conflicts between reason and faith. It had made a religion out of science by divinizing nature, and a science out of religion by naturalizing the divine. But it is precisely in these respects that Fichte and Spinoza seem utterly irreconcilable. If nature is divine, then it is infinite, and everything should fall under its laws; hence there cannot be any transcendental realm of freedom above and beyond nature. Rather than creating itself, the self simply realizes of necessity the essence given to it by the natural order of things.[15]

Ultimately, argues Beiser, the organic conception of nature is what enables the romantic fusion of Fichte and Spinoza to take place, a fusion that, as we saw in chapter 3, corrected the one-sided perspectives of both Fichte's idealism and Spinoza's realism.

As discussed in chapter 3, while Schlegel does not fully endorse Fichte's philosophy, he does recognize the important contributions of Fichte's *Wissenschaftslehre*. Schlegel was well aware of the central role of consciousness in our approximation of reality, so Fichte's work is heralded as a tendency of the age, a work that has set philosophy on a new path that has changed how we conceive of subjectivity. Yet, given that Schlegel claims that the I is only probable, not certain, it surely cannot be the absolute first principle for philosophy. Without a certain first principle, philosophy cannot be endowed with certainty, nor can it be complete. So, what begins with a point of agreement, namely, the important role of consciousness for defining the tasks of philosophy, ends with a most decisive parting of ways. After all, for Fichte, the notion of philosophy as an incomplete science was *sinnlos* (futile, senseless); indeed, an incomplete philosophy is, for Fichte, "not philosophy at all." In contrast, Schlegel *defines* philosophy in terms of its incompleteness: "If knowledge itself is infinite, and so always incomplete, then philosophy as a science can never be finished, closed, complete."[16] Our search for knowledge begins with a feeling, a longing for the infinite (*Sehnsucht nach dem Unendlichen*),[17] and we will forever long for the infinite (totality of knowledge) yet never grasp it. In a fragment, Schlegel expresses the same idea in a less poetic way: "The whole must begin with a reflection on the infinitude of the drive towards knowledge."[18] This feeling of deficit is the result of a reflection on our state of consciousness as limited and the realization that the scope of knowledge is infinite. Frank suggests that this longing, which is the result of the tension between the infinite that is posited and the finite positer, may be the middle to which Schlegel refers, when he insists that philosophy begins in the middle.[19] Hence, if Frank is right, Schlegel's claim that philosophy begins in the middle amounts to the claim that philosophy begins with a feeling of deficit. In several places, Schlegel does emphasize the importance of the *Wissenstrieb* (drive for knowledge) and *Wissbegierd* (hunger for knowledge). Certainly, this feeling of deficit is central to the activity of philosophizing and can be said to be part of the middle to which Schlegel refers.

The feeling of deficit is the result of the realization of the inherent incompleteness of knowledge; we are finite knowers with a longing to know that what is without limits, the Absolute. A feeling of incompleteness is what fuels our desire to know and to investigate.[20] Yet the middle to which Schlegel refers is not exhausted by the concepts of 'feeling' and 'longing.' To these must be added a fundamental doubt regarding the status of objects in the world and Schlegel's unusual view of consciousness.

Let us look once again at Schlegel's own description of where his philosophy begins:

> Our philosophy does not begin like the others with a first principle—where the first proposition is like the center or first ring of a comet—with the rest a long tail of mist—we depart from a small but living seed—our center lies in the middle. From an unlikely and modest beginning—doubt regarding the "thing" which, to some degree shows itself in all thoughtful people and the always present, prevalent probability of the I—our philosophy will develop in a steady progression and become strengthened until it reaches the highest point of human knowledge and shows the breadth and limits of all knowledge.[21]

The above passage is a rather florid description of Schlegel's philosophy, but in the preceding chapters I have begun to fill in the historical context that helps us to appreciate its philosophical weight. Ultimately, in what might, at first blush, seem to be nothing but a vague and vacuous metaphorical expression, we find the two central axes of Schlegel's view of philosophy's starting point: philosophy begins between belief in the I and doubt regarding the thing. This view is systematically developed in *Lectures on Transcendental Philosophy* and the Köln lectures, *The Development of Philosophy in Twelve Books*.[22] As I have already indicated, the Köln lectures are essentially a critique of all other systems of philosophy: a critique which is defined by Schlegel's view of the role of history in philosophy and by his emphasis on the search for truth as a process of approximation. According to Schlegel, the I is not certain, only probable, and the objects with which this I interacts are not static things. In short, permanence does not underlie change; rather, change itself is essential. Schlegel in fact describes the world as "an infinite I in the process of becoming."[23]

Kant and Fichte were certain that philosophy must begin with the subject and even presented proofs for this. Thus they were able to build a system around the thinking subject as a sort of starting point for philosophy. Knowledge was the result of certainty regarding primitives, for Kant the transcendental unity of apperception, that is, that "the I think must be able to accompany every thought"; for Fichte the structure of the I and its sufficiency to posit to the Non-I. Neither of these primitives depends in any way upon what follows. Hence, we can understand the whole scope of knowledge through an analysis of its parts. This may explain why neither Kant nor Fichte viewed history as central to the work of the philosopher. In contrast, Schlegel's philosophy begins *between* the likelihood of the I and doubt concerning the status of things. Neither of these is an apodictic assertion. The "system" developed around this "middle" position is quite unlike either Kant's or Fichte's. Schlegel's method is not, and indeed cannot be, analytic, but synthetic or genetic. Schlegel's move to "the middle" has important ramifications for his own philosophical commitments, and it is a move still found valuable by contemporary philosophers. Hence it points to the contemporary relevance of his thought.[24]

In the introduction to his Köln lectures, Schlegel claims that philosophy is in need of a comparative history of philosophy. In the second book of the same lectures, he claims that this historical-comparative approach is just as essential to our knowledge of the world. Philosophy must not merely analyze concepts, and the components of reality, but also provide a method for understanding these within given contexts. The only way philosophy will be equipped to do this is if it incorporates a genetic or synthetic method. "This method of observing and conceptualizing objects according to their inner connections, their elements, in their step-wise development and their inner relations can be understood as opposed to the syllogistic method which has a technical use. This method can be called genetic or due to its similarity with mathematics, a method of construction."[25] In order to clarify this reference to a conceptualization of objects according to their inner connections (or what might also be termed their "coherence"), I shall now present Schlegel's peculiar view of objects. He understood objects not as fixed, unchanging, lifeless things, but as part of an organic whole.

Destroying the Illusion of the Finite: Schlegel's Critique of the Thing

Schlegel's use of the word *Ding* can be traced to Kant. Kant's use of the concept of '*Ding*' was widely criticized, especially in its reference to the noumena or "thing-in-itself" (*Ding an sich*). Both Jacobi and Fichte rejected Kant's thing-in-itself.[26] Jacobi claims that there cannot be things-in-themselves because if we assume that a thing-in-itself is the cause of an appearance, all we produce is another appearance. And if we assume that there is a distinction between an appearance and something causing it, but which is not itself an appearance, we can never show how the two are causally related. Either way, we are left with no way out of the problem of how to explain the relation between noumena and phenomena; that is, we are left with a skepticism that many thinkers of the immediate post-Kantian generation found unacceptable. Jacobi's famous complaint captures a serious problem facing Kant's mysterious realm: "Without that presupposition (of the existence of things-in-themselves) I could not enter (Kant's) system . . . and could not remain there with that presupposition."[27]

Jacobi thus rejects Kant's transcendental idealism and, as we have discussed, embraces a type of realism, which Schlegel diagnosed as a blind leap of faith.

Fichte's objections to Kant's inaccessible realm follow another line, one that many scholars find more promising in terms of avoiding the threat of skepticism posed by Kant's appeal to the thing-in-itself. Fichte's general strategy is to show that a *susbstratum* or a bearer of properties can be an object of awareness; that such a substratum cannot be perceptually abstracted from its properties; and that the ontological distinction between a substratum and its properties collapses, leaving only the self and its sensations.[28] Fichte develops his idealism from this position, one that begins with an I and a Non-I, rather than with appearances and things-in-themselves. A virtue of his idealism is that it leaves no room for inaccessible substrata.

Schlegel's objections to Kant's thing-in-itself go deeper than the objections of both Jacobi and Fichte. Ultimately, he rejects not only Kant's thing-in-itself but also the accompanying ontology based on permanent substance.

For Kant, a thing is a set of appearances bound together by something that is perceptually unavailable to us. He defines an object as the synthesis of representations that we refer to as something according to a rule of consciousness.[29] For Kant, "the synthetic unity of consciousness is an objective condition of all knowledge."[30] This definition of objectivity rests upon the principle of permanence of substance, which Kant explicates in his first analogy. Kant claims that "[p]ermanence is a necessary condition under which alone appearances are determinable as things or objects in a possible experience."[31] Moreover, "[t]he senses represent to us something merely as it appears—this something must also in itself be a thing—an object of a non-sensible intuition, that is, of the understanding."[32] According to Kant, "[a]ll appearances contain the permanent (substance) as the object itself, and the transitory as its mere determination, that is, as a way in which the object exists."[33]

According to Schlegel, Kant uses the notion of a permanent substance or thing in order to explain appearances. Appearances are then understood as regular, law-like, and necessary, as "things" that can be explained; "The thing-in-itself is the enduring foundation of the changing appearance which itself does not appear, of that which is limited and separated."[34]

The concept 'thing' is understood to refer to some static, lifeless, ahistorical bearer of the properties that we perceive. The "thing-in-itself" propels us beyond the world of phenomena and the laws of nature, clearing space for the ideas of the supersensible realm, such as

God, freedom, and the immortality of the soul.³⁵ The thing-in-itself was central to Kant's project of carving out space for human freedom. So there seems to be a problem left in the wake of rejecting the thing-in-itself, namely, how are we to accommodate the idea of freedom? Schlegel wants to combine Fichte and Spinoza, to accommodate freedom within the realm of nature. As Beiser points out, the Romantics reject the noumenal realm as part of Kant's solution to the problem of freedom because of its dualistic implications:

> True to their anti-dualism, the romantics placed the self within nature, insisting that it is one mode of the single infinite substance, one part of the universal organism. They were no less naturalistic than Spinoza: they too affirmed that everything is within nature, and that everything in nature conforms to law. Contrary to one popular image of romanticism, they did not allow for caprice, arbitrariness, or chance in nature. Rather, they maintained that everything that happens in nature happens of necessity, such that it could not have been otherwise. The romantics also did not question that everything that happens must occur according to mechanical laws, so that for every event there will be some prior causes determining it into action.³⁶

Yet, the Romantics were not determinists, and Beiser explains the point of departure from Spinoza's philosophy quite eloquently: "Where [the Romantics] are different from Spinoza is not in exempting events from mechanical necessity but in bringing mechanical necessity itself under higher organic laws."³⁷ Schlegel endorses just the sort of holism described by Beiser, a holism that acknowledges not only a world of mechanical laws, that is, a realm of static, unchanging laws of nature, but also a world of processes of life, of genetic or organic laws. Schlegel's push toward holism and his critical stance vis-à-vis Kant's realm of the thing-in-itself as the underlying realm of reality is born of his desire to free us from the illusion of the finite.

When appearances are defined as things-for-us, which rely on some enduring, unchanging thing-in-itself so that it (in whatever form it takes in the various philosophical systems) becomes primary, then the static takes precedence over the changing, the living, and this, according to Schlegel, has been a constant source of error in philosophy.³⁸

Schlegel's critique of the thing is concentrated in books 1, 2, 3, and 4 of the lectures on the development of philosophy he delivered in Köln (1804–05). Relevant parallel critiques are found in a series of lectures on logic, which he delivered in Köln (1805–06); the second section is dedicated to a discussion of ontology. Here he distinguishes legitimate from illegitimate uses of the concept thing. Only the practical use of the concept thing is legitimate; its speculative use is not legitimate. Practical use is logical use. Logical or mathematical entities can be treated as things, for they are ahistorical and static anyway, subject to the laws of nature and limited by those laws. The rules of inference (identity, noncontradiction, etc.) all depend upon the concept of an enduring, unchanging set of laws not subject to historical developments. We can use these laws of thought to carry out mechanical operations, to follow chains of argumentation. But we must not generalize from this limited class of changeless entities, and assume that all that we come across can be understood in the same way: living entities are entities or things of a different sort than logical or mathematical entities, and laws of nature, etc. Schlegel's critique of the thing is part of his concern with creating an ontology that would do justice to life.[39] This is because in order to understand most aspects of reality, we must understand the origin and the cause of its genesis, and know their purposes, their laws of development (*Bildungsgesetze*). From these considerations, Schlegel concludes:

> We obtain all insight regarding the *essence* of a thing only insofar as we get to know its emergence according to its sources, grounds and its purposes and laws of formation; thus, taken speculatively, all concepts and all theory consists only of genetic concepts; as soon as we do not remain merely by the external characteristics, the concept of a thing as an unseeable, dead holder of characteristics vanishes and there arises only the concept, a picture of life; we obtain then something completely vital—mobile, where one comes from the other and brings forth another, in short we obtain insight into the history of the thing.[40]

To illustrate the importance of going beyond the "merely external characteristics" of a thing, Schlegel discusses a gold coin. In order to understand the coin we must understand it within a context where certain social institutions were at work—trade, money, etc.[41] Of course, we can investigate it qua gold metal, but then we have only part of the picture, for the coin is more than just a set of physical properties; it is a part of the history of humanity, and as such, it should not be reduced to its finite, empirical properties. As Schlegel tells us, "the concept of say a gold coin, if we would not look only at the external characteristics, would lead us to a study of gold in general, that is to an important part of the history of humanity in addition to an investigation of the contents of the metal."[42]

According to Schlegel, logical and mathematical objects exhaust the class of objects that can be meaningfully discussed without reference to history and laws of development. For a realist, the object qua lifeless bearers of properties is a starting point that is not in the middle of anything but rather is the point from which all else is measured. The notion of the thing enables the philosopher to treat a given object as if it were something finite, which can be exhaustively analyzed and known. Schlegel is interested in more than the external properties of objects. His critique of the thing is an important part of his claim that philosophy begins in the middle, for in this critique Schlegel emphasizes the limitations involved with reducing the objects in the world to collections of purely physical characteristics, rendering things as isolated parts unconnected to any greater whole. Schlegel's critique of the thing is part of his project to destroy the illusion of the finite and to uncover the interconnectedness that joins all individuals in the infinite chain of being.

For Schlegel, the meaning of things can only be uncovered when those things are seen as parts of a larger social whole—this social whole being a way of enlivening the objects made dead by an analysis that severs them from their connection to the whole of which they are a part. Schlegel's holism is nonempirical insofar as it postulates a social "whole" beyond the empirical set of properties that are part of our experience. Within the context of objects this leads to complications as any nonempirical approach in philosophy will. For we are faced with a search for reasonable criteria regarding the truth of the claims we make.[43] This is the problem of how we are to analyze the historical whole which contains mechanical laws but is organic so that the mechanical laws are part of the greater organic whole.

One upshot of Schlegel's commitment to capturing the "life" of objects often suffocated by philosophical analysis was that teleological approaches were rejected, and a distinct embrace of aesthetic approaches was embraced. Hence Schlegel avoided problems like the ones described by Wilhelm von Humboldt:

> Historical truth is, generally speaking, much more threatened by philosophical than by artistic handling, since the latter is at least accustomed to granting freedom to its subject matter. Philosophy dictates a goal to events. This search for final causes, even though it may be deduced from the essence of man and nature itself, distorts and falsifies every independent judgment of the characteristic working of forces. Teleological history, therefore, never attains the living truth of universal destiny because the individual

always has to reach the pinnacle of his own development within the span of his fleeting existence; teleological history can, for that reason, never properly locate the ultimate goal of events in living things but has to seek it, as it were, in dead institutions and in the concept of an ideal totality.[44]

If philosophers are guilty of freezing living reality in their move to subsume changing, living reality under fixed, final causes, then the adjective *philosophical* will indeed suggest a move away from change and life to the fixed, stable, or dead categories used to capture reality. The ideal of such philosophical methods is "some state of perfection," which, as we saw earlier, was disavowed in Schlegel's emphasis on infinite becoming. As we have seen, the romantic ideal, romantic poetry, is a poetry that is progressive because it is always in a state of becoming, never reaching completion. Romantic philosophy is inherently incomplete, and Schlegel does not attempt to use final causes (or any sort of teleological method) to put a cap on the organic forces of life. And, as we have seen, Schlegel's break from teleological closure for his system does lead him to embrace a kind of relativism—he claims in his *Lectures on Transcendental Philosophy* that "all truth is relative." Yet, as discussed in chapter 1, he immediately saw the problem with this claim, adding that, "if all truth is relative, then the claim that all truth is relative is also relative. But when everything is properly understood, then one can concede this point too."

The pressing challenge in light of these claims is, What needs to be properly understood in order to save Schlegel's claim regarding the relativity of truth from collapsing into a self-refuting claim? We can take the Absolute as the whole to which each part is related, and as I have already discussed, that whole (the Absolute) is a nonrelative orientation point if ever there were one, so there is an important sense in which the relativity of individual truths is nonrelative in relation to the Absolute or the whole of truths. As we put claims together to build the whole, as we see how they fit together, there is a degree of uncertainty. Any given claim fits relative to another piece of the puzzle, and we may change our claims as our view of the puzzle becomes clearer. But to endorse uncertainty is not to endorse indeterminancy. Schlegel endorses uncertainty, because the Absolute (that which is without limits) will never be grasped by finite human knowers (limited beings). Yet the Absolute is an orientation point in our search for knowledge, so no helpless relativism lurks on Schlegel's philosophical horizon.[45]

Schlegel's romantic philosophy is antifoundationalist, and an understanding of the implications of his particular breed of antifoundationalism enables us to appreciate a major contribution that Schlegel made to philosophy: his model of philosophy did not sacrifice living, changing reality to fixed, teleological categories, all in the name of systematic unity, but rather left the system open, incorporating change and flux into the very frame of philosophy itself. There is no concept of an ahistorical, fixed totality operative in Schlegel's "romantic" conception of philosophy. Romantic philosophy is not guilty of what Wilhelm von Humboldt accuses most philosophy of, that is, an inability to locate the goal of events in living things, fixated, as most philosophers are, by the concept of an ideal totality, which leads away from living things and toward dead institutions.[46]

Romantic philosophy does not rest on firm foundations from which it spins a deductive web of certainty. In place of a closed, grand deductive system that would provide the first and last word on the foundations of knowledge, the romantic conception of philosophy breaks with the view that philosophy must rest upon any foundation at all. In this conception of philosophy, there is no attempt to keep uncertainty out of the picture, but rather a humble acceptance of the provisional nature of all of our claims to knowledge. As I have emphasized several times throughout this book, antifoundationalists need not abandon a conception of objective truth: romantic skepticism about foundations led to reflections about our epistemological limitations, but *not* to any rejection of objectivity or truth. Admitting epistemological limitations need not lead us down the path of denying the existence of a mind-independent reality. Schlegel, with his emphasis on the critical roles that history and poetry have to play in educating humanity, did not shirk from critique, inquiry or deliberation (as the relativist, with his easy "anything goes" attitude, often does).

I have already discussed some of the criticisms that Schlegel presented of idealism, and in chapter 1, I argue that in order to better understand the contributions of the early German Romantics, we would do well to more sharply distinguish their philosophy from that of their German Idealist contemporaries. Yes, Schlegel did not reject idealism altogether, and a certain strand of idealism shapes his view of how we come to understand the world. After all, he does want to use Fichte's idealism to construct a view of reality, but Fichte's idealism will yield only a *partial* view of reality. Idealism must be combined with realism. Fichte and Spinoza must be brought together.

Schlegel does claim that idealism is the only type of philosophy that is true philosophy, that is, it is the only type of philosophy that is capable of freeing us from the tyranny of the thing.[47] This, according to Schlegel, is due to the fact that idealism begins with the I as infinite consciousness and develops a view according to which facts in the world are partially dependent upon this consciousness. This perspective enables philosophy to fulfill its task of "freeing us from the illusion of the finite and the belief in things and bring us to share a view of infinite plenitude (*unendliche Fülle*) and manifoldness."[48] This is accomplished when reality is seen as the product of an exchange (or what Schlegel calls "dialogue") between consciousness (I) and the world (not of things, but of dialogue partners). This exchange is yet another manifestation of the *Wechselerweis*, that method of mutual confirmation that enables us to bring claims together in a coherent way and approximate truth. Earlier in the Köln lectures, Schlegel writes that philosophy is "knowledge of the inner human, of the causes of nature, the relations of humans to nature and their connections with it; or when there is not yet a truly complete philosophy at hand, then a striving towards this knowledge."[49] The "inner human" is consciousness, and it is through an understanding of its structure we come to have any knowledge of the world at all, and insofar as idealism gives us a way to understand subjectivity, it provides a useful set of tools in our search for truth. Yet we fall into error if we think that our search for truth will be well served by recourse *only* to idealism, that is, if we restrict ourselves only to consciousness, only one of the two poles that frame reality. Schlegel acknowledges that in order to understand reality, we must posit a separation between consciousness and objects of consciousness, so while he does endorse idealism as part of the solution to the problem of understanding the world, he endorses it only in partnership with realism.

Schlegel has established that our belief in external things must, at best, be doubted. (In several places, he makes a stronger claim that we would do better to dispense with it altogether, rather too boldly claiming, "Ontology is nothing—there are no general, undetermined things.")[50] Schlegel's treatment of consciousness is a further critique of the thing paradigm and an explanation of why, given the structure of consciousness, we so easily fall into it. Schlegel claims that we can understand the thing as the source of error in philosophy only after we trace its roots back to the theory of consciousness from which it emerges.[51]

Despite Schlegel's criticisms of both Fichte and Kant's deductions of the I, he does endorse a view of philosophy whereby the I plays a crucial role, even claiming that the I thinking itself, or self-consciousness, is the starting point of all philosophy.[52] Yet he also claims that his philosophy does not begin like the others with one principle but with a living seed. How can we reconcile this metaphor with his statement that self-consciousness is the most secure beginning point of philosophy?

To answer this we must look carefully at his account of the structure of consciousness. Sense, reason, and will condition consciousness.[53] The process by which we come to have objects of consciousness at all is a function of intuiting, thinking, and willing. We are conscious of entities outside of us, objects, and ideas within us. Knowledge of objects outside of us presupposes knowledge of the inner objects of consciousness, the consciousness of ourselves as thinking beings; without this, there could be no knowledge of objects at all. If we take "a" to be an object of consciousness, then we must have an I to perceive or intuit this; reason, or an ability to reflect upon it; and will, or the ability to set limits to the reflection and focus attention on one object. "A" must be perceived by the I but also distinguished from it. This is where the thing enters. In order to distinguish the object of consciousness from the thinking subject, the object of consciousness is conceived as if it were enduring and static, for otherwise the manifold of sense impressions could never be ordered to produce clarity. Schlegel does not question the use of the concept thing here, but he does question its status. That we must posit the object of consciousness as something outside of us as enduring and static is justified, but that we assume that this is more than an impression, an appearance, is unjustified. When we perceive an object, in order to form a judgment about it, we freeze it, isolate it from its place in the whole, and treat it as a lone individual and whole in itself in other words, we make it a thing, but this is an illusion and cannot be the source of knowledge.

The inner life of the object is the source of knowledge.[54] Each object has an inner life because no object is a lifeless thing, but rather a dialogue partner and as such, part of the same organic whole of which the I is also a part. Schlegel's account of consciousness, coupled with his critique of the thing paradigm leads him to conclude that there are no objects distinct from subjects but rather that something common joins them. So when he claims that self-consciousness is the most secure beginning point of philosophy, he is complementing the metaphor in which he describes the beginning of his philosophy as being a small but living seed. For Schlegel, self-consciousness is consciousness of an I, which is not a solitary cogito or *Ich*, but rather part of an organic unity, part of something greater.

According to Schlegel's holism, the structure of consciousness is dynamic, and the objects of consciousness are not things, but dialogue partners. The thing paradigm creates a view of reality in which isolated subjects subsume finite, isolated objects under general rules generated by the subject's mind, in order to form judgments and to find truth.[55] Schlegel wants to abandon this paradigm for a more dynamic, vitalistic one, looking at knowledge as the result of a historical process.

> If upon reflection we cannot deny that everything is within us, then we are left with no other explanation for the feeling of limitation which always accompanies us in life than the assumption

that we are only a part of ourselves. This leads directly to a belief in a You, not as (as in life) something opposed to the I, or similar (human against human, not animal, rock against humans), but rather as a counter-I, and herewith is bound necessarily the belief in an Original-I. This Original-I is the concept which ultimately grounds philosophy. At this point, all radii of philosophy join. Our I, philosophically considered, contains within it a relation to an Original-I and a Counter-I, this is at once a You, Him, Us.[56]

This Original-I can be understood as the whole of which each individual I is only a part. This enables Schlegel to claim that each thing is related to every other thing and that the only way to understand anything of the world is through the whole of which each thing is a part. In slightly different form, we find yet another critique of Fichte's deductive method. The I is only one part of what forms the essence of philosophy. More important is the whole that transcends any particular I, and indeed, without which each individual I would be without meaning. Reality does not consist of a mass of Non-I, thing-like entities deduced from the I. The entire methodological apparatus of deduction or ahistorical, systematic derivation is replaced by a vitalistic one, and it is only against this background that Schlegel's *Wechselerweis* makes any sense at all. "From this follows too, how the external things are to be viewed in philosophy. They are not to be seen as Non-I external to the I; not merely dead, flat, empty sensible re-appearances of the I which are limited by the I in an ungraspable way, but rather, as stated, as a living, powerful, Counter-I, a You."[57] This is the living seed to which Schlegel refers in his florid description of philosophy's beginning point. The I cannot be posited absolutely, or it would become a thing. Fichte posits the I absolutely and hence commits this error. Nor can the I, Schlegel goes on to claim, be presupposed for that would be against his genetic method. The I must be found. And as the I is only part of a greater whole, the way to find it is through a historical search.[58] The search for the I involves language and community, and Schlegel ends his lectures with reference to the power that language and art have to free us from the isolation and silence of things.[59]

Wilhelm Meister: Schlegel's Model of Coherence

Schlegel's suggestion that art has the power to free us from the isolation and silence of things was not merely an empty gesture toward art. He actually applied his theory to art as both critic and artist.[60] Nowhere does his talent as a critic shine brighter than his essay on Goethe's *Wilhelm Meister*, an interpretative performance of the first rank.[61] Schlegel looked upon Goethe as an idol of sorts, an esteem not fully reciprocated by the great poet of Weimar. For though Goethe was impressed by certain aspects of Schlegel's fragments,[62] he described Romanticism in harsh terms in general (calling it a "kind of sickness"). Yet there is no doubt that Goethe shaped the entire early German Romantic generation. Schlegel was captivated, in particular, by Goethe's novel, *Wilhelm Meisters Lehrjahre*; it represented for Schlegel the paragon of what art could accomplish, immortalized, in the company of the French Revolution and Fichte's *Wissenschaftslehre*, as a tendency of the age. While Schlegel could only be partially supportive of the French Revolution (which collapsed all too soon into the Reign of Terror) and Fichte's *Wissenschaftslehre* (which had undesirable dogmatic, mystical aspects), he saw in Goethe's *Meister* a universal *Mischgattung*, a romantic model of what art could and should achieve.[63]

In what follows, I will not be interested in arguing for the virtues of Schlegel's reading of *Wilhelm Meister* as a contribution to Goethe scholarship because I am more concerned with what the piece has to tell us about Schlegel's view of knowledge than what it might be able to tell us about Goethe's work. Those who are interested in how Goethe fares under Schlegel's lens have found the essay wanting. For example, it has been characterized by Arnd Bohn as an "unexcelled rhapsody of misreading,"[64] a characterization that would have amused Schlegel for its harmony with the frequent charges of the utter incomprehensibility of his writings. Bohn claims that Schlegel was "[d]riven by the punning conviction that the novel, for which German uses the word 'Roman' is paradigmatic for a *romantic* era" and that "Schlegel sees Wilhelm's essence in 'Streben, Wollen und Empfinden' (striving, wanting, and feeling) and the world of the novel as a fantastic realm." Bohn further stresses that the ultimate organic unity of both the main character, Wilhelm, and of the succeeding sections of the book "overrides any awareness of incompleteness or gaps."[65] For Bohn, Schlegel, "[o]verwhelmed by the desire to make of *Wilhelm Meister* the work of art whose completion would attest to the triumph of a new poetic sensibility, of Romanticism, . . . missed the basic arguments Goethe was making."[66]

For my purposes, it is not really all that important whether or not Schlegel's reading of *Wilhelm Meister* was a rhapsodic misreading (which I do not think it to be). Yet, I do want to linger for a moment on what I take to be two major problems of Bohn's reading of Schlegel. First, it is misleading to claim that Schlegel somehow located the "romantic" in *Wilhelm Meister* because he read it as an innovative novel or "Roman." Furthermore, there is a problem with Bohn's claim that Schlegel stressed that the unity of *Wilhelm Meister* and of the succeeding sections "overrides" any awareness of incompleteness or gaps. What Schlegel stresses in his essay on *Wilhelm Meister* is the *Zusammenhang* present in the work, the coherence, which is a kind of unity, that comes precisely by taking the parts and piecing them together so that some sort of coherent whole is produced. The coherent whole obtained through piecing the parts together is a kind of organic unity, but there is no suggestion in anything that Schlegel claims that the incompleteness or gaps need to be overridden. And, as I shall argue, what Schlegel found romantic in Goethe's novel was not any punning conviction centered around the German word *Roman* but rather a conviction that the episodic form of the novel and the emphasis on coherence (*Zusammenhang*) led the reader of Goethe's novel to reflect more deeply on the ways in which we strive for the infinite and how we put together pieces of a puzzle to construct the whole of which we are but a part. In short, *Wilhelm Meister* is just the sort of art that Schlegel has in mind when he claims that art can help us destroy the illusion of the finite or free us from the silence of things, opening us to a world of living dialogue.

If we follow Bohm's reading, however, we lose sight of the valuable insights Schlegel's essay offers regarding what Schlegel's romantic project was all about, namely how the epistemological commitments born of Schlegel's antifoundationalism are reflected in his assessments of art. In *Über Goethes Meister* we find a brilliant merging of epistemology and aesthetics, and we see what Schlegel is after in his call to unite poetry and philosophy and why his calls were often given in fragments.

In Critical Fragment 120, Schlegel tells us, "Whoever could manage to interpret Goethe's *Meister* properly would have expressed what is now happening in literature. He could, so far as literary criticism is concerned, retire forever."[67] Early in the *Meister* essay, Schlegel tells us that in *Wilhelm Meister*, "art will become science, and life an art."[68] Given that the theme of the unity of poetry, philosophy, and science shapes so much of Schlegel's work, if *Wilhelm Meister* is indeed a novel in which such unity is achieved, we begin to see why Schlegel would identify it as a tendency of the age and further claim that an understanding of the work would reveal everything that was happening in literature. There is an important sense in which Schlegel's *Über Goethes Meister* provides us with an answer to a question posed in *Athenäum* Fragment 168, namely, "what philosophy is fittest for the poet?"[69] Schlegel begins to answer the question in the same fragment where it is raised:

> Certainly no system at variance with one's feelings or common sense; or one that transforms the real into the illusory; or abstains from all decisions; or inhibits a leap into the suprasensory regions; or achieves humanity only by adding up the externals.

This excludes eudemonism, fatalism, idealism, skepticism, materialism, or empiricism. Then what philosophy is left for the poet? The creative philosophy that originates in freedom and belief in freedom, and shows how the human spirit impresses its law on all things and how the world is its work of art.

The creative philosophy sketched in the fragment is precisely the sort of system Schlegel finds in Goethe's novel, and it is a mirror of what he thought philosophy should be: the philosophy that is "fittest for the poet" is precisely that philosophy which is all about how things fit together, namely, the antifoundationalist philosophy structured around the *Wechselerweis*.

Goethe of course never mentions a *Wechselerweis* in his novel, so where is the connection that Schlegel sees between his philosophy and Goethe's novel? Throughout the essay, Schlegel stresses the episodic character of the novel. Goethe does not tell the tale of Wilhelm's development via a linear narrative but rather via sketches of scenes, which Schlegel describes like acts of a play, all of which can be combined to form a whole. Speaking of the first book, Schlegel writes: "Introductory to the whole work, the first book is a series of varied situations and picturesque contrasts, each casting a new and brighter light on Wilhelm's character from a different, noteworthy perspective; and each of the smaller, clearly distinct chapters and blocks of narrative forms in itself more or less a picturesque whole [*malerisches Ganzes*]."[70] Schlegel emphasizes that a sense for the whole (*Sinn für das Weltall*) is critical when reading the novel, for it is a work that demands an active piecing together of the parts in order for the meaning to emerge. It is important to note that Schlegel stresses that each part of the whole is a whole in itself, so he does not hold the view that parts *only* have meaning in virtue of the whole of which they are parts. A virtue of the novel is the sense for the whole that is developed in the reader as she is exposed to the various episodes and constructs them into a coherent story of Wilhelm's *Bildung*. This is a process with both passive and active elements:

> It is a beautiful and indeed necessary experience when reading a poetic work to give ourselves up entirely to its influence, to let the writer do with us what he will; perhaps only in matters of detail is it necessary to pause and confirm our emotional response with a moment's reflection, raise it into a thought, and where there is room for doubt or dispute, decide and amplify the matter. This is the prime, the most essential response. But it is no less necessary to be able to abstract from all the details, to grasp the general meaning in its hovering [*das Allgemeine schwebend*

zu fassen], survey the extent, and take hold of the whole, investigate even the most hidden parts and to connect that which is most remote.[71]

The process of understanding the details offered by the writer is essential. A first step as it were in coming to an understanding of the piece is that we attempt to understand what the author is saying to us. We "let the writer do with us what he will." But with this openness to be guided by the author, our work is not finished. There is the matter of "abstract[ing] from all the details" or "grasp[ing] the general meaning in its hovering" of "taking hold of the whole" and "connect[ing]" the parts to make new connections. This process is not limited to the activity of reading and understanding a novel; it could very well describe what the natural scientist does in understanding the book of nature. First the eye must be on the details, the shape of the leaf being studied, its color, the pattern of its growth. Then in order to talk about the general morphology of the leaf, a process of abstraction needs to take place, where the grasp of the general meaning, the taking hold of the whole, and connecting of the particular observations to others so that new insights can be achieved. Schlegel, in fact, makes an explicit connection between understanding a work of art and understanding nature, asking, "Why should we not both breathe in the perfume of a flower and at the same time, entirely absorbed in the observation, contemplate in its infinite ramifications the vein-system of a single leaf?"[72] Whether his example is our understanding of literature or of nature, Schlegel's ultimate concerns are of an epistemological bent: he wants to understand how knowledge is acquired, and he finds in Goethe's novel a model for the coherence model of knowledge that he endorses. Goethe's *Meister* leads the attentive reader to a reflection of how we piece our beliefs together to form systems of knowledge. Goethe is the sort of writer Schlegel has in mind when he claims that; "[t]he synthetic writer constructs and creates a reader as he should be; he doesn't imagine him calm and dead, but alive and critical. He allows whatever he has created to take shape gradually before the reader's eyes, or else he tempts him to discover it himself. He doesn't try to make any particular impression on him, but enters with him into the sacred relationship of deepest symphilosophy or sympoetry."[73]

The synthetic writer is contrasted to the analytic writer, who "observes the reader as he is; and accordingly he makes his calculations and sets up his machines in order to make the proper impression on him,"[74] delivering a monologue that does not give rise to the symphilosophy stressed by Schlegel. As we shall see, the synthetic writer, needing as he does a certain level of cooperation from the reader, runs risks that the analytic writer need not face, and there is a greater margin for error in the form of misunderstanding or simple inertia on the part of the reader, who needs to be more than merely a receiver of ideas, who needs to become an active dialogue partner.

As Goethe's novel is not delivered in a standard, orderly way, with a clearly structured narrative, in order to appreciate the novel, Schlegel tells us, one must have a "true instinct" for system:

> Our usual expectations of unity and coherence [*die gewöhnliche Erwartung von Einheit und Zusammenhang*] are disappointed by this novel as often as they are fulfilled. But the reader who possesses a true instinct for system, who has a sense of totality or that anticipation of the world in its entirety which makes Wilhelm so interesting, will be aware throughout the work of what we call its personality and living individuality [*lebendiger Individualität des Werks*]. And the more deeply he probes, the more inner connections and relations and the greater intellectual coherence [*geistigen Zusammenhang*] he will discover in it.[75]

This description of the hermeneutical obstacles facing the reader of Goethe's novel could very well be a description of the task facing the reader of Schlegel's fragments. As he tells us, since Goethe's novel is "absolutely new and unique," we can "learn to understand it only on its own terms."[76] Likewise, the reader who wants to understand Schlegel's philosophical system must be prepared to engage with his texts in a far different way than the reader of Kant's *Critique of Pure Reason* and other canonical texts, for what Schlegel is up to is also "absolutely new and unique," not only at the level of content but also of literary form.

There are no transcendental deductions in Schlegel's system, no architectonic that can be charted and graphed. The reader must weave the parts together and be prepared to be disappointed with the lack of unity as often as she is pleased by the steps in the direction of the wished for unity. In Schlegel's conception of a philosophical system, change and interaction are stressed, and organic coherence is the goal. Recall that Schlegel defines system in terms of coherence and unity: "System is an integrated, connected whole of the matter of knowledge [*wissenschaftliche Stoff*] in a continuous mutual confirmation and organic coherence—a whole of a plurality that is in itself perfected and unified."[77] Organic coherence is a goal that no systematic derivation will achieve for us, and no single system either. The philosopher must work from a single system, that is, from one link in the chain of all systems, but always with a view toward the unity of which each system is but a part of the greater whole, for "even a perfect system can only be a mere approximation."[78] And "[t]he idea of philosophy can only be reached through an infinite progression."[79] The importance of recognizing that one works from within a given system but that any given system is always also part of a whole comprised of other systems is also stressed in a fragment that I have already analyzed within the context of Schlegel's critique of Fichte: "Every philosopher has his own line or tendency which is his departing point and his cycle. He who has a system is as lost as he who has none. One must therefore reconcile both."[80] As discussed in chapter 3, the dilemma that Schlegel points to in this fragment is the tension between (1) the need to set limits in order to achieve the coherence and unity necessary to establish systems of knowledge and (2) the recognition that all systems will have an element of the arbitrary imposition of limits on our search for knowledge. Schlegel emphasizes the importance of balancing the tension between limitation and unity with the whole in *Ideen* Fragment 48 when he writes that "[e]very thinking part of an organization should not feel its limits without at the same time feeling its unity in relation to the whole."[81] In *Ideen* Fragment 55, he remarks, "Versatility consists not just in a comprehensive system but also in a feeling for the chaos outside that system, like man's feeling for something beyond man."[82] Having a system provides us with the feeling of limits, and within limits there is order, yet the move beyond limits, a product of a feeling for chaos born of the state of being outside (or without) a system, propels us beyond any particular system in search of the whole, to which our instinct for system will lead us.

As I have emphasized throughout this book, Schlegel's antifoundationalism leads him to see philosophy as consisting of a plurality of systems, each of which can offer a piece of the whole of the system of knowledge but never the complete system. Schlegel rejects a foundationalist approach to the problem of knowledge and emphasizes the importance of coherence: we never have the last word on how to justify a claim, but we must try to bring our claims into some coherent scheme or whole. Our epistemological predicament is presented in the very form of Goethe's novel: "The differing nature of the individual sections [*Massen*] should be able to throw a great deal of light on the organization of the whole. But in progressing appropriately from the parts to the whole, observation and analysis must not get lost in over-minute detail . . . The development within the individual sections ensures the overall coherence, and in pulling them together, the poet confirms their variety. And in this way each essential part of the single and indivisible novel becomes a system in itself."[83] Variety without unity is chaos, and knowledge is the result of placing limits on our cognitive activity so is part of a tendency toward order and away from chaos, but complete order will never be obtained, so we will never leave chaos completely behind either.[84]

Philosophy cannot *be* a science; it is only ever in the process of becoming a science. And it is not in the process of becoming a deductive science, in which truth can be derived absolutely, but something more like the art of constructing coherent schemes from our collection of beliefs. Recall the claim made in *Athenäum* Fragment 216: from Schlegel's perspective, Fichte's philosophy is only a *tendency*, a single contribution to the problem of how we come to have knowledge of the world, but it is only a push (albeit a revolutionary one) in the right direction. There is an important sense in which what Schlegel admired in Goethe's *Meister* was just as important to the development of his own philosophy as Fichte's *Wissenschaftslehre*. In Goethe's *Wilhelm Meister*, Schlegel found precisely the balance between the feeling of limits and that which is without limits, the unity born of the relation of the parts to the whole that is for him central to the structure of our knowledge.

One way for the reader to accomplish the construction of the whole that is so important to Schlegel is by getting to the inner life of all things, which echoes the points discussed earlier concerning the importance of life for Schlegel. Goethe's novel, on Schlegel's reading, brings us closer to life and shatters the illusion of the finite: "The whole man who feels and thinks in universal terms is interested not only in the brilliant outward covering, the bright garment of this beautiful earth; he also likes to investigate the layering and the composition of the strata far within it; he would wish to delve deeper and deeper, even to the very centre, if possible, and would want to know the construction of the whole."[85] Throughout his essay on *Meister*, Schlegel speaks often of the *geistige Zusammenhang* (intellectual coherence) the work offers. Schlegel was wary of the one-sidedness (*Einseitigkeit*) of most systems and praised the dialogue form for the chorus of positions it could attain, describing the dialogue in *Athenäum* Fragment 77 as "a chain or garland of fragments,"[86] reminding us in one of his fragments on literature and poetry that "Each system only *grows* out of fragments."[87] Within philosophy, Schlegel could not find a system that grew out of fragments, one that avoided the one-sidedness that plagued most systems that were deduced mechanically from first principles. Most philosophical systems were isolated works, generated ex nihilo, and given that Schlegel believed that "every thinking part of an organization should not feel its limits without at the same time feeling its unity in relation to the whole," once philosophers become aware of the limits of their own system, they will see that "where philosophy stops, poetry has to begin."[88] It must be noted once again that romantic poetry does not denote a collection of literary forms, a historical period, or any particular set of textual characteristics at all. It is an aesthetic ideal that sheds light on our finitude and the finitude of all human creations. The limits of philosophy give rise to a perspective on this ideal, for coming up against those limits shifts our view from any particular system to the whole of which each system is just a part. It is perhaps then not surprising that Schlegel found the system that balanced having and not having a system, the system that did not trap us in the illusion of the finite or suffer from the pretense of offering us final words, not in any philosopher's system, but rather in the system Goethe presented in his novel, "Both the larger and smaller masses reveal the inate impulse of this work, so organized and organizing down to its finest detail to form a whole. No break is coincidental or without meaning; and in this novel, where everything is at the same time both means and end, it would not be wrong to regard the first part, irrespective of its relationship to the whole, as a novel in itself."[89] While Schlegel is not speaking directly of fragments in this description of the organization of Goethe's novel and how the parts are organized to construct a whole, his emphasis on the fact that individual parts can also be seen as wholes in themselves helps shed light on what he means when in *Athenäum* Fragment 206 he claims, "A fragment, like a miniature work of art, has to be entirely isolated from the surrounding world and complete in itself like a hedgehog [*Igel*]."[90] Fragments are parts of a whole; parts that have independent value or meaning but that nonetheless should be read in connection with the whole of which they are a part.[91]

Schlegel emphasizes that our standards for judging poetry are going to have to change if we wish to be fair to Goethe's innovative novel, for "to judge it according to an idea of genre drawn from custom and belief, accidental experiences and arbitrary demands, is as if a child tried to clutch the stars and the moon in his hand and pack them in his satchel."[92] For Schlegel, it would be an aesthetic crime to limit something as celestial as *Meister* to conventional genres. Schlegel, too, challenged conventional genres and indeed conventional approaches to the very discipline of philosophy, seriously questioning the tidy, traditional compartmentalizations that kept philosophy, arts, and science separate (and not at all equal).[93] Schlegel's move to bring these areas of human experience into contact with one another has too often been read to be part of an antirational, mythical, cult-like movement, a reading that, one might say, places the moon and stars in the darkness of the satchel, missing the enlightening, modern, and very rational implications of Schlegel's philosophical project.[94] Taking art more seriously did not make Schlegel less philosophical. Indeed his esteem of art gave rise to some of his most valuable philosophical contributions, which becomes clear when we look at the aesthetic consequences of his thought.

Chapter Seven

The Aesthetic Consequences of Antifoundationalism

I am not alone in finding a rich line of investigation in tracing the aesthetic consequences of Schlegel's thought. In *The Romantic Imperative*, Beiser claims that "Schlegel's romanticism grew out of his *critique* of Fichte's foundationalism.... In a nutshell, Schlegel's romanticism was the aesthetics of anti-foundationalism."[1] The story of Schlegel's antifoundationalism that I have been telling in the chapters of this book coheres well with Beiser's claim, though in my story figures such as Jacobi, Reinhold, Niethammer, and Kant join Fichte as important sources for the development of Schlegel's romantic position, which emerges not only in Schlegel's critique of the foundationalism of Reinhold and Fichte but also in his critique of the historical short-sightedness of Kant, the leap of faith embraced by Jacobi, and the appeal to common sense made by Niethammer. Beiser's talk of "the aesthetics of anti-foundationalism" is important, for it opens up a host of topics that enable some of Schlegel's most original and relevant philosophical contributions to come into focus. In exploring the aesthetic consequences of Schlegel's thought, I hope to show that the connection he makes between philosophy and romantic poetry was a modern, original contribution from which we still have much to learn.

Unfortunately, while the aesthetic dimension of Schlegel's thought makes it relevant to contemporary thinkers, from its inception, precisely that dimension has prevented his thought from receiving the attention that it deserves from philosophers. Schlegel was after a way to unify knowledge, to bring science, poetry, and philosophy into closer contact with one another in a move to help each area develop more fully. Yet far from being seriously considered, Schlegel's romantic thought has been viewed with suspicion by philosophers, who see in his calls nothing more than a disorderly collection of dilettantish outbursts against the revered figures of his day, rants aimed at unsettling the orthodox method of doing philosophy. Yet behind Schlegel's unorthodox methods there was no destructive spirit lurking; Schlegel's rebellious acts were part of a productive move to advance knowledge and to reform philosophy. Certainly he broke with what has been described by some as the deferential attitude that characterizes German philosophy.[2] If German philosophy is to be characterized as deferential in spirit, then Schlegel's impudent stance toward the views and methods of his contemporaries might be conspicuously un-Germanic, but his approach cannot thereby be deemed unphilosophical. Let us now look at the philosophical depth of Schlegel's playful, witty aesthetics of antifoundationalism.

The Modern Spirit of Romanticism

Schlegel's reaction to the Jacobi-Mendelssohn debate put him squarely on the side of reason and of the project of modernity pursued by the members of the German Enlightenment. Nonetheless, the romantic side of modernism is all too often rejected as an irrational move toward placing poetry *instead* of philosophy at the center of culture,[3] yet there is no good reason to accept the false dichotomy according to which if one embraces poetry, then one must bid farewell to philosophy. Not only can poetry and philosophy coexist peacefully, but they can also, or so argued the Romantics, mutually enhance one another.

Andrew Bowie has articulated a strong defense of the critical potential of early German Romanticism, a potential that exists not despite, but precisely *due to* the Romantics' engagement with the poetic power of language, literature, and art.[4] He defends the Romantics from "Habermas' suspicions that Romantic ideas may either rely on pre-Kantian dogmatism or involve 'an abdication of problem-solving philosophical thinking before the poetic power of language, literature, and art.'[5]"[6] For Habermas, the turn to aesthetics is a turn away from "the language of public argument," yet as Bowie indicates, Habermas overlooks the "role of those forms of world-disclosure which *are* important because of their resistance to being converted into discursivity or into scientifically verifiable theories."[7]

In a move that reveals Habermas' concerns about the turn to art to be alarmist, Bowie shows that Schlegel's interest in poetry and mythology was not the result of a desire to take a "mystical flight from the pressures of modernity."[8] As discussed in the introduction, it is the case that at the beginning of his philosophical writing, Schlegel expressed skepticism for what modern culture, especially aesthetics, had to offer. At the early stages of Schlegel's thought, modern or romantic poetry was opposed to classical poetry. It was subjective and artificial (*künstlich*), whereas classical poetry was objective and natural. In his classical phase, Schlegel viewed the limitlessness of modern poetry as negative, but he soon reversed that negative judgment and embraced the progressive spirit of modern poetry.

As we have seen, in *Athenäum* Fragment 116 Schlegel claims that "romantic poetry is a progressive, universal poetry"[9]—romantic poetry is an ideal, a poetry that is progressive because it is always in a state of becoming, never reaching completion. This view of the inherent incompleteness of poetry holds, as Schlegel's reactions to the thought of Fichte clearly demonstrates, for our knowledge claims as well: we do not build knowledge deductively from absolute foundations, but place our claims together in a coherent scheme, so absolute certainty is not an appropriate epistemological goal. Greater and greater degrees of certainty are the most for which we can hope.

A philosophy that will never be "completed," a philosophy that is always in a state of becoming, should not just develop blindly, with no critical perspective to guide it. Schlegel was not content to let the Enlightenment project proceed uncritically. In fact, well before Theodor Adorno and Max Horkheimer published their *Dialektik der Aufklärung* (published in the form favored by Schlegel, that is, in "philosophical fragments"), which was an ambitious project to make the Enlightenment reflexive, that is "to carry out its project on its own products, i.e., its own theories,"[10] Schlegel had already announced the need for a critical look at the Enlightenment itself. Because of this, that it is no overstatement to claim, as Ernst Behler does, that "Schlegel [is the] best representative for the self-reflective modernism of German romanticism.[11] Klaus Peter has also argued in support of the modern spirit of Schlegel's thought, connecting it to the philosophical project of Horkheimer and Adorno: "[A]lready with the Romantics we find a model which the *Dialectic of the Enlightenment* attempted to present, namely the two sides of reason; its profit and its prices. Here we find the contemporary relevance of Friedrich Schlegel and early Romanticism."[12] Peter presents Schlegel's critique of modernity in terms of his critique of modern poetry, which is in a state of crisis.[13] The crisis diagnosed by Schlegel can, he claims, be overcome with the creation of a "new mythology," which is no return to a dark, primitive period but rather part of the very progressive spirit of romantic thought.

Scholars of Romanticism have pointed to chaos as "one of the central concepts in Romantic thought" and have used it to explain everything from Schlegel's use of fragments to his appeal to mythology. For example, according to Karl Menges, "The term [*chaos*] is ever present, explicitly and by implication, advancing an aesthetic paradigm that harks back to the origins of mankind in an attempt to recapture and restore the vitality of an early, mythological age. To the extent that such beginnings are linked with chaos, it is important to note that they are completely free of any negative connotations associated with the conventional etymology of the word."[14] There is much textual evidence that speaks in favor of the emphasis on chaos in our understanding of Schlegel's turn to mythology, but I think that there is a side of Schlegel's engagement with mythology that is overlooked if we put too much focus on its moorings in the concept of 'chaos.' On my reading of Schlegel's philosophical project, his interest in mythology is part of his concern with *Bildung*, in particular with his goal of finding some sort of new center or unifying tradition for a society torn asunder by a variety of disruptive factors. Cohesiveness, on my reading, is more important than the concept of chaos in coming to an understanding of Schlegel's aesthetic project and his project of establishing a new mythology. As Susan Haack has observed, "cohesive" is to social groups as "consistent" is to beliefs, that is, "unlike 'consistent,' 'cohesive' is often used of social groups, such as a tribe or a society or church whose members are united by shared beliefs, attitudes, and goals."[15] True to his concern with coherence, whether it be of our knowledge claims or of the form of the novels that he claims were most characteristically "romantic," even at the level of society, Schlegel was after a way of bringing parts together to form a unified whole. And in his search for greater social cohesion, he was drawn not only to mythology but also to democracy, underscoring that the turn to mythology is not a turn away from the progressive spirit of his age and that democracy did not, as Kant had argued, amount to anarchy.[16]

A turn to mythology as a way of bringing society together was not unique to Schlegel. Indeed, next to Schlegel's famous *Athenäum* Fragment 116, another very enigmatic text, the so-called, "Oldest Programme for a System of German Idealism" (1796) is often appealed to as kind of manifesto of the early German Romantic movement, although not one of the contributors to *Das Athenäum* is a candidate for its authorship.[17] The text was published anonymously in Hegel's handwriting, but its authorship continues to be a matter of debate, with Hegel, Hölderlin, and Schelling each in contention for authorship. Given that the text swings from the use of "I" to "we," some scholars suggest it was jointly authored. The "Programme" was discovered by Franz Rosenzweig in 1917, who gave the short piece its rather misleading title. There is indeed a programmatic sketch given for something, but not for something as systematic as German Idealism *tout court*. What brims from the imperatives articulated in its lines is the revolutionary spirit that shaped the young thinkers who hoped to transform their society and unify the disparate social groups found with it. The program announced in the text is one for a new mythology, one that will unify society by presenting a set of symbols that will communicate to all members of society and help to create a new center and help develop social cohesiveness, a sense of unity.

As Bubner has recently pointed out, this short text has been analyzed so exhaustively that we can compare the literature on it to a forensic report. I will not repeat those findings here, or track all of the fascinating paths that are to be found in the short but highly suggestive text. My interest lies in the call for the development of social cohesiveness that the author(s) locate in the aesthetic realm:

> Until we make ideas aesthetic, that is, mythological, they are of no interest to the *people*, and vice versa: until mythology is rational, it will be an embarrassment to philosophy. Thus those who are enlightened and those who are not must finally make common cause, mythology must become philosophical, to make the people rational, and philosophy must become mythological, to make philosophy sensuous. Then eternal unity will reign among us. Never again the arrogant glance, never again the blind shuddering of the people, before its wise men and priests. Only then will *equal* development of *all* of our powers await us, for the particular person as well as for all individuals.[18]

The project of establishing social unity is described as the "greatest task of humanity," and it will be carried out by an aesthetic revolution of sorts. The idea of beauty taken in the "higher Platonic sense" is that which will unify all, which is why the "philosopher must possess as much aesthetic power as the poet." The mythologization of philosophy and the philosophization of mythology make no assault on reason and are not a departure from the goals of the Enlightenment but rather attempts to enlighten the Enlightenment, to bring society together into a coherent whole. Menges, with his concern for the role of chaos, reads the text as heralding a "radically anarchistic, chaos-inspired critique of the state."[19] I disagree with this diagnosis of the text. On my reading, the call for a new mythology is more like an aesthetically inspired critique of the state, which seeks through the establishment of a new mythology to establish a new sense of harmony, of social cohesiveness.

Like the author of the "Programme for a System of German Idealism," Schlegel sees his society as one that is decaying, breaking apart. Schlegel (with the voice of Ludovico), opens his *Talk on the New Mythology* with the following lament: "I call on you my friends, to ask yourselves, with the same earnestness with which you revere art: Shall the power of enthusiasm continue to be splintered [*versplittert*] even [*auch*] in poetry, and finally fall silent alone, when it has fought itself weary against the hostile enemies? Shall the highest and the holiest remain forever nameless and formless?"[20] Without social cohesiveness, art will indeed fall victim to "namelessness and formlessness," in a word, to chaos, for there will be no tradition available to provide a context, a context crucial for critical discussion; there is no dialogue possible without the unity that makes such exchange possible. Schlegel's *Rede* continues in this mood of alarm, with a feeling of nostalgia for a unity that has been lost. In modern society, there is no more community, just a collection of individuals, isolated parts with no sense of the whole. What is missing is a tradition, that which helps to create a sense of cohesiveness vital to societies: "The modern poet must work this all out from within and many have done it magnificently—each, however, alone until now; each work anew, as if creating from nothing."[21] Schlegel, as we have seen, was suspicious of attempts by philosophers to create systems ex nihilo, for such creation turns a blind eye to the historical relations that are part of the context in which ideas develop. These lines from his *Rede* reveal that he also believed that the creation of artists took place within a tradition, and that historical consciousness of that tradition formed an important element of the creative process. Mythology, he argues, will help to correct the excessive subjectivity plaguing society: "Our poetry, I maintain, lacks a midpoint as mythology was for the poetry of the ancients and modern poetic art's inferiority to classical art can be summarized in the words: we have no mythology. But I would add that we are close to attaining one, or rather, it is time that we try earnestly to take part in producing one."[22] The new mythology must be "the most artificial of all artworks"[23] but also "an artwork of nature."[24] This sounds like a variation on a familiar Schlegelian theme, namely, calls to bring together seemingly irreconcilable elements. Now he tells us that the mythology that will help bring society together into some sort of cohesive whole must be at once artificial and natural. Such dilemmas grant some sympathy to those of Schlegel's critics who charged that his writings were indeed incomprehensible. To understand what Schlegel is after here, we return once again to that odd couple that often appears to resolve conflicts in the landscape of Schlegel's thought.

Once again, Fichte and Spinoza are presented as thinkers whose ideas need to be fused: the new mythology that must combine the theory of the subject (Fichte's idealism) with the theory of nature (Spinoza's realism). The two poles of reality, consciousness and the infinite, will help to shape the new mythology (as they ultimately shape all of reality): "If a new mythology can only create itself our of the innermost depths of the spirit as if out of itself, then we find a very significant hint and a significant confirmation of that which we seek in the great phenomenon of the age—in idealism!"[25] Schlegel continues: "In every form, idealism must go outside of itself in one way or another in order to be able to return to itself and to remain what it is. Therefore, a new and equally unbounded realism must and will emerge out of the womb of idealism. Thus idealism must not and will not merely become a model for the new mythology based on its own mode of development, but rather will indirectly be a source of it. You can already perceive traces of a similar tendency nearly everywhere, particularly in physics, which no longer seems to be lacking anything but a mythological view of nature."[26] The unity of the subject and the object, that is the I and nature, can only be attained through aesthetic practices, which is the only way that we can understand the infinite by means of the finite. The interest Schlegel has in art is epistemological; ultimately he endorses the value of aesthetic reflection as a way of reconciling the finite with the infinite.[27] This reconciliation has both philosophical and social consequences. Part of my goal in this study of Schlegel's philosophical contributions has been to dispel some of the myths surrounding early German Romanticism so that the critical potential of the movement, a movement mired in misunderstandings, can finally emerge.

Understanding, Misunderstanding, and Irony

While I have attempted to liberate Schlegel's thought from the misunderstandings that have plagued a proper reception of his work, it should be kept in mind that Schlegel was almost as interested in understanding as he was in its failure, misunderstanding. His concern with misunderstanding is showcased in "Über die Unverständlichkeit" (1800), was an essay he wrote for the final volume of *Das Athenäum*.[28] As we have seen, the journal and its contributors became the object of derision, for many of the entries were said to be incomprehensible (*unverständlich*). The charges of incomprehensibility prompted Schlegel to close the journal with an essay that tackled understanding head on and comes up in fragments as well.[29] The *Unverständlichkeit* essay is more protest essay than straightforward exposition on the nature of understanding and misunderstanding. Schelgel was not only perplexed, but annoyed by the deficiencies of his readers. His playful response to the lack of cooperation from his readers would have been incomprehensible to those very readers who accused him of incomprehensibility:

> Now, it is a peculiarity of mine that I absolutely detest incomprehension, not only the incomprehension of the uncomprehending

> but even more the incomprehension of the comprehending. For this reason, I made a resolution quite some time ago to have a talk about this matter with my reader, and then create before his eyes—in spite of him as it were—another new reader to my own liking: yes, even to deduce him if need be . . . I wanted for once to be really thorough and go through the whole series of my essays, admit their frequent lack of success and complete frankness, and so gradually lead the reader to being similarily frank and straightforward with himself. . . . I wanted to show that the purest and most genuine incomprehension emanates precisely from science and the arts—which by their very nature aim at comprehension and at making comprehensible—and from philosophy and philology.[30]

Once again the theme of the active role of the reader in helping to bring forth the meaning of the text is summoned, the reader that Schlegel's work all too often did not find. Schlegel was a "synthetic writer," which he defined as a writer who created a reader as "he should be" and did not "imagine him calm and dead, but alive and critical." Schlegel sought with his writing to develop "sacred relationships of the deepest symphilosophy," yet this search was often frustrated by the lack of cooperation on the part of the readers.

Schlegel's examination of the confusion generated by his fragments is focused on a fragment I have referenced several times throughout this book, *Athenäum* 216, the "notorious fragment about the three tendencies." He discusses, and not without a strong dose of irony, some of the misunderstandings of the fragment, which he innocently claims he wrote "almost without any irony at all."[31] He notes that there is one misunderstanding related to the very term *tendency*, which particularly troubles him. Some readers may have misunderstood his use of 'tendency' as suggesting that he considered Fichte's *Wissenschaftslehre* to be a "temporary venture," which he "might perhaps have a mind to continue (only rather better) and then bring to completion." He wonders how on earth anyone could have "accused him of having had so bad an intention."[32]

I hope that by now it is clear why Schlegel would have considered a reading of his use of 'tendency' to suggest a "temporary venture," which would be completed by him as equivalent to ascribing a "bad intention" to him. For Schlegel, our knowledge claims are never rooted in an absolutely certain foundation. We cannot be so arrogant as to think that we will ever have the last word on the meaning of any given event or text or idea, and certainly, his critiques of Fichte, or of Jacobi, Reinhold, Niethammer, or Kant, for that matter, were not attempts to complete what they had not finished, for he was well aware of the inherent incompleteness of knowledge and of philosophy itself.

Moreover, Schlegel was well aware of the consequences that the incompleteness of knowledge had upon the level of comprehension attainable via any given text. As he tells us in *Lyceum* Fragment 20, "A classical text must never be entirely comprehensible. But those who are cultivated and who cultivate themselves must always want to learn more from it." Unfortunately, too many of Schlegel's readers never appreciated this point and blamed his texts for failing to be fully comprehensible (as if it were the task of a text to be *fully* comprehensible), in a way similar to the way in which his fragments were dismissed as scattered thoughts lacking rigour and philosophical worth. Yet, it would be a mistake to accuse Schlegel of seeking to confuse his readers and generate nonsense with his witty writings: incomprehension, after all, is not indeterminacy, for how could we hope to learn from anything whose meaning was utterly indeterminate? Schlegel's emphasis on incomprehension is no abandonment of a project that was central to his philosophical work—that is, the very process of coming to an understanding of a text, an idea, and so on—but rather it was part of his commitment to comprehension, understood as a never-ending historical process. These claims are in keeping with Schlegel's view of philosophy as an infinite task, something that is defined in terms of a process of becoming, rather than an accomplished or complete state of being.

As Schlegel was well aware, "a great part of the incomprehensibility of the *Athenäum* is unquestionably due to the *irony* that to a greater or lesser extent is to be found everywhere in it."[33] Irony is sure to generate misunderstandings for the reader who is not willing to attempt to understand the text "on its own terms." But irony is also a tool that serves as a hermeneutical motor, fueling the never-ending process of understanding a text. Schlegel asks, "[I]sn't this entire, unending world constructed by the understanding out of *incomprehensibility or chaos?*"[34] Irony is a tool that enables the hovering stressed in *Athenäum* Fragment 116, a "hovering [on the wings of poetic reflection] between the portrayer and the portrayed [that] can multiply in an endless succession of mirrors." Irony belongs to poetry as a mode of representation. Yet it also belongs to philosophy, for it is the result of philosophy's inability to represent the Absolute. Nothing is complete, and irony is the tool used to make the inherent incompleteness of human experience apparent. Romantic irony is playful and irreverent, but it is not the result of any lack of respect that Schlegel had for the world and reality. It is rather the result of a deep respect for and commitment to *understanding* reality. Romantic irony makes no mockery of the world; it is not a disparaging attitude toward the world; rather, it is the ultimate show of humility; it is used to show how little all humans know.[35] Romantic irony is part of the general romantic vision of reality as essentially incomplete, as an approximation toward the distant and unreachable goal of the infinite. As Schlegel puts it: "Pure thinking and cognition [*Erkennen*] of the highest can never be represented [*dargestellt*] adequately—this is the principle of the relative unrepresentability [*Undarstellbarkeit*] of the highest."[36] This difficulty of representing the highest or the infinite is overcome when philosophy gives up its haughty independence and turns to art for help.[37] The infinite can only be alluded to indirectly, which is possible only if art is able to go beyond what it represents, by alluding to that which it does not succeed in saying. Because art is able to do this through irony, Schlegel claims: "Philosophy is the real homeland of irony, which one would like to define as logical beauty: for wherever philosophy appears in oral or written dialogues—and is not simply confined into rigid systems—there irony should be asked for and provided."[38] Philosophy that is the product of a mathematical or scientific deductive method is a philosophy confined to rigid systems. The dialogue form, like the fragment, is a literary form that is part of a philosophical "system" that combines having and not having system; this "romantic combination" is part of a philosophy informed by aesthetic method, and here we find irony. Irony is a literary tool that lifts the rigid confines of language.

Irony is a sort of play that reveals the limitations of a view of reality that presumed to have the last word. With the use of romantic irony, Schlegel showed that there was no last word. And once we give up a last word, aesthetic methods become sensible alternatives to the methods of mathematics and the natural sciences. Here again, Rorty and Schlegel come into close contact with one another.

Recall Rorty's suggestion that philosophy is best seen as a kind of writing, as a kind of family romance. Such a call puts philosophy closer to literature; indeed, Rorty thinks that we should "see philosophy [as] a branch of literature."[39] Rorty, like Schlegel, sees art as completing what philosophy cannot do alone. In Rorty's story, once we give up philosophical metanarratives, what we have are historical narratives (much more contingent in nature), which are similar to Schlegel's tendencies. Given that, "the principal backup for historiography is not philosophy but the arts, which serve to develop and modify a group's self-image by, for example, apotheosizing its heroes, diabolizing its enemies, mounting dialogues among its members, and refocusing its attention,"[40] art comes to hold an important, and certainly not an irrational role, for social life.[41] Schlegel's interest in mythology is part of his concern with social cohesiveness, which can be read as the social analogue to his concern for coherence in his view of truth. Of course, unlike Rorty, Schlegel would not pit art against philosophy. Both come together to build the social cohesiveness, or solidarity. Schlegel is committed to the cultivation of nothing less than humanity itself.

In *Contingency, Irony, and Solidarity* (1989), Rorty develops his view of the sort of task before us in the wake of our departure from metanarratives. The intellectual ironist takes on a prominent role, for we need someone who can handle language in such a way that the radical doubts about the vocabulary used and language's inability to get beyond itself to what is real are revealed.

Certainly, on both Schlegel's and Rorty's accounts of irony, there is going to be a highly sophisticated level of multiplicity of meaning to be found in language, a multiplicity that is presented in a way that is playful but should not blind us to its *serious* goals. But *Witz* and *Blitz*, as Anstett reminds us, "illuminate only briefly, when they don't blind us, and the illuminated matter often appears even darker after the bright flash is extinguished."[42] Humor certainly involves a play of wit, ideas brought together in precisely that explosive way that leads to laughter, thus creating a highly charged atmosphere of the sort Anstett describes in terms of flames and darkness, all taking place rather fleetingly. Philosophers, interested in the serious construction of lasting systems, do not welcome such fiery presentation. As Richard Bernstein has pointed out, "failing to be serious" is "the ultimate philosophical sin" that leads critics to suspect the ironist of attacking the critical potential of philosophy itself.[43] Susan Haack also comments on the problems that philosophers seem to have with wit, reminding us that, we "should not fool ourselves into thinking that humor, a sense of style, or a good ear for prose rhythms are somehow inappropriate to the academic *genre*, a sign of insufficient seriousness."[44] Just as it is possible to hold a philosophical position without having a metanarrative available, it is possible to combine argumentation with wit, to use irony to critique language and to attempt to reform philosophy.

Irony, a central tool for the development of Schlegel's views deployed for the purposes of criticizing the standard discourse of the discipline has proved to be a hindrance to a proper understanding of his romantic views. Schlegel used irony to play with the limits of understanding, and when there is play involved in understanding, the possibility of serious misunderstanding is great, which can have disastrous results for the very intelligibility of the ironist's discourse. Schlegel turned to irony in order to criticize the way that language was used (but certainly *not* make it unintelligible). With the use of irony, meaning swings between the said and the unsaid, so the act of understanding must meet this oscillation of meaning. As Schlegel was well aware, the successful use of irony is not dependent only upon the author. It requires an agility of mind on the part of the audience. If the audience of the irony consists of philosophers, problems are sure to lurk on the hermeneutical horizon. The philosophical community can understand (or at least appreciate) the philosopher who is clear and concise and who presents arguments in a language of premises and conclusions that is straightforward (this is the reliable discourse of science). In contrast, there are few philosophers who are willing to grant importance to playful rhetorical moves (dreaded literary devices!) in philosophy, even if these moves are part of a critical orchestration that could lead to reforms in philosophy that might enable the discipline to better address venerable philosophical questions regarding issues such as truth, goodness, and beauty.

Irony and the Necessity of Poetry

In a private lecture of 1807, Schlegel explains the relation between philosophy and poetry: "It should be brought to mind that the necessity of poetry is based on the requirement to represent the infinite, which emerges from the imperfection of philosophy."[45] The imperfection of philosophy that Schlegel refers to here is part of what I have insisted sets his contributions apart from those of his contemporaries who were more "idealist" than Schlegel, in hoping to get a transparent look at the Absolute. Schlegel is aware that any attempts to grasp the Absolute are futile, for any intellectual grasping involves setting down limits, for knowledge involves limits, and the Absolute is defined precisely in terms of its lack of conditions or limits. The Absolute can be approximated, through something like the "chaos of combinative wit," but not via systematic derivations or deductions. Schlegel's aesthetic turn, then, is certainly no irrational move. It is born of the consequences of his antifoundationalism, and he consistently followed out the ramifications of his skepticism regarding first principles in both the content and the form of his philosophy. Schlegel's favored literary forms (fragments, dialogues, novels), devices (irony, wit), and even the narrative structure of his experimental novel, *Lucinde*, are the particular ways he came to terms with our inability to grasp the Absolute and our need to try to represent the unrepresentable.[46]

Romantic poetry is not only "progressive and universal," but it also can "hover at the midpoint between the portrayed and the portrayer . . . on the wings of poetic reflection again and again to a higher power" and "multiply [the world] in an endless succession of mirrors."[47] A poetry that hovers at the midpoint between portrayer and portrayed, on the wings of poetic reflection, is created by a poet who has discovered the secret and value of lightness and is not bound to simply producing copies of what there is in the world, but is able to use the wings of poetic reflection to reflect upon how what there is in the world is represented in the first place and then reflect on this reflection, and reflect upon the reflection of the reflection, and so on, ultimately creating "an endless succession of mirrors."

This new way of understanding the nature of philosophy gave rise to the need for a new method. This method involved a kind of hovering "between the portrayed and the portrayer," with the philosopher as the portrayer and reality as the portrayed. Only a philosophy that is rooted in irony has the agility and lightness necessary to hover between reality and the philosopher. This sort of philosophy is intimately related to poetry indeed, it finds its completion in poetry.

Schlegel uses the relation between the portrayer and the portrayed in order to discuss representation. He was well aware of the value of irony and the lightness it granted to the representation of ideas, and it is in connection to irony that Schlegel's connection to Socrates-Plato is strongest.

Schlegel claims that Socratic irony "contains and arouses a feeling of indissoluble antagonism between the absolute and the relative, between the impossibility and the necessity of complete communication" (*Lyceum* Fragment 108). In chapter 1, I discussed some of the problems with Beiser's move to classify the early German Romantics as absolute idealists and his accompanying insistence that the strongest aspect of their Platonic heritage was in the development of their idealism. I believe that the best case for the Platonic legacy of the early German Romantics can be located in what Beiser so well describes as "the ironic smile of Socrates," found "beneath the surface of Schlegel's . . . skepticism about first principles and complete systems,"[48] rather than in Plato's theory of ideal forms.

The form of irony that inspired Schlegel was Socratic irony. Plato's Dialogues provide many examples of the sort of irony that leaves one wondering what the words used to express an idea really mean; the reader is left suspended between the portrayer, Socrates, and the portrayed, his claims, never quite sure that one has captured the meaning. For example, in the *Phaedrus* when we are given a scathing critique of the written word, this is given in writing. But after we have been told that the written word is deceptive, on what grounds can we accept written claims against the written word?[49] Ironically, in order to understand irony itself, we must have already the sort of agility that irony requires. Schlegel expresses this paradox eloquently: "Socratic irony is the only involuntary and yet completely deliberate dissimulation . . . In this sort of irony, everything should be playful and serious, guilelessly open and deeply hidden."[50] Irony became the cornerstone of Schlegel's romantic philosophy, reflecting a view of philosophy as an infinite task, as a kind of longing for the infinite that could never be expressed by using the unplayful method of the natural sciences, but rather by uniting philosophy with poetry.

In "Works of Art and Mere Real Things," Arthur Danto talks about the various ways in which the mimetic function of art has been looked upon.[51] After discussing Socrates and his "aversion to mirror images and mimesis," Danto moves to what may have been overlooked by Socrates' narrow view of what artistic representation entailed, namely, that "mirrors and then, by generalization, artworks, rather than giving us back what we already can know without benefit of them, serve [...] as instruments of self-revelation."[52] To illustrate the mirror functioning of art as a mode of self-revelation, Danto discusses Shakespeare's *Hamlet*, a figure and a work close to Schlegel's philosophical heart.[53]

Hamlet and the play within the play meant to "catch the conscience of the king" figure prominently in Danto's discussion of the mimetic function of art. In Shakespeare's play, we have two different representations of the murdered king of Denmark: the character that Shakespeare creates who is only present to us as a memory and possibly as a ghost and the player-king in the play that Hamlet has arranged to have staged. This double mirroring makes the issue of representation a theme of the play. Hamlet uses a play, a representation of what he believes transpired between his dead father and his Uncle Claudius, to demonstrate to his uncle that he knows the truth about the circumstances surrounding his father's death. The play put on by Hamlet (Hamlet's play) is a play within Shakespeare's play and is consciously used by Hamlet as a mirror to reflect the circumstances surrounding his father's death and to "catch the conscience" of his uncle, to see his uncle's face cloud with guilt as it becomes clear that Hamlet knows the truth about Claudius' deeds. Before Hamlet's play is over, Claudius rises and leaves the performance. He cannot stand to see such a story represented. We can conclude on the basis of Claudius' action that Hamlet has indeed used his play to successfully catch the conscience of the king. This sort of maneuver, a kind of revelation of the mimetic function of art, reflects the great power of literature and art in general. It is a kind of maneuver that enables us to achieve the metaperspective that Schlegel believed was so important for philosophers to have.

There is nothing "narcissistic" about these representations. While Hamlet's intention with his play might have been exclusively to elicit feelings of guilt in his uncle, clearly, Shakespeare's intentions with his play are not merely to elicit sentimental reactions in us. Shakespeare's play leads us to reflect upon the nature of art and representation. Moreover Shakespeare's play forces us to give *rational consideration* to human emotions and character traits. When one reads Shakespeare's play, one reflects rationally about the nature of, say, betrayal. One does not *feel* betrayed.[54] Art can represent reality. And an artist can make the act of representation visible in the work of art, especially through the use of irony, which enables us to look critically at art itself.

For Schlegel irony is linked to lightness and agility. He found this agility exemplified in the age of Cervantes and Shakespeare. Recall that Schlegel locates the Romantic in the work of Shakespeare and Cervantes: "This is where I look for and find the Romantic—in the older moderns, in Shakespeare, Cervantes, in Italian poetry, in that age of knights, love, and fairy-tales where the thing and the word originated."[55] A central reason why Schlegel is drawn to Cervantes' *Don Quixote* and Shakespeare's *Hamlet* is because these works lead us directly to irony, where he locates the root of the relationship between poetry and philosophy. One function of irony is that of providing a kind of distancing device that enables the characters to reflect on the power of the mirroring that is one central aspect of art, namely, representation. Irony is a mimetic device that enables Shakespeare's characters to make the issue of the power of representation explicit. In a review, Schlegel discusses the importance of acknowledging that over and above being an artist who can represent a full spectrum of feelings to an audience, Shakespeare is "one of the most intentional artists" (*einer der absichtsvollsten Künstler*).[56] That is, the play within the play that we find in Hamlet does not occur by accident nor simply to intensify the intellectual joys associated with the great sorrow we may feel as we read of Hamlet's plight. The play within the play is ironic; it is an intentional mimetic structure that is put into the play by one of the "most intentional artists" in order to make us reflect upon the very nature and power of art (in addition to reflecting on such lofty things as human suffering, revenge, loyalty, etc.).

The use of irony requires that the author know how to move from a representation of the subject matter at hand to a reflection of the representation of that subject matter, creating a kind of frame in which the subject matter is seen at a different level. This makes the subject matter move between two levels of meaning or even more if we are to take Schlegel's reference to "an infinitely teeming chaos" seriously.[57] Irony is a tool that puts us on the trail of the Absolute, helping us to approximate it. Moreover, it has an important role to play in the critique of philosophy that Schlegel was after; the hovering function of irony was seen by him to be instrumental in helping us to look critically at philosophy itself.

Friedrich Schlegel employed unconventional forms for the expression of his ideas in order to challenge the general view of philosophy as something that should be modeled on the natural sciences. A central goal of his romantic project was to bring philosophy into closer contact with poetry and history, odd bedfellows in the wake of Kant's *Critique of Pure Reason*, a work that celebrated philosophy's relation to the ahistorical sciences.

The present book has been an attempt to present Schlegel's *philosophical* views as they developed during his romantic phase and in response to the *philosophical* disputes that dominated during the post-Kantian period. I emphasize the adjective 'philosophical,' for the prejudices against bringing philosophy too close to poetry still linger in the intellectual air we breathe, condemning Schlegel and the early German Romantics to the literary sidelines. I hope that the story I have told of the emergence of Schlegel's romantic philosophy has helped to dispel the myth that early German Romanticism was some sort of mystical movement out to enchant the world. What emerges from my portrait of Schlegel's romantic philosophy, a philosophy that was certainly filled with a strong dose of *Witz* and *Blitz*, is an even stronger dose of enduring skepticism that challenged traditional notions of the nature of philosophy. Schlegel's challenge is one we would do well to take more seriously.

Notes

Introduction

1. Loci classici of works dealing with the literary strengths of early German Romanticism are Rudolf Haym, *Die Romantische Schule* (Berlin, 1928); Richarda Huch, *Die Blütezeit der Romantik—Ausbreitung, Blütezeit und Verfall der Romantik* (Tübingen: Rainer Wunderlich, 1951); Georg Lukács, *Die Seele und die Formen* (Berlin, 1911); Oskar Walzel, *German Romanticism*, translated by Alma Elsie Lussky (New York: Capricorn Books, 1966).

2. Evidence of this renewed interest is the abundant work done by philosophers in Germany and in the United States on early German Romanticism. See Manfred Frank, *Einführung in die frühromantische Ästhetik* (Frankfurt: Suhrkamp, 1989); "Alle Wahrheit ist Relativ, Alles Wissen Symbolisch," *Revue Internationale de Philosophie* 50 (1996): 403–436; *Unendliche Annäherung: Die Anfänge der philosophischen Frühromantik* (Frankfurt: Suhrkamp, 1997). The last twelve lectures of *Unendliche Annäherung* have been translated into English by Elizabeth Millán-Zaibert, under the title *The Philosophical Foundations of Early German Romanticism* (Albany: State University of New York Press, 2004). Manfred Frank also edited a special volume on the philosophical foundations of early German Romanticism for the *Revue Internationale de Philosophie* 50 (1996), with articles by Ernst Behler, Violetta Waibel, Jürgen Stolzenberg, Wilhelm Baum, and Andrew Bowie. See also Dieter Henrich, "Jakob Zwillings Nachlass: Eine Rekonstruktion," *Hegel Studien Beiheft* 28 (1986); *Konstellationen: Probleme und Debatten am Ursprung der idealistischen Philosophie (1789–1795)* (Stuttgart: Klett-Cotta, 1991); and *Der Grund im Bewußtsein: Untersuchungen zu Hölderlins Denken (1794–1795)* (Stuttgart: Klett-Cotta, 1992). Examples of recent Anglophone interest in early German Romanticism include *The Cambridge Companion to German Idealism*, ed. Karl Ameriks (Cambridge: Cambridge University Press, 2000); Frederick Beiser, *The Romantic Imperative: The Concept of Early German Romanticism* (Cambridge, MA: Harvard University Press, 2003); and *German Idealism: The Struggle against Subjectivism, 1791–1801* (Cambridge, MA: Harvard University Press, 2002); Isaiah Berlin, *The*

Roots of Romanticism (Princeton: Princeton University Press, 1999); Terry Pinkard, *German Philosophy, 1760–1860: The Legacy of Idealism* (Cambridge: Cambridge University Press, 2002); Robert Richards, *The Romantic Conception of Life: Science and Philosophy in the Age of Goethe* (Chicago: University of Chicago Press, 2002). A recent volume of *Pli: The Warwick Journal of Philosophy*, entitled *Crises of the Transcendental: From Kant to Romanticism*, volume 10 (2000), was dedicated to a discussion of key figures and themes of the movement. Another mark of renewed interest in this period of intellectual history is found in the launching of a new journal, *Internationales Jahrbuch des Deutschen Idealismus/International Yearbook of German Idealism*, ed. Karl Ameriks and Jürgen Stolzenberg. For a detailed discussion of the recent literature, see E. Millán-Zaibert, "The Revival of *Frühromantik* in the Anglophone World," *Philosophy Today* (Spring 2005): 96–117.

3. Goethe's famous claim, *"Das Klassische nenne ich das Gesunde und das Romantische das Kranke"* ("I call the classical that which is healthy and the romantic that which is sick") and other fascinating aspects of the complicated relation between the Romantics and Goethe are discussed and analyzed in Arnd Bohn, "Goethe and the Romantics," *The Literature of German Romanticism*, ed. Dennis F. Mahoney, pp. 35–60 (Rochester, NY: Camden House, 2004).

4. For more on the details of the true story of the relation between German Romanticism and National Socialism, see Ralf Klausnitzer, *Blaue Blume unterm Hakenkreuz: Die Rezeption der deutschen literarischen Romantik im Dritten Reich* (Paderborn: Ferdinand Schöningh, 1999). Klausnitzer's thick, well-researched volume helps to correct insidious misconceptions regarding the nature of German Romanticism and its relation to Nazism. He helps break down the general and seriously flawed conception of Romanticism, whereby it is seen as an anti-Enlightenment movement that privileged feelings over reason, glorified the "German Spirit," endorsing the sort of nationalism that would rear its ugly head in the fascism of twentieth-century Germany. In a recently published collection of lectures by Isaiah Berlin, *The Roots of Romanticism* (Princeton University Press, 1999), German Romanticism is characterized as a movement bent on a path of the destruction of reason and science, culminating in a pernicious nationalism that gave way to fascism. A more traditional source for the misreading of Romanticism as a conservative, nationalistic political movement is Georg Lukács's *Destruction of Reason*, where he goes so far as to create a history that directly links Hitler to Schelling. But, as Manfred Frank has shown, Lukács's history is riddled with error, because Schelling was no Romantic, and the Nazis, as can be shown in detail, hated the protagonists of early German Romanticism. See Manfred Frank, "Wie reaktionär war eigentlich die Frühromantik? (Elemente zur Aufstörung der Meinungsbildung)," in *Athenäum. Jahrbuch für Romantik* (Paderborn: Schöningh, 1997): 141–66.

5. Albuquerque: Living Batch Press, 1989.

6. Albany: State University of New York Press, 1988. This study was pivotal for opening discussions of the meaning and significance of early German Romanticism. Lacoue-Labarthe and Nancy argue that early German Romanticism *must* be approached philosophically if its significance for literature is to be fully appreciated. As they write, "[A]lthough it is not entirely or simply philo-

sophical, romanticism is rigorously comprehensible (or even accessible) only on a philosophical basis, in its proper and in fact unique (in other words, entirely new) articulation with the philosophical. Neither a simple "literary movement" nor—still less—the appearance of some "new sensibility," nor even the reading (in any sense) of the classical problems of the theory of art or aesthetics, romanticism cannot be approached with a model of seamless evolution or progress . . . If romanticism is approachable . . . it is approachable only by means of the "philosophical path," if it is true that crisis is fundamentally philosophical and that the crisis at stake here, as we will see, is opened by nothing other than Criticism itself" (p. 29, cf. p. 103). While I do not agree with all of the details of Lacoue-Labarthe and Nancy's account of the emergence of Romanticism from the crisis of criticism, I think that we would do well to keep in mind their insistence that we approach the movement via a philosophical path. As we shall see, this path intersects in important and fruitful ways with the literary and scientific paths, but the philosophical path provides a way to see the whole toward which the Romantics were striving, and that view is crucial for an accurate assessment of the movement's contributions. When Lacoue-Labarthe and Nancy claim that "Philosophy controls romanticism" (p. 29), they explain this in terms of Kant's role in opening up the "possibility of romanticism" (p. 29). Since my main thesis is that antifoundationalism and the concomitant embrace of a coherence view of truth open up the possibility of Romanticism, Kant and the Romantics end up in close company, but several figures other than Kant (e.g., Jacobi, Fichte, Reinhold) turn out to be just as important as Kant for opening up the possibility of Romanticism. I must disagree with them when they begin to characterize Romanticism in terms of an overcoming of Kant (pp. 33ff.).

7. *This New Yet Unapproachable America: Lectures after Emerson and Wittgenstein*, op. cit., pp. 4–6.

8. Richard Eldridge, "A Continuing Task: Cavell and the Truth of Skepticism" (p. 76), in *The Sense of Stanley Cavell*, ed. Richard Fleming and Michael Payne (Lewisburg: Bucknell University Press, 1989).

9. A recent article by Richard Eldridge draws important connections between naturalism and Romanticism ("Some Remarks on Logical Truth: Human Nature and Romanticism," *Midwest Studies in Philosophy* 19 (1994): 220–42). Although Eldridge does not directly discuss early German Romanticism, his claim that "Romanticism is one reasonably accurate name for the sense that human beings are thus perenially between the aspiration to establish the ultimate terms of human responsibility and that aspiration's disappointment" (ibid., p. 238) nicely captures a major theme in Schlegel's thought, that of the tension between the infinite and the finite and the feeling of longing that arises from this state of eternal longing after that which can never be attained, a theme to which I shall return several times throughout the course of this book.

10. Theodor Ziolkowski, *Das Wunderjahr in Jena. Geist und Gesellschaft 1794–95* (Stuttgart: Klett-Cotta, 1998).

11. Hans Eichner begins his introduction to volume 18 of the critical edition of Schlegel's works with the following claim: "In contrast to the other representatives of the Romantic School, Friedrich Schlegel was the philosopher of

this movement. While August Wilhelm Schlegel was devoted primarily to philology, Novalis and Tieck to poetry, and Schleiermacher to theology, Friedrich Schlegel could say of himself that since 1790, metaphysics was the primary occupation of his life" (*KA* 18, ix). In his recent review of a new book on Felix Mendelssohn, Charles Rosen refers to Schlegel as the thinker "who gave us our first definition of Romanticism" (*Times Literary Supplement*, no. 5268 (March 19, 2004): 3. In *Enlightenment, Revolution and Romanticism*, chapter 9, Frederick Beiser writes, "If any single figure could claim to be the leader of the romantic circle, it would indisputably be Friedrich Schlegel. His energy, enthusiasm, and enterprise were the creative forces behind the *Athenäum*, the journal of the group; and his thinking laid the foundation for the aesthetics of romanticism. It was indeed Schlegel who formulated the concept of romantic poetry, from which the movement took its name and much of its inspiration" (p. 245). In *Enlightenment, Revolution and Romanticism*, Beiser focuses only upon Schlegel's contributions to political philosophy and aesthetics. In another study, entitled *The Fate of Reason: German Philosophy from Kant to Fichte* (Cambridge, MA: Harvard University Press, 1987), Beiser gives an excellent account of the philosophical context surrounding early German Romanticism yet does not go into detail regarding Schlegel's epistemological or metaphysical positions. Beiser's two most recent works on the early German Romantics explore central aspects of Schlegel's philosophy in great detail. See, for example, *German Idealism: The Struggle against Subjectivism, 1791–1801* (Cambridge, MA: Harvard University Press, 2002) and *The Romantic Imperative: The Concept of Early German Romanticism* (Cambridge, MA: Harvard University Press, 2003). In both of these works, Beiser analyzes Schlegel's central philosophical positions in great detail, and, moreover, in such provocative ways that his work opens up new debates concerning the philosophical commitments of the early German Romantics, just the sort of productive debate that helps augment scholarship in the area.

12. See esp. *German Idealism: The Struggle against Subjectivism, 1791–1801* (Cambridge, MA: Harvard University Press, 2002) and *The Romantic Imperative: The Concept of Early German Romanticism* (Cambridge, MA: Harvard University Press, 2003).

13. See for example, Andrew Bowie, ed. and trans., *Schleiermacher: Hermeneutics and Criticism and Other Writings* (Cambridge: Cambridge University Press, 1998) and *Schelling: On the History of Modern Philosophy* (Cambridge: Cambridge University Press, 1994).

14. Bowie's recent *Introduction to German Philosophy: From Kant to Habermas* (Oxford: Polity, 2003) is good reflection of his impressive grasp of the historical streams of German philosophy. In this work, he provides an analysis of the controversies that shaped German philosophy in the long and incredibly diverse span from Kant to Habermas (and to his credit includes the early German Romantics in his account).

15. See especially "German Philosophy Today: Between Idealism, Romanticism, and Pragmatism," in *German Philosophy Since Kant*, ed. Anthony O'Hear (Cambridge: Cambridge University Press, 1999): 357–98.

16. Vol. 3, no. 197 (1996), pp. 515–54.

17. The McDowell connection to German Idealism and *Frühromantik* is further strengthened by a recent collection of essays, *Reading McDowell: On Mind and World*, ed. Nicholas H. Smith (Routledge, 2002), where there are several provocative articles exploring the connections between McDowell's work and the philosophical concerns of the post-Kantians (mainly Hegel). In the collection several philosophers who have been important contributors to the discussions regarding German Idealism and early German Romanticism offer their thoughts on McDowell's work (J. M. Bernstein, R. J. Bernstein, R. Brandom, R. Bubner, M. Friedman, C. Larmore, R. Pippin, and C. Taylor)—as do philosophers whose work falls more squarely in the analytic tradition (H. Putnam, B. Stroud, C. Wright)—thus the collection represents a productive move to bring together voices from the continental tradition and the analytic tradition.

18. See Wilhelm Dilthey, *Leben Schleiermachers, Vol. I, Book 2* (Berlin: de Gruyter, 1970) and *Die Entstehung der Hermeneutik* (Göttingen, 1961). Both Dilthey and Hans-Georg Gadamer acknowledge that Schlegel's thought was an important turning point in the history of hermeneutics, the point at which the act of understanding became its own subject.

19. Ernst Behler, "Friedrich Schlegels Theorie des Verstehens: Hermeneutik oder Dekonstuktion?" in *Die Aktualität der Frühromantik* (Paderborn: Ferdinand Schöningh, 1987), pp. 141–60. Also, Klaus Peter, "Friedrich Schlegel und Adorno. Die Dialektik der Aufklärung in der Romantik und heute," ibid., pp. 219–35.

20. Walter Benjamin, *Der Begriff der Kunstkritik in der deutschen Romantik, Band I Gesammelte Schriften* (Frankfurt am Main: Suhrkamp, 1974). Lacoue-Labarthe and Nancy give Benjamin due credit for his penetrating insights regarding the affinities between early German Romanticism and modernism: "A veritable romantic *unconscious* is discernible today, in most of the central motifs of our 'modernity.' Not the least result of romanticism's indefinable character is the way it has allowed this so-called modernity to use romanticism as a foil, without ever recognizing—or in order not to recognize—that it has done little more than rehash romanticism's discoveries. To suspect a trap in the imprecision of the Schlegels, and to comprehend that the trap had worked perfectly, required all the lucidity of a Benjamin" (*The Literary Absolute*, op. cit., p. 15).

21. *Friedrich Schlegel Kritische Ausgabe* (*KA*), in thirty-five volumes, edited by Ernst Behler in collaboration with Jean-Jacques Antstett, Jakob Baxa, Ursula Behler, Liselotte Dieckmann, Hans Eichner, Raymond Immerwahr, Robert L. Kahn, Eugene Susini, Bertold Sutter, A. Leslie Wilson, and others (Paderborn: Schöningh, 1958ff.).

22. See especially *Frühromantik. Die Frühromantik als literaturgeschichtliche Phänomen* (Berlin: de Gruyter, 1992) and *German Romantic Literary Theory* (Cambridge: Cambridge University Press, 1993).

23. Given this purported wide range of interpretations, it seems strange that so little attention has been paid to the second.

24. Behler, *German Romantic Literary Theory*, op. cit., pp. 2–3.

25. Ibid., p. 5. This claim regarding the independence of Romantic theory from historical considerations is puzzling particularly because later (p. 11) Behler

says something quite different: "Always engaged in an active relationship with historical events, early Romantic theory also remained in lively contact with the literary life of its own time." This criticism of Behler in no way suggests that nothing he says of Schlegel or early German Romanticism is valid. Quite the contrary, his work, both as a translator and as a researcher in this area has been tremendously important. Nonetheless, his mistakes, based as they are on a one-sided approach to certain aspects of Schlegel's thought, point to a widespread problem involved in attempts to study a movement that was both literary *and* philosophical.

26. *Die Entwicklung der Philosophie in zwölf Büchern* (The Development of Philosophy in twelve volumes) in *KA* 12. This was part of a series of private lectures given in Köln (1804–05).

27. Behler, *German Romantic Literary Theory*, op. cit., p. 8.

28. F. Beiser, *Romantic Imperative*, op. cit., p. 7.

29. Ibid.

30. Ibid., p. 8.

31. Ibid.

32. Ibid.

33. Ibid., p. 22.

34. See *Konstellationen. Probleme und Debatten am Ursprung der idealistischen Philosophie (1789–1795)* (Stuttgart: Klett-Cotta, 1991) and *Der Grund im Bewusstsein. Holderlin's Denken in Jena 1794–95* (ibid., 1995).

35. Especially *Unendliche Annäherung. Die Anfänge der philosophischen Frühromantik* (Frankfurt/M: Suhrkamp, 1997); *Philosophische Grundlagen der Frühromantik* in *Athenäum Jahrbuch fur Romantik* (1994); *Einführung in die frühromantische Ästhetik*, (Frankfurt/M: Suhrkamp, 1989); *Das Problem "Zeit" in der deutschen Romantik: Zeitbewußtsein und Bewußtsein von Zeitlichkeit in der frühromantischen Philosophie und in Tiecks Dichtung* (München: Winkler, 1972).

36. Gabriele Rommel, "Romanticism and Natural Science," in *The Literature of German Romanticism*, ed. Dennis F. Mahoney (Rochester, NY: Camden House, 2004): 216. Rommel's article, aside from this claim, which, in light of recent studies, is not compelling, is an excellent overview of the contributions the German Romantics (not just the *Frühromantiker*) made to science and our conception of nature.

37. Robert Richards, *The Romantic Conception of Life* (Chicago: University of Chicago Press, 2002), p. xix.

38. In current work, I have begun to draw lines between Schlegel and Novalis' romantic thought and the conception of nature developed by Alexander von Humboldt, a leading scientist of Schlegel's time. Robert Richards is one of the few authors to discuss Humboldt's work and to connect it to the intellectual work of the early German Romantics.

39. Another good example of a work that highlights the philosophical relevance of the movement is *Die Aktualität der Frühromantik*, ed. Ernst Behler (Paderborn: Schöningh, 1987). This is comprised of a series of articles by the leading scholars in this field (e.g., R. Brinkmann, J. Hörisch, R. Bubner, M. Frank, E. Behler, K. Peter, and H. Schanze). Most of these articles deal with specific philosophical issues of early German Romanticism.

40. This is not to say that there have been no valuable English-language studies on Schlegel's thought. See, for example, Michel Chaouli, *The Laboratory of Poetry: Chemistry and Poetics in the Work of Friedrich Schlegel* (Baltimore: Johns Hopkins University Press, 2002). This is an excellent study of the theme of experimentation that emerges from Schlegel's fragments, and it does offer keen insights on the conception of a system that emerges from Schlegel's early Romantic period. Chaouli does an impressive job of linking Schlegel's thought to eighteenth-century developments in chemistry, yet he is not specifically interested in the details of Schlegel's philosophical positions.

41. The best source here is Ernst Behler's and Ursula Struc-Oppenberg's introduction of 1975 to volume 8 of the *Kritische Ausgabe* (*KA*) of Schlegel's work, pp. 15–232.

42. I borrow this expression from Manfred Frank's characterization of the phases of Schlegel's thought. The expression is used by Schlegel to describe his early phase; see *Lyceum* Fragments, especially nos. 7 and 66 but also 11, 60, 84, 91, 93, and 107 in *KA* 2, pp. 147–63. In translation by Peter Firchow (Minneapolis: University of Minnesota Press, 1991), pp. 1–16.

43. My claim may seem too nonchalant to some students of Schlegel's work, for there is some controversy regarding how the different phases relate or do not relate to one another. In *The Romantic Imperative* (op. cit.), Fred Beiser presents Schlegel as a "mysterious romantic" precisely because of the various conversions one finds in Schlegel's work, and he provides a well-detailed account of the tensions, nuances, and shifts in Schlegel's positions. There are interesting and important stories to be told about the various shifts in Schlegel's thought, but my interest in the following chapters is on his romantic phase and on the notion of philosophy born of that phase of Schlegel's thought, with full recognition that there are many other important corners of Schlegel's thought yet to be fully explored.

44. Cf. *KA* 1, p. 28; *KA* 2, p. 68, 69; *KA* 8, p. 6.

45. The University of Jena had a student population of approximately 900. Count Carl August of Weimar was the chief administrator of the university and was rather liberal concerning matters of the human sciences. This made the university in Jena open to receive the new ideas of the time. Chief among these ideas was Kant's critical philosophy. Kant's philosophy was taught by Karl Leonhard Reinhold, Gottlieb Hufeland, and Carl Christian Erhard Schmid. These scholars attracted many students. One of the most important journals of the time, the *Allgemeine Literatur Zeitung* was published in Jena. These two factors coupled with Jena's proximity to Weimar, a cultural center, attracted a broad range of thinkers.

46. See *KA* 8: pp. 55, 82, and 155. This was his "Rezension der vier ersten Bande von F.I. Niethammers *Philosophischen Journal*" (1797), *KA* 8, pp. 12–37.

47. Especially harsh was Schlegel's criticism of Schiller's poem "The Worth of Women," which appeared in Schiller's journal *Musenalmanach* in 1796. In that review, Schlegel ridiculed Schiller's celebration of the domestic functions of women (see *KA* 2, p. 6). Despite his harsh criticisms of some of the conservative views he perceived in Schiller's work, Schlegel did acknowledge his indebtedness to Schiller's work on aesthetics, especially the essay "On Naive and Sentimental Poetry." For more on Schlegel's love-hate relationship with Schiller, see Eichner's introduction to *KA* 2.

48. For more on Schlegel's relation with Reichhardt, see Frederick Beiser, *Enlightenment, Revolution and Romanticism* (Cambridge: Harvard University Press, 1992), pp. 253–60.

49. See Eichner's introduction to *KA* 2, esp., 42–71. In Berlin, Schlegel established a relation with Friedrich Schleiermacher (1768–1834) and met the daughter of Moses Mendelssohn, Dorothea Veit (1763–1839), whom he married in 1804. Both Schleiermacher and Veit became important figures for the development of Schlegel's thought. '*Symphilosophie*,' that is, philosophy as the product of thinking and sharing thoughts with another, was an important concept for the early Romantics. Schleiermacher became a contributor to *Das Athenäum*. Veit and Schlegel published a novel together (*Florentin*), and one of Schlegel's most important statements regarding the emancipation of women was written in the form of an open letter to Veit ("Über die Philosophie. An Dorothea" (1799), *KA* 8, pp. 41–62).

50. Letter to his brother, cited by Eichner in *KA* 2, 42.

51. Schlegel's apology for the journal and its "incomprehensible" entries is found in his essay "Über die Unverständlichkeit," *KA* 2, pp. 363–72. The place of incomprehensibility in Schlegel's romantic philosophy will be discussed in chapter 7.

52. These appeared in three different issues of the journal: in vol. 1, no. 1 (Berlin, 1798): 73, 75, 77–78, 79–80; in vol. 1, no. 2 (Berlin, 1798): 3–146; in vol. 3, no. 1 (Berlin, 1800): 4–33. Altogether there were 451 fragments written by Novalis (13), Schleiermacher (29), A. W. Schlegel (85), Friedrich Schlegel (219). Four of the fragments were written jointly, and the authorship of the remaining ninety-seven have not yet been determined (Eichner, *KA* 2, 111–114). See Ernst Behler, *Die Zeitschriften der Brüder Schlegel* (Darmstadt: Wissenschaftliche Buchgesellschaft, 1983). He remarks at length upon the origin of the fragment, indicating that although the influence of the French moralist Chamfort is indisputable (a collection of his aphorisms appeared in German translation in 1797), the stronger influence is to be found in a more German "root" of this literary tradition. He writes: "In the German tradition, above all in the 18th century, there appears a peculiar metaphysical need regarding the fragment in its sense as inaccessible, limited, merely human knowledge. Probably this comes from a particular nuance of Luther's translation of the bible, in particular from the influence of the sentence, *ex parte enim cognoscimus* from the First Letter of Corinthiam (13, 19) which Luther translated with the familiar words: 'Our knowledge is the work of parts' " (p. 38).

In his discussion of the German "roots" of the fragment tradition, Behler also mentions Goethe's reference to literature as a "fragment of all fragments" and Lessing's reference to some of his writings as fragments. Lavater and Herder (1766) also refer to some of their work as fragments. Behler writes: "It is recommended when determining the significance of the romantic fragments, to keep in mind the particular German tradition of fragmentary thinking, so that this literary form is not measured according to models with which they do not accord"(p. 38). Behler's historical explanation is valuable, but I believe that it is necessary to supplement this with a consideration of the fragment as a consequence of Schlegel's view of philosophy; my analysis of the fragment will be presented in chapters 6 and 7, when I discuss the aesthetic consequences of early German Romanticism.

53. See Rodolphe Gasché "Ideality in Fragmentation," foreword to Peter Firchow's translation of Friedrich Schlegel's *Philosophical Fragments* (Minneapolis: University of Minnesota Press, 1991), vii–xxxii. According to Gasché, fragmentation constitutes the properly Romantic vision of the system (xiii). His analysis takes its theoretical starting point from the work of Walter Benjamin (*Der Begriff der Kunstkritik in der deutschen Romantik*) and Lacoue-Labarthe/Nancy (*The Literary Absolute*) yet goes beyond these in finding a common thread between "idea" and "fragment" and tracing this to Kant's discussion of representation (*Vorstellung*) and presentation (*Darstellung*) in the *Critique of Judgment*. He concludes that fragments are ideas in presentation.

54. See Eichner's introduction to *KA* 2, 39–64.

55. Es ist gleich tödlich für den Geist, ein System zu haben, und keins zu haben. Es wird sich also wohl entschließen müssen, beides zu verbinden (*KA* 2, p. 173, no. 53). I have consulted Peter Firchow's translation of the *Fragments* (Minneapolis: University of Minnesota Press, 1991) and Ernst Behler and Roman Struc's translation of sections from Schlegel's *Dialogue on Poetry* (New York: Continuum, 1982). Many of Schlegel's texts have not yet been translated into English. When I am dealing with texts, from Schlegel or other thinkers, that have not yet been translated into English, I shall give the German in the note. When there is a translation available, unless I disagree with the translation, I shall simply give the English, while, of course, also giving the reference of the original German source.

56. An excellent analysis of this theme is provided by Christiane Schildknecht, *Philosophische Masken. Literarische Formen der Philosophie bei Platon, Descartes, Wolff und Lichtenberg* (Stuttgart: Metzler Verlag, 1990) and Gottfried Gabriel and Christiane Schildknecht, ed. *Literarische Formen der Philosophie* (Stuttgart: Metzlersche Verlag, 1990).

57. See, for example, *'Romantic' and Its Cognates: The European History of a Word*, ed. Hans Eichner (Toronto: University of Toronto Press, 1972). Nicholas V. Riasanovsky, *The Emergence of Romanticism* (Oxford: Oxford University Press, 1992) is a comparative study of British and early German Romanticism. Riasanovsky locates the origins of Romanticism in a particular period, the 1790s, and two particular geographical areas, England and Germany, focusing upon thinkers such as Wordsworth, Coleridge, Novalis, Friedrich Schlegel, and Wackenroder as they struggled with a central problem: pantheism. Riasanovsky's essay provides a compelling story of why the "burst" of activity found in the specific period of his study was doomed from the start to implode faster than it exploded.

58. A. O. Lovejoy, "The Meaning of 'Romantic' in Early German Romanticism" and "Schiller and the Genesis of German Romanticism," in *Essays in the History of Ideas* (Baltimore: Johns Hopkins University Press, 1948), pp. 183–206 and 207–27.

59. Ibid., p. 203.

60. Ibid.

61. Dennis F. Mahoney, introduction to *The Literature of German Romanticism*, p. 7 (Rochester, NY: Camden House, 2004).

62. A reference to "Über das Studium der griechischen Poesie" (written in 1795 and published in 1797).

63. *KA* 2, 147–48/Firchow p. 1. See also *Lyceum* Fragments 65, 66, 84, 93, and 107.

64. *KA* 2, p. 182, no. 116.

65. For a thorough dissection of this fragment, see Eichner's introduction to *KA* 2, 59–64.

66. Behler, *Irony and the Discourse of Modernity* (Seattle: University of Washington Press, 1990), p. 61.

67. Ibid.

68. Behler, ibid., p. 50.

69. For more on the genesis and use of this term see René Welleck, "The Concept of Romanticism in Literary History," in *Concepts of Criticism* (New Haven: Yale University Press, 1963), pp. 128–98, and Hans Eichner "Romantisch—Romantik—Romantiker," in *'Romantic' and Its Cognates—The European History of a Word*, ed., Hans Eichner, pp. 98–156 (Toronto: University of Toronto Press, 1972).

70. Behler, *German Romantic Literary Theory* (op. cit.), p. 25.

71. Da suche und finde ich das Romantische, bei den ältern Modernen, bei Shakespeare, Cervantes, in der italiänischen Poesie, in jenem Zeitalter der Ritter, der Liebe und der Märchen, aus welchem die Sache und das Wort selbst herstammt (*KA* 2, p. 335).

72. Behler, *German Romantic Literary Theory* (op. cit.), p. 26.

73. Denn nach meiner Ansicht and nach meinem Sprachgebrauch ist eben das romantisch, was uns einen sentimentalen Stoff in einer fantastischen (d.h., in einer ganz durch die Fantasie bestimmten) Form darstellt (*KA* 2, p. 333).

74. *KA* 2, p. 216. Behler uses the reaction to the French Revolution to make a broad claim about Romanticism throughout Europe: "[T]he transformation of the French Revolution into a universal and philosophical emancipation of humanity is a dominant attempt by the Romantics in all European countries of that time and explains basic features of the literary modernity manifesting itself in the romantic age. Here we are at the beginning of critical reflections about the French Revolution which constitute perhaps the most important response to this event. These reflections are inseparable from the spirit of modernity as it arose during the romantic age and from the notion of an infinite perfectibility of the human race" (Ernst Behler, *Irony and the Discourse of Modernity* (op. cit.), p. 51). Behler is quite right to highlight the connection between the French Revolution, a radical political event, and the development of Romanticism. This relation between poetry and politics is essential to understanding the modern, progressive spirit of early German Romanticism. I will return to the theme of early German Romanticism's relation to modernism in the final chapter.

75. Behler, *German Romantic Literary Theory* (op. cit.), p. 30. 'Romantic' took on a polemical, caricaturing designation later, with the advent of the Heidel-

berg Romantics. The Homer translator Johann F. Voss applied the term disparagingly to the proponents of this style and thus it took on a negative connotation. In the 1830s and 1840s there arose a group of ardent opponents of Romanticism. These representatives of the "New Germany" (das Junge Deutschland) included Heinrich Heine, Arnold Ruge, and Theodor Echtermeyer (ibid., p. 32). Hegel was also highly critical of Romanticism, deeming it a type of subjectivity without any continents, the "apex of subjectivity separating itself from the unifying substance" (ibid.). In the late 1800s and early 1900s several efforts were undertaken to investigate the contributions of the early Romantics. Important contributors to this endeavor include Richarda Huch, Carl Schmitt, Georg Lukács, Oskar Walzel, Josef Körner, Paul Kluckhohn. It was within this context that the term *Romantic School* became broken down into early Romanticism or Jena Romantics, Middle Romanticism or Heidelberg Romantics, and late Romanticism.

76. The manuscript of these lectures consists of student notes. It was found in 1927 by Josef Körner. Körner prepared the first printing of these lectures and then gave the manuscript to the University of Bonn Library. Unfortunately, the manuscript is now missing; as a result, all subsequent editions must rely upon that of Körner. See Jean-Jacques Anstatt, *KA* 12, 20–21.

77. Behler notes that the awareness of a national consciousness that arose in Schlegel during his years in Paris played a role in his religious conversion. In Köln, after returning from Paris, Schlegel became intensely interested in German history, especially the medieval period. This interest found expression in his lectures on history (1811). His friendship with Sulpiz and Melchior Boissereé [(1783–1854) (1786–1851)] was also influential in his conversion; they were Catholics, and the city of Köln, also known at the "German Rome," was strongly influenced by Catholicism. His wife, Dorothea, who converted from Judaism to Protestantism in 1804, and then to Catholicism in 1808, was also an important influence in his decision to convert to Catholicism.

The Schlegel of this late phase is markedly different from the revolutionary, "romantic" Schlegel. The problem of reconciling these two phases of thought is more difficult than that of relating the early "classical" period with the middle "romantic" period. In his work on Indian thought (*Über die Sprache und Weisheit der Indier* [1808]) Schlegel makes his break with pantheism explicit (*KA* 8, 229, 243). In an essay on Fichte from this period ("Die Fichtesche Lehre im Verhältnis zum Zeitalter" [1808]), Schlegel claims that the pantheistic concept of religion that he had developed in *Das Athenäum* was a type of aesthetic religion, which in the present political climate could no longer be taken seriously (*KA* 8, p. 70). In the late period, Schlegel's enthusiasm for the French Revolution is replaced by an enthusiasm for Catholicism. This replacement entails the development of some new conceptual frameworks. This is not to say, of course, that his romantic leanings altogether disappear, but their traces do diminish. For a good summary of the themes of his late philosophy, see *Concordia* (the journal he edited from 1820 through 1823), especially, "Von der Seele" (On the Soul) and "Signatur des Zeitalters" (The Marks of the Age).

78. Cited in *KA* 8, 131.

79. Katholisch werden ist nicht Religion verändern, sondern überhaupt nur, sie anerkennen.

80. For a discussion of this phenomenon, see Benno von Wiese, "Fr. Schlegel. Ein Beitrag zur Geschichte der romantischen Konversionen," in *Ph. Forschungen*, Heft 6 (Berlin, 1927), and Karl Mannheim, "Das konservative Denken," in *Archiv für Sozialwissenschaften* 57, nos. 1–2. A thorough study of the reception of German Romanticism during the Nazi period is provided in Ralf Klausnitzer, *Blaue Blume unterm Hakenkreuz: Die Rezeption der deutschen literarischen Romantik im Dritten Reich* (Paderborn: Ferdinand Schöningh, 1999). In his highly suggestive essay, *The Emergence of Romanticism* (Oxford: Oxford University Press, 1992), Nicholas V. Riasanovsky links the short burst of activity that characterized early German and English Romanticism in terms of an endorsement of pantheism and the prompt rejection of its implications, which led the romantics on both the island and the continent to seek refuge from their failed vision in political and religious conservatism. Beiser also addresses the issue of the conservative turn of the early German Romantics in "Religion and Politics in *Frühromantik*," the final chapter of his *Romantic Imperative* (op. cit.), pp. 171–86. Beiser claims that the quietistic consequences of romantic pantheism are one source of the early Romantics' later convervatism: "The more the romantics saw the divine order everywhere, even in present social and political institutions, and the more they regarded that order as the product of necessity, the less motivation they had to change things, the more resigned they became. Schleiermacher's shift from activity to contemplation marks the beginning of the end of the early progressive period of *Frühromantik*" (p. 186).

81. I am thankful to Newton Garver, who urged me to clarify the term with some examples in order to strip it of its aura of mystery, to make it less forbidding. I hope that I have succeeded. I am also grateful to Fred Beiser for valuable criticism of earlier attempts to analyze this term.

82. See esp. Susan Haack, *Evidence and Inquiry: Towards a Reconstruction in Epistemology* (Oxford: Blackwell, 1993).

83. *KA* 18, pp. 506–07, esp. nos. 12, 15.

84. Cf. *KA* 18, p. 509 (Ph.Lj., Beil. 1, 45), p. 518 (Beil. 2, 13) and *KA* 2, p. 243, no. 412.

85. In his article, "Hegel, German Idealism, and Antifoundationalism," in *Antifoundationalism: Old and New*, ed. Tom Rockmore and Beth J. Singer, pp. 105–26 (Philadelphia: Temple University Press, 1992), Rockmore links the focus on the problem of knowledge that dominated during the post-Kantian period with the interest in foundationalism and antifoundationalism: "From Kant onward, the entire German idealist tradition is centrally concerned with the problem of knowledge. Hence, it is not surprising that an interest in foundationalism and antifoundationalism runs throughout the thought of the period" (p. 106).

86. *KA* 2, p. , no. 216/Firchow, p. 46.

87. See *KA* 2, pp. 12–37.

88. *KA* 18, pp. 506–07, nos. 12, 15.

89. See Beiser, *The Romantic Imperative* (op. cit.), p. 108. I am also grateful to Fred Beiser for encouraging me to develop this notion in more detail than I had in an earlier draft of this work.

One. Finding Room for the Romantics between Kant and Hegel

1. We see this sort of critique of the poets in Plato. See *The Republic*, Book 10, esp., 595a–602b and 607b–d. Plato's views on the nature and importance of poetry are infused with Socratic irony, so it would be unfair to read him as an enemy of art, yet his criticisms of art are part of a tradition that has informed Western philosophy. The "ancient quarrel between philosophy and poetry" to which Socrates makes reference in Book 10 (607b–c) of *The Republic* was settled in favor of a philosophy modeled on the methods of mathematics and the natural sciences and distinctly *against* any methods even remotely related to poetry. The early German Romantics remove the very battlefield that gives rise to the quarrel in the first place.

2. In "Die Überwindung der Metaphysik durch die logische Analyse der Sprache," *Erkenntnis*, vol. 2 (1931): 219–41, p. 240. Translated by Arthur Pap as "The Elimination of Metaphysics through Logical Analysis," in *Logical Positivism*, ed. A. J. Ayer, pp. 79–80 (New York: Free Press, 1959).

3. "The Necessity of Inspired Reading," in *The Chronicle of Higher Education*, vol. 42, no. 22, February 9, 1996, p. A48.

4. Richard Rorty, "Philosophy as a Kind of Writing: An Essay on Derrida," in *Consequences of Pragmatism* (Minnesota: University of Minnesota Press, 1982), p. 92.

5. Rorty began his career with great sympathy for the conception of 'philosophy' outlined by the logical positivists and their emphasis on linguistic method. It is hard to imagine that the same philosopher who edited *The Linguistic Turn* in 1967, would publish something like *Philosophy and the Mirror of Nature* in 1979 and eventually develop a conception of philosophy that embraced philosophy as a kind of writing.

6. This "unconventional" style has also been employed by a host of diverse thinkers, from Blaise Pascal to Ludwig Wittgenstein. Interestingly, however, a superficial view whereby the employment of this style reveals either the nonphilosophical, or the philosophical-but-irrational-and-sloppy, nature of the project surrounds Schlegel in ways quite unlike the received views regarding other authors who employed this style.

7. Italo Calvino refers to the relationship in such terms, while also emphasizing that there are much more productive ways to view the relationship. Calvino, "Philosophy and Literature," in *The Uses of Literature*, trans. Patrick Creagh (New York: Harcourt Brace, 1982). For the affinities between Schlegel and Calvino's view of philosophy's relation to poetry, see Elizabeth Millán-Zaibert, "A Method for the New Millennium: Calvino and Irony," in *Literary Philosophers: Borges, Calvino, and Eco*, eds. J. Gracia, and C. Korsmeyer, pp. 129–48 (London: Routledge, 2002).

8. Cf. Georg Lukács, *The Destruction of Reason*, trans. Peter Palmer (Atlantic Highlands, NJ: Humanities, 1980), and Peter Viereck, *Meta-politics. The Roots of the Nazi Mind* (New York: Capricorn Books, 1941).

9. At first blush, it seems counterintuitive to read German Idealism as leading to a robust realism. Yet a closer look reveals that the most prototypical absolute idealist of the period, Hegel, did hold that human thought reflects the nature of reality itself, not its own subjectivity, which would seem to be a kind of absolute realism or materialism, rather than any form of idealism at all. Yet, since Hegel holds that the "deepest fact about the nature of reality is that it is a product of God's thought" (Paul Guyer, "Absolute Idealism and the Rejection of Kantian Dualism," in *The Cambridge Companion to German Idealism*, ed. Karl Ameriks, p. 37 (Cambridge: Cambridge University Press, 2000)), Hegel's position remains a form of absolute idealism, though not one that takes anything away from the real but rather one that attempts to make the real accessible to us in a way that Kant's dualism between appearance and reality did not.

10. Karl Ameriks, ed., *The Cambridge Companion to German Idealism* (Cambridge: Cambridge University Press, 2000), p. 8.

11. Frederick Beiser, *German Idealism: The Struggle against Subjectivism, 1781–1801* (Harvard University Press, 2002), p. 6.

12. Ibid., p. 6; emphasis added.

13. For more on this matter, see Paul Guyer, "Absolute Idealism and the Rejection of Kantian Dualism," in *The Cambridge Companion to German Idealism*, ed. Karl Ameriks, pp. 37–56 (Cambridge: Cambridge University Press, 2000).

14. Fred Beiser, "The Enlightenment and Idealism," in *The Cambridge Companion to German Idealism*, ed. Karl Ameriks, 18 (Cambridge: Cambridge University Press, 2000).

15. This is how Beiser refers to Kant's project in his article "The Enlightenment and Idealism," in op. cit., p. 22.

16. Andrew Bowie, "German Philosophy Today: Between Idealism, Romanticism, and Pragmatism," in *German Philosophy Since Kant*, ed. Anthony O'Hear, p. 366 (Cambridge: Cambridge University Press, 1999).

17. Andrew Bowie, "John McDowell's *Mind and World*, and Romantic Epistemology," *Revue Internationale de Philosophie* 50, no. 197 (3/1996): 516. This is a fascinating article in which Bowie shows that issues that are very much on the minds of contemporary analytic philosophers, for example, the question of "how to ground what we hold true of the world" (p. 518), have much in common with the philosophical project of the early German Romantics, a group of thinkers perennially ignored by analytic philosophers.

18. Ibid., p. 519.

19. In his article "Hegel, German Idealism, and Antifoundationalism" (op. cit.), Tom Rockmore acknowledges that Hegel is after some unity of thought and being but that Hegel's antifoundationalism makes such a unity impossible: "Hegel holds that [the problem of the relation of thought and being] must be resolved through a demonstration of the unity of the two relata, which has in previous thinkers only been claimed. But this unity is indemonstrable in terms of the

doctrine of circularity" (p. 122). If Rockmore is right that Hegel is indeed an antifoundationalist, then he and Schlegel share much more than either thinker ever acknowledged. It is beyond the scope of the present volume to focus on the relation and affinities between Hegel and Schlegel, for I am interested in tracing Schlegel's antifoundationalism as it develops in his reactions to the thinkers of his period. Hegel's work does not figure prominently in Schlegel's reactions. Nonetheless, I fully endorse Rockmore's claim that it is crucially important to explore the nuances of German Idealism so that a clearer image of the movement can emerge. Beiser's recent volume, *German Idealism: The Struggle against Subjectivity*, is a most productive move in this direction, as is Karl Ameriks' recent *Cambridge Companion to German Idealism*.

20. Bowie, "John McDowell's *Mind and World*, and Romantic Epistemology," op. cit., p. 529.

21. *KA* 18, p. 511, no. 64. "The Absolute" simply means that which is unconditioned.

22. As Bowie puts this: "There is then, for Kant, an essential opacity inherent in an ineluctable aspect of the subject's spontaneous 'talent' for judgment which is the condition of 'experience' [...]. The talent in question is, of course, 'schematism' " (see KrV, 179–80 A) ("John McDowell's *Mind and World*, and Early Romantic Epistemology," op. cit., p. 532).

23. Bowie, "John McDowell's *Mind and World*, and Romantic Epistemology," op. cit., pp. 532–33.

24. Warum erkennt K[ant] die coexistente Nullität d[er] Welt und nicht auch der succeßive? Die histor[ische] Approximation?—Hat er etwas Divinatorisches?—Er weiß oft, da *ist was*, aber nicht was es ist. Er ist d[er] Spürhund der [Philosophie] Fichte d[er] Jäger. Ahndung von Realen im Gegensatz des Logischen, auch eine falsche Antithese (*KA* 18, p. 61, no. 420).

25. A recent article by Richard Littlejohns helps to correct this pernicious antirational reading of the early German Romantics. In his article "Early Romanticism," in *The Literature of German Romanticism*, ed. Dennis F. Mahoney, pp. 61–78 (Rochester: Camden House, 2004), Littlejohns stresses the rational project of the early German Romantics, while acknowledging their embrace of uncertainty. He writes: "There is a long tradition of misrepresenting Early Romanticism by interpreting it as a revolt against the *Aufklärung* (Enlightenment) and as plunge into irrationalism . . . Yet . . . for Schlegel and Novalis at least the emphasis on self-expression is on the importance of reason, on—to use one of their favorite terms—circumspection ("Besonnenheit"), the detached self-criticism that serves to prevent thought from petrifying into one-dimensional certitude and complacency" (pp. 61–62).

26. In *The Cambridge Companion to German Idealism*, ed. Karl Ameriks, pp. 200–218 (Cambridge: Cambridge University Press, 2000). Zöller's article gives much-deserved credit to Schopenhauer, who, as Zöller points out, with the publication of *The World as Will and Representation* (1818), was "the author of the first completely executed post-Kantian philosophical system" (p. 200). Hegel is more often given the credit for this achievement.

27. Ibid., p. 201.
28. Ibid., p. 202
29. Ibid.
30. Ibid., p. 207.
31. Charles Larmore, "Hölderlin and Novalis," in *The Cambridge Companion to German Idealism*, ed. Karl Ameriks, pp. 141–60 (Cambridge: Cambridge University Press, 2000).
32. Ibid., p. 141.
33. Ibid.
34. Andrew Bowie puts this well when he reminds us, "The leading role in the modern German controversy over the ground of philosophy is generally attributed to Hegel, who is still too often interpreted as simply having overcome the failures of his idealist and Romantic predecessors, and thus as having obviated their potential 'irrationalism' "("German Philosophy Today: Between Idealism, Romanticism, and Pragmatism," op. cit., p. 369).
35. Andrew Bowie, "John McDowell's *Mind and World*, and Early Romantic Epistemology," *Revue Internationale de Philosophie*, 3, no. 197 (1996), p. 544.
36. Andrew Bowie, "John McDowell's *Mind and World*, and Early Romantic Epistemology," op. cit., p. 551.
37. Terry Pinkard, "Hegel's *Phenomenology* and *Logic*: An Overview," in *The Cambridge Companion to German Idealism*, ed. Karl Ameriks, pp. 161–79 (Cambridge: Cambridge University Press, 2000).
38. Terry Pinkard, ibid., p. 164.
39. See Manfred Frank, *The Philosophical Foundations of Early German Romanticism*, trans. Elizabeth Millán-Zaibert (Albany: State University of New York Press, 2004), pp. 75, 178.
40. Ibid., p. 28.
41. F. Beiser, *The Romantic Imperative* (op. cit.), p. 59.
42. Ibid., p. 4.
43. *Ohne* die Tendenz aufs Absolute könnte sich die Philosophie gegens Endliche nicht 'polemisch' verhalten. Und darum täuscht sich, wer die eigentlich radikale Moderne (oder gar Post-Moderne) mit der Ablösung von Gedanken des Absoluten beginnen lassen möchte. Gäbe es nicht die Orientierung auf ein nicht-relatives Eins, so könnten die verschiedenen in der Geschichte in Erscheinung getretenen Ausdeutungen desselben gar nicht in Widersprüche zu einander treten und sich also auch nicht vernichten (M. Frank, "*Alle Wahrheit ist relativ alles Wissen Symbolisch*—Motive der Grundsatz-Skepsis in der frühen Jenaer Romantik [1796]," *Revue Internationale de Philosophie* 50, no. 197 [1996], pp. 434–35).
44. M. Frank, *The Foundations of Early German Romanticism*, p. 175.
45. F. Beiser, *German Idealism: The Struggle against Subjectivism*, op. cit., p. 352.
46. Ibid., p. 353.
47. Ibid., pp. 657–58, note 2.
48. M. Frank, *The Philosophical Foundations of Early German Romanticism*, p. 178.

49. Absoluter idealismus ohne allen Re[alismus] ist Spiritualismus (*KA* 18, p. 33, no. 151).

50. Der halbe Kritiker ist mehr Idealist—Kant, Fichte—oder mehr Realist—Jacobi, Mohr; denn eins absolut zu sein im Gegensatz und getrennt von andern ist unmöglich. Nur der absolute Idealist ist absoluter Realist und umgekehrt (*KA* 18, p. 80, no. 606).

51. F. Beiser, *German Idealism: The Struggle against Subjectivity* (op. cit.), p. 355.

52. F. Beiser, *The Romantic Imperative* (op. cit.), pp. 65–66.

53. F. Beiser, ibid., p. 67.

54. This is a play on the title of an article by Otto Pöggeler, "Ist Hegel Schlegel? Friedrich Schlegel und Hölderlins Frankfurter Freundenkreis," in *Frankfurt aber ist der Nabel dieser Erde. Das Schicksal einer Generation der Goethezeit*, ed. Christoph Jamme and Otto Pöggeler, pp. 325–48 (Stuttgard: Klett-Cotta, 1983). Pöggeler explores the connections between Schlegel and Hegel's work, from the early Jena period, at which time it is rumored that Hegel sat in on Schlegel's lectures on transcendental philosophy (1800–01) to the more mature period of both thinkers' work: Hegel's Berlin period and Schlegel's Vienna period. Reflecting some of the prejudices that mar the article, Hegel is referred to as the "Berliner Philosoph," while Schlegel merely is the "Wiener Schriftsteller" (p. 327).

55. G. Zöller, op. cit., p. 200

56. See for example, Frederick Neuhauser, *Fichte's Theory of Subjectivity* (Cambridge: Cambridge University Press, 1990); Daniel Breazeale and Tom Rockmore, eds., *New Perspectives on Fichte* (Atlantic Highlands, NJ: Humanities, 1996); Wayne Martin, *Idealism and Objectivity: Understanding Fichte's Jena Project* (Stanford: Stanford University Press, 1997); Günter Zöller, *Fichte's Transcendental Philosophy: The Original Duplicity of Intelligence and Will* (Cambridge: Cambridge University Press, 2002).

57. Frederick Beiser, *German Idealism: The Struggle against Subjectivism, 1781–1801* (Harvard University Press, 2002).

58. Ibid., p. 11.

59. Ibid., p. 467.

60. Ibid., p. 553.

61. Ibid., p. 10.

62. R. Bubner, *The Innovations of Idealism* (Cambridge: Cambridge University Press, 2003), p. 33.

63. Es ist gleich tödlich für den Geist, ein System zu haben, und keins zu haben. Es wird sich also wohl entschließen müssen beides zu verbinden (*KA* 2, p. 173, no. 53/Firchow, p. 24). Cf. "Every philosopher has his line or tendency, that which is his departure point and his cycle. He who has a system is as spiritually lost as he who has none. One must indeed combine both" (Jeder Philosoph hat auch seine Linie—Tendenz was sein Punctum (saliens) und seinen Cycluz. Wer ein System hat, ist so gut geistig verlohren, als wer keins hat. Man muß eben beides verbinden) (*KA* 18, p. 80, no. 614).

64. Andrew Bowie, "John McDowell's *Mind and World*, and Early Romantic Epistemology," op. cit., p. 553.

65. Alle Wahrheit ist relativ; alles Wissen [ist] symbolisch, and die Philosophie [ist] unendlich (*KA* 12, p. 232).

66. Der Satz, dass alle Wahrheit relativ sey, könnte leicht auf eine allgemeine Skepsis hinleiten. Z. B. Wenn alle Wahrheit relativ ist, so ist auch der Satz relativ, dass alle Wahrheit relativ sey. Wenn alles richtig verstanden wird, so kann man dies auch zugeben. Es ist damit nichts gewonnen; man kann nicht nur diesen Satz zugeben, sondern auch das, dass das ganze System der Philosophie relativ sey (*KA* 12, p. 237).

67. For an extensive treatment of the nuances of Schlegel's relativism, see Manfred Frank, "Alle Wahrheit is Relativ, Alles Wissen Symbolisch: Motive der Grundsatz-Skepsis in der frühen Jenaer Romantik (1796)," *Revue Internationale de Philosophie* 197 (1995): 403–36. In this article he offers this very important observation regarding the sense in which we are to understand Schlegel's appeal to relativism, "Die Wahrheit ist übrigens nicht relativ in dem Sinne, wie zeitgenössische Relativisten das wollen, nämlich abhängig von einem bestimmten Weltbild oder Begriffschema. Schlegel vertritt vielmehr—ebenso wie Novalis—eine Kohärenztheorie der Wahrheit. Danach ist wahr, 'was sich aufs ganze bezieht'" (416–17).

68. Absolute Wahrheit kann nicht zugegeben werden; und dies ist die Urkunde für die Freyheit der Gedanken und des Geistes. Wenn die absolute Wahrheit gefunden wäre, so wäre damit das Geschäft des Geistes vollendet, und er müsste aufhören zu seyn, da er nur in der Thätigkeit existiert (*KA* 12).

69. Bowie describes the romantic position well: "There is little doubt that Novalis, like both Schelling and Schlegel, does assume a coherence theory of truth, in which particular truths are constituted via the relationships within a totality; given that the totality could not in Romantic terms ever be said to be complete, truth is open to constant revision and will consist in fallibilistic consensus . . . Hegel is also at first sight a coherence theorist, but the completion of his system of reflection turns coherence into correspondence: if the end really is the truth of what seemed immediate at the beginning the two must in fact correspond. If Hegel's form of correspondence is, as the Romantic arguments suggest, unrealizable, truth becomes instead a regulative idea which we understand via our feeling of the lack of being inherent in all reflection, thus by the impossibility of correspondence and the need for the ever renewed praxis of interpretation in new contexts" ("John McDowell's *Mind and World*, and Early Romantic Epistemology," op. cit., pp. 548–49).

70. *KA* 2, p. 178.

71. Den Anfangspunkt für die Philosophie provisorisch nachweisen zu wollen, mag einer angehen, als das Grundpinzip (wenn es übrigens ein Grundprinzip gibt) von der Philosophie abgesondert angeben, wie das wirklich in einigen wissenschaftlichen Einleitungen ist versucht worden. Man kann zugeben, daß in einer vorläufigen Abhandlung der Punkt, von wo aus man zu philosophieren beginnen muß, aufgesucht und nachgewiesen werde (*KA* 12, p. 110).

72. The reception of Schlegel's journal, *Das Athenäum*, was not warm. Many philosophers, especially those targeted in its pages, took offense at their portray-

als. There were also frequent complaints about the *Unverständlichkeit* of the entries, especially the fragments. The essay on incomprehensibility was published in the last issue of the journal, a kind of swan song.

73. F. Beiser, *The Romantic Imperative* (op. cit.), p. 67

74. This is a far cry from Berlin's claims in *The Roots of Romanticism* (Princeton, NJ: Princeton University Press, 1999). Berlin characterizes Romanticism (not distinguishing between early, middle, or late) as an anti-Enlightenment movement that was rooted in irrationalism and the blind forces of the will and led to a kind of poetic mythology that culminated in a glorified nationalism. He argues that the two most prominent consequences of Romanticism were existentialism and fascism. See my review of this work in *Essays in Philosophy: A Biannual Journal* 3, no. 1 (January 2002).

75. "In einer Kritik der Philosophie muß die Philosophie als Kunst betrachtet werden" (*KA* 18, p. 79, no. 601).

76. Es gibt Wirklichkeit, die man nicht besser behandeln kann, als indem man sie wie Poesie behandelt. Feindschaft, sogenanntes Unglück, Mißverhältniß. Dergleichen gibt es sehr viel in der Welt. Alle Mitteldinge zwischen Mensch und Sachen sind Poesie (*KA* 18, p. 89, no. 719).

77. In a manner quite similar to that of Schlegel, Adorno saw the literary form as connected to philosophical method and so to the conception of truth: "Im emphatischen Essay entledigt sich der Gedanke der traditionellen Idee von der Wahrheit. Damit suspendiert er zugleich den traditionellen Begriff von Methode" (In *Der Essay als Form*, Noten zur Literaratur 1, Schriften Band 11 (Frankfurt a.Main: Suhrkamp, 1958), p. 25). For an excellent treatment of the philosophical relevance of literary form, see *Literarische Formen der Philosophie*, ed. Gottfried Gabriel and Christiane Schildknecht (Stuttgart: Metzlersche Verlag, 1990).

Two. Searching for the Grounds of Knowledge

1. George di Giovanni describes this in his article, "The First Twenty Years of Critique: The Spinoza Connection," in *The Cambridge Companion to Kant*, ed. Paul Guyer, pp. 417–48 (Cambridge: Cambridge University Press, 1995).

2. In his analysis of the period between 1781 and 1794, Frederick Beiser claims that "philosophers devoted themselves to a single fundamental problem . . . If we were to formulate this issue in a single phrase, we might call it the authority of reason" (Frederick Beiser, *The Fate of Reason* (Cambridge, Mass: Harvard University Press, 1987), p. 1.

3. Frederick Beiser, "Early Romanticism and the Aufklärung," in *What Is Enlightenment? Eighteenth Century Answers and Twentieth Century Questions*, ed., James Schmidt, p. 323 (Berkeley: University of California Press, 1996).

4. For more on this debate, see Alexander Altmann, *Moses Mendelssohn: A Biographical Study* (University, Alabama: University of Alabama Press, 1973), pp. 593–759; Frederick Beiser, *The Fate of Reason: German Philosophy from Kant to Fichte* (Cambridge: Harvard University Press, 1987), esp. chap. 2, "Jacobi and the Pantheism Controversy," pp. 44–91; Stephen Bell, *Spinoza in Germany from 1670 to the Age of Goethe* (University of London: Institute of Germanic Studies, 1984); and Dale Snow, "F. H. Jacobi and the Development of German Idealism," *Journal*

of the History of Philosophy 25, no. 3 (July 1987): 397–416; and ibid., "Jacobi's Critique of the Enlightenment," in *What Is Enlightenment?* op. cit., pp. 306–16.

5. This was *Morgenstunde oder Vorlesungen über das Daseyn Gottes* (Morning Hours or Lectures on the Existence of God), which was eventually published in October 1785.

6. It is not insignificant that this is four years after the publication of the first edition of Kant's *Critique of Pure Reason* (1781) and two years before the publication of the second edition (1787). In fact, George di Giovanni indicates that Kant's emphasis on the tension between reason and faith in the second edition was probably influenced by Jacobi's publication. Cf. Di Giovanni, "The First Twenty Years of Critique: The Spinzoa Connection," in *The Cambridge Companion to Kant*, ed. Paul Guyer, pp. 417–48 (Cambridge: Cambridge University Press, 1992).

7. *Über die Lehre des Spinoza in Briefen an Herrn Moses Mendelssohn* (Breslau: Loewe, 1789), pp. 215ff. The translation is mine, though I have consulted George di Giovanni's translation in *Friedrich Heinrich Jacobi: The Main Philosophical Writings and the Novel Allwill*, op. cit., p. 230.

8. "The Unfinished Philosophy of Friedrich Heinrich Jacobi," in *Friedrich Heinrich Jacobi: The Main Philosophical Writings and the Novel Allwill* (op. cit.), p. 43.

9. Ibid., p. 43.

10. Ibid., p. 49.

11. Jacobi himself introduces this term in his *Spinoza Büchlein*. Yet, di Giovanni cautions us against translating this as any version of a "leap of faith," which does not appear anywhere in Jacobi's work, suggesting instead that we understand the appeal to a *salto mortale* as the inversion necessary to return us to our feet after being led by those thinkers addicted to explanation and who must walk on their heads (op. cit., p. 195, note). There is some irony in the fact that the very phrase that Jacobi used to try to return philosophers to their senses, and away from what he perceived to be an irrational approach to understanding reality, became the phrase that his critics used to brand him an irrationalist, making leaps of faith instead of carefully reasoned moves. See especially Kant's essay, "What Does It Mean to Orient Oneself in Thought?" (1786).

12. *KA* 18, p. 511, no. 64. "The Absolute" is nuanced and, as we saw in chapter 1, developed differently by each thinker who uses it, but its basic meaning remains very much the same, pointing to the unconditioned. See for example, Kant's definition in the *Critique of Pure Reason*, A 324/B 380ff.

13. Most recently, Isaiah Berlin, *The Roots of Romanticism*, op. cit., esp. pp. 21–45.

14. This was published in 1796 and is found in *KA* 2, pp. 57–77. For more on Schlegel's reception of Jacobi's work, see *KA* 8, pp. xxx–xxxvii; *KA* 2, pp. 57–77; *KA* 18, p. 3, no. 3; p. 6, no. 26; pp. 7–8, no. 41; p. 9, no. 60; p. 13, no. 104; p. 21, no. 34; pp. 54–56, no. 353, 356, 361, 364, 368, 371.

15. *KA* 2, p. 227 *Athenäum* Fragment 346/ Firchow, p. 70.

16. Altmann, op. cit., p. 679.

17. *KA* 18, p. 108, no. 941. See also *KA* 18, p. 112, no. 998.
18. *KA* 2, pp. 71–72.
19. Die erste subjecktive Bedingung alles echten Philosophierens ist—Philosophie im alten Sokratischen Sinne des Worts: Wissenschaftsliebe, uneigennütziges, reines Interesse an Erkenntnis und Wahrheit: man könnte es *logischen Enthusiasmus* nennen; der wesentlichste Bestanteil des philosophischen Genies. Nicht *was* sie meinen, underscheidet den Philosophen und den Sophisten: sondern *wie* sie's meinen. Jeder Denker, für den Wissenschaft und Wahrheit keinen unbedingten Wert haben, der ihre Gesetze seinen Wünschen nachsetzt, sie zu seinen Zwecken eigennützig missbraucht, ist ein *Sophist*; mögen diese Wünsche und Zwecke so erhaben sein, und so gut scheinen, als sie wollen (*KA* 2, p. 69).
20. *KA* 2, p. 77.
21. Wenn die wissenschaftliche Untersuchung nicht von der gerechten Voraussetzung, daß Wahrheit sein soll ausgeht, mit dem festen Entschluß und der Kraft, sie zu nehmen, wie sie gefunden wird, sondern von einer trotzigen Forderung, daß dies und jenes wahr sein soll: so muß sie mit Unglauben und Verzweifeln, oder mit Aberglauben und Schwärmerei endigen, je nachem der Untersucher mehr Mut hat, der Erfahrung oder der Vernunft Hohn zu sprechen (*KA* 2, p. 70).
22. *KA* 2, p. 69.
23. Di Giovanni, "The First Twenty Years of Critique: The Spinoza Connection," op. cit., p. 426.
24. *KA* 2, p. 72. For the most recent discussion of the central role of this concept in Schlegel's philosophy, see Manfred Frank, "*Wechselgrundsatz*: Friedrich Schlegels Philosophischer Ausgangspunkt," *Zeitschrift für philosophische Forschung* 50 (1996): 26–50.
25. *KA* 2, p. 161, no. 115; p. 178, no. 84; p. 182, no. 116.
26. Volume 1 of the letters appeared in *Der Teutsche Merkur* between August 1786 and 1787. There were eight of them.
27. Schlegel was critical of these attempts to popularize philosophy. He writes: "Through his confused popularising, Reinhold has been responsible for the misfortune that philosophy has excited a cry among non-philosophers" (Reinhold hat auch durch sein verfluchtes Popularisieren das Unglück gestiftet daß die Philosophie ein Geschrei unter den Nichtphilosophen erregt hat) (*KA* 18, p. 8, no. 44). In the commentary to this fragment, Behler claims that, because of the *Letters*, Reinhold remained in Schlegel's eyes the prototype of a mere popularizer of philosophy (*KA*, p. 375, note 44). Cf. *KA* 18, pp. 19, 20, 56, 510, 512, nos. 5, 25, 368, Beilage 1, nos. 53, 74.
28. Cf. Beiser, *The Fate of Reason* (op. cit.), p. 231.
29. I limit myself to a discussion of these two critiques because in them we find parallels and contrasts which shaped the discussion to follow and directly influenced the development of Schlegel's thought. For an account of Carl Immanuel Diez's critique of Reinhold, see Dieter Henrich, *Konstellationen. Probleme und Debatten am Ursprung der idealistischen Philosophie (1789–1795)* (Klett-Cotta, 1991), pp. 236–44.

30. *The Foundation of Philosophical Knowledge*, trans. George di Giovanni, in *Between Kant and Hegel: Texts in the Development of Post-Kantian Idealism*, ed. G. di Giovanni and H. S. Harris, p. 61 (Albany: State University of New York Press, 1985).

31. Ibid., p. 63.

32. Ibid., p. 67.

33. Ibid., p. 68.

34. Ibid., p. 57.

35. Reinhold, der erste unter den kantischen Sophisten hat eigentlich den Kantianismus organisiert und auch das Mißverstehen gestiftet (*KA* 18, p. 19, no. 5).

36. Kant geht nicht von der Tatsache aus; Erfahrung ist; wie Niethammer, Reinhold, Erhard ihn mißverstanden haben; sondern von dem unerwiesenen aber zu erweisenden Satze Erfahrung MUSS SEYN wie Beck, Schelling und Fichte ihn richtig verstanden haben. Dieser Satz muß aber durchaus erwiesen werden (*KA* 18, p. 20, no. 25).

37. Translated by George di Giovanni as *"Aenesidemus"* in *Between Kant and Hegel* (op. cit.), pp. 104–35.

38. Beiser indicates that Schulze's historical influence went beyond the controversy surrounding Reinhold's philosophy. In 1803, Hegel wrote a review of Schulze's *Kritik der theoretischen Philosophie*, a work that refined and systematized the criticisms of Kant developed in *Aenesidemus*. According to Beiser, Schulze's skepticism caused Hegel to rethink the relation between philosophy and skepticism. Beiser claims that "the conclusion of these reflections—that a true skepticism plays a positive role in every system of philosophy—was an important step toward the development of Hegel's dialectic in the *Phänomenologie*" (*The Fate of Reason*, op. cit., p. 268). Schulze also influenced Arthur Schopenhauer, who was his student at the Unversity of Göttingen in 1810. Beiser notes in particular the influence of Schulze's critique of Kant and Schopenhauer's mention of this in *Die Welt als Wille und Vorstellung* (ibid., p. 268).

39. *Aenesidemus*, op. cit., p. 109.

40. Etwas das sich bewußt is, und Subjekt heißt, etwas, dessen man sich bewußt ist und Objekt heißt und etwas wodurch man sich bewußt ist, und *Vorstellen* heißt (*The Foundation of Philosophical Knowledge*, op. cit., p. 64).

41. Cf. C. I. Diez's critique 1792.

42. *Aenesidemus*, op. cit., p. 111.

43. Ibid., p. 132.

44. The work is divided into four parts. Part 1 is dedicated to a defense of the fact of consciousness as the first principle for philosophy. Part 2 is a discussion of the status of metaphysics. Part 3 discusses the type of skepticism that can properly be directed against the *Critique of Pure Reason*. Part 4 is dedicated to the development of the concept of 'will' that Reinhold had begun to develop in vol. 2 of his *Letters on Kantian Philosophy* (*Vorrede*, vi–vii). All references to this work are from the edition published in Jena by Johann Michael Mauke, 1794. All translations are my own.

45. Ibid., p. iv.

46. Aenesidemus wird finden, dass sein Wunsch, bey meiner bisherigen Begründung der Elementarphilosophie nicht stehen zu bleiben, auch der meinige ist (pp. vi–vii).

47. Atlas indicates that Reinhold, in contrast to another great Kantian of the time, Maimon, misunderstood Kant's purposes. Maimon criticized Kant's distinction between the concepts of understanding, which he claimed to be intuitively demonstrable, and the purely systematic idea of reason (cf. *Critique of Judgment*, sections 75–78). Kant was not searching for the source nor trying to determine the cause of cognition. The *Critique of Pure Reason* was meant to be an investigation of the content of cognition. Reinhold's search for a first principle, then, is based on a creative misunderstanding of Kant's project.

48. Verstand in der engsten Bedeutung dieses Wortes, das Vermögen der Denkkraft, das sich unmittelbar mit sinnlichen Vorstellungen beschäfftigt; und aus denselben neuen Vorstellungen die Begriffe in engster Bedeuten heissen und Verknupfung der sinnlichen Vorstellungen sind—erzeugt (*Beyträge*, op. cit., p. 4).

49. Cf. ibid., pp. 5–7.

50. Cf. ibid., pp. 18–21.

51. Vernunft in engster Bedeutung, das Vermögen der Denkkraft das sich zunächst mit übersinnlichen Vorstellungen beschäfftigt, und aus denselben neue Vorstellungen, die Ideen heissen, erzeugt, die sich entweder durch Begriffe und sinnliche Vorstellungen auf Objekte der äußeren Erfahrung oder unmittelbar auf das Vorstellende Subjekt und durch dasselbe auf die Tatsachen der inneren Erfahrung beziehen (ibid., pp. 4–5).

52. Ibid., pp. 17–18.

53. Uneinig mit sich selbst (ibid., pp. 24, 57).

54. So lange die philosophierende Vernunft die gegebenen absoluten letzten Gründe durch ihre allmähligen Fortschritte noch nicht entdeckt hat, hält sie relativ lezte Gründe für die absoluten, bloß angenommene für die gegebene; ein Mißverständnis welches sich durch ihre Uneinigkeit mit sich selbst in den Streitigkeiten zwischen ihren Repräsentaten, und in der Verschiedenheit der angenommen lezten Gründe die von denselben aufgestellt werden genugsam ankündiget (ibid., p. 57).

55. Beym Suchen der letzten Grunde muss die philosophierende Vernunft zuerst von der Überzeugungen des gemeinen Verstandes ausgehen durch welcher sie nur insoferne sicher geleitet werden kann, als dieselben gesund sind (ibid., p. 17). Understanding is healthy as long as it remains within the realm of the given.

56. According to Daniel Breazeale, "The Aenesidemus review turned out to be much more than a defense of Kantianism against skepticism. It implies a fundamental reassessment of both Kant's and Reinhold's work and—in tentative but unmistakable terms—announces the discovery of a new standpoint and of a new foundation for transcendental philosophy. Fichte's review of Aenesidemus thus not only signals a revolution in his own philosophical development but marks a genuine watershed in the history of German Idealism" ("Fichte's Aenesidemus Review and the Transformation of German Idealism," *Review of Metaphysics* 34 (1980–81): 546).

57. *Review of Aenesidemus*, trans. George di Giovanni, in *Between Kant and Hegel* (op. cit.), p. 142.

58. Ibid., p. 135. This is precisely what Fichte attempts to show in his *Wissenschaftslehre*. Di Giovanni refers us specifically to the *Grundlage* (1794), pp. 97–98 and sections 8–10, pp. 102–03.

59. Ibid., p. 140.

60. Ibid., p. 141.

61. Breazeale details the "delicate position" in which Fichte finds himself throughout the review of having to agree with many of the skeptics' objections while at the same time defending the fundamental correctness of the search for the "highest principle of philosophy." In Daniel Breazeale, "Fichte's Aenesidemus Review," op. cit., pp. 545–68.

62. *Review of Aenesidemus*, op. cit., p. 141.

63. Als Propädeutik zur Wissenschaftslehre ist der Reinholdianismus nur sehr gut, und in so fern sollte man ihn werben lassen (*KA* 18, p. 512, no. 74).

64. See D. Henrich, *Konstellationen* (op. cit.), p. 244ff.

Three. Fichte's *Wissenschaftslehre*

1. Although this talk of "starting points" and "first principles" of philosophy may sound hazy to some contemporary ears, during the post-Kantian period, such issues, also described in terms of a search for grounds, guided philosophical discourse. See Robert Pippin, *Hegel's Idealism: The Satisfactions of Self-Consciousness* (Cambridge: Cambridge University Press, 1989). Pippin focuses almost exclusively on Hegel's contributions to the problem of the grounds of knowledge, offering little regarding the way with which this problem was dealt by the romantic philosophers. For a detailed presentation of how the constellation of thinkers surrounding early German Romanticism dealt with this cluster of issues, see the work of Dieter Henrich, especially *Der Grund im Bewußtsein. Untersuchungen zu Hölderlins Denken (1794–1795)* (Stuttgart: Klett-Cotta, 1992) and *Konstellationen: Probleme und Debatten am Ursprung der idealistischen Philosophie (1789–1795)* (Stuttgart: Klett-Cotta, 1991).

2. For references to Fichte's work, see "First Introduction to the *Wissenschaftslehre*" in *J. G. Fichte: Introductions to the* Wissenschaftslehre *and Other Writings (IWL)*, trans. and ed. Daniel Breazeale (Indianapolis: Hackett, 1994) (hereafter *IWL*). *J. G. Fichte, Gesamtausgabe der bayerischen Akademie der Wissenschaften*, ed. R. Lauth, Hans Gliwitzky, Erich Fuchs, and H. Jakob (Stuttgart: Frommann, 1964ff.) (hereafter *GA*).

3. Cf. Daniel Breazeale, ed. and trans. *J. G. Fichte, Introductions to the* Wissenschaftslehre *and Other Writings (1797–1800)* (Indianapolis: Hackett, 1994), p. xiii. Breazeale explains Fichte's choice to publish his *Wissenschaftslehre* in a series of installments for the *Philosophisches Journal* by emphasizing Fichte's publication record in that journal and his role as coeditor. It is, however, also important to emphasize that the journal was dedicated to questioning the feasibility of a philosophy based on first principles and that Fichte's philosophy was the main target

for many of the criticisms voiced in its various contributions. Hence, Fichte was compelled to answer in order to protect his system from these skeptical attacks, and replying to his critics in the same journal where the critics voiced their concerns was a clever strategy.

4. Dieter Henrich, *Fichtes ursprüngliche Einsicht* (Frankfurt am Main: Vittorio Klostermann, 1967).

5. *IWL*, p. 51/*GA*, p. 468.

6. Roger Scruton, *Kant* (Oxford: Oxford University Press, 1982), p. 93.

7. For a more thorough analysis of this, especially with respect to how Fichte's foundation establishes a life philosophy over and against an ontology, see Martin Heidegger, *Der Deutsche Idealismus (Fichte, Schelling, Hegel) und die philosophische Problemlage der Gegenwart* (Frankfurt am Main: Vittorio Klostermann, 1997), especially pp. 49–175. This move away from ontology and toward life is something that Fichte and Schlegel share, though the reasons motivating their moves are different.

8. As we shall see in chapter 6, Schlegel was also skeptical of any Kantian thing-like entities, but not only because of the epistemological problems they posed (viz., that they are beyond the grasp of the subject), but rather because of his organic holism.

9. Hans J. Verweyen, "New Perspectives on J. G. Fichte," *Idealistic Studies* 6, no. 2 (1976): 123.

10. Ibid., pp. 123–24.

11. Das Ich setzt sich nicht weil es sich setzt, sondern weil es sich setzen soll; das ist ein sehr großer Unterschied (*KA* 18, p. 35, no. 176).

12. Das *Ich setzt sich selbst* und das *Ich soll sich setzen* sind wohl mit nichten abgeleitete Sätze aus einem höhern, einer ist so hoch als der andre; auch sind es zwei Grundsätze nicht einer. Wechselgrundsatz (*KA* 18, p. 36, no. 187).

13. Carl Christian Erhard Schmid, "Bruchstücke aus einer Schrift über die Philosophie und ihre Prinzipien," *Philosophisches Journal*, Bd. 3, Heft 2 (1795), pp. 95–132, and Fichte's response "Vergleichung des von Herrn Prof. Schmid aufgestellten Systems mit der Wissenschaftslehre," ibid., Bd. 3, Heft 4 (1796), pp. 267–320.

14. Dass wir etwas vorstellen, dass wir einen Wille haben, dass es Gegenstände gibt. Alles diese lasst sich nicht philosophisch aus Prinzipien sondern unmittelbar erkennen ("Bruchstücke," op. cit., p. 109).

15. Ibid., p. 110.

16. Ibid., p. 101.

17. [D]en neuen und kühnen Versuch, den Anfangs und den Endpunkt alles Philosophierens zu vereinigen, in dem man dem Begriffe von einem erkennenden Subjekte, welches im Selbstbewusstsein vorkommt; ein idealistisches Absolutum unterschob, und aus der Fülle dieser erdichteten Unendlichkeit jedesmal gerade das und gerade so viel hervorzog, als man nötig zu haben glaubte, um alles, was im Bewusstsein vorkommt, daraus herzuleiten. So wird die Philosophie eine unendliche Dichtung und der Philosoph erhob sich zur Würde eines Selbstschöpfers einer Welt, eines Innbegriffs aller Dinge aus sich selbst und für sich selbst (ibid., p. 106).

18. Dass es Verstand, dass es einen Willen gebe und dass durch diese beiden Kräfte mannigfaltige Tätigkeiten und Handlungen möglich sind, das ist Tatsache, etwas Gegebenes, aber a priori gegeben, ein Objekt der Vernunft—schlechthin a priori (ibid., p. 119).

19. Auch als Naturkräfte in Verbindung mit der Natur, und in dieser Rücksicht sind dieselben a posteriori gegeben und das Bewusstseins von denselben ist mit dem ursprünglichen Selbstbewusstsein zufällig und auf eine wandelbare Weise verbunden (ibid., p. 120).

20. "Vergleichung des vom Herrn Prof. Schmid aufgestellten Systems mit der Wissenschaftslehre," *Philosophisches Journal* 3, no. 4 (1796): 267–320.

21. Manfred Frank, *The Philosophical Foundations of Early German Romanticism* (op. cit.), p. 37.

22. Meines Erachtens ist die Frage, welche die Philosophie zu beantworten hat, folgende: wie hängen unsere Vorstellungen mit ihren Objecten zusammen; in wiefern kann man sagen, dass denselben etwas, unabhängig, und überhaupt von uns, ausser uns entspreche? ("Vergleichung," op. cit., p. 287).

23. Ich gebe zuvorderst einen kurzen Abriss dieses Systems, der beiläufig dazu beitragen kann, gerade durch seine Kurze, die Leser, die sich vor dem als ungeheuer schwer verufenen Buche selbst scheinen, mit dem Systeme ihn etwas bekannt zu machen (ibid., p. 295).

24. Welches ist der Grund unsrer Behauptung, dass unsern Vorstellungen etwas ausser uns entspreche? Diese Aufgabe, die eigentliche Aufgabe aller Philosophie . . . nimmt die Wissenschaftslehre auf, und beantwortet sie folgendermassen: Die Vorstellung und das Objekt das ihr entsprechen soll, sind Eins, und eben dasselbe, nur angesehen aus zwei verschiedenen Gesichtspunkten, dass es aber aus diesen zwei verschiedenen Gesichtspunkten angesehen werden muss, liegt in der erkennbaren und darzustellenden Natur der Vernunft, ist sonach nothwendig, und ist einzusehen, als nothwendig. Die Wissenschaftslehre giebt die Einsicht, wie und warum das vernünftige Wesen beides, das doch nur eins ist, unterscheiden, und hinterher doch urtheilen müsse, dass beide, den Charakter der Freiheit, den die Vorstellung als solche hat, und den der Notwendigkeit, den das Objekt als solches hat, abgerechnet, völlig gleich sind (ibid., pp. 295–96).

25. Das Verfahren der Wissenschaftslehre ist folgendes: Sie fodert jeden auf zu bemerken, was er überhaupt und schlechthin nothwendig (darauf kommt alles an, aber gerade zu diesem Absoluten, mit gänzlicher Abstraction von aller Individualität, können wenigsten Menschen sich erheben) was er nothwendig thue, wenn er sich sagt: Ich . . . Sie postulirt: jeder der nur die geforderte Handlung wirklich vornehme, werde finden, dass er sich selbst setze, oder welches manchem klärer ist, daß er Subject und Object zugleich sei. In dieser absoluten Identität des Subjekts und Objects besteht die Ichheit (ibid., p. 296).

26. Durch sie wird der kritische Idealismus gleich zu Anfange aufgestellt, die Identität der Idealität und Realität, der kein Idealismus ist, nach welchem das Ich nur als Subjekt, und kein Dogmatismus, nach welchen es nur als Object betrachtet wird (ibid., p. 297).

27. Die Wissenschaftslehre stellt mit ihrem ersten Satze nicht nur alle Philosophie, sondern auch die Bedingungen alles Philosophierens auf; sie weist

durch ihn ab, nicht nur Alles, sondern auch Alle, die nicht in ihren Umkreis gehören (ibid., p. 298).

28. Was denkt man sich eigentlich, wenn man jenen Satz sich denkt? fragt der Philosoph weiter; und die erschöpfende Beantwortung dieser Frage ist die ganze Philosophie (ibid., p. 300).

29. Der Zweck der letztern Wissenschaft ist nicht der, ein System von Dingen zu rechtfertigen, sondern eine Reihe von Handlungen zu beschreiben (ibid., p. 302).

30. Dadurch allein aber leistet auch die Wissenschaftslehre was von der Philosophie zu fodern war. Es ist uns z.B. zur Genüge gefaßt worden, welche Prädicate der Vorstellung zukommen; was aber das Vorstellen eigentlich sei, wollten wir wissen. Dies aber läßt sich nur genetisch darstellen, so daß man den Geist zum Vorstellen selbst in Handlung setze (ibid., p. 303).

31. Es ist auch nicht Factum des Bewusstseins, daß Dinge sind; nicht Factum desselben, daß Menschen sind, Thiere, Bäume, u.s.f, sondern nur, daß dieser bestimmte einzelne Mensch, dieses bestimmte Thier, dieser bestimmte Baum ist, die vor meinem Auge schweben. Jeder Gemeinbegriff setzt eine Abstraktion durch Freiheit voraus (ibid., pp. 306–07). Cf. n. on p. 301 regarding the schematism and problem of thing-in-itself.

32. Denn das Ich bleibt gar nicht als ein gefundenes, als ein Object übrig: sondern, wenn es doch ja nach der Analogie des bisherigen philosophischen Sprachgebrauchs benennt werden sollte, nach welchem sich die bisherige Darstellung der Wissenschaftslehre nur zu sehr gerichtet und sich dadurch den Verdrehungen der Buchstäbler bloss gestellt—eine Tathandlung (ibid. p. 307).

33. Ibid., p. 307.

34. It is essential to keep in mind that Fichte's use of "imagination" comes from Kant. It is a formative capacity of the mind (not a synonym for "fantasy" or anything of the like). When he speaks of the formative power of the imagination, he is referring to the schematism, which is that process that allows us to subsume a particular under a general category. All of the concepts that Fichte mentions are empirical concepts, so the schematism works from these particulars in order to form a general concept (compare this to how it works in the case of the pure concepts of the understanding). Kant would not agree that abstracting from a particular tree to the concept of a tree in general is a product of the imagination in its freedom. Kant is careful to distinguish the free schematism from the determinant one. The former leads to our experience of the beautiful, for here the imagination "plays" with the concepts of the understanding. In the latter, the imagination is bound by these concepts. Fichte fails to distinguish between these two processes, and hence, it is easy to sympathize with charges such as Schmid's that Fichte's philosophy is an infinite poem, in which reality becomes the product of the creative powers of the mind and the connection to objective becomes tenuous. Schlegel was also critical of Fichte's neglect of the objective world.

35. Ich abstrahiere von dem Besondern in jedem Erkennen, und setze mich als das Erkennende überhaupt, gerade so wie ich vorher einen Baum überhaupt setzte; sondere diese Vorstellung von den übrigen Prädicaten, die ich mir

zuschreibe, ab, und fixiere sie in dem Begriffe eines Erkenntnisvermögens, oder eines Verstandes, gebe diesem Begriffe ein Bild, und sage: siehe, das ist mein Verstand (ibid., p. 308).

36. Setzt unter ihren Augen zusammen, was durch die Abstraction getrennt war (ibid., p. 310).

37. Auf dem Wege der Abstraction können Glieder übersprungen werden, auf dem Wege der Zusammensetzung nie (ibid., p. 310).

38. Die Wissenschaftslehre endet mit Aufstellung der reinen Empirie; sie bringt ans Licht, was wir wirklich erfahren können, nothwendig erfahren müssen, begründet sonach wahrhaft die Möglichkeit aller Erfahrung. Über diese reine Erfahrung nun kann weiterhin rasonniert, dieselbe combiniert und systematisch werden; und dies heißt mir Wissenschaft, welch da angeht, wo die Philosophie sich endet und von unendlichen Umfange ist. Wissenschaft und Philosophie sind mir sonach gar nicht einerlei (ibid., p. 317).

39. "Versuch einer neuen Darstellung der Wissenschaftslehre," *Philosophisches Journal* 7 (1797): 1–20.

40. *IWL*, p. 61.

41. "Nur dadurch, dass man den Act angiebt, durch welchen ein Begriff zu Stande kommt, wird derselbe vollkommen bestimmt" (*GA*, p. 523).

42. Alles mögliche Bewusstseyn, als Objectives eines Subjects, setzt ein unmittelbares Bewusstseyn, in welchem Subjectives und Objectives schlechthin Eins seyen, voraus; ausserdem ist das Bewusstseyn schlechthin unbegreiflich. Man wird immer vergeblich nach einem Bande zwischen dem Subjecte und Objecte suchen, wenn man sie nicht gleich ursprünglich in ihrer Vereinigung aufgefasst hat. Darum ist alle Philosophie, die nicht von dem Puncte, in welchem sie vereinigt sind, ausgeht, nothwendig seicht und unvollständig, und vermag nicht zu erklären, was sie erklären soll, und ist sonach keine Philosophie (*IWL*, p. 114/*GA*, p. 528).

43. *IWL*, pp. 31–32/*GA*, p. 446.

44. This review of the first four issues of Niethammer's *Philosophisches Journal* was published in the *Allgemeine Literatur Zeitung* (1798). See, "Rezension von Niethammers Philosophischen Journal," *KA* 8, pp. 11–32, esp., p. 26.

45. *IWL*, p. 4/*GA*, p. 420.

46. Auch in der Wissenschaftslehre muss die Methode kritisch sein; das ist Fichte nicht (*KA* 18, p. 8, no. 52).

47. Absoluter Idealismus ohne allen Realismus ist Spiritualismus (*KA* 18, p. 33, no. 151); Cf. ibid., p. 37, no. 201.

48. I do not linger here on the topic of mysticism, yet I do want to indicate its importance for the early German Romantic philosophers. Although Schlegel is highly critical of mysticism as a philosophical position, several mystical thinkers influenced him. Two of the best works on this topic are Marshall Brown, *The Shape of German Romanticism* (Ithaca, NY: Cornell University Press, 1979), and Ernst Benz, trans., Blair Reynolds and Eunice M. Paul, *The Mystical Sources of German Romantic Philosophy* (Allison Park, PA: Pickwick, 1983).

49. F. Beiser, *The Romantic Imperative* (op. cit.), p. 149.

50. *KA* 18, p. 511, no. 64.

51. Er will zu viel demonstriren und lange nicht genug... (*KA* 18, p. 32, no. 140).

52. Den Anfangspunkt für die Philosophie provisorisch nachweisen zu wollen, mag einer angehen, als das Grundpinzip (wenn es übrigens ein Grundprinzip gibt) von der Philosophie abgesondert angeben, wie das wirklich in einigen wissenschaftlichen Einleitungen ist versucht worden. Man kann zugeben, daß in einer vorläufigen Abhandlung der Punkt, von wo aus man zu philosophieren beginnen muß, aufgesucht und nachgewiesen werde (*KA* 12, p. 110).

53. Gänzlich von allen vorhergegangen Systemen und Ideen abstrahieren, und dies alles verwerfen, wie Descartes versucht hat, ist durchaus unmöglich. Eine solche ganz neue Schöpfung aus dem eigenen Geist, ein gänzliches Vergessen alles Vorhergedachten hat freilich auch Fichte versucht, ist ihm aber ebenso mißlungen (*KA* 12, p. 111).

54. Unsere Philosophie fängt nicht wie andere mit einem ersten Grundsatze an, wo der erste Satz gleichsam der Kern oder erste Ring des Kometen, das übrige ein langer Schweif von Dunst zu sein pflegt—wir gehen von einem zwar kleinen, aber lebendigen Keime aus, der Kern liegt bei uns in der Mitte (*KA* 12, p. 328).

55. *IWL*, p. 31/*GA*, p. 446.

56. Schlegel's most developed treatment of what the method of philosophy should be is found in *Die Entwicklung der Philosophie in zwölf Büchern* (*KA* 12–13). See especially his discussion at *KA* 12, pp. 307ff.

57. *KA* 2, p. 178.

58. Weil ein philosophisches System sich aus das andere stützt, zur Verständigung des einen immer wieder Kenntnis des anderen vorhergehenden erforderlich ist, und die Philosophien eine zusammenhängende Kette bilden, wovon die Kenntnis eines Glieder immer wieder zur Kenntnis des anderen nötigt (*KA* 12, p. 111).

59. System ist eine durchgängig gegliederte Allheit von wissenschaftlichem Stoff in durchgehender Wechselwirkung und organischen Zusammenhang—*Allheit* ein in sich selbst vollendete und vereinigte Vielheit (*KA* 18, p. 12, no. 84).

60. Jeder Philosoph hat auch seine Linie—Tendenz was sein Punctum (saliens) und seinen Cyclus. Wer ein System hat, ist so gut geistig verlohren, als wer keins hat. Man muß eben beides verbinden (*KA* 18, p. 80, no. 614). Cf. "It's equally fatal for the mind to have system and to have none. It will simply have to decide to combine the two" (Es ist gleich tödlich für den Geist, ein System zu haben, und keins zu haben. Es wird sich also wohl entschließen müssen beides zu verbinden (*KA* 2, p. 173, no. 53).

61. F. Beiser, *The Romantic Imperative* (Cambridge, MA: Harvard University Press, 2003), p. 126.

62. While my concern in this chapter is to present Schlegel's reading of Fichte's *Wissenschaftslehre*, it is only fair to point out that Schlegel's emphasis on the isolation of Fichte's Ich and of the entire *Wissenschaftslehre* is not shared by contemporary Fichte scholars. Consider Dan Breazeale's recent description of Fichte's *Wissenschaftslehre* (a description that would have put Schlegel right back

under Fichte's spell): "Like the self it describes, the Jena *Wissenschaftslehre* is a system that remains forever open to the 'infinite richness of experience.' For this is a philosophy that acknowledges the presence within the I itself, of a realm of irreducible otherness, absolute contingency, and ultimate incomprehensibility" ("Fichte's Abstract Realism," in *The Emergence of German Idealism*, ed. Michael Baur and Daniel O. Dahlstrom, p. 113 [Washington, DC: Catholic University of America Press, 1999]).

63. Cf. *KA* 18, p. 36, no. 185: "Construction is far more than deduction" (Construction ist weit mehr als Deduction); ibid., p. 31, no. 129: "Deduction never has an end and should never have an end (Das Deducieren hat nirgends ein Ende soll nirgends ein Ende haben). Of course, Fichte emphasizes "systematic derivation" and not deduction, and not all systematic derivation is deductive, so there are problems with some of the details of Schlegel's charges that Fichte is guilty of deduction, but the general picture of philosophy endorsed by Fichte is at odds with Schlegel's conception of philosophy.

64. *IWL*, p. 12/*GA*, p. 426.

65. Ich habe noch niemand gefunden, der an Fichte glaubte. Viele die ihn bewundern, einige die ihn kennen, einen oder den andern, der ihn versteht. Fichte ist eigentlich wie der Besoffne, der nicht müde wird von der einen Seite auf das Pferd zu steigen und darüber transcendierend herunter zu fallen.—Er idealisirt sich seine Gegner zu vollkommen Respräsentanten der reinen Unphilosohie. (*KA* 18, p. 32, no. 138).

66. This critique is concentrated in two series of fragments entitled *Zur Wissenschaftslehre* 1796 (*KA* 18, pp. 3–14, nos. 1–125) and *Geist der Wissenschaftslehre 1797–1798* (*KA* 18, pp. 31–39, nos. 126–227).

67. Postulirt man Wissenschaft und sucht nur die Bedingung ihrer Möglichkeit, so geräth man in den Mysticism und die consequenteste von diesem Standpunkte einzig mögliche Auflösung der Aufgabe ist—*das Sezten eines absoluten Ich*—wodurch Form und Inhalt der absoluten Wissenschaftslehre zugleich gegeben wird. (*KA* 18, p. 7, no. 32).

68. Hat man die Erlaubniss etwas Unbedingtes willkührlich zu setzen; so ist nichts leichter als alles zu erklären. Der Mystiker erreicht daher wirklich den positiven Theil der philosophische Aufgabe. Das hat niemand so gut begriffen als die Griechischen Sophisten und die neuern Mystiker und unter ihnen Fichte.—Dieß ist ein neuer Grund warum der Mystizismus unheilbar ist. Er hat eigentlich durchaus kein Interesse für das Technische und Historische. Bringt ihm aber was ihr wollt aus diesem Gebiete um ihn in Verlegenheit zu setzen oder stutzig zu machen und zu einer Bekehrung vorzubereiten; er wird lächeln und alles kinderleicht durch seinen *Talisman* erklären, lösen—vernichten. Er ist eigentlich *Pabst* in seinem Gebiete, und hat die unfehlbare Machte, Himmel und Hölle durch seinen Schlüssel zu öffnen und zu schliessen. Das ist inconsequent an Fichte, daß er sich für die Verbreitung seiner Philosophie interessiert (*KA* 18, p. 3, no. 2).

69. *Die Philosophie* im eigentlichen Sinne hat weder einen Grundsatz, noch einen Gegenstand, noch eine bestimmte Aufgabe. Die *Wissenschaftslehre* hat einen bestimmten Gegenstand (Ich und NichtIch und deren Verhältniße) einen bestimmten

Wechselgrund und also auch eine bestimmte Aufgabe (*KA* 18, p. 7, no. 36).
70. *KA* 18, p. 3, no. 2.
71. *KA* 18, p. 5, no. 10.
72. "Mysticism produces itself. Its ESSENCE and also its BEGINNING is the arbitrary positing of an Absolute" (*KA* 18, p. 4, no. 7). "Mysticism is self-defeating because it is sophistical and cannot tell us anything about the world" (*KA* 18, p. 3, no. 2).
73. Cf. *KA* 18, p. 32, nos. 141, 143; p. 33, no. 148. See also, *KA* 23, p. 333, and *KA* 2, p. 284.
74. Über keinen Gegenstand philosophieren sie seltner als über die Philosophie (*KA* 2, p. 165, no. 1).
75. Da die Philosophie jetzt alles was ihn vorkommt kritisiert, so wäre eine Kritik der Philosophie nichts als eine gerechte Repressalie (*KA* 2, p. 173, no. 56). Cf. Da die Philosophie so vieles je fast alles im Himmel und auf Erden Kritisiert hat; so kann sie sichs je wohl gefallen lassen, daß man sie auch einmal kritisiert (*KA* 18, p. 40, no. 228).
76. Cf. *KA* 18, p. 33, no. 143: Another one of [Fichte's] major errors is that philosophy and philosophy of philosophy are not blended; each stands alone (Auch ist ein großer Fehler daß Philosophie und Philosophie der Philosophie nicht genug *verschmolzen* ist; beides steht einzeln.). Nr. 148: Fichte is analytic and synthetic but both only in an isolated way, not blended. Therefore he is only critical not yet historical or systematic (Fichte ist analytisch und synthetisch aber beydes nur isolirt nicht verschmolzen. Also nur Kritiker, noch nicht Historischer Systematiker.). P. 37, no. 197: The spirit of a philosophy is its philosophy of philosophy (Der Geist einer Philosophie ist ihre Philosophie der Philosophie.)
77. *German Romantic Literary Theory* (op. cit.), p. 190.
78. Die Wissenschaftslehre ist... eine *Fichtesche Darstellung des Fichteschen Geistes in Fichteschen Buchstaben* (*KA* 18, p. 33, no. 144). Cf. *KA* 18, p. 3, no. 2.
79. "Antifoundationalism, Circularity, and the Spirit of Fichte," in *Fichte: Historical Contexts/Contemporary Controversies*, ed. Daniel Breazeale and Tom Rockmore, pp. 96–97 (Atlantic Highlands, NJ: Humanities, 1994).
80. Ibid., p. 100.
81. Ibid.
82. Ibid., p. 101.
83. Ibid., p. 105.
84. Ibid.
85. Ibid.
86. Ibid., p. 110.

Four. Niethammer's Influence on the Development of Schlegel's Skepticism

1. The *Ankündigung* appeared in the *Intelligenzblatt der Allgemeine Literatur Zeitung*, no. 1 on 3 January 1795, the *Vorbericht* appeared with the first issue of the *Philosophisches Journal*, mid-May, 1795.

2. Originally, Niethammer planned to call the journal one of *Jenesischer Gelehrten*, intending to limit his team of collaborators to the intellectual community of Jena. Those he planned to include were: Schiller, Fichte, Schmid, Humboldt, Heusinger, and Weisshuhn. Subsequently, he broadened the scope of possible contributors to include Erhard, Hufeland, Maimon, and Reinhold, who did not reside in Jena and changed the name to the more general one of *deutscher Gelehrten*. Cf. Marcelo Stamm, "Mit der Überzeugung der Entbehrlichkeit eines höchsten und einzigen Grundsatzes. Ein Konstellationsporträt um Friedrich Immanual Niethammers Philosophisches Journal einer Gesellschaft teutscher Gelehrten" (Munich: upublished manuscript, 1992), p. 16.

3. All references to this article are to "Von den Ansprüchen des gemeinen Menschenverstandes an die Philosophyie," *Philosophisches Journal einer Gesellschaft teutscher Gelehrten* 1, vol. 1 (1795): 1–45.

4. This is Schlegel's claim in his review of the first four volumes of the journal. *KA* 8, p. 13.

5. In his attempt to answer his critics, Reinhold was led to develop a theory of "common, healthy understanding," according to which we always begin to philosophize with a store of preknowledge that we acquire through common or healthy understanding. The crisis of his philosophy of elements and his theory of representation led him to this point. Niethammer also turned to common, healthy understanding in order to address the perceived crisis of a philosophy based on first principles. In this way, empiricism was brought in to correct the empty speculations of philosophisizing reason, that is, a reason too abstract to tell us anything about experience in the world. On Reinhold's development of a theory of common, healthy understanding, see Dieter Henrich, *Konstellationen. Probleme und Debatten am Ursprung der idealistischen Philosophie (1789–1789)* (Stuttgart: Klett-Cotta, 1991), pp. 240–44.

6. *Gemeiner Verstand* is the German term of the latinized phrase *sensus communis*. As Latin was the lingua franca in German philosophy up until the publication of Kant's *Critique of Pure Reason* (1781), both terms were used to refer to "common sense." In addition, there are references to *gesunder Menschenverstand* (common, healthy understanding). This term, too, refers to "common sense" and contains an implicit reference to that which the term *gesunder Menschenverstand* was formulated to combat, the sickness of a philosophy too removed from experience and hence given to empty flights of speculation.

7. Those written from 1796 to 1798 in Dresden, Jena, and Berlin, which were not written to be published, but rather to serve as sketches for a more complete treatment later. In a letter to his brother August Wilhelm in late 1795, he writes: "Du wirst höchst begreiflich finden, daß mir für jetzt Ausführung und Vollendung unaussprechlich schwer wird; meine Absichten müßten weniger umfassend und groß sein, wenn das nicht so wäre." The less elaborate form of expression was the fragment. Of course, as Behler indicates, there were periods of Schlegel's thought during which he defended the fragment as his specific form of presentation (*KA* 18, p. xix–xxi and p. 79, no. 601; p. 89, no. 719; p. 97, no. 815; p. 100, no. 858; p. 102, no. 880; p. 108, nos. 950, 955). By the time of his

death in 1842, Schlegel had filled 137 notebooks with fragments discussing a wide array of topics. For purposes of understanding his romantic period, however, the fragments from the "Philosophische Lehrjahre" (Philosophical Apprenticeship) and the accompanying "Beilage" (appendixes) are most relevant. The "Lehrjahre" is divided into seven sections: (I) "Philosophische Fragmente. Erste Epoche. 1" [1796]; (II) "Philosophische Fragmente. Erste Epoche 2" [1796–1798]; (III) "Philosophische Fragmente. Erste Epoche 3" [1797–1801]; (IV) "Philosophische Fragmente. Zweite Epoche 1" [1798–1799]; (V) "Philosophische Fragmente. Zweite Epoche 2" [1798–1801]; (VI) "Zur Philosophie Nr. 1. Paris. 1802 Jul"; (VII) "Zur Philosophie Nr. 2." *Paris. 1802. December <October 1803>*. This chapter concerns only those fragments written before 1798 and the accompanying "Beilage" from this period (i.e., the first two of eight "Beilage" written). These are all from *KA* 18. References will be to the volume followed by the page number.

    8. See Dieter Henrich, *Der Grund im Bewußtsein. Untersuchungen zu Hölderlins Denken (1794–1795)* (Stuttgart: Klett-Cotta, 1993), pp. 113–26.

    9. Wo ist Kants erster Grundsatz, Kritik der Vernunft, habt ihr daran nicht genug, so ist euch nicht zu helfen! Ja, mein lieber Niethammer, ich bitte, ich beschwöre Sie, brauchen Sie Ihr vorzügliches Talent, Kants Lehre klar und deutlich darzustellen, dazu, daß Sie es thun; brauchen Sie aus Reinholds, Fichte's und eigener Weise, eine Sache begreiflich zu machen, so viel dazu, als es frommt; sein Sie der Advokat der guten Sache, nur möge Sie der gesunde Menschenverstand vor einem einzigen absoluten Prinzip bewahren, da, wenn es eins gäbe, es doch überflüssig wäre. [. . .] Von nun an erkläre ich mich zum unversöhnlichsten Feinde aller sogenannten ersten Grundsätze der Philosophie, und denjenigen, der einen braucht, zu einem Narren, der, wenn ihn der Paroxysmus angreift, aus seinem Grundsatz deduciert und syllogistisiert. Meines Erachtens soll die Maxime und (wegen meiner mag das Kind den Namen tragen) der erste Grundsatz eines jeden Menschen und Philosophen dieser sein: "Ich wünsche ein moralisches Wesen zu sein," und kann ihm der Stoff, den ihm das menschliche Vorstellungsvermögen apriori und a posteriori (wenn es noch nöthig wäre) darbietet. Die Möglichkeit beweisen, d.h. reiniget er diesen Gedanken von allem Widerspruch, so hat er alles gethan, was sich in diesem Gebiete thun läßt. (*Denkwürdigkeiten des Philosophen und Arztes Johann Benjamin Erhard* [hg. von K. A. Varnhagen von Ense, Stuttgart und Tuebingen 1830], p. 394).

    10. Weiter als Kant läßt sich nicht gehen, wenn man bloß auf Erkenntnis sieht, aber höher kann man hinaufseigen, wenn man nur auf die Übersicht dieser Erkenntnis sieht. Die höheren Prinzipien sind dann weder des Seins noch des Erkennens sondern bloss des Darstellens. [. . .] und da stehe ich nun, und muß wieder hinab, wenn ich nicht bloss einen unendlichen Horizont haben, sondern wirklich Gegenstande sehen will. Will ich aber in meiner höhen Region bleiben, so habe ich freilich Raum für alles logische Mögliche, aber ich muss nicht zurnen, wenn mir der Untenstehende hinaufruft, dass es nicht wirklich ist (ibid.).

    11. Herbert hat über das eine Prinzip von einer Seite ganz recht. Die Philosophie, die von einem Grundsatz ausgeht und sich anmaßt, alles daraus abzuleiten, bleibt auf immer ein sophistisches Kunststück, allein die Philosophie,

die bis zum höchsten Grundsatz hinaufsteigt, und alles andere mit ihm in vollkommener Harmonie darstellt, nicht daraus ableitet, ist die wahre (Ibid., p. 396).

12. Cf. Henrich, *Grund im Bewußtsein*, op. cit., p. 117. Henrich emphasizes the kinship between the conclusion of this metaphilosophical inquiry concerning the beginning of philosophy, namely, that there can be no absolute fixed starting point but only an infinite progess of approximation, with Kant's notion of the infinite moral perfectability of humans.

13. Aenesidemus ist ein dergleichen fataler Plazregen der dem Reinhold sein allgemeingültiges Fundament unter den Füßen weggespühlt hat (In Henrich, *Der Grund im Bewußtsein*, op. cit., p. 828).

14. Wo wir vorstellen, denken und empfinden, da sind wir und die Welt, wo wir nicht vorstellen denken und empfinden, da sind wir nicht und die Welt (wenigstens für uns) nicht (ibid., p. 830).

15. Ibid., p. 831.

16. Mit dieser Überzeugung der Entbehrlichkeit eines höchsten und Einzigen Grundsatzes alles Wissens, sehe ich dem Ringen der philosophierenden Urteilskraft (Vernunft passt hier nicht, die Vernunft philosophiert nicht) und ihren Repräsentanten mit großer Ruhe zu. Das Gelingen oder Misslingen ihres Beginnens geht mich als Mensch nicht an (ibid., p. 832).

17. Aber daraus folgt nicht, dass ich das suchen nach einem solchen allgemeingültigen Fundament des Wissens nicht sehr hoch achte, und ob ich gleich glaube, dass ein Satz—was immer für einer es sei—schwerlich jemals ein solches Fundament für das ganze Gebäude abgeben werde, so ist doch nicht zu leugnen dass die Philosophie durch diese Anstrengungen, einen Schlussstein des ganzen Gewölbes oder einen Grundstein des ganzen Gebäudes zu finden, schon um vieles weiter gebracht worden ist (ibid., p. 832).

18. Deswegen also ist das Aufsuchen eines oder mehrerer ersten Grundsätze für die ganze Menschheit wichtig inwiefern jene Einigkeit der Philosophie mit sich selbst für die Menschheit wichtig ist (ibid., p. 833).

19. Verhnachlässigung der Empirie and Unbekanntschaft mit der Erfahrung.

20. Fur die Vollendung der Philosophie als Wissenschaft arbeiten heisst auf die einzig zweckmässige Art die Philosophie gemeinnutzig machen.

21. Die Philosophie muss also vor allen Dingen Wissenschaft seyn, ehe sie gemeinnutzing werden kann.

22. In the fragments he wrote during this time, Schlegel also complains about the hypercritics. See *KA* 18, p. 506, no. 6; p. 512, nos. 68, 77, 78.

23. Aber es ist nicht alles was für die Philosophie zu leisten ist, dass sie selbst von aussen durch ein sicheres Fundament begründet und von innen ihren einzelnen Theilen nach zusammenhangend und vollständig ausgebildet als Wissenschaft vollendet werde. Man erwartet von der Philosophie, dass sie durch Aufstellung deutlicher Begriffe und einleuchtender Grundsätze über den Endzweck alles Wissens und Handelns, dem Menschen die bestimmte und unwandelbaren Richtung nach seinem Ziele gebe, in welcher er sich unter der blossen Leitung des Gefühles niemals unverrückt erhalten kann.

24. Sie aus den ursprünglichen Gesetzen des menschlichen Geistes ableiten.

25. Allein diese Vollendung der Philosophie als Wissenschaft ist eine Idee, der wir uns nur mit allmählichen Schritten annähern konnen.

26. Wir müssen für die Vollendung der Philosophie als Wissenschaft arbeiten und auf jedem Punkte um den wir diesem Ziele näher geruckt sind, die erweiterte Übersichten oder die großere Bestimmtheit sogleich auf das ganze System der Wissenschaften überzutragen.

27. Bei der Forderung einen oberersten Grundsatz alles Wissens aufzustellen und darauf die Philosophie als Wissenschaft zu grunden—gerade in der Hauptsache in der Bestimmung dieses Grundsatzes, vollig von einander abweichen.

28. Es ist also in dem ganzen Umfang unsers gesammten Wissens kein Satz zu finden, der die erforderliche apodictische unbedingte Gewißheit hätte, um ein solches System unsers Wissens darauf zu gründen, das in allen seinen Theilen vollendet, den Grundsatz selbst gleich, völlig unzweifelhaft und unwidersprechlich gewiß wäre ("Von den Ansprüchen des gemeinen Menschenverstandes," op. cit., pp. 44–45).

29. Diese unmittelbare Gewissheit von den Auspruchen des gemeinen Verstandes, welche aller wissenschaftlichen Untersuchung vorhergeht scheint auch allerdings fur sich allein völlig hinreichend zu sein, und einer anderweitigen Bestätigung durchaus nicht zu bedürfen (ibid., p. 3).

30. Mithin hat es allerdings den Anschein, dass der gemeinen Verstand die Hilfe der Philosophie, welche diese Allgemeingültigkeit unsers Wissens und Handelns erst zu begründens macht, gänzlich entbehren können und—wie man auch in der Populärphilosophie stillschweigend vorausgesetzt hat—alle Philosophie uberflüssig mache. Das Verhältnis des gemeinen Verstandes zur Philosophie in dieser Rücksicht betrachtet scheint der gemeinen Verstand auf den ersten Anblick die oberste Stimme unbedingt behaupten zu können (ibid.).

31. Wie sollen die Aussprüche des gemeinen Verstandes Allgemeingültigkeit unser Wissens begrunden, da sie selbst kein anders Fundament haben, als ein Gefühl (unmittlebares Bewusstsein) ihrer Allgemeinheit und Notwendigkeit? (ibid., p. 4).

32. Es ist ein grosser Unterschied zwischen dem Gefühl des Allgemeinen und Notwendigen in einem Urtheile, und der Allgemeinheit und Notwendigkeit dieses Gefühles selbst. Woran soll ich erkennen, dass das was mir als allgemein und notwendig vorkommt auch wirklich allgemein und notwendig sei? (ibid.).

33. Cf., ibid., pp. 38–39.

34. Ist von dem Factum wichtig geschlossen? Sind die Bedingungen, welche die Kritik, um das Factum zu erklären, als nothwendig in dem Subjecte voraussetzt, wirklich die notwendigen und einzigen Bedingungen jenes Factums? Ist Erfahrung nur auf diese Art einzig möglich? Es kommt also alles darauf an, das Gesetzen der bestimmten Bedingung a priori zu einem a posteriori gegebenen Bedingten, als allgemeingültig zu erweisen (ibid., p. 27).

35. Niethammer antizipiert hier die Kritik die in der heutigen Philosophie oft gegen transzendentale Argumente geltend gemacht worden ist. Transzendentale Argumente suchen apodiktische Ermöglichungsbedingungen durch Ableitung kontingenter, also nicht apodiktisch gewisser, vielmehr theorie-relativer Sätze.

36. Von einer Tatsache kann man weiter keinen Beweis fordern, als den des unmittlebaren Bewussteseins, es ist sogar widersprechenden, fur etwas historisches

einen philosophischen Beweis zu verlangen; ein Faktum kann man zwar im Bewusstsein nachweisen, aber ein philosophischer Beweis kann weder die Wirklichkeit noch die Nothwendigkeit derselben verbürgen ("Von den Ansprüchen," op. cit., p. 24).

37. Ibid., p. 23.

38. So ist die jedem Moment des Bewusstseins unmittelbar gegenwärtige Thatsache "daß Erfahrung ist" allerdings eine feste Grundlage, von welcher aus die Philosophie seinen Schrittes in der Reihe der Bedingungen aufwärts gehen kann (ibid., p. 25).

39. According to Niethammer, the fact that there is experience is not open to philosophical skepticism.

40. Mithin wird man allerdings von den Ansprüchen des gemeinen Verstandes wieder an die Philosophie verwiesen, und muß gestehen, daß nur dann, wenn die Philosophie ihre Beweise allgemeingültig und vollständig führen kann, die völlige Überzeugung von der Allgemeingültigkeit unsers Wissens statt finde (ibid., p. 38).

41. Es kommt also hier alles darauf an, wiefern die Philosophie ihre eigen Gewissheit feststellen kann; welchen lediglich von dem Satze abhängt, auf den sie alles baut. Ein Urtheil ist bewiesen wenn ich die Allgemeingültigkeit desselben, die man unmittelbar in Anspruch genommen hat, mittelbar aus der Allgemeingültigkeit eines andern Urtheils ableite (ibid., p. 41).

42. Aber allein es fragt sich erst, ob es auch einen solchen schlechthin unbedingt gewisser Satz gebe, der als Grundsatz unsers gesammter Wissens aufgestellt werden könnte (ibid., p. 44).

43. Ob sich dieser Mangel der apodiktischen Gewissheit dadurch ersetzen lasse, daß man aus einem solchen Satz das System des gesammter Wissens ableitet, den man einstweilen als Satz postuliert und durch den Erfolg selbst—indem man zeigt, dass das aus ihm abgeleitete System ein Ganzen ausmache, in welchem als dem Miettelpunkt alle Radien des Cirkels zusammmenlaufen—als Grundsatz erweist; d.h. ob die blosse Form der Philosophie als Wissenschaft die gesuchte apodiktische Gewissheit unsers Wissens begründen könne: darüber werden wir uns bei einer andern Gelegenheit umständlicher erklären (ibid., p. 45).

44. Vor aller und ohne alle wissenschaftliche Belehrung vorhanden und mithin von denselben völlig unabhängig.

45. *Ich bin zufrieden mit der Recension des Niethammerschen "Journals" nicht weil sie gelobt wird, sondern weil ich meine innerste Absicht vollkommen dabey erreicht. Das wollte ich eben: Niethammer sollte mich verstehen, Fichte aber nicht. Herr Jedermann sollte es vollkommen verstehn, aber jeder anders. Ganz klar und doch unergründlich tief. Doch mündlich mehr darüber. Da es nun mein Debut auf dem philosphischen Theater war, und ich von so unzähligen äußern Ketten geengt war: so erlaubst Du mir immer, diese leichte Formation (denn als Recension und nach ihrem Zweck ist diese nach meinem Urteil besser als irgendeine meiner Schriften) als einen wichtigen Fortschritt meines Geistes, anzusehn. Alles was ich vorher schrieb (Du weißt, welch Katastrophe ich meine), betrachte ich jetzt als Kinderei* (Jena, 5 May 1797). Letter number 31 in *Friedrich*

Schlegel und Novalis: Biographie einer Romantikerfreundschaft in ihren Briefen, ed. Max Preitz (Darmstadt: Hermann Gentner Verlag, 1957), p. 84.

46. Cf. His earliest work was more philological than philosophical. Characteristic texts from his early period include *Vom Wert des Studiums der Griechen und Romer* (1795–1796) [*KA* 1, pp. 621–42] and *Von der Schönheit in der Dichtkunst* (1795)[*KA* 16, pp. 5–31]. However, even his philological work had a strong philosophical tendency; this is seen most clearly in his review of Jacobi's novel *Woldemar* (1796), discussed in chapter 2.

47. Der Reichtum dieser Zeitschrift an wichtigen Abhandlungen, welche jeder, der sich fur die Fortschritte der Philosophie interessiert, selbst nicht bloß lesen, sondern studieren muss.

48. Niethammer's articles "Von den Anspruchen des gemeinen Verstandes an die Philosophie" and his "Briefe über den Religionsindifferentismus"; Weißhuhn's "Beiträge zur Synonymisitk"; Erhard's "Apologie des Teufels"; Maimon's "Über den Gebrauch der Philosophie zur Erweiterung der Erkenntnis"; Schelling's "Briefe über Kritizismus und Dogmatismus"; Schmid's "Bruchstücke über die Philosophie und ihre Prinzipien" and Fichte's response to this article, "Vergleichung des von Herrn Prof. Schmid aufgestellten Systems mit der Wissenschaftslehre." as well as his *Versuch einer neuen Darstellung der Wissenschaftslehre*.

49. Jede philosophische Recension muß zugleich Philosophie der Recension sein, d.h., Recension 1/0. (*KA* 18, p. 86, no. 680).

50. Wie sollte es ein Wissenschaftsurteil geben, wo es noch keine Wissenschaft gibt? Zwar müssen auch alle übrigen Wissenschaften oszillieren, so lange es an einer positiven Philosophie fehlt. Indessen gibt es in ihnen doch wenigstens etwas relativ Festes und Allgemeingeltendes. In der Philosophie is nichts ausgemacht, wie der Augenschein lehrt. Es fehlt hier noch aller Grund und Boden ... Wo soll also eine philosophische Rezension anfangen und endigen? (*KA* 8, pp. 30–31).

51. In several fragments from this period (1796–1798), we find references to Schlegel's discontent with any appeal to common sense. Cf., *KA* 18: pp. 11ff. nos. 75, 78, 111, 117, 119; p. 22, no. 43; p. 30, no. 124; p. 516, no. 110.

52. Diese Tendenz musste bei einem gerechtigkeitsliebenden Philosophen noch sehr durch das Gefühl verstärkt werden, daß er in diesem Rechtshandel zugleich Partei und Richter sein: wenn er sich einmal den gemeinen Verstand und die Philosophie als streitende Parteien dachte. Daß man aber sie sich so denken dürfe, ist es eben, was Rez. bezweifelt (*KA* 8, p. 13).

53. Niemand kann weniger beurteilen; ja niemanden interessiert es weniger, was der gemeine Verstand (in der letzten Bedeutung) eigentlich will und sagt, als den gemeinen Verstand (in der ersten Bedeutung) selbst. Die Ausspruche desselben nicht etwa zu deduzieren, sondern nur aus allen übrigen zahlosen Ausspruchen auszusondern und vollständing anzugeben, ist kein leichtes Geschäft; aber nur der Philosoph vermag es, und zwar nur durch Philosophie. Dies ist freilich ein Zirkel. Daher sagt denn auch der gemeine Verstand in jeder Philosophie etwas ganz andres, welches gewöhnlich mit dieser Philosophie vortrefflich übereinzustimmen pflegt.

54. Grundsatz der Empiriker das Allgemeingeltende ist allgemein gültig.—Das *Allgemeine* in der Aussage des unphilosophischen Verstandes kann man nur durch positive Principien aufsuchen und ausmitteln;—entweder nach der *demokratischen Fiction der Majorität*, oder durch ein *aristokratisches Patriciat.*—Man muß die Stimmen zählen oder wiegen (*KA* 18, p. 11, no. 78).

55. Wenn es möglich wäre, die Ansprüche des nicht spekulierenden Verstandes auf dem allgemeinen Gebiet und in den besondern Fächern rein historisch zu bestimmen: so müsste die Nichtübereinstimmung seines Systems den echten Philosophen zu der praktischen Voraussetzung nötigen, dass der Fehler an ihm liege, und er sich nicht bei den Möglichkeiten, die sich immer anbieten, oder doch hoffen lassen, jene Nichtübereinstimmung, unbeschadet des Systems, leidlich zu erklären, beruhigen dürfe (*KA* 8, p. 14).

56. Die *Anwendbarkeit* ist eben so wenig ein Kriterium der ächten Philosophie wie die *Mittheilbarkeit*. Wer sie zum Kriterium macht, der setzt voraus, daß die philosophische Auflösung einer bestimmten Aufgabe zur Erreichung einer bestimmten Absicht dienen soll; und widerspricht sich selbst (*KA* 18, p. 9, no. 54). See also, *KA* 18, p. 14, no. 110: here Schlegel observes that the criterion of applicability is flawed from the start for philosophy has not yet been found, and so it cannot be applied or distributed, nor does it need to be in order to be verified. He asks: "And how could one know in advance whethter truth would be communicable and applicable?" (Und wie könnte man im voraus wissen ob die Wahrheit mittheilbar und anwendbar sein wurde).

57. Eine philosophische Streitfrage kann nur vor einem philosophischen Richterstuhl ausgemacht, ein philosophischen Urtheil nur von einem philosophischen Richter gefällt werden; diejenigen welche an den gesunden Menschenverstand appelliren, legen also damit ein öffentliches Bekenntniß ihrer Unphilosophie ab— oder sie läugnen die Möglichkeit der Philosophie überhaupt. Aber freilich ist nicht jeder Streit mit einem Philosophen über seine Philosophie philosophisch (*KA* 18, p. 11, no. 75).

58. My gratitude to Leo Zaibert for raising this objection.

59. Die Philosophie, welche Zweck an sich sein soll, kann nicht ihre Bestimmung darin setzen, die Anspruchen des gemeinen Verstandes gegen den Skeptizismus zu rechtfertigen, oder zu dem gegebnen Wissen die wissenschaftliche Einheit zu suchen, ohne ihre hohe Würde ganz zu verlieren (*KA* 8, p. 13).

60. Das Wesen der Philosophie ist die *Allheit des Wissens* zu suchen. Darin liegt schon die Verneinung alles willkührlichen Setzens (was dem Wissen entgegengesetzt) und aller Widersprüche (was der Einheit und also der Allheit entgegensteht). Also sind Skeptizismus, Empirismus, Mystizismus nur *philosophierende Unphilosophie* (*KA* 18, p. 13, no. 101).

61. The most developed account of Schlegel's taxonomy is found in the lectures he delivered in Cologne (1804–1805) entitled *The Development of Philosophy in Twelve Books* (*Die Entwicklung der Philosophie in zwölf Büchern*) (*KA* 12 and 13). In the following discussion we shall focus primarily on book 1, "Introduction and Historical Characteristics of Philosophy according to Its Successive Development" (*KA* 12, pp. 107–41), for this provides the best overview of what Schlegel achieved with his historical, taxonomical approach to philosophy.

Notes to Chapter Four   213

62. On his view of critical philosophy see *KA* 18, p. 9, no. 57; p. 12, nos. 84 and 93; p. 14, no. 108; p. 91, no. 748; on his definition of dogmatism see, *KA* 18, p. 7, no. 36; p. 9, no. 57.

63. Die drei Abarten mag im Gegensatz des Kriticismus auch *Dogmatismus* nennen. Fichte ist ein Dogmatiker und Kant ein halber Kritiker (*KA* 18, p. 5, no. 10).

64. Cf. *KA* 18, p. 10, no. 67.

65. Die aller consequentesten Skeptiker, Mystiker, Empiriker sind also die welche wirklich und in der That aufhören zu philosophieren... Fichte ist so sehr Philosoph als es der Mystiker nur sien kann... Vom Mysticism ist es klar, dass er sich selbst erzeugt. Sein WESEN und auch sein ANFANG ist das willkührliche Setzen des Absoluten. Des consequenten Eklektizismus Wesen und Anfang ist das willkührliche Vernichten des Absoluten Unbegränzten, das willkührliche Setzen einer absoluten Gränze (*KA* 18, p. 4, no. 7).

66. Die drei Abarten vernichten sich nicht nur gegenseitig sondern auch jede selbst. Dass der consequenste Skeptiker mit Stillschweigen und Nichtdenken endigen müßte = 0, versteht sich von selbst. Er müßte auch aufhören zu widerlegen, weil er sich selbst widerspricht, es nicht der Mühe werth achten, aus Zwecklosigkeit—oder vielmehr auch wissen dass er nur Widerlegbares widerlegen kann. Die Mystiker endigen mit dumpfen Hinbruten in sich selbst. Der empirische Eklektiker widerspricht sich selbst dadurch, daß er philosophieren will, also *unbegränzt wissen* und doch *mit einer Gränze des Wissens abhebt*. Er behauptet etwas Widersprechendes; eine absolute sich selbst setzende Gränze des Wissens, da die Gränze doch nur aus dem Unbedingten entspringen kann (*KA* 18, p. 4, no. 6).

Die Einheit, Vielheit, Allheit der Widersprüche in Mystizismus, Empirismus, Skeptizismus deuten auf ein Abetheilung a priori—*Genealogie der Irrthümer* (*KA* 18, p. 13, no. 95).

67. Hat man die Erlaubniss etwas Unbedingtes willkührlich zu setzen, so ist nichts leichter als *alles zu erklären*. Der Mystiker erreicht daher wirklich den *positiven Theil der philosophische Aufgabe*. Das hat niemand so gut begriffen als die Griechischen Sophisten und die neuern Mystiker und unter ihnen Fichte.—Dieß ist ein neuer Grund warum der Mystizismus unheilbar ist. Er hat eigentlich durchaus kein Interesse für das Technische und Historische. Bringt ihm aber was ihr wollt aus diesem Gebiete um ihn in Verlegenheit zu setzen oder stutzig zu machen und zu einer Bekehrung vorzubereiten; er wird lächeln und alles kinderleicht durch seinen *Talisman* erklären lösen—vernichten. Er ist eigentlich *Pabst* in seinem Gebiete, und hat die unfehlbare Macht, Himmel und Hölle durch seinen Schlüssel zu öffnen und zu schliessen. Das ist inconsequent an Fichte, daß er sich für die Verbreiten seiner Philosophie interessirt (*KA* 18, p. 3, no. 2).

68. *KA* 18, p. 509, no. 42.

69. Der Mystiker ist von dem Zustand der übrigen Bildung und andrer Wissenschaften am unabhängigsten. Die Empiriker und Eklektiker verstehen sich allein aufs Historische und Technische und darum sind sie am meisten geignet wissenschaftliche Revoluzionen zu stiften (*KA* 18, p. 6, no. 28).

In Rücksicht der Anwendbarkeit und Mittheilbarkeit ist der Eklektiker am vorzüglichsten, der Empiriker philosophisch gründlicher. Da sie aber beide eigentlcih eine UN*philosophie* und technische Anwendbarkeit ihr Princip ist, so ist der Eklektiker der consequenteste. Der consequente Empiriker endigt mit einer eignen Art Mystizismus—Voltaires *Le bout de tout le monde est rien* (*KA* 18, p. 10, no. 72).

70. Der Skeptiker und Mystiker sind philosophische Idealisten. Der Eklektische Unphilosoph ein Realist (*KA* 18, p. 509, no. 42). See also *KA* 18, p. 6, no. 28; p. 11, no. 77.

71. Die Philosophie an sich ist gar keine Wissenschaft—in sofern aber alle Wissenschaften ein System machen, und philosophisch behandelt werden sollen, kann man den Inbegriff derselben auch Philosophie nennen (*KA* 18, p. 7, no. 37).

72. Die Philosophie ist weit mehr als eine evidente Wissenschaft; auch mehr als Kunst (*KA* 18, p. 104, no. 900).

73. Jeder Philosoph hat auch seine Linie—Tendenz was sein Punctum (saliens) und seinen Cyclus. Wer ein System hat, ist so gut geistig verlohren, als wer keins hat. Man muß eben beides verbinden (*KA* 18, p. 80, no. 614).

Five. Critique as Metaphilosophy

1. Karl Ameriks has recently argued that Reinhold, far from adopting the ahistorical perspective of Kant, actually initiated the historical turn in Germany. Ameriks does convincingly show that in many of his writings Reinhold integrates history into philosophy. Yet, in those writings dedicated to "completing" Kant's critical philosophy, history does not play a significant role in Reinhold's work. Hence, my claim must be appropriately limited to the positions Reinhold developed in *Beyträge zur Berichtigung der bisherigen Mißverständnisse der Philosophie* (1790) and *Über das Fundament des philosophischen Wissens* (1791). See Karl Ameriks, "Reinhold on Systematicity, Popularity, and the Historical Turn," in *Luzern Reinhold Kongress Proceedings*, 2002.

2. See Rüdiger Bubner, "Kant, Transcendental Argument and the Problem of Deduction," *Review of Metaphysics* 28, no. 3 (1975): p. 466.

3. *KA* 2, p. 366.

4. Schlegel wrote this critique of Kant's *Perpetual Peace* for F. I. Niethammer's *Philosophisches Journal*. However, because of editorial differences, it was published instead in F. Reichardt's journal *Deutschland* 3, no. 7 (1796): pp. 10–41.

5. When we begin to understand the implications of such a shift, early German Romanticism's relation to the development of the field we know today as the human sciences (*Geisteswissenschaften*) emerges and aspects of the philosophical revolution they initiated are brought to light. For more on the relation between early German Romanticism and the development of hermeneutics, see Ernst Behler, "Friedrich Schlegels Theorie des Verstehens: Hermeneutik oder Dekonstruktion?" in *Die Aktualität der Frühromantik* (Paderborn: Ferdinand Schöningh, 1987), pp. 141–60, and Klaus Peter, "Friedrich Schlegel und Adorno. Die Dialektik der Aufklärung in der Romantik und heute," ibid., pp. 219–35. Wilhelm Dilthey's work was informed considerably by the romantic view of philosophy as an essentially historical enterprise. See, for example, Wilhelm Dilthey, *Leben Schleiermachers*, vol. I, book 2 (Berlin: de Gruyter, 1970) and *Die Entstehung der Hermeneutik* (Göttingen, 1961).

6. Schlegel's charge that Kant is a half critic appears in his *Philosophical Fragments*: "As opposed to criticism, the three positions [skepticism, mysticism, empiricism] may be called dogmatism. Fichte is a dogmatic and Kant a half-critic" (Die drei Abarten mag im Gegensatz des Kriticismus auch Dogmatismus nennen. Fichte ist ein Dogmatiker und Kant ein halber Kritiker) (*KA* 18, p. 5, no. 10).

7. Eine gute Vorrede muß zugleich die Wurzel und das Quadrate ihres Buch sein (*KA* 2, p. 148, Lyceum no. 8).

8. All references are to the *Critique of Pure Reason*, trans. Norman Kemp Smith (New York: MacMillan, 1929) and are made to the A or first version of 1781 and to the B or second version of 1787.

9. Of course, a deductive method in general had not been *initiated* by Kant: both Euclid and Newton use deductive method in their thought and served as models for Kant's thought.

10. *KA* 2, p. 178.

11. For example, Michael Elsässer, in his introduction to Schlegel's *Transcendentalphilosophie*, claims that Schlegel's romantic philosophy, with its focus on the unconscious activities of consciousness, turns against the tradition of rational philosophy (Friedrich Schlegel, *Transcendentalphilosophie*, ed. Michael Elsässer [Hamburg: Verlag, 1991], p. xvi).

12. See especially *KA* 18, p. 511, no. 64.

13. The full claim goes as follows: "Ist die Erkenntnis des Unendlichen selbst *unendlich*, also immer nur unvollendet, unvollkommen, so kann auch die Philsophie als Wissenschaft nie geendigt, geschlossen und vollkommen sein, sie kann immer nur nach diesem hohen Ziele streben, und alle mögliche Wege versuchen, sich ihm mehr und mehr zu nähern. Sie ist überhaupt mehr ein *Suchen, Streben* nach Wissenschaft, als selbst eine Wissenschaft" (*KA* 12, p. 166).

14. *KA* 12, p. 328.

15. Weil ein philosophisches System sich aus das andere stützt, zur Verständigung des einen immer wieder Kenntnis des anderen vorhergehenden erforderlich ist, und die Philosophien eine zusammenhängende Kette bilden, wovon die Kenntnis eines Gliedes immer wieder zur Kenntnis des anderen nötigt (*KA* 12, p. 111).

16. R. Bubner, *The Innovations of Idealism*, trans. Nicholas Walker (Cambridge: Cambridge University Press, 2003), p. 33.

17. Absolute Abstraction findet Statt in der Elem[entar] [Philosophie]—bedingte Abstraktion (hist[orisches] Urtheil) und bedingte Spek[ulation] (Beobachtungsgeist) in der Hist[orischen] [Philosophie] Absolute Spekul[ation] in d[er] Tr[anszendentalen] [Philosophie] (*KA* 18, p. 66, no. 461).

18. A 856/B 884.

19. For more on the relevance of history for philosophy, see Whitaker T. Deininger, "Some Reflections on Epistemology and Historical Inquiry," *The Journal of Philosophy* 53, no. 14 (1956): 429–42.

20. Es hat Philosophen gegeben, welche die freilich sehr richtige Behauptung, der Philosoph müsse *Selbstdenker* sein, so stark übertrieben, daß sie vorgaben, der Philosoph müsse sich um die Meinungen und Ideen andrer gar nicht bekümmern diesen gar keinen Einfluß auf die eigne Denkart gestatten, ganz unabhängig von

fremden Unterrichte, mit absoluter Selbständigkeit seine eigne Denkart bis zur höchsten Vollkommenheit entwickeln und ausbilden, und seine Philosophie *rein* aus sich selbst erschaffen. Zu diesem Zwecke müsse er alles früher Gelernte gänzlich zu vergessen suchen. Dieses Vergessen alles früher Gehörten und Gelernten, wenn es auch schon an sich nicht *ganz unmöglich* wäre und der Natur des menschlichen Geistes entgegen wäre, würde den Philosophen nur einem *blinden Einflusse* fremder Meinungen auf seine Denkart aussetzen (*KA* 12, p. 168).

21. *Die Philosophie ist ein Experment*, und daher muß jeder, der philosophieren will, immer wieder von vorne anfangen. (Es ist nicht in der Philosophie wie in andern Wissenschaften, daß man das, was andere schon in der Wissenschaft geleistet haben, nimmt, und darauf fortbaut. Die Philosophie ist, schon ein für sich bestehendes Ganze, und jeder, der philosophiren will, muß schlechthin vorne anfangen) (*KA* 12, p. 3).

22. Es kommt auf die Ideen, Meinungen, und Gedanken der verschiedenen Philosophen an, welche zu untersuchen, zu erklären und zu beurteilen nicht Sache der Geschichte, sondern der Kritik ist (*KA* 12, p. 112).

23. Über keinen Gegenstand philosophieren sie seltner als über die Philosophie (*KA* 2, p. 165, no. 1).

24. Da die Philosophie jetzt alles was ihn vorkommt kritisiert, so wäre eine Kritik der Philosophie nichts als eine gerechte Repressalie (*KA* 2, p. 173, no. 56). Cf., Da die Philosophie so vieles je fast alles im Himmel und auf Erden Kritisiert hat; so kann sie sichs je wohl gefallen lassen, daß man sie auch einmal kritisire (*KA* 18, p. 40, no. 228).

25. Daß eine Kritik der philosophierenden Vernunft ohne Geschichte der Philosophie nicht gelingen kann, beweist uns Kant selbst, da sein Werk, das als Kritik der philosophierenden Vernunft durchaus nicht historisch genug doch schon voller historischen Beziehungen ist und er verschiedene Systeme zu konsturieren sucht (*KA* 12, p. 286).

26. An original and fruitful line of research on the contemporary relevance of early German Romanticism is found in attempts to connect the work of the early German Romantics to the area of comparative literature. This line of interpretation can be traced to Walter Benjamin's doctoral dissertation, *Der Begriff der Kunstkritik in der deutschen Romantik* (op. cit.). See also Philippe Lacoue-Labarthe and Jean-Luc Nancy, *The Literary Absolute*, trans., Phillip Barnard and Cheryl Lester (Albany: State University of New York Press, 1998) and the recent collection of essays edited by Beatrice Hanssen and Andrew Benjamin, *Walter Benjamin and Romanticism* (New York: Continuum, 2002). Schlegel does devote much time in his fragments and essays to the relation between critique and poetry, emphasizing that critique is the common pillar upon which the entire edifice of knowledge and language rests linking a lack of critique with the decline of poetry, and suggesting that culture and cultivation depend upon developing a critical attitude, especially with respect to poetry. See especially *Concerning the Essence of Critique* (*KA* 3, 51–60). Yet this focus on the connection between poetry and criticism does not entail an exclusive interest with literary criticism. After all, Schlegel sees poetry and philosophy as intimately related. Schlegel's explicit interest in philo-

sophical critique and in Kant's shortcomings as a critical philosopher is related to his concern with the very nature of philosophy.

27. Ein naturforschender Beobachter der philosophierenden Vernunft endlich könnte vielleicht bloß als solcher, und unabhängig von jedem besondern System, die Produkte derselben klassifizieren (wie der Pflanzenkenner, welcher den innern Grund der Natureinteilungen seines Gegenstandes doch auch nicht zu deduzieren vermag), ihre Krisen bestimmen, die Tendenz ihres Ganges und die Indikationen ihres Strebens auffassen und bezeichnen. Solche historischen Andeutungen über Alles, was jeder in seinem Kreise *Geist des Zeitalters* nennt, sind es vorzüglich, was man, als Präliminarien einer künftigen Geschichte, in *Übersichten* erwartet. Um jedoch für die Produkte der philosophierenden Vernunft Sinn zu haben, müßte er selbst Philosoph sein. Wäre er aber das: so würde er uns doch wieder nur die Ansicht seiner individuellen Philosophie geben können; wenn er nicht auch mehr als Philosoph wäre; "welches," um uns eines Kantischen Ausdrucks zu bedienen, "mehr sagen will, als ein bescheidner Mann sich selber anmaßen wird" (*KA* 8, pp. 31–32).

28. *KA* 2, p. 213, *Athenäum*, no. 281.

29. In several fragments from this period (1796–1798) Schlegel describes the critique of philosophy as a process in which philosophy is treated as art. For example, "In einer Kritik der Philosophie muß die Philosophie als Kunst betrachtet werden" (*KA* 18, p. 79, no. 601); "Es gibt Wirklichkeit, die man nicht besser behandeln kann, als indem man sie *wie Poesie* behandelt. Feindschaft, sogenanntes Unglück, Mißverhältniß. Dergleichen Poesie giebt es sehr viel in der Welt. Alle Mitteldinge zwischen Mensch und Sachen sind Posie. Theoretisch und artistisch muß sich der Mensch auf jede beliebige Weise stimmen können" (ibid., p. 89, no. 719).

30. Schlegel indicates that in the ancient world, philosophy was treated as an art : "Es ist Tatsache, daß die Philosophie bei dem gebildesten Volk des Altertums als Kunst getrieben wird" (*KA* 8, p. 31). In the ancient world, both art and philosophy were judged according to objective standards: art was judged according to objective standards of beauty and philosophy according to objective standards of logic.

31. He writes: "Erst mit dem Romantikern setzte sich der Ausdruck Kunstkritiker gegenüber dem älteren Kunstrichter endgültig durch" (*Der Begriff der Kunstkritik in der deutschen Romantik, Bd. I Gesammelte* Schriften, Frankfurt a. Main: Suhrkamp, 1974, p. 51). Translated into English as "The Concept of Criticism in German Romanticism," in *Walter Benjamin: Selected Writings. Volume 1— 1913–1926*, ed. Marcus Bullock and Michael W. Jennings (Cambridge, MA: Harvard University Press, 1996), pp. 116–200.

32. Cf. G. Tonelli, "*Critique* and Related Terms Prior to Kant: A Historical Survey," *Kant-Studien* 69 (1978), pp. 119–48. He gives some examples of how 'critique' was defined before the publication of Kant's *Critique of Pure Reason* that are much closer to Schlegel's view of critique than the one developed by Kant. See especially pp. 142–44.

33. Cf. *KA* 18, p. 34, no. 163: "The critical method is at one and the same time philosophical and philological" (Die kritische Methode ist zugleich philosophisch und philologisch).

34. Der Kritiker hat viel Verwandschaft mit dem Polemiker; nur geht er nicht darauf aus zu vernichten, sondern bloß zu sichten, die vorhandenen Philosophien von ihren Schlacken zu reinigen.—Kants Zweck ist nun auch nicht bloß polemisch; er sagt der Kritiker müsse sich mit der größten Vielseitigkeit und Universalität in den Standpunkt eines jeden Systems zu versetzen suchen, einem jeden Recht widerfahren lassen, was aber bei ihm nicht oft geschieht. Die Idee jedoch, daß eine Kritik der Philosophie selbst vorangehen müsse, ist ganz Kants Erfindung und gewiß sehr verdienstlich; auch hat er sich seinem Ideal hie und da genähert; dies wäre indessen noch mehr der Fall gewesen, wenn er mehr Philolog gewesen wäre und mehr philologische, kritische Rücksicht auf die Geschichte der Philosophie genommen hätte (*KA* 12, p. 291).

35. Kant im Grund höchst unkritisch (*KA* 18, p. 21, no. 35). Cf. "Die Erklärung eines *organischen* Produkts, eines *organischen* Wesens, muß HISTORISCH sein" (*KA* 18, p. 21, no. 36).

36. Die Philosophie muß kritisch sein, aber in einem ganz anderen und viel höheren Sinne als bei Kant, nach einer *lebendigen* Kritik des *Geistes* (*KA* 19, p. 346, no. 296).

37. Indeed, Schlegel offers a harsh criticism of Reinhold for having sowed confusion of Kant's philosophy with his obstinate insistence on establishing a first principle for it: "Reinhold, the first of the Kantian sophists, was really the one to organize Kantianism and also to establish misunderstanding.—searcher for a first principle" (Reinhold, der erste unten den Kantischen Sophisten hat eigentlich den Kantianmus organisiert und auch das Mißverstehen gestiftet.—Grundsucher) (*KA* 18, p. 19, no. 5).

38. He was, of course, not the only one to have such an insight. F. I. Niethammer shared this conviction, even while his solution to the problems posed by it were quite different.

Six. Philosophy *in Media Res*

1. *Philosophische Lehrjahre* (1796–1806), Beilage II Aus der ersten Epoche. Zur Logik und Philosophie 1796 (*Jena*). *KA* 18, pp. 517–21.

2. *Unendlichkeit* der Fortschritte, die nun noch bleiben. Nicht bloß der Stoff ist unerschöpflich, sondern auch die Form, jeder Begriff, jeder Erweis, jeder Satz unendlich perfektibel. Auch die Mathematik ist davon nicht abgeschlossen, kann davon nicht ausgeschlossen seyn. Aeußerst wichtig ist die *Perfektabilität der Mathematik* für die Philosophie (*KA* 18, p. 518, no. 9).

3. *Bildung* ist das Einzige, was gegen Schwärmerei sichert. Es giebt keine *Grundsätze*, die allgemein zweckmäßige Begleiter und Führer zur Wahrheit wären. Auch die gefährlichsten lassen sich für gewisse Stufen und geistige Bildung rechtfertigen und auch die sichersten und besten können in einem Abgrund von Irrthümmer führen (*KA* 18, p. 518, no. 13).

4. Es muß der Philosophie nicht bloß ein Wechselbeweis, sondern auch ein *Wechselbegriff* zum Grunde liegen. Man kann bei jedem Begriff wie bei jedem Erweis nach einem Begriff und Erweis desselben fragen. Daher muß die Philosophie

wie das epische Gedicht in der Mitte anfangen, und es ist unmöglich dieselbe so vorzutragen und Stück für Stück hinzuzählen, daß gleich das Erste für sich vollkommen begründet und erklärt wäre. Es ist ein Ganzes, und der Weg es zu erkennen ist also keine grade Linie, sondern ein Kreis. Das Ganze der Grundwissenschaft muß aus zwei Ideen, Sätzen, Begriffen, Anschauung ohne allen weiteren Stoff abgeleitet seyn (*KA* 18, p. 518, no. 16).

5. Das *Widerlegen aller andern* und der *vollendete innere Zusammenhang* sind die eigentlichen Kriterien des Systems. *Philosophie* der eigentlichste Name für die Prolegomene aller Wissenschaften (*KA* 18, p. 520, no. 21).

6. In meinem System ist der letzte Grund wirklich ein Wechselerweis (*KA* 18, pp. 520–521, no. 22).

7. Cf., *CPR* A 133/B 172.

8. In his introduction to Schlegel's philosophical lectures, Jean-Jacques Anstett describes Schlegel's concern with the problem of *Bildung* as the problem of "harmonizing the reciprocal [gegenseitig] relation between I and the world," "for Bildung is conceived by [Schlegel] as the overcoming of the finite, fragmentary [*zerstückelte*] condition of the I through a broadening, perfecting harmony with the opposing [*gegenüberstehende*] organic, infinite universe" (*KA* 12, xiii). Anstett captures one aspect of the problem of *Bildung* in Schlegel's philosophy, but more needs to be said about it in the search for knowledge and in the development of social cohesiveness, issues that I shall discuss in this chapter and in chapter 7. Behler describes *Bildung* in Schlegel's own words as a process of an "alternating action between freedom and nature" ("Friedrich Schlegel's Theory of an Alternating Principle," op. cit., p. 395).

9. "Endlich etwas Ganzes zu geben, wo man auch kein Glied supplieren muß" (*KA* 12, p. xix).

10. Ein Wissen von dem Ursprünglichen oder Primitiven gibt uns *Prinzi*pien. Und ein Wissen der Totalität giebt Ideen. Ein Prinzip ist also ein Wissen des Ursprüglichen. *Eine Idee ist* ein Wissen des Ganzen (*KA* 12, p. 4).

11. Manfred Frank, "*Wechselgrundsatz*. Friedrich Schlegels philosophischer Ausgangspunkt," *Zeitschrift für philosophische Forschung* 50 (1996): 37–38.

12. Und nun haben wir gleichsam die Elemente, die eine Philosophie geben können; es sind nämlich: *Bewusstsein* und *das Unendliche*. Es sind dies gleichsam die beyden Pole, um die sich alle Philosophie dreht (*KA* 12, p. 5).

13. Die beyden Elemente machen eine geschlossene Sphäre, in deren Mitte Realität liegt (*KA* 12, p. 6).

14. Die *Fichtische Philosophie* geht auf das *Bewußtsein*. Die Philosophie *des Spinoza* aber geht auf *das Unendliche* (*KA* 12, p. 5).

15. F. Beiser, *The Romantic Imperative* (op. cit.), p. 134.

16. Ist die Erkenntnis selbst *unendlich* also immer nur unvollendet, so kann auch die Philosophie als Wissenschaft nie geendigt, geschlossen und vollkommen sein (*KA* 12, p. 166).

17. *KA* 12, p. 7.

18. Das Ganze muss anfangen mit einer Reflexion über die Unendlichkeit des Wissentriebes (*KA* 18, p. 283, no. 1048).

19. Frank, "Wechselgrundsatz," op. cit., p. 42.
20. Cf. *KA* 12, p. 330. For Schlegel, the concept of '*Wißbegierde*' or 'desire to know' is of central importance in explaining how our knowledge grows.
21. Unsere Philosophie fängt nicht wie andere mit einem ersten Grundsatze an, wo der erste Satz gleichsam der Kern oder erste Ring des Kometen, das übrige ein langer Schweif von Dunst zu sein pflegt,—wir gehen von einem zwar kleinen, aber lebendigen Keime aus, der Kern liegt bei uns in der *Mitte*. Aus dem unscheinbaren geringen Anfange, dem Zweifel an dem Ding, der sich doch zum Teil bei allen nachdenkenden Menschen äußert,—und der doch immer vorhandenen überwiegenden Wahrscheinlichkeit des Ichs wird sich unsere Philosophie nach und nach entwickeln und in steter Progression sich selbst verstärken, bis sie zu dem höchsten Punkte menschlicher Erkenntnis durchdringt und den Umfang so wie die Grenzen alles Wissens zeigt (*KA* 12, p. 328).
22. *Die Entwicklung der Philosophie in zwölf Büchern*. The first book contains the introduction and historical characteristics of philosophy according to its successive development. Books 2, 3, and 4 treat psychology and the theory of consciousness. Books 5, 6, and 7 treat the theory of nature, theory of man, theory of godness (*Gottheit*), respectively. Book 8 is a critique of moral principles Book 9 is on morality. Book 10 focuses on natural and state law, and book 11, on politics. Book 12 deals with civil law and contains the conclusion to the lectures.
23. Die Welt ist also ein unendliches Ich im Werden (*KA* 12, p. 339).
24. This "middle" position finds many contemporary defenders. Michael Krausz writes: "We are never 'prior to' communities. We find ourselves *in* them, at least in virtue of being involved in particular practices and more generally in virtue of our ability to use language and to manipulate symbol systems at all. Here we do not start in the beginning; we start in the middle" ("Relativism and Foundationalism," *The Monist* 67, no. 3 (July, 1984): 395–404). See also J. Margolis, *Pragmatism without Foundations* (Oxford: Blackwell, 1986); Richard Rorty, *Philosophy and the Mirror of Nature* (Prinectorn: Princeton University Press, 1981); and Donald Davidson, "A Coherence Theory of Truth and Knowledge," in *Kant oder Hegel*, ed. Dieter Henrich, pp. 423–32 (Stuttgart: Klett-Cotta, 1983). The holism that Donald Davidson and Richard Rorty endorse brings with it problems similar to the problems facing Schlegel's holism. Davidson accepts a coherence theory of truth as a way to circumvent what he calls "the unintellegibility of the dualism of a conceptual scheme and a 'world' waiting to be coped with" (p. 425). Yet in overcoming this dualism, the problem of getting out of the web of beliefs to the world seems to threaten, for "nothing can count as a reason for holding a belief except another belief," something that Rorty also stresses in his *Philosophy and the Mirror of Nature*. "[N]othing counts as justification unless by reference to what we already accept, and there is no way to get outside our beliefs and our language so as to find some test other than coherence" (cited in D. Davidson, ibid., p. 426). Nonetheless, "while we cannot 'get outside our beliefs and our language so as to find some test other than coherence'—we nevertheless can have knowledge of and talk about an objective public world which is not of our own making" (D. Davidson, ibid., pp. 426–27). So we find ourselves in a position both comforting and tense,

that is, not being able to "get outside our beliefs and our language" (which could be understood, to return to Schlegel's *Athenäum* Fragment 53, as "having a system") yet able to "talk about an objective public world not of our own making" (the position of "not having a system").

25. Diese Methode, die Gegenstände nach ihrer innern Zusammensetzung und ihren Elementen, ihrer stufenweisen Entwicklung und ihren innern Verhältnissen zu sich selbst zu betrachten und zu begreifen, kann man als entgegengesetzt der syllogistischen, bloß für den subaltern, technischen Gebrauch gültigen, die *genetische* oder wegen der Ähnlichkeit mit der Mathematik die *Methode der Konstruktion* nennen (*KA* 12, pp. 322–23; cf. ibid., p. 307).

26. For an excellent treatment of these critiques as well as of the critiques of Schopenhauer and Hegel, see Moltke S. Gram, "Things in Themselves: The Historical Lessons," *Journal of the History of Philosophy* 18, no. 4 (1980): 407–31. Gram's central conclusion is that most historical critiques of Kant's thing-in-itself rest on a failure to distinguish the issues surrounding the dichotomy between the thing-in-itself and appearance, on the one hand, and the perceptual thing and its properties, on the other hand. The latter concerns the transcendental object, which cannot be known because it does not designate any kind of object. The former concerns the thing-in-itself, which cannot be given to us because we are limited to our forms of intuition (p. 423); Cf. *Critique of Pure Reason*, A 493–94/B 521–22.

27. Jacobi, *Werke*, ed. F. Roth, 6 vols. (Leipzig: Fischer, 1815), vol. 2, "Über den transzendentalen Idealismus," p. 304.

28. Gram, "The Things in Themselves," op. cit., p. 409.

29. *Critique of Pure Reason*, op. cit., B 137–38.

30. Ibid., B 137.

31. Ibid., A 189/B 232.

32. Ibid., A 249.

33. Ibid., A 182.

34. Das Ding-an-sich ist die beharrliche, selbst nicht erscheinende Grundlage der wechselnden Erscheinungen an einem durchgängig Beschränkten und Abgesonderten (*KA* 12, p. 306).

35. Bei Kant ist wieder der Begriff des Dings, zwar nicht so der Begriff des Dings überhaupt, als vielmehr der Begriff des Dings an sich. Kant halt dies identisch mit dem Übersinnlichen, welches nach seiner Behauptung, die er verantworten mag, dem Menschen unerkennbar bleibt (*KA* 12, p. 307).

36. F. Beiser, *The Romantic Imperative*, op. cit., p. 150.

37. Ibid.

38. An interesting contemporary concern for this problem is voiced by W. V. Quine in his essay "Things and Their Place in Theories," in *Theories and Things* (Cambridge, Mass.: Harvard University Press, 1981), pp. 1–23. In this essay, he defines naturalism as part of his attempt to rescue philosophy from the abyss of the transcendental. More specifically, naturalism is presented as a "project of a rational reconstruction of the world from sense data," a "project of positing a realm of entities intimately related to the stimulation of sensory surfaces" and

the accompanying construction of a language adequate to this (pp. 22–23). Naturalism, then, eliminates the question whether or in how far our science measures up to the *Ding an sich* (p. 22). It is within science itself rather than in some prior philosophy that reality is to be identified and described (p. 21). Schlegel, too, wants to rescue philosophy from the trappings of a *Ding an sich*. Of course, the way in which he does it is quite different from Quine's. Yet what they share is the conviction that reality is framed by something other than our subjectivity so that philosophy must find some way of dealing with the world that is "out there," independently of the knowing subject. Quine takes the naturalist route, whereas Schlegel blends naturalism with idealism, or Spinoza with Fichte.

39. See *KA* 12, pp. 307ff.

40. Alle Einsicht in das *Wesen* eines Dings erhalten wir indessen nur dadurch, dass wir seine Entstehung nach seiner Quelle, seinem Grunde und nach seinen Zwecken und Bildungsgesetzen erkennen; daher sind auch alle Begriffe spekulativ genommen genetische Begriffe und alle Theorie besteht nur in genetischen Begriffen;—sobald wir nicht bloss bei den äußern Merkmalen stehenbleiben, verschwindet der Begriff des Dings, als eines unsichtbaren, toten Tragers der Merkmale, und entsteht uns nur der Begriff, ein Bild des Lebens; wir erhalten dann etwas durchaus Lebendiges—Bewgliches, wo eins aus dem andern entsteht und hervorheht, kurz wir erhalten die Einsicht in die Geschichte des Dinges (*KA* 12, p. 307).

41. This cluster of philosophical problems is finally receiving attention again. Cf. John Searle, *The Construction of Social Reality* (New York: Free Press, 1995), a much-needed contribution to the problem of understanding social reality.

42. So würde uns z.B. der Begriff einer goldenen Münze, wenn wir nicht bloß auf die äußern Merkmale sähen, einesteils in Rücksicht der Form zu einer Abhandlung vom *Golde* überhaupt, d.h. also zu einem wichtigen Teile der Geschichte der Menschheit, andernteils in Rücksicht auf den Inhalt zu einer Untersuchung der Elemente der Metalle führen (*KA* 12, pp. 308–09).

43. Yet this is not an insurmountable problem as Dilthey, Heidegger, Gadamer, and other representatives of the hermeneutic tradition in Germany have shown and more recent work on the structure of social reality from Anglo-American philosophers indicates.

44. Wilhelm von Humboldt, "On the Historian's Task," in *The Theory and Practice of History: Leopold von Ranke*, ed. G. Iggers and K von Moltke (Indianapolis: Bobbs-Merrill, 1972), p. 15.

45. Manfred Frank discusses this in his article, "Alle Wahrheit ist relative, alles Wissen symbolisch," *Revue Internationale de Philosophie* 50 (1996): 403–36, see esp. pp. 435ff.

46. There is also the danger, when a philosopher deals in teleological systems, of placing a cultural prejudice within the closed system itself, that is, of measuring all by a supposedly "universal" standard that is all too local. This may very well have been the cause of many a charge of inferiority that plagued and continues to plague interpretation of other cultures. Schlegel was a multiculturalist long before the term existed to describe him as such: he and his fellow Romantics

showed an enthusiastic interest and appreciation for other cultures, not only within Europe (translating authors such as Cervantes and Shakespeare), but also for the East, showing keen interest in Indian philosophy.

47. Aus der Charakteristik der vier ersteren Arten [Empiricismus, Materialismus, Skeptizismus, Päntheismus] wird sich ergeben, dass die letztere [Idealismus] die einzige, welche auf wahrem Weg, d.h. recht eigentlich philosophisch ist. Daher muss die Untersuchung der ersteren auch notwendig jener der letzteren vorangehen (*KA* 12, p. 115).

48. Die Philosophie muss eigentlich damit anfangen, uns von dem Scheine des Endlichen und dem Glauben an die Dinge zu befreien und uns zu einer Ansicht der unendlichen Fülle und Mannigfaltigkeit erkennen lehren (*KA* 12, p. 335).

49. Erkenntnis des innern Menschen, der Ursachen der Natur, des Verhältnisses des Menschen zur Natur und seines Zusammenhangs mit ihr; oder, wenn noch keine wirkliche vollendete Philosophie vorhanden, ein Streben nach jener Erkenntnis (*KA* 12, p. 110).

50. *Ontologie* is nichts—es gibt keine allgemeinen unbestimmten Dinge (*KA* 18; *Beilage* 8, p. 561 *Zur Philosophie* no. 7).

51. *KA* 12, pp. 300, 307.

52. *KA* 12, p. 299.

53. *KA* 12, p. 326.

54. *KA* 12, pp. 307, 331.

55. *KA* 12, pp. 151, 345.

56. Wenn wir uns beim Nachdenken nicht leugnen können, daß *alles in uns ist*, so können wir uns das Gefühl der Beschränktheit, das uns im Leben beständig begleitet, nicht anders erklären, als indem wir annehmen, *daß wir nur ein Stück von uns selbst sind*. Dies führte geradewegs zu einem *Glauben an ein Du*, nicht als ein (wie im Leben) dem Ich Entgegengesetztes, Ähnliches (Mensch gegen Mensch, nicht Tier, Stein gegen den Menschen), sondern überhaupt als ein Gegen-Ich, und hiermit verbindet sich denn notwendig der Glaube an ein *Ur-Ich*. Dieses Ur-Ich ist der Begriff, der eigentlich die Philosophie begründet. Hier in diesem Punkte greifen all Radien der Philosophie zusammen. Unser Ich, philosophisch betrachtet, enthält also eine Beziehung auf ein Ur-Ich, und ein Gegen-Ich; es ist zugleich ein Du, Er, Wir (*KA* 12, p. 337).

57. Hieraus folgt nun auch, wie die Außendinge in der Philosophie anzusehen sind. Sie sind nicht Nicht-Ich außer dem Ich; nicht bloß ein toter, matter, leerer, sinnlicher Widerschein des Ichs, der dies auf eine unbegreifliche Art beschränkt, sondern, wie gesagt, ein lebendiges, kräftiges Gegen-Ich, ein Du (*KA* 12, p. 337).

58. Das Ich kann nicht gegeben sein, sonst würde es sich in ein Ding verwandeln. Es darf auch nicht vorausgesetzt werden; das wäre gegen die Methode (*KA* 12, p. 339).

59. Das bewegliche der Worte befreit uns immer mehr von der Starrheit der Dinge, und das Gemeinsame, allgemein Mittelsame von der Einsamkeit der Anschauung (*KA* 12, p. 345).

60. See *KA* 2 for his essays on literature and *KA* 5 for his novel, *Lucinde* (1799).

61. I am not alone in my esteem for the piece. For more on this see, Hans Eichner's introduction to *KA* 2, 71–79 and Andreas Huyssen, "Republikanismus und ästhetische Revolution beim jungen Friedrich Schlegel," in *Friedrich Schlegel. Kritische und theoretische Schriften*, ed. Andreas Huyssen, pp. 227–43, esp. p. 241 (Stuttgart: Reclam, 1978).

62. E. Mason contrasts Goethe's reception of Schlegel's impudent fragments to Schiller's repulsion of the same (Schiller claimed that Schlegel's "pert, opinionated, sarcastic, one-sided manner" made him "feel physically ill" [Letter to Goethe, 23 July 1798]). Goethe, Mason tells us, "took considerable pleasure in the polemical aspects of the *Fragmente*, commented genially on the Schlegels as a 'wasps' nest' and defended them against Schiller. They may well have played some part in suggesting to him the idea of his own *Maximen und Reflexionen* ('Maxims and Reflections')" (p. 213), in Eudo C. Mason, "The Aphorism," in *The Romantic Period in Germany*, ed. Siegbert Prawer, pp. 204–34 (London: Cox and Wyman, 1970).

63. Its only fault was that it was not obscene enough for Schlegel's taste; see *Literary Notebooks, KA*, p. 575. An exploration of this charge would take us too far afield—it is, among other things, an indication of how important provocation was to Schlegel. My focus in this study of Schlegel's work is on his antifoundationalism, yet his philosophical project was part of a larger concern with a reform of society, which involved shaking off the prudishness that Schlegel believed hampered social progress, especially for women. For more on his progressive view of gender roles, see Gisela Dischner, *Friedrich Schlegels Lucinde und Materialien zu einer Theorie des Müßiggangs* (Hildesheim: Gesternberg, 1980); Sara Friedrichsmeyer, *The Androgyne in Early German Romanticism* (Bern: Peter Lang, 1983); Lisa C. Roetzel, "Feminizing Philosophy," in *Theory as Practice. A Critical Anthology of Early German Romantic Writings*, ed. and trans. Jochen Schulte-Sasse et al. (Minneapolis: Universtiy of Minnesota Press, 1997); and Winfried Menninghaus, ed., *Friedrich Schlegel. Theorie der Weiblichkeit*. Frankfurt am Main: Insel, 1983.

64. Arnd Bohn, "Goethe and the Romantics," in *The Literature of German Romanticism*, ed. Dennis F. Mahoney, p. 42 (Rochester, NY: Camden House, 2004).

65. Ibid.

66. Ibid.

67. *KA* 2, p. 162/Firchow, p. 15.

68. The essay has been translated into English as "On Goethe's *Meister*," appearing in *Classic and Romantic German Aesthetics*, ed. J. M. Bernstein (Cambridge: Cambridge University Press, 2003): 269–86 (hereafter OM). I give the references to both the German original (*KA* 2, pp. 126–46) and to the Cambridge translation (OM). *KA* 2, p. 128/OM, p. 271.

69. *KA* 2, pp. 191–92/Firchow, p. 39.

70. *KA* 2, pp. 128–29/OM, p. 271.

71. *KA* 2, pp. 130–31/OM, p. 273.

72. *KA* 2, p. 130/OM, p. 273.
73. Critical Fragment no. 112, *KA* 2, p. 161/Firchow, p. 14
74. Ibid.
75. *KA* 2, p. 134/OM, p. 276.
76. *KA* 2, p. 133/OM, p. 275.
77. System ist eine durchgängig gegliederte Allheit von wissenschaftlichem Stoff in durchgehender Wechselwirkung und organischen Zusammenhang—*Allheit* ein in sich selbst vollendete und vereinigte Vielheit (*KA* 18, p. 12, no. 84).
78. *KA* 12, p. 10.
79. Die Idee der Philosohie ist nur durch eine Unendliche Progression von Systemen zu erreichen (*KA* 12, p. 10).
80. Jeder Philosoph hat auch seine Linie—Tendenz was sein Punctum (saliens) und seinen Cyclus. Wer ein System hat, ist so gut geistig verlohren, als wer keins hat. Man muß eben beides verbinden (*KA* 18, p. 80, no. 614). Cf. *KA* 2, p. 173, no. 53.
81. *KA* 2, p. 261/Firchow, p. 98.
82. *KA* 2, p. 262/Firchow, p. 99.
83. *KA* 2, p. 135/OM, pp. 276–77.
84. While the role of chaos in Schlegel's philosophy is important, I think that some authors overestimate its importance. Azade Seyhan, for example, grants to chaos a transcendental role, claiming that "Schlegel... defines chaos as the condition for the possibility of knowledge" (p. 133) in *Representation and Its Discontents: The Critical Legacy of German Romanticism* (University of California Press, 1992). There is a significant difference between Schlegel's claim that we will never leave chaos completely behind and Seyhan's claim that chaos is a condition for the possibility of knowledge.
85. *KA* 2, p. 131/OM, p. 273.
86. *KA* 2, p. 176 /Firchow, p. 27.
87. *KA* 16, no. 496.
88. *KA* 2, p. 261; *Ideen* Fragment 48.
89. *KA* 2, p. 131/OM, pp. 273–74.
90. KA 2, p. 197, *Athenäum* Fragment 206 /Firchow, p. 45.
91. One way in which the fragment differs from the aphorism is in the way that it is meant to be received: the aphorism need not be read as part of a whole. Whereas the fragment is part of the whole, system is defined as a garland of fragments so that if the fragments are not connected, pieced together, then no system emerges. Andreas Huyssen describes the difference in terms of the responses demanded of the reader by the aphorism versus the fragment, telling us that the fragment was a vehicle used by Schlegel to actively involve the reader in romantic thinking. See "Republikanismus und ästhetische Revolution beim jungen Friedrich Schlegel," in *Friedrich Schlegel. Kritische und theoretische Schriften*, ed. Andreas Huyssen, pp. 227–43, esp. p. 239 (Stuttgart: Reclam, 1978).
92. *KA* 2, p. 132/OM, p. 275.
93. The "progressive universal poetry," endorsed by Schlegel would, as Bubner points out, "gradually lead to the dissolution of all distinctions of genre,

to the unification of art and philosophy, and to the intensification of social communication" (*The Innovations of Idealism*, op. cit., pp. 32–33).

94. See, for example, Nicholas Saul, "The Pursuit of the Subject: Literature as Critic and Perfecter of Philosophy 1790–1830," in *Philosophy and German Literature 1700–1990*, ed. Nicholas Saul, pp. 57–101 (Cambridge: Cambridge University Press, 2003). He writes, for example, that "[w]henever Romantic writers use the term 'Poesie,' it connotes this implicit critique of philosophy. In the end, poetry becomes for the Romantics a mythical entity. Their texts are not only to realize philosophy's project but also to incarnate absolute poetry. In this sense poetry becomes a cult, and the cult of poetry comes to embody Germany's postrevolutionary answer to the French religion of reason. The abstract quality of some of these procedures should not mask their political status as a response to the Revolution. 'Poesie,' said Friedrich Schlegel, is a republican discourse" (p. 72).

Seven. The Aesthetic Consequences of Antifoundationalism

1. Frederick C. Beiser, *The Romantic Imperative: The Concept of Early German Romanticism* (Cambridge, MA: Harvard University Press, 2003), p. 108.

2. See Barry Smith, "Textual Deference," *American Philosophical Quarterly* 28, no. 1 (1991): 1–12.

3. See for example Habermas's treatment of Schlegel's call for a new mythology, in *Der Philosophische Diskurs der Moderne* (Frankfurt am Main: Suhrkamp, 1988), especially lecture 4, "Eintritt in die Postmoderne: Nietzsche als Drehscheibe" and lecture 5, "Die Verschlingung von Mythos und Aufklärung: Horkheimer und Adorno." In lecture 4, Habermas writes: "Under the modern conditions of reflection, which is pushed to an extreme, it is art and not philosophy that protects the flames of that absolute identity, which first were ignited in the festive cults of religious communities of faith. Art, which recovers its public character in the form of a new mythology, is no longer merely an organon of philosophy, but rather goal and future of philosophy" [Unter den modernen Bedingungen einer ins Extrem getriebenenen Reflexion hütet die Kunst, und nicht die Philosophie, die Flamme jener absoluten Identität, die sich einst in den festlichen Kulten von religiösen Glaubensgemeinschaften entzündet hatte. Die Kunst, die in Gestalt einer neuen Mythologie ihren öffentlichen Charakter zurückgewänne, wäre nicht mehr nur Organon, sondern Ziel und Zukunft der Philosophie"] (p. 111).

4. Andrew Bowie, "German Philosophy Today: Between Idealism, Romanticism, and Pragmatism," in *German Philosophy since Kant*, ed. Anthony O'Hear, pp. 357–98 (Cambridge University Press, 1999).

5. Habermas, *Texte und Kontexte* (Frankfurt: Suhrkamp, 1991), p. 90.

6. Bowie, op. cit., pp. 389–90.

7. Ibid.

8. Ibid., p. 397.

9. *KA* 2, p. 182, no. 116.

10. Jürgen Habermas discusses this work in lecture 5 of *Der philosophische Diskurs der Moderne: Zwölf Vorlesungen* (Frankfurt am Main: Suhrkamp, 1988), "Die Verschlingung von Mythos und Aufklärung: Horkheimer und Adorno," pp.

130–57. (This has been translated by Thomas Y. Levin and appeared as "The Entwinement of Myth and Enlightenment: Re-Reading Dialectic of Enlightenment," in *New German Critique*, no. 26 [1982]: 13–30.) Habermas, as stated above, treats early German Romantics with suspicion, as he reads their moves toward completing philosophy in and as poetry as pushing philosophy toward the realm of the irrational; this is part of his general concern with leveling the boundaries between literature and philosophy. For more on this, see "Exkurs zur Einebnung des Gattungsunterschiedes zwischen Philosophie und Literatur," in *Der philosophische Diskurs der Moderne* (op. cit.), pp. 219–46.

11. Behler, *Irony and the Discourse of Modernity* (op. cit.), p. 60.

12. Klaus Peter, "Friedrich Schlegel und Adorno: Die Dialektik der Aufklärung in der Romantik und heute," in *Die Aktualität der Frühromantik*, ed. Ernst Behler, ed., pp. 219–35 (Paderborn: Schöningh, 1987).

13. As Lacoue-Labarthe and Nancy observe, the emergence of early German Romanticism was a response to a triple crisis: an economic crisis, a political crisis (caused by the collapse of the progressive spirit of the French Revolution), and the crisis occasioned by Kant's *Critique*. "The characters we see assembling at Jena participated in this triple crisis in the most immediate manner. Thus their project will not be a literary project and will open up not a crisis *in* literature, but a general crisis and critique (social, moral, religious, political: all of these aspects are found in the *Fragments*) for which literature or literary theory will be the privileged locus of expression" (*The Literary Absolute*, op. cit., p. 5).

14. Karl Menges, "Romantic Anti-foundationalism and the Theory of Chaos," in *Romanticism and Beyond: A Festschrift for John F. Fetzer*, ed. C. A. Berned, I. Henderson, and W. McConnell, pp. 33–56 (New York: Lang, 1996). See also Dietrich Mathy, *Poesie und Chaos. Zur anarchistischen Komponente der frühromantischen Ästhetik* (Munich: Weixler, 1984).

15. S. Haack, "Coherence, Consistency, Cogency, Congruity, Cohesiveness, &c.: Remain Calm! Don't Go Overboard!" *New Literary History* 35 (2004): 174.

16. Cf. Schlegel's *Versuch über den Begriff des Republicanismus* (1796).

17. See Elizabeth Mittman and Mary S. Strand, "Representing Self and Other in Early German Romanticism," in *Theory as Practice: A Critical Anthology of Early German Romantic Writings*, ed. Jochen Schulte-Sasse, et. al., pp. 47–71 (Minneapolis: University of Minnesota Press, 1997), and Azade Seyhan, *Representation and Its Discontents: The Critical Legacy of German Romanticism* (Berkeley: University of California Press, 1992). Philippe Lacoue-Labarthe and Jean-Luc Nancy begin their study, *The Literary Absolute: The Theory of Literature in German Romanticism*, trans. Philip Barnard and Cheryl Lester (Albany: State University of New York Press, 1988), with a discussion of this text, using it as a kind of "overture" to the early German Romantic movement.

18. The essay has been translated into English as "Oldest Programme for a System of German Idealism," in *Classic and Romantic German Aesthetics*, ed. J. M. Bernstein (Cambridge: Cambridge University Press, 2003), pp. 186–87.

19. K. Menges, "Romantic Anti-foundationalism and the Theory of Chaos," in *Romanticism and Beyond: A Festschrift for John F. Fetzer*, ed. C. A. Berned, I. Henderson, and W. McConnell, p. 46 (New York: Lang, 1996).

20. Translated as "Speech on Mythology," in *Theory as Practice. A Critical Anthology of Early German Romantic Writings*, ed. and trans. Jochen Schulte-Sasse et al. (Minneapolis: University of Minnesota Press, 1997), p. 182.

21. Ibid.

22. Ibid.

23. Ibid., p. 183.

24. Ibid., p. 186.

25. Ibid., p. 183.

26. Ibid., p. 184.

27. Cf. *Athenäum* Fragment 304; *Ideen* nos. 41, 59, 62, 80, 108.

28. References are to the English translation of the essay, "On Incomprehensibility," in *Classic and Romantic German Aesthetics*, ed. J. M. Bernstein (Cambridge: Cambridge University Press, 2003), pp. 297–308 (hereafter, OI).

29. See esp. *Lyceum* nos. 20 and 108, *Blütenstaub* no. 2, *Athenäum* no. 78, *Ideen* no. 129, all in *KA* 2.

30. OI, p. 298.

31. OI, p. 300.

32. OI, p. 301.

33. OI, p. 302.

34. OI, p. 305.

35. At the end of chapter 3 of his book, *Leading a Human Life: Wittgenstein, Intentionality, and Romanticism*, Eldridge, after having given a brilliant account of Schlegel's use of irony, comes to a conclusion that is misleading. He claims that Schlegel's views empty the spontaneity of the human being of content, "reducing it to something more nearly resembling an animal function," and then goes on to talk of "Schlegelian nihilism." It is important to realize that, just as Schlegel's irony does not make a mockery of the world, his acknowledgement of the openness of all philosophical inquiry and the incompleteness of our knowledge does not make him any sort of nihilist. Eldridge, *Leading a Human Life: Wittgenstein, Intentionality, and Romanticism* (Chicago: University of Chicago Press, 1997), esp. pp. 83–85.

36. *KA* 12, p. 214.

37. *KA* 13, pp. 55ff. and 173ff.

38. *KA* 2, *Kritische* Fragmente 42/Firchow translation, p. 5.

39. Richard Rorty, "Thugs and Theorists: A Reply to Bernstein," *Political Theory* 15, no. 4 (1987): 572.

40. Ibid., p. 587.

41. With his view that philosophy is slowly being replaced by the arts, Rorty comes close to the view that Lacoue-Labarthe and Nancy attribute to the early German Romantics. See *The Literary Absolute* (op. cit.), *passim*, esp. pp. 35–37. I disagree with this reading of the early German Romantics. Philosophy is completed *in* and *as* poetry, but not replaced by it.

42. *KA* 12, p. xix.

43. Richard J. Bernstein, *Beyond Objectivism and Relativism* (Oxford: Blackwell, 1983), p. 255, note 38.

44. "Coherence, Consistency, Cogency, Congruity, Cohesiveness, &c.: Remain Calm! Don't Go Overboard!" *New Literary History* 35 (2004): 180.

45. Cited in Manfred Frank, *Unendliche Annäherung. Die Anfänge der philosophischen Frühromantik* (Frankfurt am Main: Suhrkamp, 1997), p. 944.

46. Richard Littlejohns provides an excellent analysis of the novel, telling us that *"Lucinde* contains thirteen independent sections—letters, allegory, Idyll, pen-portraits, dialogue—that represent variations on a set of themes relating above all to sexuality and marriage. In form it offers, and boasts about, decorative profusion or confusion (*"reizende Verwirrung" KA* 5, p. 9 and *passim*); and it rejoices in flouting pedantic order, both in the structure of the novel and in the permissive social and sexual relations which it advocates. Whimsical subjectivity and digression are the principle of *Lucinde*, as in Schlegel's theory, held together by the 'intellectual coherence' that he had first identified in *Wilhelm Meisters Lehrjahre* (Richard Littlejohns, "Early Romanticism," in D. Mahoney, ed., *The Literature of German Romanticism*, pp. 69–70).

47. *Athenäum* Fragment 116; *KA* 2, p. 182.

48. F. Beiser, *The Romantic Imperative* (op. cit.), p. 67.

49. *Phaedrus*, 274b–277a.

50. *KA* 2, *Kritische* Fragmente 108/Firchow translation, p. 13.

51. In Arthur Danto, *The Transfiguration of the Commonplace: A Philosophy of Art* (Cambridge, MA: Harvard University Press, 1981), pp. 1–32.

52. Ibid., p. 9.

53. *Hamlet* also figures prominently in Goethe's *Wilhelm Meister*, something that of course did not escape Schlegel's attention. In "On *Meister*," he refers to it as the play that "offers the occasion for such varied and interesting debate on what the secret intention of the artist might be, or what the accidental flaws in the work are" (OM, p. 280) and further comments that *"Hamlet* can seem so closely related to *Wilhelm Meister* as to be mistaken for it" (OM, p. 280).

54. Recently, Colin McGinn, who notes that in light of the fact that "fiction fails to conform to any of the methodological paradigms that have dominated philosophy at large," the contributions of literary fiction to the realm of ethics have been neglected, has tried to remedy this situation. The result of his attempt to remedy this neglect is his book *Ethics, Evil, and Fiction* (Oxford: Clarendon, 1997). In the course of the book, important connections between aesthetics and ethics are made. Schlegel's keen awareness of the philosophical relevance of literature was ahead of its time.

55. *KA* 2, p. 335.

56. *KA* 2, *Über Tiecks Don Quixote*, pp. 281–83.

57. Schlegel claims, "Irony is the clear consciousness of eternal agility, of an infinitely teeming chaos" (*KA* 2, *Ideen* 69/Firchow translation, p. 100).

Bibliography

Primary Sources

Feuerbach, Paul Johann Anselm. "Über die Unmöglichkeit eines ersten absoluten Grundsatzes der Philosophie, " *Philosophisches Journal 2*, no. 4 (1795): 306–22.
Fichte, J. G. *Gesammtausgabe der bayerischen Akademie der Wissenschaften*, R. Lauth and H. Jakob, ed. Stuttgart: Fromann, 1970.
———. "Recension des Aenesidemus oder über die Fundamente der vom Herrn Prof. Reinhold in Jena gelieferten Elementarphilosophie," *Jenaer Allgemeine Literaturzeitung* 1794, nos. 47–49.
———. "Vergleichung des vom Hrn. Prof. Schmid aufgestellten Systems mit der Wissenschaftslehre," *Philosophisches Journal 3*, no. 4 (1796): 267–320.
———. "Versuch einer neuen Darstellung der Wissenschaftslehre," *Philosophisches Journal 7*, no. 1 (1797): 1–20.
Jacobi, Fr. Heinrich. *David Hume über den Glauben oder Idealismus und Realismus ein Gespräch*. Breslau: Gottl. Löwe, 1787.
———. *Über die Lehre Spinozas in Briefen an Herrn Moses Mendelssohn*. Neue vermehrte Auflage, Breslau: Löwe, 1789.
Kant, Immanuel. *Kritik der reinen Vernunft*. Hamburg: Meiner, 1956.
———. *Critique of Pure Reason*, trans., with an introduction by Norman Kemp Smith. New York: Modern Library, 1958.
———. *Was heißt sich im Denken orientieren?* (1786).
Körner, Josef, ed. *Krisenjahre der Frühromantik. Briefe aus dem Schlegel-Kreise*. 3 volumes. Brün/Wien/Leipzig/Bern: 1936–1958.
Maimon, Salomon. *Gesammelte Werke*, ed. Valerio Verra. Hildesheim: Olms, 1965–1976.
Mendelssohn, Moses. *Schriften zur Philosophie, Aesthetik und Politik*, ed. M. Brach. Kildesheim: Olms, 1968.
Niethammer, Friedrich Immanuel. "Ankündigung: Philosophisches Journal einer Gesellschaft deutscher Gelehrten," herausgegeben von F. I. Niethammer,

Professor der Philosophie, in *Intelligenzblatt der Allgemeinen Literatur-Zeitung* (Jena), no. 1, Mittwochs, den 7ten Jauar 1795, 46–48.

———. "Die Hauptmomente der Reinholdischen Elementarphilosophie, in Beziehung auf die Einwendung des Aenesidemus untersucht," *Philosophisches Journal* 2, no. 3 (1795): 237–62.

———. "Von den Ansprüchen des gemeinen Verstandes an die Philosophie," *Philosophisches Journal* 1, no. 1 (1795): 1–45.

———. "Vorbericht über Zweck und Einrichtung dieses Journals," *Philosophisches Journal einer Gesellschaft Teutscher Gelehrten* 1 (May 1795). Reprinted in Marcel Stamm, l.c., pp. 77–80.

Preitz, Max, ed. *Fr. Schlegel und Novalis. Biographie einer Romantikfreundschaft in ihren Briefen*. Darmstadt: Wisseschaftliche Buchgesellschaft, 1957.

Reinhold, K. L. *Beyträge zur Berichtigung bisheriger Mißverständnisse der Philosophen. Zweyter Band die Fundamente des philosophischen Wissens, der Metaphysik, Moral, moralischen Religion und Geschmackslehre betreffend*. Jena: Widtmann and Mauke, 1790–1794.

Schlegel, F. *Kritische Ausgabe*, 35 volumes, ed. Ernst Behler (in collaboration with Jean-Jacques Anstett, Jakob Baxa, Ursula Behler, Liselotte Dieckmann, Hans Eichner, Raymond Immerwahr, Robert L. Kahn, Eugene Susini, Bertold Sutter, A. Leslie Wilson, and others). Paderborn: Schöningh, 1958ff.

Schmid, Carl Christian Erhard. "Brüchstücke aus einer Schrift über die Philosophie und ihre Principien. Zu vorläufiger Prüfung vorgelegt," *Philosophisches Journal* 3, no. 2 (1795): 95–132.

Schulze, Gottlob Ernst. *Aenesidemus oder über die Fundamente der von Herrn Professor Reinhold gelieferten Elementar-Philosophie*, ed. A. Liebert. Neudrucke seltener philosophischer Werke, Herausgegeben von der Kantgesellschaft, Band I. Berlin: Reuther and Reichard, 1911.

Wackenroder, W. H., and Ludwig Tieck. *Herzensergießungen eines kunstliebenden Klosterbruders*. 1797.

———. *Phantasien über die Kunst*. 1799.

Secondary Sources

Alford, Steven E. *Irony and the Logic of the Romantic Imagination*. New York: Lang, 1984.

Allison, Henry E. *The Kant-Eberhard Controversy*. Baltimore: Johns Hopkins, 1973.

Altmann, Alexander. *Moses Mendelssohn: A Biographical Study*. Alabama: University of Alabama Press, 1973.

Ameriks, Karl. "Hegel's Critique of Kant's Theoretical Philosophy," *Philosophy and Phenomenological Research* 46, no. 1 (1985): 1–35.

———. "Reinhold and the Short Arguments to Idealism," in *Proceedings of the Sixth International Kant Congress*, ed. G. Funke and T. M. Seebohm, pp. 441–53. Press, 1985.

———. "Kant, Fichte, and Short Arguments to Idealism," *Archiv für Geschichte der Philosophie* 72 (1990): 63–85.

———. *Kant and the Fate of Autonomy: Problems in the Appropriation of the Critical Philosophy*. Cambridge: Cambridge University Press, 2000.
———, ed. *The Modern Subject: Conceptions of the Self in Classical German Philosophy*. Albany: State University of New York Press, 1995.
———, ed. *The Cambridge Companion to German Idealism*. Cambridge: Cambridge University Press, 2000.
Aris, R. *History of Political Thought in Germany: From 1789 to 1815*. New York: Russell and Russell, 1965.
Arndt, Dieter, ed. *Der Nihilismus als Phänomen der Geistesgeschichte in der wissenschaftlichen Diskussion unseres Jahrhunderts*. Darmstadt: Wissenschaftliche Buchgesellschaft, 1974.
Atlas, Samuel. *From Critical to Speculative Idealism: The Philosophy of Salomon Maimon*. The Hague: Nijhoff, 1964.
Bauer, Günther. *Der absolute Idealismus als Voraussetzung einer historischen Philosophie. Ein Versuch über die Philosophie des jungen Fr. Schlegel*. München: Study, 1966.
———. *Vernunft und Erkenntnis. Die Philosophie F. H. Jacobis*. Bonn: Bouvier, 1969.
Baum, Willhelm. "Der Klagenfurter Herbert Kreis zwischen Aufklärung und Romantik," *Revue Internationale de Philosophie* 50, no. 197 (1996): 483–514.
Baumann, Peter. *Fichtes Wissenschaftslehre: Probleme ihres Anfanges*. Bonn: Bouvier, 1974.
Baur, Michael, and Daniel Dahlstrom, eds. *The Emergence of German Idealism*. Washington, DC: Catholic University of America Press, 1999.
Beck, Lewis White. *Early German Philosophy*. Cambridge, MA: Harvard University Press, 1969.
Behler, Ernst. "Friedrich Schlegels Vorlesungen über Transzendentalphilosophie Jena 1800–1801," in *Transzendentalphilosophie und Spekulation. Der Streit um die Gestalt einer Ersten Philosophie (1799–1807)*, ed. Walter Jaeschke. Hamburg: Meiner, 1953.
———. "Der Wendepunkt Fr. Schlegels," *Philosophische Jahrbuch der Görresgesellschaft*, 1956, pp. 256ff.
———. "Friedrich Schlegels Theorie des Verstehens: Hermeneutik oder Dekonstuktion?" in *Die Aktualität der Frühromantik*, ed. Ernst Behler, pp. 141–60. Paderborn: Schöningh, 1987.
———. *Irony and the Discourse of Modernity*. Seattle: University of Washington Press, 1990.
———. *Frühromantik Die Frühromantik als literaturgeschichtliche Phänomen*. Berlin: de Gruyter, 1992.
———. *German Romantic Literary Theory*. Cambridge: Cambridge University Press, 1993.
———. "Friedrich Schlegel's Theory of an Alternating Principle Prior to His Arrival in Jena (6 August 1796)," *Revue Internationale de Philosophie* 50, no. 197 (1996): 383–402.
———, trans. *Friedrich Schlegel's Dialogue on Poetry and Literary Aphorisms*. University Park: Pennsylvania State University Press, 1966.
———, ed. *Die Europäische Romantik*. Frankfurt am Main, 1972.

———, ed. *German Romantic Criticism: Novalis, Schlegel, Schleiermacher and Others*. New York: Continuum, 1982.

———. *Die Zeitschriften der Brüder Schlegel*. Darmstadt: Wissenschaftliche Buchgesellschaft, 1983.

———, ed. *Die Aktualität der Frühromantik*. Paderborn: Schöningh, 1987.

———, ed. *Fichte, Jacobi and Schelling: Philosophy of German Idealism*. New York: Continuum, 1987.

Behrens, Klaus. *Fr. Schlegels Geschichtsphilosophie (1794–1808)*. Tübingen: Niemayer, 1984.

Beierwaltes, Werner, ed. *Schelling. Texte zur Philosophie der Kunst*. Stuttgart: Reclam, 1982.

Beiser, Frederick C. *The Fate of Reason: German Philosophy from Kant to Fichte*. Cambridge, MA: Harvard University Press, 1987.

———. *Enlightenment, Revolution, and Romanticism: The Genesis of Modern German Political Thought, 1790–1800*. Cambridge, MA: Harvard University Press, 1992.

———. "Early Romanticism and the Aufklärung," in *What Is Enlightenment? Eighteenth Century Answers and Twentieth Century Questions*, ed., James Schmidt, pp. 317–29. Berkeley: University of California Press, 1996

———. "The Enlightenment and Idealism," in *The Cambridge Companion to German Idealism*, ed. Karl Ameriks, pp. 18–36. Cambridge: Cambridge University Press, 2000.

———. *German Idealism: The Struggle against Subjectivism, 1781–1801*. Cambridge, MA: Harvard University Press, 2002.

———. *The Romantic Imperative: The Concept of Early German Romanticism*. Cambridge, MA: Harvard University Press, 2003.

———, ed., trans. *The Early Political Writings of the German Romantics*. Cambridge: Cambridge University Press, 1996.

Bell, Stephen. *Spinoza in Germany from 1670 to the Age of Goethe*. London: Institute of Germanic Studies, 1984.

Benjamin, Walter. *Der Begriff der Kunstkritik in der deutschen Romantik. Bd. I Gesammelte Schriften*. Frankfurt am Main: Suhrkamp, 1974. English translation: *The Concept of Criticism in German Romanticism*, in *Walter Benjamin: Selected Writings. Volume 1, 1913–1926*, ed. Marcus Bullock and Michael W. Jennings, pp. 116–200. Cambridge, MA: Harvard University Press, 1996.

Benz, Ernst. *The Mystical Sources of German Romantic Philosophy*, trans. Blair Reynolds and Eunice M. Paul. Allison Park, PA: Pickwick, 1983.

Benz, Richard. *Die Zeit der deutschen Klassik*. Stuttgart: Reclam, 1953.

Bergman, Samuel Hugo. *The Philosophy of Solomon Maimon* (translated from the Hebrew by Noah J. Jacobs). Jerusalem: Magnes, Hebrew University, 1967.

Berlin, Isaiah. *Vico and Herder: Two Studies in the History of Ideas*. London: Hogarth, 1976.

———. *The Magus of the North: J. G. Hamann and the Origins of Modern Irrationalism*, ed. Henry Hardy. New York: Farrar, Straus, and Giroux, 1993.

———. "The Romantic Revolution: A Crisis in the History of Modern Thought," in *The Sense of Reality*, ed. Henry Hardy, pp. 168–93. New York: Farrar, Straus, and Giroux, 1996.

———. *The Roots of Romanticism*, ed. Henry Hardy. Princeton: Princeton University Press, 1999.

Bernstein, J. M., ed. *Classic and Romantic German Aesthetics*. Cambridge: Cambridge University Press, 2003.

Bernstein, Richard J. *Beyond Objectivism and Relativism*. Oxford: Blackwell, 1983.

Bohn, Arnd. "Goethe and the Romantics," in *The Literature of German Romanticism*, ed. Dennis F. Mahoney, pp. 35–60. Rochester, NY: Camden House, 2004.

Bondeli, Martin. Das Anfangsproblem bei Karl Leonhard Reinhold: eine systematische und entwicklungs-geschictliche Untersuchung zur Philosophie Reinholds in der Zeit von 1789 bis 1803. Frankfurt am Main: V. Klostermann, 1994.

Bowie, Andrew. *Aesthetics and Subjectivity: From Kant to Nietzsche*. Manchester, 1993.

———. *Schelling and Modern European Philosophy: An Introduction*. London: Routledge, 1993.

———. "Romanticism and Technology," *Radical Philosophy* 72 (1995): 5–16.

———. "John McDowell's Mind and World, and Early Romantic Epistemology," *Revue Internationale de Philosophie* 50, no. 197 (1996): 515–54.

———. "Rethinking the History of the Subject: Jacobi, Schelling, and Heidegger," in *Deconstructive Subjectivities*, ed. Simon Critchley and Peter Dews, pp. 105–26. Albany: State University of New York Press, 1996.

———. *From Romanticism to Critical Theory: The Philosophy of German Literary Theory*. London: Routledge, 1997.

———. "German Philosophy Today: Between Idealism, Romanticism and Pragmatism," in *German Philosophy since Kant*, ed. Anthony O'Hear, pp. 357–98. Cambridge: Cambridge University Press, 1999.

———. "German Idealism and the Arts," in *The Cambridge Companion to German Idealism*, ed. Karl Ameriks, pp. 239–57. Cambridge: Cambridge University Press, 2000.

Brandt, Reinhard. "Fichtes Erste Einleitung in die Wissenschaftslehre (1798)," *Kant Studien* 69 (1978): 67–89.

Breazeale, Daniel. "Fichte's Aenesidemus Review and the Transformation of German Idealism," *Review of Metaphysics* 34 (March 1981): 545–68.

———. "Between Kant and Fichte: Karl Leonard Reinhold's Elementary Philosophy," *Review of Metaphysics* 35, no. 4 (1982): 785–822.

———. "How to Make an Idealist: Fichte's 'Refutation of Dogmatism' and the Problem of the Starting Point of the *Wissenschaftslehre*," *The Philosophical Forum* 19, nos. 2–3 (W-S, 1987–88): 97–123. This is a special issue devoted to a discussion of Fichte's thought and includes articles by Walter E. Wright, Robert B. Pippin, Alexis Philonenko, Stanley Rosen, Tom Rockmore, John Lachs, Luc Ferry, and A. J. Mandt.

———. "Fichte on Skepticism," *Journal of the History of Philosophy* 88 (1991): 524–31.
———. "Fichte's Abstract Realism," in *The Emergence of German Idealism*, ed. Michael Baur and Daniel Dahlstrom, pp. 95–115. Washington, DC: Catholic University of America Press, 1999.
———, trans., ed. *Fichte, Early Philosophical Writings*. Ithaca: Cornell University Press, 1988.
———, trans., ed. *Fichte, Foundations of Transcendental Philosophy, Wissenschaftslehre nova methodo (1796/99)*. Ithaca, NY: Cornell University Press, 1992.
———, trans., ed. *Introduction to the Wissenschaftslehre and Other Writings 1797–1800*. Indianapolis: Hackett, 1994.
——— and Tom Rockmore, eds. *Fichte: Historical Contexts/Contemporary Controversies*. New Jersey: Humanities, 1994.
Briegleb, Klaus. *Ästhetische Sittlichkeit. Versuch über Fr. Schlegels Systementwurf zur Begründung der Dichtungskritik*. Tübingen: Niemayer, 1962.
Brinkmann, Richard. *Frühromantik und französische Revolution. Die deutsche Literatur und die französische Revolution*. Göttingen, 1974.
Brown, Marshall. *The Shape of German Romanticism*. Ithaca: Cornell University Press, 1979.
Brüggen, Michael. "Jacobi, Schelling und Hegel," in *Friedrich Heinrich Jacobi, Philosoph und Literatur der Goethezeit*, ed. Klaus Hammacher. Frankfurt, 1971.
Bubner, Rüdiger, ed. "Das Älteste Systemprogram. Studien zur Frühgeschichte des deutschen Idealismus," *Hegel Studien*. Bonn, 1973.
———. "Kant, Transcendental Argument and the Problem of Deduction," *Review of Metaphysics* 28, no. 3 (1975): 453–67.
———. *Innovationen des Idealismus*. Göttingen: Vandenhoek and Ruprecht, 1995.
———. *The Innovations of Idealism*, trans. Nicholas Walker. Cambridge: Cambridge University Press, 2003.
Calvino, Italo. "Philosophy and Literature," in *The Uses of Literature*, trans., Patrick Creagh. New York: Harcourt Brace, 1982.
Capen, Samuel Paul. *Friedrich Schlegel's Relations with Reichhart and his Contributions to Deutschland*. Publications of the University of Pennsylvania: Series in Philology and Literature, vol. 9, no. 2. Boston: Ginn, 1903.
Carnap, Rudolf. "Die Überwindung der Metaphysik durch die logische Analyse der Sprache," *Erkenntnis*, 2 (1931): 219–41. Translated by Arthur Pap as "The Elimination of Metaphysics through Logical Analysis," in *Logical Positivism*, ed. A. J. Ayer, pp. 60–81. New York: Free Press, 1959.
Cassirer, Ernst. *Das Erkenntnisproblem in der Philosophie und Wissenschaft der neueren Zeit. Dritter Band, Die Nachkantischen Systeme*. Darmstadt: Wissenschaftliche Buchgesellschaft, 1991 (3rd edition).
Cavell, Stanley. *In Quest of the Ordinary: Lines of Skepticism and Romanticism*. Chicago: University of Chicago Press, 1988.
———. *This New Yet Unapproachable America: Lectures after Emerson and Wittgenstein*. Albuquerque, NM: Living Batch, 1989.

Cragg, Gerald R. *Reason and Authority in the Eighteenth Century*. Cambridge, MA: Harvard University Press, 1964.
Dällenbach, Lucien, and Christian L. Hart, eds. *Fragment und Totalität*. Frankfurt am Main: Suhrkamp, 1984.
Danto, Arthur. *The Transfiguration of the Commonplace. A Philosophy of Art*. Cambridge, MA: Harvard University Press, 1981.
Davidson, Donald. "The Structure and Content of Truth," *The Journal of Philosophy* 87, no. 6 (1990): 279–328.
Deininger, Whitaker T. "Some Reflections on Epistemology and Historical Inquiry," *The Journal of Philosophy*, 53, no. 14 (1956): 429–42.
DeMan, Paul. *The Rhetoric of Temporality*. New York: Columbia University Press, 1984.
———. *The Romantic School and Other Essays*, ed. Joan Hermond and Robert Holub. New York: Continuum, 1985.
di Giovanni, G., and H. S. Harris, eds. and trans. *Between Kant and Hegel: Texts in the Development of Post-Kantian Idealism*. Albany: State University of New York Press, 1985.
———. "From Jacobi's Novel to Fichte's Idealism: Some Comments on the 1798–99 Atheism Dispute," *Journal of the History of Philosophy* 27, no. 1 (1989): 75–100.
———. "The First Twenty Years of Critique: The Spinoza Connection," in *The Cambridge Companion to Kant*, ed. Paul Guyer, pp. 417–48. Cambridge: Cambridge University Press, 1992.
———, trans. *The main philosophical writings and the novel Allwill of Fr. Heinrich Jacobi*. Montreal: McGill-Queen's University Press, 1994.
Dieckmann, L. "Fr. Schlegel and Romantic Concepts of the Symbol," *Germanic Review* 34 (1959): 276–83.
Dilthey, Wilhelm. *Die Entstehung der Hermeneutik*. Göttingen, 1961.
———. *Das Leben Scheiermachers*. Berlin: de Gruyter, 1970.
Dischner, Gisela. *Friedrich Schlegels Lucinde und Materialien zu einer Theorie des Müßiggangs*. Hildesheim: Gesternberg, 1980.
Dummett, Michael. "Truth," *Proceedings of the Aristotelian Society* 59 (1959): 141–62.
Eichner, Hans. "Romantisch-Romantik-Romantiker," in *'Romantic' and Its Cognates: The European History of a Word*, ed. Hans Eichner, pp. 98–156. Toronto: University of Toronto Press, 1972.
Eldridge, Richard. "Some Remarks on Logical Truth: Human Nature and Romanticism," *Midwest Studies in Philosophy* 19 (1994): 220–42.
———. *Leading a Human Life: Wittgenstein, Intentionality, and Romanticism*. Chicago: University of Chicago Press, 1997.
———. *The Persistence of Romanticism. Essays in Philosophy and Literature*. Cambridge: Cambridge University Press, 2001.
———, ed. *Beyond Representation. Philosophy and Poetic Imagination*. Cambridge: Cambridge University Press, 1996.
Elsässer, Michael, ed. *Friedrich Schlegel, Transcendentalphilosophie*. Hamburg: Felix Meiner Verlag, 1991.
———. *Friedrich Schlegels Kritik am Ding* (with an introduction by Werner Beierwaltes). Hamburg: Felix Meiner Verlag, 1994.

Enders, Karl. *Fr. Schlegel—Die Quellen seinse Wesens und Werdens.* Leipzig, 1913.
Feifel, Rosa. *Die Lebensphilosophie Fr. Schlegels.* Bonn, 1938.
Fischer, Michael. "Accepting the Romantics as Philosophers," *Philosophy and Literature* 12 (October, 1988): 179–89.
Folwartsehny, Helmut. *Friedrich Schlegels Verhältnis zur Philosophie.* Breslau, 1930.
Frank, Manfred. *Das Problem "Zeit" in der deutschen Romantik: Zeitbewußtsein und Bewußtsein von Zeitlichkeit in der frühromantischen Philosophie und in Tiecks Dichtung.* München: Winkler, 1972.
———. *Der kommende Gott. Vorlesungen über die Neue Mythologie.* Frankfurt am Main: Suhrkamp, 1982.
———. *Eine Einführung in Schellings Philosophie.* Frankfurt am Main: Suhrkamp, 1985.
———. *Einführung in die Frühromantische Ästhetik: Vorlesungen.* Frankfurt am Main: Suhrkamp, 1989.
———. *Selbstbewußtseinstheorie von Fichte bis Sartre.* Frankfurt am Main: Suhrkamp, 1991.
———. "Kant und die Anfänge des deutschen Idealismus. Vorlesung WS 1991/92 und SS 1992." Unpublished manuscript.
———. "Two Centuries of Philosophical Critique of Reason and its 'Postmodern' Radicalization," in *Reason and Its Other: Rationality in Modern German Philosophy and Culture,* ed. Dieter Freundlieb and Waynne Hudson, pp. 67–86. Berg European Studies Series. Rhode Island: Berg, 1993.
———. "Vorlesungen über die philosophischen Grundlage der Frühromantik. WS 1992/93 und SS 1993." Unpublished manuscript.
———. "Philosophische Grundlage der Frühromantik," *Athenäum, Jahrbuch für Romantik* 4 (1994): 37–130.
———. "*Alle Wahrheit ist relativ, alles Wissen symbolisch*—Motive der Grundsatz-Skepsis in der frühen Jenaer Romantik (1796)," *Revue Internationale de Philosophie* 50, no. 197 (1996): 403–36.
———. "Wechselgrundsatz: Friedrich Schlegels philosophischer Ausgangspunkt," *Zeitschrift für philosophische Forschung* 50 (1996): 26–50.
———. "Wie reaktionär war eigentlich die Frühromantik? (Elemente zur Aufstörung der Me-inungsbildung)," in *Athenäum. Jahrbuch für Romantik.* Paderborn: Schöningh, 1997): 141–66.
———. *Unendliche Annäherung. Die Anfänge der philosophischen Frühromantik.* Frankfurt/M: Suhrkamp, 1997 (The third part of this work has been translated by Elizabeth Millán-Zaibert as *The Philosophical Foundations of Early German Romanticism.* Albany: State University of New York Press, 2004.)
Fried, Jochem. *Die Symbolik des Reden. Über alte und neue Mythologie in der Frühromantik.* München, 1985.
Friedrichsmeyer, Sara. *The Androgyne in Early German Romanticism.* Bern: Lang, 1983.
Fries, Johann Friedrich. *Reinhold, Fichte, Schelling.* Leipzig, 1803.
Frischmann, Bärbel. *Vom transzendentalen zum frühromantischen Idealismus. J. G. Fichte und Fr. Schlegel.* Paderborn: Schöningh, 2005.

Gabriel, Gottfried, and Christiane Schildknecht. *Literarische Formen der Philosophie*. Stuttgart: J. B. Metzler Verlag, 1990.
Gadamer, Hans Georg. *Die Aktualität des Schönen*. Stuttgart: Reclam, 1977.
———. *Truth and Method*, trans. Joel Weinsheimer and Donald G. Marshall. New York: Crossroad, 1991.
Gardiner, Patrick L. *Nineteenth Century Philosophy*. London: Free Press, 1969.
Gasché, Rodolphe. "Ideality in Fragmentation," foreword to *Philosophical Fragments Friedrich Schlegel*, Peter Firchow, trans., pp. vii–xxxii. Minneapolis: University of Minnesota Press, 1991.
———. "Comparatively Theoretical," in *Germanistik und Komparistik*, ed. H. Birus, pp. 417–32. Stuttgart: J. B. Metzler Verlag, 1995.
Glawe, Walther. *Religionsphilosophischen Ansichten Fr. Schlegels*. Berlin: Tronwitzsch and Sohn, 1905.
Goodman, Russell B. *American Philosophy and the Romantic Tradition*. New York: Cambridge University Press, 1991.
Gram, Moltke S. "Things in Themselves: The Historical Lessons," *Journal of the History of Philosophy* 18, no. 4 (1980): 407–31.
Griswold, Charles. "Fichte's Modification of Kant's Transcendental Idealism in the *Wissenschaftslehre* of 1794 and Introductions of 1797," *Auslegung* 4, no. 2: 132–51.
Grunnet, Susanne Elisa. *Die Bewußtseinstheorie Friedrich Schlegels*. Paderborn: Schönigh, 1994.
Guyer, Paul. "Kant's Intentions in the Refutation of Idealism," *The Philosophical Review* 92, no. 3 (1983): 329–83.
———. "Absolute Idealism and the Rejection of Kantian Dualism," in *The Cambridge Companion to German Idealism*, ed. Karl Ameriks, pp. 37–56. Cambridge: Cambridge University Press, 2000.
———, ed. *The Cambridge Companion to Kant*. Cambridge: Cambridge University Press, 1995.
Haack, Susan. *Evidence and Inquiry: Towards Reconstruction in Epistemology*. Oxford: Blackwell, 1993.
———."Coherence, Consitency, Cogency, Congruity, Cohesiveness, &c.: Remain Calm! Don't Go Overboard!" *New Literary History* 35 (2004): 167–83.
Habermas, Jürgen. *Der philosophische Diskurs der Moderne*. Frankfurt am Main: Suhrkamp, 1985.
———. *Wahrheit und Rechtfertigung*. Frankfurt am Main: Suhrkamp, 1999.
Hammacher, Klaus, ed. *Der transzendentale Gedanke. Die gegenwärtige Darstellung der Philosophie Fichtes*. Hamburg: Felix Meiner Verlag, 1981.
Hartmann, Nicolai. *Die Philosophie des deutschen Idealismus*. Berlin: de Gruyter, 1923–1929.
Haym, Rudolf. *Die Romantische Schule*, 5th edition. Berlin: Gaertner, 1870.
Hebeisen, Alfreditor. *Friedrich Heinrich Jacobi: Seine Auseinandersetzung mit Spinoza*. Bern: Haupt, 1960.
Hegel, Hannelore. *Issak von Sinclair zwischen Fichte, Hölderlin und Hegel. Ein Beitrag zur Entstehungsgeschichte der idealistischen Philosophie*. Frankfurt am Main: Klostermann, 1971.

Heidegger, Martin. *Der Deutsche Idealismus (Fichte, Schelling, Hegel) und die philosophische Problemlage der Gegenwart*. Frankfurt am Main: Klostermann, 1997.

Heiner, Hans-Jochem. *Das Ganzheitsdenken Fr. Schlegels. Wissensoziologische Deutung einer Denkform*. Stuttgart: Metzler, 1971.

Heinrich, Gerda. *Geschichtsphilosophische Positionen der deutschen Frühromantik: Fr. Schlegel und Novalis*. Berlin: Verlag, 1971.

Hendrix, Gerd Peter. *Das politische Weltbild Fr. Schlegels*. Bonn: Bouvier, 1962.

Henrich, Dieter. *Fichtes ursprungliche Einsicht*. Frankfurt am Main: Klostermann, 1967.

———. *Identität und Objektivität: Eine Untersuchung über Kants transzendentale Deduktion*. Heidelberg: Winter, 1976.

———. *Selbstverhältnisse. Gedanken und Auslegungen zu den Grundlagen der klassischen deutschen Philosophie*. Stuttgart: Reclam, 1982.

———. "Die Anfänge der Theorie des Subjekts (1789)," in *Zwischenbetrachtung. Im Prozeß der Aufklärung, Festschrift für Jürgen Habermas*, ed. Axel Honneth, pp. 106–70. Frankfurt am Main: Suhrkamp, 1989.

———. *Konstellationen: Probleme und Debatten am Ursprung der idealistischen Philosophie (1789–1795)*. Stuttgart: Klett-Cotta, 1991.

———. *Aesthetic Judgment and the Moral Image of the World: Studies in Kant*. Stanford: Stanford University Press, 1992.

———. *Der Grund im Bewußtsein. Untersuchungen zu Hölderlins Denken (1794–1795)*. Stuttgart: Klett-Cotta, 1992.

———. *The Unity of Reason: Essays on Kant's Philosophy*, trans. Richard L. Velkey. Cambridge, MA: Harvard University Press, 1994.

———. *Between Kant and Hegel: Lectures on German Idealism*, ed. David S. Pacini. Cambridge, MA: Harvard University Press, 2003.

———, and Christoph Jamme, eds. *Jakob Zwillings Nachlass: Eine Rekonstruktion; mit Beiträge zur Geschichte des spekulativen Denkens*. Hegel-Studien 28 (1986).

———, ed. *Fr. Heinrich Jacobi. Präsident der Akademie, Philosoph, Theoretiker der Sprache*. München, 1993.

Helfer, Martha B. *The Retreat of Representation: The Concept of Darstellung in German Critical Discourse*. Albany: State University of New York Press, 1996.

Hettner, Hermann. *Die romantische Schule in ihrem Zusammenhänge mit Goethe und Schiller*. Braunschweig, 1850.

Hörisch, Jochem. *Die fröhliche Wissenschaft der Poesie: der Universalitätsanspruch von Dichtung in der frühromantischen Poetologie*. Frankfurt am Main: Suhrkamp, 1976.

———. "Herrscherwort, Geld und geltende Sätze—Adornos Aktualisierung der Frühromantik und ihre Affinität zur poststrukturalistischen Kritik des Subjekts," in B. Linder and M.W. Lüdke eds., *Materialen zur ästhetischen Theorie Adornos*, pp. 397–414. Frankfurt am Main: Suhrkamp, 1980.

Huch, Richarda. *Die Blützeint der Romantik—Ausbreitung, Blützeit und Verfall der Romantik*. Tübingen: Wunderlich, 1951.

Huge, Richard. *Poesie und Reflexion in der Ästhetik des frühen Fr. Schlegels*. Stuttgart: Metzler, 1971.

Humboldt, Wilhelm von. "On the Historian's Task," in *The Theory and Practice of History: Leopold von Ranke*, ed. G. Iggers and K von Moltke. Indianapolis: Bobbs-Merrill, 1972.

Huyssen, Andreas, ed. *Fr. Schlegel. Kritischen und theoretische Schriften*, with an afterword, "Republikanismus und ästhetische Revolution beim jungen Fr. Schlegel." Stuttgart: Reclam, 1978.

Imle, F. *Fr. Schlegels Entwicklung von Kant zum Katholizismus*. Paderborn: Schöningh, 1927.

Immerwahr, Raymond. "The Word Romantisch and Its History," in *The Romantic Period in Germany: Essays by Members of the London University Institute of Germanic Studies*, ed. Siegbert Prawer, pp. 34–63. London: Weidenfeld and Nicolson, 1970.

Jaeschke, Walter, ed. *Transzendentalphilosophie und Spekulation: Der Streit um die Gestalt einer Ersten Philosophie (1799–1807). Quellenband und Referatband*. Hamburg: Verlag, 1993.

Jaeschke, Walter, and Helmut Holzheg, eds. *Früher Idealismus und Frühromantik: Der Streit um die Grundlagen der Ästhetik (1795–1805)*. Hamburg: Felix Meiner Verlag, 1990.

Jauß, Hans Robert. *Studien zum Epochenwandel der ästhetischen Moderne*. Frankfurt am Main: Suhrkamp, 1989.

Kalleinke, Gerhard S. *Das Verhältnis von Goethe und Runge im Zusammenhang mit Goethes Auseinandersetzung mit der Frühromantik*. Hamburg: Buske, 1973.

Kaufmann, Walter. "Goethe and the History of Ideas," *Journal of the History of Ideas* 10 (October, 1949): 503–16.

Kircher, Erwin. *Philosophie der Romantik*. Jena, 1908.

Kirkham, Richard L. *Theories of Truth: A Critical Introduction*. Cambridge: MIT Press, 1995.

Klausnitzer, Ralf. *Blaue Blume unterm Hakenkreuz: Die Rezeption der deutschen literarischen Romantik im Dritten Reich*. Paderborn: Schöningh, 1999.

Klemmt, Alfreditor *K. L. Reinholds Elementarphilosophie. Eine Studie über den Ursprung des spekulativen deutschen Idealismus*. Hamburg: Meiner, 1958.

Korf, H. A. *Geist der Goethezeit: Versuch einer ideallen Entwicklung der klassisch-romantisch Literaturgeschichte*, 2d ed., 4 vols. Leipzig: Köhler and Asnelany, 1955.

Körner, Josef. *Romantiker und Klassiker. Die Brüder Schlegel in ihren Beziehungen zu Schiller und Goethe*. Darmstadt: Wissenschaftliche Buchgesellschaft, 1971.

Krämer, Hans. *Fichte, Schlegel und der Infinitismus in der Platondeutung*. Stuttgart: Metzler, 1988.

Kroner, Richard. *Von Kant bis Hegel*. Tübingen: Mohr, 1921.

Küstler, B. *Transzendentale Einbildungskraft und ästhetische Phantasie. Zum Verhältnis von philosophische Idealismus und Romantik. Monographien zur philosophischen Forschung* 185. Königstein, 1979.

Lachs, John. "Fichte's Idealism," *American Philosophical Quarterly* 9 (1972): 311–18.

Lacoue-Labarthe, Philippe, and Jean-Luc Nancy. *The Literary Absolute: The Theory of Literature in German Romanticism* (translated from the French by Phillip Barnard and Cheryl Lester). Albany: State University of New York Press, 1988.

Larmore, Charles. *The Romantic Legacy*. New York: Columbia University Press, 1996.

———. "Hölderlin and Novalis," in *The Cambridge Companion to German Idealism*, ed. Karl Ameriks, pp. 141–60. Cambridge: Cambridge University Press, 2000.

Lauth, Reinhard. "Die Bedeutung der fichteschen Philosophie für die Gegenwart," *Philosophisches Jahrbuch* 70 (1963): 253–54.

———. "J. G. Fichte's Gesamtidee der Philosophie," *Philosophisches Jahrbuch* 71 (1964): 255–56.

———. *Zur Idee der Tanszendentalphilosophie*. München, 1965.

Leddy, Thomas. "Moore and Shustermann on Organic Wholes," *The Journal of Aesthetics and Art Criticism*, 49, no. 1 (1991): 63–73.

Lederbogen, F. *Fr. Schlegels Geschichtsphilosophie*. Leipzig, 1908.

Lerch, Paul. *Friedrich Schlegels philosophische Anschauungen in ihrer Entwicklung und systematischen Ausgestaltung*. Inaugural-Study zur Erlangung der Doktorwürde der hohen philosophischen Fakultät der Fr. Alexanders Universität Erlangen. Berlin: Germania, 1905.

Littlejohns, Richard. "Early Romanticism," in *The Literature of German Romanticism*, ed. Dennis F. Mahoney, pp. 61–78. Rochester: Camden House, 2004.

Loewe, Johann Heinrich. *Die Philosophie Fichtes nach den Gesammtergebnisse ihrer Entwicklung und ihrem Verhältnisse zu Kant und Spinoza*. Hildesheim: Olms, 1976.

Lovejoy, A. O. "The Meaning of 'Romantic' in Early-German Romanticism," *Essays in the History of Ideas*, pp. 183–206. Baltimore: Johns Hopkins Press, 1948.

———. "Schiller and the Genesis of German Romanticism," *Essays in the History of Ideas*, pp. 207–27. Baltimore: Johns Hopkins Press, 1948.

Lukács, G. *Die Seele und die Formen*. Berlin, 1911.

———. *The Destruction of Reason*, trans. Peter Palmer. Atlantic Highlands, NJ: Humanities, 1980.

Mahoney, Dennis F., ed. *The Literature of German Romanticism*. Rochester, NY: Camden House, 2004.

Mandt, A. J. "Fichte's Idealism in Theory and Practice," *Idealistic Studies* 14 (1984): 127–47.

Mann, Otto. *Der junge Fr. Schlegel*. Berlin, 1932.

Mannheim, Karl. "Das konservative Denken," in *Archiv für Sozialwissenschaften* 57, no. 1–2.

Margolis, Joseph. *Pragmatism without Foundations*. Oxford: Blackwell, 1986.

Martin, Wayne. *Idealism and Objectivity: Understanding Fichte's Jena Project*. Stanford, CA: Stanford University Press, 1997.

Mason, Eudo C. "The Aphorism," in *The Romantic Period in Germany*, ed. Siegbert Prawer, pp. 204–34. London: Cox and Wyman, 1970.

Mathy, Dietrich. *Poesie und Chaos. Zur anarchistischen Komponente der frühromantischen Ästhetik*. Munich: Weixler, 1984.

McGinn, Colin. *Ethics, Evil, and Fiction*. Oxford: Clarendon, 1997.

Menges, Karl. "Romantic Anti-foundationalism and the Theory of Chaos," in *Romanticism and Beyond: A Festschrift for John F. Fetzer*, ed. C. A. Berned, I. Henderson, and W. McConnell, pp. 33–56. New York: Lang, 1996.
Mennemeier, F. N. "Fragment und Ironie beim jungen Fr. Schlegel, " *Poetica* 2 (1968): 310–48.
Menninghaus, Winfried, ed. *Friedrich Schlegel. Theorie der Weiblichkeit*. Frankfurt am Main: Insel, 1983.
———. *Unendliche Verdopplung: Die frühromantische Grundlegung der kunsttheorie im Begriff absoluter Selbstreflexion*. Frankfurt am Main: Suhrkampt, 1987.
Mettler, Werner. *Der junge Fr. Schlegel und die gr. Literatur*. Zürich: Atlantis, 1955.
Michel, W. *Ästhetische Hermeneutik und Frühromantische Kritik. Fr. Schlegels fragmentarische Entwürfe, Rezensionen, Charakteristiken und Kritiken (1795–1801)*. Göttingen, 1982.
Millán-Zaibert, Elizabeth. "Romantic Rationality," *Pli: The Warwick Journal of Philosophy*, special volume, *Crises of the Transcendental: From Kant to Romanticism* 10 (2000): 141–55.
———. "A Method for the New Millennium: Calvino and Irony," in *Literary Philosophers: Borges, Calvino, and Eco*, ed. J. Gracia, and C. Korsmeyer, pp. 129–48. London: Routledge, 2002.
———. "What Is Early German Romanticism?" introduction to Manfred Frank, *The Philosophical Foundations of Early German Romanticism* (Albany: State University of New York Press, 2004): 1–25.
———. "The Revival of *Frühromantik* in the Anglophone World," *Philosophy Today* (Spring 2005): 96–117.
———. "Romanticismo e postmoderno: Variazioni incompresse sulla critica della modernità," (Romanticism and Post-Modernism: Misunderstood Variations on a Critique of Modernity), in *Prospettive sul Postmoderno, Volume One*, Considerazioni epistemologiche, ed. N. Limantis and L. Pastore. Milano: Mimesis, 2006, pp. 27–59.
Mues, Albert, ed. *Transzendentalphilosophie als System: Die Auseinandersetzung zwischen 1794 und 1806*. Hamburg: Felix Meiner Verlag, 1987.
Müller, Karl. *Friedrich Schlegels Konversion im Zusammenhang seiner weltanschaulichen Entwicklung*. Giessen: Nitschkowski, 1928.
Neuhauser, Frederick. *Fichte's Theory of Subjectivity*. Cambridge: Cambridge University Press, 1990.
Nüsse, Heinrich. *Die Sprachtheorie Fr. Schlegels*. Heidelberg: Carl-Winter, 1962.
Oesch, Martin. *Aus der Frühzeit des deutschen Idealismus. Texte zur Wissenschaftslehre Fichtes 1794–1804*. Würzburg: Königshausen and Neumann, 1987.
Peter, Klaus. *Fr. Schlegels ästhetischer Intellektualismus. Studien über die paradoxe Einheit von Philosophie und Kunst in den Jahren vor 1800*. Frankfurt am Main, 1965.
———. "Objektivität und Interesse: Zu zwei Begriffen Fr. Schlegels," *Ideologie: Kritische Studien zur Literatur*. Frankfurt, 1972.
———. *Idealismus als Kritik. Fr. Schlegels Philosophie der unvollendeten Welt*. Stuttgart: Kohlhammer, 1973.

———. *Friedrich Schlegel*. Stuttgart: Metzler, 1978.
———. *Studien der Aufklärung. Moral und Politik bei Lessing, Novalis und Fr. Schlegel*. Wiesbaden: Verlagsgesellschaft Athenaion, 1980.
———. "Friedrich Schlegel und Adorno. Die Dialektik der Aufklärung in der Romantik und heute," in *Die Aktualität der Frühromantik*, ed. Ernst Behler, pp. 219–35. Paderborn: Schöningh, 1987.
———, ed. *Romantikforschung seit 1945*. Königstein: Hain, 1980.
———, ed. *Die politische Romantik in Deutschland*. Stuttgart: Reclam, 1985.
———, and Otto Pöggeler, eds. *Frankfurt aber ist der Nabel dieser Erde' Das Schicksal einer Generation der Goethezeit*. Stuttgart: Klett-Cotta, 1983.
Pikulik, Lothar. *Frühromantik: Epoche-Werke-Wirkung*. München: Beck, 1992.
Pinkard, Terry. "Hegel's *Phenomenology* and *Logic*: An Overview," in *The Cambridge Companion to German Idealism*, ed. Karl Ameriks, pp. 161–79. Cambridge: Cambridge University Press, 2000.
———. *German Philosophy 1760–1860: The Legacy of Idealism*. Cambridge: Cambridge University Press, 2002.
Pippin, Robert. *Hegel's Idealism: The Satisfactions of Self-Consciousness*. Cambridge: Cambridge University Press, 1989.
Pöggeler, Otto. "Ist Hegel Schlegel? Friedrich Schlegel und Hölderlins Frankfurter Freundenkreis," in *Frankfurt aber ist der Nabel dieser Erde' Das Schicksal einer Generation der Goethezeit*, ed. Christoph Jamme and Otto Pöggeler, pp. 325–48. Stuttgart: Klett-Cotta, 1983.
Pupi, Angelo. *La formazione della filosofia di K. L. Reinhold, 1784–94*. Milan: Societa Editrica Vita e Pensiero, 1966.
Quine, W. V. "Things and Their Place in Theories," in *Theories and Things*, pp. 1–23. Cambridge, MA: Harvard University Press, 1981.
Reill, Peter. *The German Enlightenment and the Rise of Historicism*. Berkeley: University of California Press, 1975.
Reiss, Hans. *Politisches Denken in der deutschen Romantik*. Munich: Francke, 1966.
Riasnovsky, Nicholas V. *The Emergence of Romanticism*. Oxford: Oxford University Press, 1992.
Richards, Robert. *The Romantic Conception of Life*. Chicago: University of Chicago Press, 2002.
Rockmore, Tom, and Beth J. Singer, eds. *Antifoundationalism Old and New*. Philadelphia: Temple University Press, 1992.
———. "Hegel, German Idealism, and Antifoundationalism," in *Antifoundationalism: Old and New*, ed. Tom Rockmore and Beth J. Singer, pp. 105–26. Philadelphia: Temple University Press, 1992.
———. "Antifoundationalism, Circularity, and the Spirit of Fichte," in *Fichte: Historical Contexts/Contemporary Controversies*, ed. Daniel Breazeale and Tom Rockmore, pp. 96–117. Atlantic Highlands, NJ: Humanities, 1994.
Roetzel, Lisa C. "Feminizing Philosophy," in *Theory as Practice: A Critical Anthology of Early German Romantic Writings*, ed. and trans. Jochen Schulte-Sasse, Haynes Horne, Andreas Michel, Elizabeth Mittman, Assenka Oksiloff, Lisa C. Roetzel, and Mary R. Strand, pp. 361–81. Minneapolis: Universtiy of Minnesota Press, 1997.

Röhr, Sabine. *A Primer on German Enlightenment: With a Translation of K. L. Reinhold's "The Fundamental Concepts and Principles of Ethics."* Columbia: University of Missouri Press, 1985.

Rommel, Gabriele. "Romanticism and Natural Science," in *The Literature of German Romanticism*, ed. Dennis F. Mahoney, pp. 209–28. Rochester, NY: Camden House, 2004.

Rorty, Richard. *Philosophy and the Mirror of Nature*. Princeton: Princeton University Press, 1981.

———. "Philosophy as a Kind of Writing: An Essay on Derrida," in *Consequences of Pragmatism*. Minnesota: University of Minnesota Press, 1982.

———. "Thugs and Theorists: A Reply to Bernstein," *Political Theory* 15, no. 4 (1987): 564–90.

———. *Contingency, Irony, and Solidarity*. Cambridge: Cambridge University Press, 1989.

———. "The Necessity of Inspired Reading," *The Chronicle of Higher Education* 42, no. 22, February 9, 1996, p. A48.

Rosen, Charles. Review of Felix Mendelssohn Biography. *Times Literary Supplement*, no. 5268 (March 19, 2004): 3–4.

Roth, Stefanie. *Friedrich Hölderlin und die deutsche Frühromantik*. Stuttgart: Metzler, 1991.

Rothermal, Otto. *Fr. Schlegel und Fichte*. Amsterdam: Stets and Zeitlinger, 1966.

Roubiczek, Paul. "Some Aspects of German Philosophy in the Romantic Period," *The Romantic Period in Germany: Essays by Members of the London University Institute of Germanic Studies*, ed. Siegbert Prawer, pp. 305–26. London: Weidenfeld and Nicolson, 1970.

Sandkaulen-Bock, Birgit. *Ausgang vom Unbedingten. Über den Anfang in der Philosophie Schellings*. Göttingen: Vandenhoeck and Ruprecht, 1990.

Schanze, Helmut. *Romantik und Aufklärung. Untersuchungen zu Fr. Schlegel und Novalis*. Nürnberg: Hans Carl Verlag, 1966.

Schildknecht, Christiane. *Philosophische Masken. Literarische Formen der Philosophie bei Platon, Descartes, Wolff und Lichtenberg*. Stuttgart: J. B. Metzler Verlag, 1990.

Schlusser, Ingeborg. *Die Auseinandersetzung von Idealismus und Realismus in Fichtes Wissenschaftslehre, Grundlage der gesammte Wissenschaftslehre, 1794/5, Zweite Darstellung der Wissenschaftslehre, 1804*. Frankfurt am Main: Klostermann, 1972.

Schmidt, James, ed. *What Is Enlightenment? Eighteenth Century Answers and Twentieth Century Questions*. Berkeley: University of California Press, 1996.

Searle, John. *The Construction of Social Reality*. New York: Free Press, 1995.

Seidel, George J. *Activity and Ground: Fichte, Schelling and Hegel*. New York: Olms, 1976.

———. *Fichte's Wissenschaftslehre of 1794: A Commentary on Part I*. West Lafayette: Purdue University Press, 1993.

Sennewald, Lothar. *Carl Christian Erhard Schmid und sein Verhältnis zu Ficthe. Ein Beitrag zur Geschichte der kantischen Philosophie*. Study, Leipzig, 1929.

Seth, Andrew. *The Development from Kant to Hegel*. New York: Garland, 1976.

Seyhan, Azade. *Representation and Its Discontents: The Critical Legacy of German Romanticism*. Berkeley: University of California Press, 1992.

Silz, Walter. *Early German Romanticism*. Cambridge: Harvard University Press, 1929.

Simon, W. M. "The Historical and Social Background of the Romantic Period in Germany," in *The Romantic Period in Germany. Essays by Members of the London University Institute of Germanic Studies*, ed. Siegbert Prawer, pp. 17–33. London: Weidenfeld and Nicolson, 1970.

Smith, Barry. "Textual Deference," *American Philosophical Quarterly* 28, no. 1 (1991): 1–12.

Smith, Nicholas H., ed. *Reading McDowell: On Mind and World*. London: Routledge, 2002.

Snow, Dale Everett. "F. H. Jacobi and the Development of German Idealism," *Journal of the History of Philosophy* 25, no. 3 (July 1987): 397–416.

———. "Jacobi's Critique of the Enlightenment," in *What Is Enlightenment? Eighteenth Century Answers and Twentieth Century Questions*, ed. James Schmidt. Berkeley: University of California Press, 1996: pp. 306–16.

———. *Schelling and the Ends of Idealism*. Albany: State University of New York Press, 1996.

Soames, Scott. "What Is a Theory of Truth?" *The Journal of Philosophy* 81, no. 8 (1984): pp. 411–29.

Sprigge, T. L. S. *The Vindication of Absolute Idealism*. Edinburgh: Edinburgh University Press, 1983.

Stamm, Marcelo. *Die Reorganisation der Philosophie aus einem Prinzip*. Stuttgart: Klett-Cotta, forthcoming.

———. "Mit der Überzeugung von der Entbehrlichkeit eines höchsten und einzigen Grundsatzes ... " Ein Konstellationsporträt um Fr.I. Niethammers, 'Philosophisches Journal einer Gesellschaft teutscher Gelehrten.' " Unpublished manuscript, Munich, 1992.

Stoljar, Margaret. *Athenäum: A Critical Commentary*. Bern: Lang, 1973.

Summerer, Stefan. *Wirklichkeit, Sittlichkeit und ästhetische Illusion: Die Fichterezeption in den Fragmenten und Aufzeichen Fr. Schlegel und Hardenbergs*. Bonn: Bouvier, 1974.

Szondi, Peter. "Fr. Schlegel und die romantische Ironie," *Euphorion* 48 (1954): pp. 397–411.

———. *Poetik und Geschichtsphilosophie*. Frankfurt am Main: Suhrkamp, 1977.

Thalmann, Marianne. *The Literary Sign Language of German Romanticism*, trans. Harold A. Basilius. Detroit: Wayne State University Press, 1972.

Tonelli, G. "*Critique* and Related Terms Prior to Kant: A Historical Survey," *Kant-Studien* 69 (1978): 119–48.

Unger, Rudolf. *Hamann und die Aufklärung. Studien zur Vorgeschichte der romantischen Geistes im 18 Jahrhundert*. Darmstadt: Wissenschaftliche Buchgesellschaft, 1963.

Vallée, G., intro. and trans. (with J. B. Lawson, and C. G. Chapple). *The Spinoza Conversations between Lessing and Jacobi: Text with Excerpts from the Ensuing Controversy*. Lanham, MD: University Press of America, 1988.

Verweyen, Hans J. "New Perspectives on J. G. Fichte," *Idealistic Studies* 6, no. 2 (1976): pp. 117–59. The entire volume is devoted to a discussion of the philosophy of J. G. Fichte.
Walzel, Oskar. *German Romanticism*, trans. Alma Elsie Lussky. New York: Capricorn Books, 1966.
Weiland, Werner. *Der junge Fr. Schlegel oder die Revolution in der Frühromantik*. Stuttgart: Kohlhammer, 1968.
von Weise, Benno. "Fr. Schlegel. Ein Beitrag zur Geschichte der romantischen Konversionen," *Philosophische Forschungen*, Heft 6, 1927.
Welleck, René. "The Concept of Romanticism in Literary History," *Concepts of Criticism*, pp. 128–98. New Haven: Yale University Press, 1963.
———. "Between Kant and Fichte: Karl Leonhard Reinhold," *Journal of the History of Ideas* 45 (April–June, 1984): 323–27.
Wheeler, Kathleen M. "Kant and Romanticism," *Philosophy and Literature* 13 (April, 1989): 42–56.
Wirz, Ludwig. *Fr. Schlegels philosophische Entwicklung*. Bonn: Hanstein, 1939.
Wundt, M. *Die Deutsche Schulphilosophie im Zeitalter der Aufklärung*. Tübingen: Mohr, 1945.
Zammito, John H. *The Genesis of Kant's Critique of Judgment*. Chicago: University of Chicago Press, 1992.
———. "Reconstructing German Idealism and Romanticism: Historicism and Presentism," *Modern Intellectual History* 1, 3 (2004): 427–38.
Zeuch, Ulrike. *Das Unendliche: Höchste Fülle oder Nichts? Zur Problematik von Fr. Schlegels Geist-Begriff und dessen geistesgeschichtlichen Voraussetzungen*. Würzburg: Königshausen und Neumann, 1991.
Ziolkowski, Theodor. *Das Wunderjahr in Jena. Geist und Gesellschaft 1794–95*. Stuttgart: Klett-Cotta, 1998.
Zöller, Günter. *Fichte's Transcendental Philosophy. The Original Duplicity of Intelligence and Will*. Cambridge: Cambridge University Press, 1998.
———. "German Realism: The Self-limitation of Idealist Thinking in Fichte, Schelling, and Schopenhauer," in *The Cambridge Companion to German Idealism*, ed. Karl Ameriks, pp. 200–18. Cambridge: Cambridge University Press, 2000.
Zovko, Jure. *Verstehen und Nichtverstehen bei Fr. Schlegel: Zur Entstehung und Bedeutung seiner hermeneutischen Kritik*. Stuttgart: Frommann und Holzboog, 1990.
Zynda, Max von. *Kant-Reinhold-Fichte. Studien zur Geschichte des Transzendental Begriffs*. Berlin: Reuther and Reichard, 1910.

Index

Absolute, the, 32–37, 122–23, 130, 139, 167, 170, 173; Bowie on, 32–33; Frank on, 39–41, 47; mysticism and, 89; Niethammer on, 106; relativism and, 49, 146–47; Schlegel on, 47, 57–58, 61, 82, 95, 115, 136
Adorno, Theodor, 161, 193n77
Aenesidemus (Schulze), 65–70, 99–100
Allgemeine Literatur Zeitung, 22, 66, 68, 109, 181n45
Ameriks, Karl, 29, 214n1
analytic philosophy, 4, 26, 133, 154–55
Anstett, Jean-Jacques, 219n8
antifoundationalism, 17–20, 37, 46, 50, 83–87, 122–26; aesthetics of, 23, 153, 159–74; coherence and, 156–57; first principles and, 18–20, 49–50, 123; Hegel's, 188n19; holism and, 137; implications of, 146–48; objectivity and, 59–61, 147; Rockmore on, 91–93. *See also* skepticism
aphorism. *See* fragment
Archimedes, 40
Arnim, Achim von, 3
art, 2, 8–9; antifoundationalism and, 23, 153, 159–74; Carnap's views on, 25; criticism of, 4, 128, 158;
inarticulable in, 42, 47; mimetic theory of, 172–73; Schelling's view of, 33; Schiller's views of, 14; Schlegel's views of, 14–15, 128, 150–53; science and, 9, 25; "sophistical," 99, 115; *Wilhelm Meisters Lehrjahre* and, 150–58
atheism, 17, 21, 55
Athenäum (journal), 2, 17, 46, 182n52; founding of, 12, 178n11; Fragment 1 from, 90, 127; Fragment 53 from, 12, 221n24; Fragment 77 from, 157; Fragment 84 from, 49, 84, 122; Fragment 116 from, 15, 47, 161, 162, 167; Fragment 168 from, 152–53; Fragment 206 from, 158; Fragment 216 from, 16, 86, 119, 151, 157, 166; Fragment 346 from, 58

Baader, Franz, 3
Beck, Jakob Sigismund, 64
Behler, Ernst, 3–8, 161; on French Revolution, 184n74; on modernism, 15; on "romantic," 15, 17; on Schlegel's critique of Fichte, 90
Beiser, Frederick, 1, 3, 8–10, 18, 23, 159, 178n11; on Manfred Frank, 41–43, 49; on German Idealism, 29–31, 37; on philosophical

Beiser, Frederick *(continued)*
  systems, 85; on Platonic idealism, 29–30, 42–44, 50–51, 171; on Reinhold, 64; on romanticism, 15, 16, 40–45, 138–39, 143, 186n80
belief. *See* faith
Benjamin, Walter, 4, 216n26
Berkeley, George, 28–29, 125
Berlin, Isaiah, 176n4, 193n74
Bernstein, Richard, 169
Bertram, Johann Baptist, 17
Bildung, 134–36, 144, 153–54, 219n8
Bohn, Arnd, 151–52
Boisserée brothers, 17, 185n77
Bowie, Andrew, 1, 3–4, 10, 50, 160; on analytic philosophy and romanticism, 133, 154–55; on Hegelian idealism, 37; on Hegel's "resolution" of Kant, 32–33; on the inarticulable in art, 47; on Kant's "opacity," 33, 39
Breazeale, Daniel, 197n56, 198n61, 203n62
Brentano, Clemens, 3
Brown, Marshall, 202n48
Bubner, Rüdiger, 46, 118, 124, 163, 225n93

Calvino, Italo, 187n7
Carnap, Rudolf, 25–26, 28
Catholicism, Schlegel's conversion to, 2, 11, 17–18, 185n77, 186n80
Cavell, Stanley, 1–3
Cervantes, Miguel de, 9, 15, 58, 173
Chamfort, Sébastien-Roch Nicolas, 182n52
chaos, 156–57, 161–64, 173, 225n84
Chaouli, Michel, 181n40
coherence, 17, 40, 61, 86, 133, 152, 155, 192n69, 220n24; antifoundationalism and, 156–57; of knowledge, 154; *Wilhelm Meister* as model of, 150–58. *See also* holism; understanding
Cologne lectures. *See Entwicklung der Philosophie in zwölf Büchern*

common sense: Niethammer's appeal to, 72, 96–97, 101–14, 159; Reinhold and, 68; Schlegel's critique of, 110–14, 134. *See also* knowledge
consciousness, 42, 83–85, 142; act of, 68–70, 72–74, 77, 88, 95; fact of, 64–70, 72–74, 78, 95; holism of, 149–50; infinite and, 137–38, 147–48; object of, 149; principle of, 62–64, 99, 117, 137–38; self, 66, 99, 148–50; "systematic derivation" of, 79–80, 84–85. *See also* ego
Copernicus, Nicolaus, 117
critique, 12, 46, 102, 119–31; Bubner on, 118; critique of, 48, 81, 89–90, 110–11, 116, 127–29, 136

Danto, Arthur, 172
Darwin, Charles, 10, 133
Davidson, Donald, 39, 220n24
deductive method. *See* philosophy, as science
de Man, Paul, 39
Derrida, Jacques, 26, 39
Descartes, René, 31, 56, 90, 126; foundationalism of, 83, 92, 149; modernism and, 93
Deutschland (journal), 11
Diez, Carl Immanuel, 195n29
di Giovanni, George, 56–57, 60, 193n1, 194n6
Dilthey, Wilhelm, 4, 214n5, 222n43
Dischner, Gisela, 224n63
dogmatism, 78, 86, 92, 215n6; mysticism and, 88–89, 100–1; philosophy versus, 73–74, 81, 88–90, 94, 114–15

ego, 124, 143, 147–50; absolute, 88, 90; Descartes', 83, 126, 149; Non-I and, 72–73, 88, 140, 142, 150; self-positing, 72–78, 81, 88, 126, 138–40. *See also* consciousness
Eichendorff, Johann von, 3
Eichner, Hans, 12, 177n11

Eldridge, Richard, 177n9
Elsässer, Michael, 215n11
empiricism, 31, 70, 80, 102, 105–6, 112–18, 120, 153
Encyclopedists, 6
Enlightenment, 10–11, 15, 21, 39, 160, 161, 163; Lessing controversy and, 54–61; Littlejohns on, 189n25
Entwicklung der Philosophie in zwölf Büchern (Schlegel), 17, 50, 123, 140–44, 148
Erhard, J. B., 64, 97–102
Euclid, 215n9

faith: atheism and, 17, 21, 55; reason and, 22, 54–61, 120, 138–39
Fichte, Johann Gottlieb, 11, 15, 17, 45–46, 51, 142; first principles and, 18, 53, 68–74, 82–84, 88–94, 121–24, 135–36; foundationalism of, 83, 91–94, 159; Hegel and, 39; idealism of, 21, 81–82, 87, 138–39, 143, 147, 164–65, 222n38; Kant and, 30–35, 48, 64, 71, 80–81, 85, 117–22, 201n34; mysticism and, 81–82, 86–91, 136; Niethammer and, 71, 72, 101, 109, 198n3; Reinhold and, 71, 79, 99, 130; Schlegel and, 4–7, 21, 71–72, 79–91, 128, 136, 138, 156, 185n77; Schmid's critique of, 75–79; *Wissenschaftslehre* of, 16, 20, 21, 46, 70–94, 101–2, 110, 119, 139, 157, 166; Zöller on, 34–36
first principles, 5, 47, 53–70, 114–15, 140; antifoundationalism and, 18–20, 49–50, 123; Fichte and, 18, 53, 68–74, 82–84, 88–94, 121–24, 135–36; Herbert and, 97–98; Kant and, 18–21, 62–64, 97–100, 119, 121–22; mysticism and, 115; Niethammer and, 97–103, 107–8; Reinhold and, 64, 67, 121–22, 135–36; *Wechselerweis* and, 134–39
foundationalism, 37, 126; Descartes', 83, 92, 149; Fichte's, 83, 91–94, 159; Jacobi's, 57–61. *See also* antifoundationalism
fragment, as literary form, 9, 12, 27, 45–47, 51–52, 158, 206n7, 225n91; Behler on, 182n52; Gasché on, 183n53; Mason on, 224n62
Frank, Manfred, 4, 9, 47, 137–39, 175n1, 181n42, 222n45; on analytic philosophy's relation to romanticism, 133; Beiser on, 41–43, 49; on Nazism, 176n4; on Niethammer, 105; on Reinhold, 99; on relativism, 192n67; on romantic realism, 38–41
French Revolution: Behler on, 184n74; Beiser on, 138; Lacoue-Labarthe on, 227n13; Schiller and, 14; Schlegel on, 16, 86, 119, 151, 185n77
Friedrich, Caspar David, 3

Gadamer, Hans-Georg, 179n18, 214n5
Gasché, Rodolphe, 183n53
Geisteswissenschaften, 4, 214n5
genetic method. *See* synthetic method
genre, 86, 151–52, 158, 168, 169, 193n77
Goethe, Johann Wolfgang von, 6, 182n52, 224n62; on romanticism, 1, 176n3; *Wilhelm Meisters Lehrjahre*, 9, 13–16, 22–23, 86, 119, 134, 150–58
Gram, Moltke S., 221n26

Haack, Susan, 19, 162
Habermas, Jürgen, 160, 226n3, 226n10
Hamann, Johann Georg, 91
Hamlet (Shakespeare), 172–73, 229n53
Hardenberg, Friedrich von. *See* Novalis
Haym, Rudolf, 13–14, 175n1
Hegel, G. W. F., 10, 21, 41, 162, 192n69; *Aufhebung* of skepticism in,

252 Index

Hegel, G. W. F. *(continued)*
  48; Fichte and, 39; Hölderlin and, 37–39; Kant and, 27–31, 35, 188n9; *Phänomenologie des Geistes*, 28, 46; on romanticism, 185n75; Schlegel and, 44–48, 189n19, 191n54; Schulze and, 196n38
Heidegger, Martin, 199n7, 214n5
Henrich, Dieter, 72, 97, 198n1
Herbert, Franz P. von, 97–102, 105, 108
Herder, Johann Gottfried, 91, 182n52
hermeneutics, 50–51, 126, 179n18, 214n5, 222n43; irony and, 167, 170; obstacles to, 155
Hippocrates, 125
Historical Characteristics of Philosophy (Schlegel), 82–83, 123–24
history, 15–16, 22, 127–31; of philosophy, 7, 46, 50–51, 60, 82–84, 90, 123–31; taxonomy and, 114–16; teleological, 45, 145–46
Hoffmann, E. T. A., 3
Hölderlin, Friedrich, 9, 36–37, 162; Hegel and, 37–39; Schelling and, 45
holism, 9, 18–19, 22–23, 43, 137, 143, 220n24; of consciousness, 149–50; *Jäger* versus *Spürhunde* types of, 32–38, 79; *Wilhelm Meisters Lehrjahre* and, 152–58. *See also* coherence; synthetic method
Horen (journal), 11, 14
Horkheimer, Max, 161
Hufeland, Gottlieb, 181n45
human sciences, 4, 214n5
Humboldt, Alexander von, 180n38
Humboldt, Wilhelm von, 145–47
Hume, David, 31, 62, 65
Huyssen, Andreas, 225n91

I, self-positing. *See* ego
idealism, 29, 34–36, 44–45, 162–63; absolute, 37–38, 40–44, 133, 188n9; Berkeley's, 28–29; critical, 78, 81, 86; definitions of, 28–32; Fichte's, 21, 81–82, 87, 138–39, 143, 147, 164–65, 222n38; materialism versus, 32, 73–74; Platonic, 29–30, 42–44, 50–51, 133, 171; realism and, 42, 48, 82, 87, 138–43, 147, 164–65; romanticism versus, 6–7, 30–32, 37–45, 48, 51–52, 133, 147; subjectivity and, 29–30, 32–33, 36–38, 77, 139. *See also* transcendental philosophy
Ideen Fragments, 156
infinite, 15, 76, 94, 110, 134, 145, 156; consciousness and, 137–38, 147–48; longing for, 47, 139–41, 171–72
intuition, 31, 33, 66
irony, 90, 127; hermeneutics and, 167, 170; necessity of poetry and, 170–74; romantic, 30; Socratic, 30, 50, 171; understanding and, 165–74

Jacobi, Friedrich Heinrich, 15, 21, 42, 53–61, 91, 141–42, 160; di Giovanni on, 56–57, 60; Niethammer and, 103–4, 106, 108; *salto mortale* of, 57–61, 108, 136, 159, 194n11; *Woldemar*, 58–60, 211n46
Jena circle, 2–3, 11, 17, 45, 181n45, 227n13
judgment, 37–38, 107, 110; aesthetic, 4, 128, 158; of objects, 149

Kant, Immanuel, 26–27, 53, 155, 159, 174; critical project of, 120–31; Erhard and, 97–99; Fichte and, 30–35, 48, 64, 71, 80–81, 85, 117–22, 201n34; first principles and, 18–21, 62–64, 97–100, 119, 121–22; Hegel and, 27–31, 35, 188n9; Herbert and, 97–99; Niethammer and, 64, 97–98, 105–6; political views of, 119–20; principle of consciousness in,

62–64; Reinhold and, 62–65, 99–100, 102, 117–22; Schelling and, 35, 64; Schlegel and, 4–6, 22, 87–90, 119–31, 136, 142–50; Schmid and, 102
Klausnitzer, Ralf, 176n4, 186n80
knowledge, 3–4, 7, 17, 37–40, 53–70, 128, 133, 154; "conditioned," 82, 125; drive for, 125, 139–40; foreknowledge and, 108; objective, 142, 148–49; systems of, 18, 22–23, 27–28, 43–44, 84–86, 92–94, 101–3, 156–57. *See also* common sense; science
Köln lectures. *See Entwicklung der Philosophie in zwölf Büchern*
Körner, Josef, 185n76
Krausz, Michael, 220n24
Kroner, Richard, 44–45

Lacoue-Labarthe, Philippe, 1, 227n13, 227n17, 228n41
Larmore, Charles, 33, 36–37, 39
Lavater, Johann Kaspar, 182n52
Lectures on Transcendental Philosophy. See transcendental philosophy
Leibniz, Gottfried Wilhelm, 58, 62–63
Lessing, Gotthold Ephraim, 21, 53–55, 182n52
"Letter on the Novel" (Schlegel), 15–16
Littlejohns, Richard, 189n25, 229n46
Locke, John, 62–63
logical positivism, 25–26, 187n5
Lovejoy, A. O., 13–14
Lucinde (Schlegel), 23, 170, 229n46
Ludwig, Wilhelm H., 2–3
Lukács, Georg, 175n1, 176n4
Luther, Martin, 182n52
Lyceum der schönen Künste (journal), 14, 50, 167, 171

Mahoney, Dennis, 14
Maimon, Salomon, 91, 197n47
Man, Paul de. *See* de Man, Paul

Mason, Eudo, 224n62
materialism, 32, 73–74, 153. *See also* realism
mathematics, 4, 25–27, 42, 121–22, 134, 144, 145, 168
McDowell, John, 3–4, 179n17
McGinn, Colin, 229n54
Mendelssohn, Moses, 21, 53–61, 160, 182n49
Menges, Karl, 161–63
Metternich, Klemens von, 18
mimesis, 172–74
mise-en-abyme, 167, 170–71
misunderstanding, 25–26, 31, 50–51, 66–68, 83, 88–89, 118, 165–74. *See also* coherence
modernism, 4, 160–65; Behler on, 15, 161; Fichte and, 93; postmodernism and, 39–40, 49
Moore, G. E., 29
mysticism, 45, 114–16, 202n48; dogmatism and, 88–89, 100–1; Fichte and, 81–82, 86–91, 136
mythology, 161–65, 168–69, 193n74, 226n3

Nagel, Thomas, 39
Nancy, Jean-Luc, 1, 227n13, 227n17, 228n41
Naturphilosophie, 10, 42–43, 133, 143–44
Nazism, 1, 14, 28, 176n4, 186n80, 193n74
Newton, Isaac, 62, 215n9
Niethammer, Friedrich Immanuel, 109–14, 136–37; appeal to common sense by, 72, 96–97, 101–14, 159; Fichte and, 71, 72, 101, 109, 198n3; first principles and, 97–103, 107–8; Kant and, 64, 97–98, 105–6; skepticism of, 96–101; "Von den Ansprüchen des gemeinen Verstandes an der Philosophie," 96, 97, 103, 105, 107–8, 110, 111. *See also Philosophisches Journal*

Non-I, 72–73, 88, 140, 142, 150. *See also* ego
nonsense. *See* misunderstanding
noumenal world, phenomenal versus, 31, 41, 141–43
Novalis, 2–3, 16, 17, 109, 137, 192n69; *Athenäum* and, 12; Beiser on, 45; on communication of a thought, 50; critque of idealism by, 36–37; Manfred Frank on, 38–40; Littlejohns on, 189n25

objectivity, 32–33, 48; antifoundationalism and, 59–61, 147; consciousness and, 80, 99; Kant's definition of, 142; representation and, 63–64, 77. *See also* thing
ontology, 30, 39, 142, 144, 148
opacity. *See* transparency

pantheism, 18, 21, 54–61, 138, 183n57, 185n77, 186n80. *See also* Spinozism
Parmenides, 26
Pascal, Blaise, 187n6
Peter, Klaus, 161
Phaedrus (Plato), 171
phenomenal world, noumenal versus, 31, 41, 141–43
philology, 11, 129, 166, 211n46
Philosophische Lehrjahre (Schlegel), 134, 207n7
Philosophisches Journal, 7, 11, 72, 198n3; "Ankündigung" for, 21, 96, 102, 103, 106; contributors to, 206n2; founding of, 21–22, 96, 100; Schlegel's review of, 22, 81, 109–14; Schmid's critique of Fichte in, 75–79; "Vorbericht" of, 22, 96, 102–5, 111. *See also* Niethammer, Friedrich Immanuel
philosophy: analytic, 4, 26, 133, 154–55; definitions of, 75–76, 80; dogmatism versus, 73–74, 81, 88–90, 94, 114–15; hermeneutical dimensions of, 50–51; history of, 7, 46, 50–51, 60, 82–84, 90, 123–31; philosophy of, 48, 81, 89–90, 110–11, 116, 119, 127–29, 136; poetry and, 2–7, 12–13, 25–28, 36, 49–52, 122–23, 152–53, 159–65, 170–74, 187n1; as science, 25–27, 52, 86–89, 101–3, 115–16, 123; speculative, 100, 102. *See also specific types*, *e.g.*, transcendental philosophy
Pinkard, Terry, 37–38
Pippin, Robert, 198n1
Plato, 125, 163; German Idealism and, 29–30, 42–44, 50–51, 133; *Phaedrus*, 171; *Republic*, 187n1; Socratic irony and, 30, 50, 171
poetry: classical, 13, 14; mythology and, 161–65; philosophy and, 2–7, 12–13, 25–28, 36, 49, 122–23, 152–53, 159–65, 170–74, 187n1; romantic, 8–9, 13–16, 157–58, 170–71, 178n11; universal, 161, 170, 225n93
Pöggeler, Otto, 191n54
postmodernism, 39–40, 49. *See also* modernism
Putnam, Hillary, 39

Quine, W. V., 221n38

rationalism, 41
realism, 34–35, 62, 145; absolute, 42, 188n9; antirealism and, 29, 30; empirical, 31, 80, 115; epistemological, 39; idealism and, 42, 48, 82, 87, 138–43, 147, 164–65; materialism and, 32, 73–74, 153; metaphysical, 74; ontological, 39; romantic, 38–41; Spinoza's, 21, 81–82, 87, 138–39, 143, 147, 164–65, 222n38
reason, 51, 121, 149; faith and, 22, 54–61, 120, 138–39; "philosophiz-

Index 255

ing," 67, 96; transparency and, 32–39, 43–44, 48–49, 57–58, 83, 170
regulative idea, 40, 44
Reichhardt, C. F., 11, 12
Reinhold, K. L., 18, 21, 71, 79, 159, 181n45, 214n1; *Beyträge zur Berichtigung der bisherigen Misverständnisse der Philosophie*, 66–68; *Briefe über die kantische Philosophie*, 62; *Elementarphilosophie*, 53, 62–66; Fichte and, 71, 79, 99, 130; first principles and, 64, 67, 121–22, 135–36; Kant and, 62–65, 99–100, 102, 117–22; Schulze's critique of, 65–70, 99–100; *Über das Fundament des philosophischen Wissens*, 53; *Versuch einer neuen Theorie des menschlichen Vorstellungsvermögens*, 53, 62
relativism, 27, 48–49, 146–47, 192n67
representation: Fichte on, 68–70, 77–79; Gasché on, 183n53; objectivity and, 63–64, 77; Reinhold on, 62–68; Schlegel on, 171
Republic (Plato), 187n1
Revue International de Philosophie (journal), 3–4
rhetoric, 25
Riasanovsky, Nicholas, 183n57, 186n80
Richards, Robert, 133, 180n38
Rockmore, Tom, 91–93, 186n85, 188n19
romanticism, 61, 160–65; aesthetics and, 159–74; Beiser on, 40–45, 133, 138–39, 143; Bohn on, 151–52; definitions of, 2, 8, 10–18, 38–39; Manfred Frank on, 38–41, 133; Goethe on, 1, 176n3; idealism versus, 6–7, 30–32, 37–45, 48, 51–52, 133, 147; Klaus Peter on, 161; realism and, 38–41; unity of thought and being in, 32–38

Rommel, Gabriele, 180n36
Rorty, Richard, 26, 168–69, 187n5, 220n24
Rosen, Charles, 178n11
Rosenzweig, Franz, 162

salto mortale. *See* Jacobi, Friedrich Heinrich
Saul, Nicholas, 226n94
Schelling, Caroline. *See* Schlegel Schelling, Caroline
Schelling, Friedrich von, 3, 6, 7, 17, 28, 41, 162; Beiser on, 44–46; Bowie on, 33; Hölderlin and, 45; Kant and, 35, 64; Zöller on, 34–36
Schildknecht, Christiane, 183n56
Schiller, Friedrich von, 6; Schlegel and, 11, 14, 181n47, 224n62; "Über die ästhetische Erziehung des Menschen," 14; "Über naive und sentimentalische Dichtung," 14, 181n47
Schlegel, August Wilhelm, 2, 11, 16, 206n7; *Athenäum* and, 12, 46; as philologist, 178n11
Schlegel, Dorothea, 2–3, 12, 18, 182n49, 185n77
Schlegel Schelling, Caroline, 2, 12
Schleiermacher, Friedrich, 2–4, 12, 16, 30
Schmid, Carl Christian Erhard, 75–79, 96, 102, 181n45
Schopenhauer, Arthur, 34–35, 189n26, 196n38
Schulze, Gottlob Ernst, 53, 79, 91; *Aenesidemus*, 65–71, 99–100; Reinhold's critique of, 65–70; skepticism of, 95–96, 196n38
science, 133, 166; art and, 9, 25; philosophy as, 25–27, 52, 86–89, 101–3, 115–16, 123; religion and, 138–39. *See also* knowledge; *Wissenschaftslehre*
Scruton, Roger, 73

Searle, John, 222n41
Sehnsucht nach dem Unendlichen, 47, 139–41, 171–72
self-consciousness. *See* consciousness
self-positing I. *See* ego
Seyhan, Azade, 225n84
Shakespeare, William, 9, 15, 172–73, 229n53
skepticism, 2, 5, 21, 75, 114–16, 153; Hegel's, 48; Hume's, 31, 62, 65; Kant's, 141–42; Niethammer's, 96–101; romantic, 33, 47–52, 94, 147; Schulze's, 65–70, 95–96. *See also* antifoundationalism
Socratic irony, 30, 50, 171
sophism, 60, 64, 99, 115
speculation, 100, 102; "conditioned," 82, 125
Spinozism: determinism and, 143; fatalism and, 74, 81; Lessing and, 53–55; realism and, 21, 58, 81–82, 87, 138–39, 143, 147, 164–65, 222n38. *See also* pantheism
spiritualism, 42
subjectivity: idealism and, 29–30, 32–33, 36–38, 77, 139; Jacobi's view of, 59–61; Reinhold's view of, 99
synthetic method, 2, 7, 9, 12, 22–23, 69, 141–42, 154–55, 166. *See also* holism

Talk on the New Mythology (Schlegel), 163–65
taxonomy, historical, 114–16
thing, 15, 141–50. *See also* objectivity
Tieck, Ludwig, 12, 17
Tieck, Sophie, 3
transcendental philosophy, 6–7, 30–31, 46; Fichte's, 91; Kant's, 30–33, 71, 80, 102, 118, 120–21, 130, 142; Niethammer's, 105–6; Schlegel's lectures on, 7, 17, 48, 126, 137, 140, 146, 191n54

transparency, 32–39, 43–44, 48–49, 57–58, 83, 170

"Über die Unverständlichkeit" (Schlegel), 50, 83, 165–70
"Über Goethes Meister" (Schlegel), 14, 151–55, 224n68, 229n53
"Über naive und sentimentalische Dichtung" (Schiller), 14, 181n47
unconditioned, paradox of, 106
understanding, 50–51, 83, 87; of criticism, 118; "from the inside," 2, 148–49; irony and, 165–74; Reinhold on, 66–68. *See also* coherence; misunderstanding
unity of thought. *See* holism

Veit, Dorothea. *See* Schlegel, Dorothea
"Versuch über den Begriff des Republikanismus" (Schlegel), 120
Verweyen, Hans, 74
vitalism, 41, 149–50
Voss, Johann F., 185n75

Wackenroder, Wilhelm H., 3
Walzel, Oskar, 175n1
Wechselbegriff, 135
Wechselerweis, 22, 60–61, 95, 134–37, 148; art and, 153; definitions of, 19–20, 135, 137; first principles and, 134–39; Niethammer and, 108
Wechselgrundsatz, 74, 88
Wilhelm Meisters Lehrjahre (Goethe), 9, 13–16, 22–23, 86, 119, 134, 150–58
Wissenschaftslehre (Fichte), 16, 20, 21, 46, 70–94, 101–2, 110, 119, 139, 157, 166
Wittgenstein, Ludwig, 187n6
women's rights, 14, 181n47, 182n49, 224n63

Zöller, Günter, 33–36, 39
Zusammenhang, 155. *See* coherence

www.ingramcontent.com/pod-product-compliance
Lightning Source LLC
Chambersburg PA
CBHW020644230426
43665CB00008B/308